TENNYSON

TENNYSON

TO STRIVE | TO SEEK | TO FIND

JOHN BATCHELOR

PEGASUS BOOKS
NEW YORK LONDON

TENNYSON

Pegasus Books LLC
80 Broad Street, 5th Floor
New York, NY 10004

ISBN: 978-1-60598-490-2

10 9 8 7 8 6 5 4 3 2 1

Printed in the United States of America
Distributed by W. W. Norton & Company, Inc.

Contents

List of Illustrations

Tennyson family tree

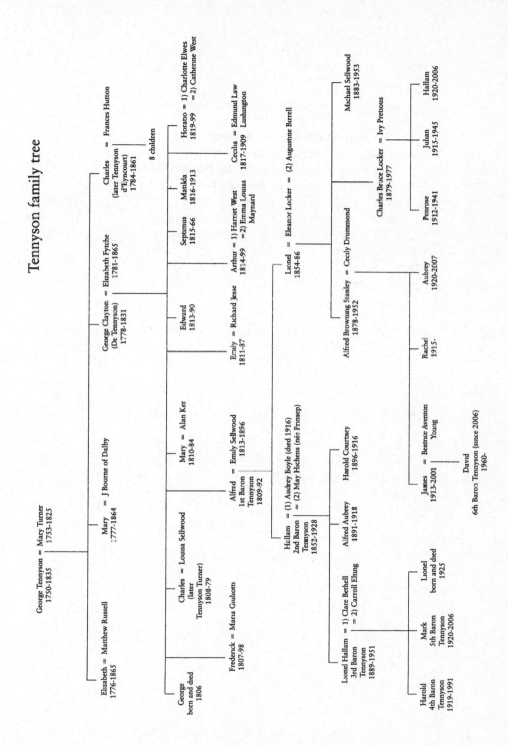

. . . that which we are, we are;
One equal temper of heroic hearts,
Made weak by time and fate, but strong in will
To strive, to seek, to find, and not to yield.

For Henrietta, with love

Preface

This biography presents an Alfred Tennyson who is stronger, more self-reliant, more businesslike, tougher and more centrally Victorian than previous biographies have displayed. Like many successful Victorians, he was a provincial determined to make good in the capital while retaining his provincial strengths; in his particular case he never lost his Lincolnshire accent and in his relationships he remained close to his Lincolnshire roots. As the major poet of the age he determined the literary taste of the mid- to late-Victorian period; and then, strategically and with a secure instinct for the market, he fed that taste. The ascendancy of Tennyson was neither the irresistible triumph of pure genius nor an accident of history; he skilfully crafted his own career and his relationship with his audience.

Tennyson was Queen Victoria's Laureate, and this book begins and ends with his direct contacts with her. He first came to know the Queen personally at an audience at Osborne House on the Isle of Wight in 1862, 150 years before the publication of this present biography.

Since 1980, when Robert Bernard Martin published *Tennyson: The Unquiet Heart*, the work of editors and archive scholars has made available a good deal of new information.

Tennyson at Aldworth: The Diary of James Henry Mangles, edited by Earl A. Knies (1984), reveals in the diary of a non-literary friend aspects of the poet's personality hitherto unsuspected; the diary of George Stovin Venables, which provides much of the material in *A Circle of Friends: The Tennysons and the Lushingtons of Park House*, edited by John O. Waller (1986), is a similarly fruitful source; the Kemble letters, a collection of correspondence among Tennyson's Cambridge friends which is now in New Zealand, give new information about Tennyson's Spanish adventure of 1830 (and provide the basis of an excellent recent article by Marion Shaw, 2009); important work on the Tennyson family papers, especially those of Tennyson's father, George Clayton Tennyson, and his uncle, Charles Tennyson d'Eyncourt, is presented in *Poems by Two Brothers: The Lives, Work and Influence of George Clayton Tennyson and Charles Tennyson d'Eyncourt*, edited by Christopher Sturman and Valerie Purton (1993). Among the other sources that have become available are the complete and updated three-volume Longman's annotated edition of Tennyson's *Poems*, edited by Christopher Ricks (1987); the *Letters* of Tennyson in three volumes edited by Cecil Lang and Edgar Shannon (1982, 1987, 1990); the *Letters* of Edward Fitzgerald in four volumes edited by Alfred McKinley Terhune and Annabelle Burdick Terhune (1980, the year in which Martin's biography was published); the *Letters* of Arthur Henry Hallam, edited by Jack Kolb (1981); the new research published by the Tennyson Society in the annual *Tennyson Research Bulletin* and in the Tennyson Society monographs. *Tennyson's Camelot*, a study of *Idylls of the King* and its medieval sources, by David Staines (1982), extended our understanding of Tennyson's huge final work. Leonée Ormond's *Alfred Tennyson: A Literary Life* (1993), together with her essays and short monographs on him, has brought out much that was hitherto unknown or misunderstood about Tennyson's relationship with the fine arts. Ann Thwaite's biography of Emily Tennyson (1996) gave a fresh perspective on the Tennyson marriage.

The story of Tennyson, then, is ready for a narrative which takes into account the material that has become available in the last thirty years. The major manuscript collections for this book have been at the Tennyson Research Centre, Lincoln; the Lincolnshire Archives in the Lincolnshire County Record Office; the Houghton Library, Harvard; Boston Public Library; the Beinecke Rare Book and Manuscript Library, Yale; Trinity College Library, Cambridge and Cambridge University Library; the Fitzwilliam Museum, Cambridge; the Bodleian Library, Oxford.

For anyone seeking to write such a biography there is the well-known difficulty that most of the correspondence between Tennyson and his wife Emily in the 1830s and 1840s was destroyed. In justice to Emily (and to their son Hallam) it needs to be remembered that when they burnt these piles of correspondence after Tennyson's death, they were acting on what they saw as his wishes. Tennyson regarded the activity of biographers as offensive and intrusive, and he would certainly have approved the determination that Hallam Tennyson showed in the two-volume *Memoir* to present the poet as he and his immediate family wished him to be remembered. It was not until 1949 that Tennyson's grandson, Charles, published a biography which acted as a corrective to Hallam's partial portrait.

I am grateful to David, Lord Tennyson, for permission to quote from Tennyson's unpublished manuscripts; to Grace Timmins, librarian and archivist of the Tennyson Research Centre at Lincoln, for invaluable and constant help with the sources and the images for this book; to the Tennyson Research Centre and Trinity College, Cambridge, for permission to use images belonging to their collections; to the Beinecke Rare Book and Manuscript Library, Yale, for access to their Tennyson collection and for permission to quote from the Prinsep papers; to the Houghton Library, Harvard, Boston Public Library, Cambridge University Library, the library of the Fitzwilliam Museum, Cambridge, and the Wren Library of Trinity College, Cambridge, for access to their Tennyson collections; to Newcastle University Library, the Literary & Philosophical Society, Newcastle, Durham University Library, and to the support staff of the Newcastle University School of English for their help with my ongoing writing and preparation of the typescript; and to the British Academy for funding which enabled me to visit British locations connected with Tennyson and, especially, the Tennyson archives at Harvard and Yale.

I also have particular debts to the following: Professor Leonée Ormond and Professor J. R. (Dick) Watson, both of whom read my text with great care and made a number of helpful suggestions; Penelope Hoare at Chatto & Windus for the expertise and dedication with which she has undertaken major editorial work on my typescript, and to Parisa Ebrahimi for her invaluable work on the later stages of the editorial process; to Felicity Bryan, my agent, for her unfailing encouragement; and to my wife, Henrietta, for the love and patience with which she has supported me during the writing of this book.

John Batchelor, Newcastle, June 2012

Prologue: The Tennysons and the Queen, 1862–1863

Wordsworth died in May 1850. The Poet Laureateship was promptly offered by Prince Albert to the obvious 'senior' poet in literary London, a banker who was also a distinguished man of letters and a celebrated host and man-about-town, Samuel Rogers. For many years Rogers had wished for this court appointment, but as he was now eighty-seven years old, he felt obliged to decline. Once he had withdrawn, a group of younger figures, including Alfred Tennyson, Leigh Hunt and Elizabeth Barrett Browning, were in the frame. Tennyson's son, Hallam, wrote in his *Memoir*:

> On November 19th my father was appointed Poet Laureate, owing chiefly to Prince Albert's admiration for 'In Memoriam'. Wordsworth had been now dead some months; and my father, as he has assured me, had not any expectation of the Laureateship, or any thought upon the subject: it seemed to him therefore a very curious coincidence, that the night before the offer reached him he dreamt that Prince Albert came and kissed him on the cheek, and that he said in his dream, 'Very kind, but very German.'[1]

On 6 March 1851, the new Poet Laureate was formally presented to the Queen at a levee at Buckingham Palace. His grandson Charles tells us that he 'had missed the first levee of the new year because he hadn't been able to borrow a Court suit and he couldn't afford to buy one'. When he attended the second levee, he was wearing a Court suit lent to him by the ancient Samuel Rogers (who by this date was a long-standing friend of Tennyson's). It is a mark of old Rogers's essential decency and generosity that although he had always wanted the office for himself, he had lent the same suit to Wordsworth when Wordsworth was appointed Laureate in 1843. Rogers was considerably smaller than Tennyson. Although the suit was a tight fit, Tennyson 'was delighted with the cocked hat and with the appearance of his magnificent legs in black silk stockings'. He called on his friend Thackeray, who found him 'as pleased and innocent as a child about the whole affair'.[2]

Tennyson took the role seriously, and was writing his first Laureate poem within a few days of his presentation to the Queen:

> Revered Victoria, you that hold
>   A nobler office upon earth
>   Than arms, or power of brain, or birth
> Could give the warrior kings of old,
>   I thank you that your Royal grace [. . .]

The whole thing is couched in terms that could not fail to please. The tiny passionate monarch was in the prime of life and physically fit; 'May you rule us long', her Laureate wrote with confidence:

> And leave us rulers of your blood
>   As noble till the latest day!
>   May children of our children say,
> 'She wrought her people lasting good [. . .]'[3]

And so on, in its blameless and decorous way.

Charles Tennyson gives his own balanced view of the young Queen herself:

There is no evidence that Queen Victoria took any special interest in the appointment of her Poet Laureate. She had little knowledge of contemporary literature and it is unlikely that she had read Tennyson's volumes of 1842 or *The Princess* [his narrative poem of 1847]. She had been married to Albert for just over ten years, during which she had gradually devolved on him more and more of her official duties. She still loved him with unabated intensity and, in spite of her dislike of the process of child-bearing ('the shadow side of marriage,' she called it), had already borne him six children, the sixth (Prince Arthur) making its appearance in May 1850 and no doubt occupying most of her activity and attention during the last half of this crucial year.

Prince Albert was 'King in all but name' and had done a great deal to retrieve the monarchy from the somewhat shabby and discredited image that it had when William IV died and Victoria, aged eighteen, succeeded. He had reorganised the Royal Household, put right the finances of the Duchy of Cornwall and the Windsor Estates, and acquired

Osborne on the Isle of Wight and Balmoral in Scotland for the monarchy. He was magnificent-looking, physically splendid, and devoted to his wife. 'He shared her love of music and dancing. It was small wonder that his young wife (she was still only thirty years old [in 1850]) adored him and left more and more responsibility in his hands.'[4]

In November 1861, however, Albert became ill with symptoms that he did not understand ('heavy catarrh', as he put it, 'headache and pains in my limbs'). His doctors diagnosed typhoid. Such was Queen Victoria's horror of the disease that they did not dare tell her, and the situation was cruelly ambiguous to the last. On 13 December, one of the Prince's doctors came to her to say that there was hope that he would recover. But on the evening of the following day, the Queen and her daughter Princess Alice sat by the Prince's bedside watching him steadily sinking. Victoria took his left hand and found that it was already cold; this was the point at which she lost her self-command and shrieked in an agony of fear, 'Oh! this is death!' And so it proved. The Prince died at a quarter to eleven on the night of 14 December 1861, the Queen holding his hand, Princess Alice on the other side of the bed, and the Prince of Wales and his sister Princess Helena at the foot.[5]

By the time Albert died, Tennyson had been Poet Laureate for ten years, and a private secretary, Sir Charles Phipps, sent him a message from Princess Alice asking him to write something. After a good deal of hesitation and anxiety (recorded in a draft letter of Tennyson's which was much revised and never sent), he decided to create a new dedication to his Arthurian project, *Idylls of the King*, a work which was still being extended. The dedication began as follows:

> These to His Memory – Since he held them dear,
> Perchance as finding there unconsciously
> Some image of himself – I dedicate,
> I dedicate, I consecrate with tears –
> These Idylls.

and closed with a fulsome recognition of the Queen's personal grief:

> Break not, O woman's-heart, but still endure;
> Break not, for thou art Royal, but endure,
> Remembering all the beauty of that star
> Which shone so close beside Thee that ye made
> One light together, but has past and leaves

> The Crown a lonely splendour.
> May all love,
> His love, unseen but felt, o'ershadow Thee,
> The love of all Thy sons encompass Thee,
> The love of all Thy daughters cherish Thee,
> The love of all Thy people comfort Thee,
> Till God's love set Thee at his side again!

Matthew Arnold remarked of these lines that they were 'very just – but so was one of The Times leaders about the same subject – and above the merit of just remark and proper feeling these lines do not appear to rise'.[6] Nor did they need to. They admirably fulfilled their purpose: they spoke directly to the Queen's feelings and to her immediate emotional need.

Meanwhile, the Queen was reading *In Memoriam*, Tennyson's extended elegy for his long-dead friend Arthur Hallam. In February 1862, she asked the Duke of Argyll* to let Tennyson know how much *In Memoriam* meant to her personally, giving him her copy to show 'how well it was read' and how many passages she had marked. The Duke wrote that she had 'substituted "widow" for "widower" and "her" for "his"' in the lines:

> Tears of the widower, when he sees
> A late-lost form that sleep reveals,
> And moves his doubtful arms, and feels
> Her place is empty, fall like these.

This was building up to a personal audience, and in a letter of 25 March, the Duke, who had 'long red hair loose over his shoulders' and whose mother-in-law was Victoria's mistress of the robes, communicated to Tennyson the Queen's 'command' that he should visit her at Osborne House. Tennyson was alarmed at the prospect, and wrote back: 'I am a shy beast and like to keep in my burrow. Two questions, what sort of salutation to make on entering Her private room? and whether to retreat backward? or sidle out as I may?' Argyll's counsel was that 'as you have already been "presented" at Court, no other Salutation is expected than a low bow . . . Don't let yourself be a "shy beast" – and "come out of your burrow".'[7] He added reassuringly: 'I think She likes all natural signs of devotion and sympathy. In this be

---

*The lively young duke was an able supporter of liberal and radical policies in the House of Lords. His 'arrogance and conceit', though, largely blocked him from office.

guided entirely by your own feelings – All formality and mere ceremony breaks down in the presence of real sorrow.'

The private audience took place in April 1862 at Osborne House. It was a momentous occasion for Tennyson and he was very nervous, but his nature was genuinely simple and easily moved, and the meeting went well. The theme of bereavement provided rewarding common ground for these two self-centred personalities. For the Queen, the meeting was an occasion of powerful emotions. She wrote in her diary (14 April 1862):

> I went down to see Tennyson who is very peculiar looking, tall, dark, with a fine head, long black flowing hair and a beard – oddly dressed, but there is no affectation about him. I told him how much I adored his glorious lines to my precious Albert [the new dedication to the *Idylls*] and how much comfort I found in his *In Memoriam*. He was full of unbounded appreciation of beloved Albert. When he spoke of my own loss, of that to the Nation, his eyes quite filled with tears.[8]

The Queen was a young widow longing for fellow feeling, but she was at the same time a public institution. There could never be anything informal or spontaneous about an audience with her, but she loved to link Tennyson's writings with her own emotions; *In Memoriam* reflected her grief. 'Next to the Bible, *In Memoriam* is my comfort,'[9] she told Tennyson; she also said, 'I am like your Mariana* now.' Wholly inappropriately – given that her husband could never have been other than Consort – Tennyson said of Prince Albert: 'He would have made a great King.' The Queen tactfully ignored this, and replied at a tangent: 'He always said it did not signify whether he did the right thing or not, so long as the right thing was done.' Tennyson reported this to an old Cambridge friend: 'As soon as it was out of my mouth I felt what a blunder I had made. But, happily, it proved to be the very right thing to have said.'[10]

That first meeting was followed by gifts of books and other marks of notice sent to him by the Queen, and Tennyson rose to another Laureate occasion with a tribute to Alexandra of Denmark. His poem

---

*Tennyson's early poem about Mariana in the moated grange, obliquely based on a sub-plot in Shakespeare's *Measure for Measure*, explores the feelings of a woman who has been abandoned by her lover and is suffering loneliness and despair.

for the young princess was published in *The Times* on the day of her wedding to the Prince of Wales, 10 March 1863, and begins:

> Sea-kings' daughter from over the sea, Alexandra!
> Saxon and Norman and Dane are we,
> But all of us Danes in our welcome of thee, Alexandra!

As it proceeds, it successfully brings out the freshness of this slim and lovely girl:

> Welcome her, all things youthful and sweet,
> Scatter the blossom under her feet!
> Break, happy land, into earlier flowers!
> Make music, O bird, in the new-budded bowers!

It is an engaging and well-judged Laureate poem, and the Queen loved it. On the day of the wedding, the Tennysons as a family held their own celebration by lighting a bonfire on the down near their home in the Isle of Wight.

Tennyson once more obeyed a summons to Osborne House, this time with his two sons and his wife Emily. After lunch with Lady Augusta Bruce* and a visit to the dairy ('very pretty it is, lined with white Dutch tiles with a wreath of convolvulus round and a fountain in the middle'), they were presented to the Queen in the drawing room.[11]

At this second audience, Tennyson was self-possessed and at his ease with the Queen. His wife Emily by contrast was apprehensive and somewhat gauche: when the Queen entered the drawing room to receive them, she 'found myself on my knee kissing the hand which was given to me but I do not know how I came there'.[12]

The Tennysons' two young sons, Hallam and Lionel, observed the whole scene very carefully. Ten-year-old Hallam wrote: 'The Queen is not stout. Her Majesty has a large mind and small body to contain it.'† Emily, however, was enthralled:

---

*A lady-in-waiting and the Queen's personal friend; later in 1863 she would upset the Queen by marrying Arthur Stanley, Dean of Westminster, but the breach was healed and she would remain close to the Queen. Arthur and Lady Augusta Stanley became long-standing friends of the Tennysons.
†Queen Victoria was four feet eleven inches tall at this date. She would become even shorter, and a great deal stouter, as she grew older. In later years she developed the 'pepperpot' profile beloved of caricaturists.

The Queen's face is beautiful. Not the least like her portraits but small and childlike, full of intelligence and ineffably sweet and of a sad sympathy. A. [Alfred Tennyson] was delighted with the breadth and penetration of her mind. One felt that no false thing could stand before her. [. . .] One feels that the Queen is a woman to live and die for.[13]

The Queen recorded her own feelings about Tennyson after this second audience. She responded warmly to his emotional sympathy, but at the same time she saw him as a shambling and untidy figure, a man of genius inside a kind of performing bear: 'Had some interesting conversation with him and was struck with the greatness and largeness of his mind, under a certainly rough exterior.'[14]

Had Albert lived, he might quickly have become a personal friend of Tennyson. But while the Prince was a European intellectual with a serious interest in the arts, the Queen was limited in outlook and education. In addition, the Laureate was part of her household, and she possessed a strong sense of her own standing in relation to him. Their friendship developed slowly, becoming over the years a matter of warm mutual regard. That first meeting of 1862, forged in their joint experience of bereavement, can be held in the mind as a sunny plateau of recognition and fame, the point at which Alfred Tennyson could stand back and acknowledge that he had advanced immeasurably beyond the child who had been born in Lincolnshire in 1809.

CHAPTER 1

Somersby, 1809–1827

What shall sever me from the love of home?

Alfred Tennyson, born 6 August 1809, came into the world at a point in history when a brilliant generation of poets destined for premature extinction was reaching full strength. Keats, Shelley and Byron would all die in young manhood; Blake, Wordsworth and Coleridge would live longer but were relatively muted voices by the time Tennyson came of age. Two extraordinary men were born in that same year. They were Felix Mendelssohn – another short life, but nevertheless a genius who would be Queen Victoria's favourite composer, as Alfred Tennyson would be her favourite poet – and Charles Darwin, whose intellectual legacy paralleled Tennyson's lifelong interest in the sciences, and whose great works published from 1859 onwards were directly relevant to Tennyson's preoccupation with the tensions between Christianity and evolution.

The young Alfred Tennyson loved both the poetry and the political daring of Byron and Shelley; he identified personally with Keats's lyricism and was jealously protective of Keats's privacy (as of his own). The Romantics, then, both nurtured him and made way for him, and his work between 1830 and 1850 was in a sense filling a vacancy created by the early deaths of their first generation.* In literary terms, much of the nineteenth century would be the age of Tennyson. He would become a national monument.

Alfred Tennyson was the third son of the Rev. George Clayton Tennyson, rector of Somersby. Somersby is a cluster of old buildings with just two significant houses: a fine eighteenth-century castellated brick house thought to be designed by Vanbrugh (at that date owned by the Burton family, patrons of the Sombersby living), and the rectory, where Tennyson was born, which stands opposite the ancient grey church. The hamlet lies some thirty miles east of Lincoln and twenty miles west of the North Sea, in a landscape of farms, woodland and rolling countryside which Tennyson was to love intensely from a very early age.

---

*John Keats died in 1821, Percy Bysshe Shelley in 1822 and George Gordon, Lord Byron, in 1824.

The rectory was and still is an attractive house, but it was small for the needs of what would become an exceptionally large family (Alfred was one of eleven children), and it must have been crowded and inconvenient. Nevertheless, Tennyson's experience of it was as of a primal paradise, and its memory was fresh for him throughout his long life.

The story of Tennyson's immediate family begins with his great-grandmother, Elizabeth Tennyson, the daughter of George Clayton of Grimsby in north Lincolnshire. In 1719, George Clayton had married Dorothy Hildeyard (or Hildyard). The Hildeyards* were an ancient family who claimed descent from both Edward I and Edward III, and from the Barons d'Eyncourt (a name that would come to figure ominously in the life of the young Alfred Tennyson). Elizabeth Clayton married Michael Tennyson (1721–96), the poet's great-grandfather, who worked as an apothecary at Hedon in Holderness (in his will he described himself as a surgeon). By his marriage to Elizabeth, he substantially enhanced his position in Lincolnshire, and was sufficiently prosperous to leave his son George Tennyson, the poet's grandfather, an income of £700 a year.

George Tennyson, a commanding and baleful presence in the life of his grandson Alfred, was known to his intimidated family as 'The Old Man of the Wolds'. With the Clayton connection and the Hildeyard ancestry, he had been born into a family where social ascendancy was seen both as a legitimate object of desire and as a confirmation of hereditary entitlement.

As a young man, George was apprenticed to a solicitor in Market Rasen. He built up a legal practice there and also became a small banker in the town, and in June 1776 he made a good marriage to Mary Turner (1753–1825), who was the daughter of a significant landowner, John Turner, Esquire, of Caistor. Mary was tall, dark, beautiful, very sensitive and pious, and was interested in literature and music. Her tastes and sympathies were in marked contrast with those of her practical, managing, bullying husband. Tennyson's father, George Clayton Tennyson, and many of Mary's grandchildren, including the poet himself, owed much of their temperament to the Turner rather than the Tennyson line.

Having made this astute marriage, the thrusting provincial lawyer rapidly prospered. He acquired land and property in Lincolnshire, and given that many of his clients were landowners, it followed naturally enough that by the 1790s, Old George (as it is convenient to call him)

---

*The same family, now spelt Hildyard, flourishes in Yorkshire and Lincolnshire today.

was a significant force in local Tory politics.[1] The county's gentry, though, did not see him as one of themselves, and there would always be resentful snobbish mutterings about the annoying prosperity of the 'Market Rasen attorney'.

There was, however, a vulnerable side to this energetic, self-seeking man. Sir Charles Tennyson (Alfred Tennyson's grandson and thus Old George's great-great-grandson) wrote:

George Tennyson's apparent hardness and self-control masked a morbid and ungovernable sensibility. This shewed itself partly in an extreme fussiness about his health – perhaps with some reason, for, although according to family tradition he was a staunch teetotaller, he became a martyr to gout at a comparatively early age. He was also easily depressed and liable to moods of indecision and fretfulness, stuttering when embarrassed and easily losing self-control. This tendency perplexed his friends who found it hard to understand why he so often allowed his vanity or vexation or fears of defeat to provoke him to impolitic answers or actions. His daughter-in-law Fanny came nearer to the truth when she wrote many years later, 'It is his nature to be active and when in the course of everyday events things do not go smoothly his mind is perturbed and that morbid sensibility prevails'. In such moods he would explode into violence and sarcasm which were excessively wounding. He himself gave a slightly different explanation: 'you know I am too much alive to fear and a thousand times to one anticipate what never happens'.[2]

Nervous or not, George Tennyson continued to be driven by his hunger for wealth and status. In the 1780s, while still in his thirties, he bought the manor of Beacons at Tealby, in Lincolnshire. It had once been the property of Lord Lovel and d'Eyncourt, an ancestor of the Hildeyards, and it still showed the remains of the original castle. Local tradition gave Beacons an older name, 'Bayons' (in turn thought to be a corruption of 'Bayeux'), and George Tennyson renamed his property accordingly, in order to bring out its flavour of ancestral vintage.

George Tennyson's four children were markedly diverse characters, and their several narratives all have a bearing on the poet's beginnings. His daughter Elizabeth, born in 1776, was her parents' darling, a vivacious, funny and attractive girl who grew up to marry the son of an extremely rich County Durham mine-owner. In due course she became the mistress of Brancepeth Castle, near Durham, rebuilt virtually stone by stone on the strength of her husband's wealth from coal. Her sister Mary, born in 1777, spent most of her childhood away from her parents, living with her mother's parents, the wealthy Turners, until she was eleven years old (this seemingly heartless practice was common in the eighteenth century). As an adult, Mary – 'Aunt Bourne' of family legend – became a gloomy, pessimistic Calvinist. '"Has [God] not damned," she cried, "most of my friends? But *me, me* He has picked out for eternal salvation, *me* who am no better than my neighbours."' Tennyson remembered her saying to him: 'Alfred, Alfred, when I look at you, I think of the words of Holy Scripture – "Depart from me, ye cursed, into everlasting fire."'[3]

Alfred's father, George Clayton Tennyson, was born in 1778. When choosing these names, Old George undoubtedly saw the 'Clayton' as conferring gentility on his first-born son, but whatever hopes he may have had for him did not last. George Clayton was intelligent, healthy and very good-looking, but headstrong. Openly disliked by his father, he was bullied, disparaged and humiliated. Not surprisingly, he grew up unmannerly and aggressive. Like his sister Mary, he was sent away to grandparents, in his case to his paternal grandfather. Like Mary, George Clayton seems to have been a troubled child, and when he came back to the parental home at the age of seven, his mother singled him out for comment (in a letter of 1785 to her own mother): 'our house is all noise and distraction since George and his grandfather [Michael Tennyson] came, I think I never saw a child so rude and ungovernable as he is'.[4] Old George worried about the boy, and it seems that he had decided as early as 1791, when George Clayton was only thirteen, that he should become a clergyman. It is clear that Old George already saw his elder son as unfit to carry on the family's upward ascent. To be a clergyman was at least a gentlemanly profession, and one that ensured an income for someone who was essentially incompetent.

This was horribly unfair. George the younger was certainly wayward and disobedient, but he was far from incompetent. As a young man he developed a loyal circle of Lincolnshire friends whose memories were that he was talented, accomplished and – when not sinking under his difficulties – very good company. He was sent first, aged eleven, to the free grammar school in York (where he was noted as a gifted schoolboy poet), and then to a private tutor in Huntingdonshire to be prepared for entrance to Cambridge. In 1796 he went up to Trinity College, Cambridge.

George Clayton Tennyson's younger brother Charles, born in 1784, had a different and happier education: first at York with his brother, but then in Lincoln, and finally at Louth Grammar School, where he was much admired. He always lived with his parents, and was clearly the favourite son just as his sister Elizabeth had established herself as the favourite daughter. He was handsome, intelligent, good with people and had a calm and sunny temperament. The headmaster at Louth said of him in 1798 that 'his disposition is so amiable, that it will probably procure general esteem from mankind as he goes into the world'.[5] Old George agreed, and Charles basked in his father's good opinion. Although they were treated so differently, and were six years apart in age, George and Charles Tennyson were good friends. It is a credit to both of them that the fraternal relationship survived.

Market Rasen, where Old George Tennyson had established his many business interests, was a drab little place which became too narrow a base for his expanding ambitions. In 1791, he and his wife moved to a substantial house at the top of the hill in Lincoln, near the cathedral, an area devoted to prosperous merchants and the leading men of the city. This was not a success – the Tennysons did not fit in. It was a disadvantage that they spoke with the distinctive rural Lincolnshire accent, and with his new money and his reputation for ruthlessness, George was kept at a distance. After a while, the Tennysons moved to a property George had inherited in Grimsby; in the meantime he had commissioned a Hull architect called George Pycock to build a new house at Tealby. His lively daughter Elizabeth wrote to her grandmother Turner (on 17 September 1797):

We shall be at Grimsby for some time [. . .] We none of us regret quitting Lincoln – every body agreeable seems tired of the place & talk of leaving [. . .] we must own that the generality of Lincoln people are not pleasant.[6]

Despite his father's withering treatment, George Clayton Tennyson grew up a strong, handsome, bookish and intellectually enquiring young man. He did well in his first year at Trinity, surprising everyone by being placed in the first class in his first-year examinations. He then transferred to St John's because he preferred that college's syllabus for the undergraduate degree, but the mathematics required for his finals defeated him, and he left the university in 1801 with a pass rather than an honours degree. He did at least graduate (which his son Alfred, later, would be unable to do).

On 11 May 1801, he was ordained deacon. An Anglican clergyman at this date did not require more than nominal commitment to the faith. Patronage of Anglican livings was, in effect, in private hands; in the gift of either the young man's immediate family, or, as in the case of the Tennysons, a wealthy landowning acquaintance. The incumbent passed his days fulfilling light religious duties but otherwise enjoying the gentlemanly life for which his upbringing had prepared him. But this of course was the way to provide for *younger* sons. George Clayton Tennyson naturally expected to be his father's principal heir, and as he was gradually forced to recognise that this was not Old George's intention, he became increasingly bitter. The fact that he was forced into the Church while his younger brother was groomed for a career in public life was intensely galling. Even worse was the growing realisation that most of his father's wealth would go to his brother, not to him.

Old George felt guilty – as well he might – and to assuage this guilt he allowed his son one last gentlemanly excursion before putting his neck under the yoke of ordination. In the autumn of 1801, he funded George Clayton to go to the coronation of the new tsar, Alexander. The young man arrived too late for the coronation itself, but Tennyson family tradition has it that he got into such dangerous scrapes that he went into hiding and had to escape disguised as a servant, on an English frigate sailing from Odessa.[7]

On later trips abroad, when already an incurable alcoholic, George Clayton would invent fantastic tales about himself. His alleged adventures in Russia could well be early instances of such tales, told with the sad purpose of lending his own life some colour and interest before he settled to the obscure and unwelcome profession to which his father had sentenced him.

George Clayton was given three livings – Benniworth, Somersby and Bag Enderby – but his many letters to his father are dominated by anxiety about money. In 1805 he married Elizabeth Fytche. An excellent choice for a clergyman, she was daughter of a vicar of Louth and niece to a bishop of Lincoln. Since the Fytches were an old family of some distinction in Lincolnshire, George in fact was thus far following in his father's footsteps by making a socially advantageous marriage. The old man did not see it that way, though: Elizabeth did not bring the kind of money he was looking for as a daughter-in-law's dowry. He settled some land on his son to mark the marriage, but he did not go to the wedding, and Elizabeth and her father-in-law were destined never to get on. Elizabeth was a sweet-natured woman who would need deep reserves of patience in her marriage.

The rectory at Somersby, which remained the private property of Robert Burton from whom Old George had secured the joint living for his son, needed refurbishment and enlargement. This took a while, but the Tennysons were finally able to move to Somersby (from Benniworth) in 1808. Eliza Tennyson was known seldom to assert herself or do anything decisive; one good reason for her passivity is that she was pregnant more or less continuously for fifteen years. Her sons were Frederick (1807), Charles (1808), Alfred (1809),* Edward (1813), Arthur (1814), Septimus (1815) and Horatio (1819), and her daughters were Mary (1810), Emilia (1811), Matilda (1816) and Cecilia (1817).

The costs of his large family meant that however generous his father's allowances – and they became increasingly generous – George Clayton was always short of money. He decided to take the education of his sons upon himself, so that for a good ten years he had to be a hard-working self-taught schoolmaster. It is not hard to see why he was in constantly poor health, nor indeed why he took to drink. He felt trapped, with his clamorous family and his unsuitable job, and though he had many friends, few of them were his intellectual equals. He consoled himself with his books, his music and his architectural designs. Later, as his financial position eased somewhat, he was able to build a considerable library to help with the education of his children. The extensive notes in his 'Commonplace Book'† indicate his intellectual liveliness and also give examples of the topics that he would have discussed with his older sons.[8] They include the history of Western art and the impact of geology on Christianity, with reference to William Paley's *Evidences of Christianity* (1794) and *Natural Theology* (1802).[9]

George Clayton was liked and respected in the county: he played the harp and had a magnificent voice, and was noted for his wit, charm and striking good looks. He became a magistrate, which led to sociability within Lincolnshire and gave him some personal confidence; he was a popular speaker at Assize dinners. He enhanced his status by applying for the degree of Doctor of Civil Law at Cambridge in 1813 (he was invariably known as 'Dr Tennyson' thereafter).[10] He and his brother Charles remained on good terms, but he also needed close friends outside the family, and one such friendship was established in 1814 when he called on Thomas Hardwicke Rawnsley, a young curate who had just arrived to take up his post at Spilsby.

---

*Strictly, Alfred was his parents' fourth son, not their third: their first child had died when he was only a few weeks old.
†This leatherbound book, which survives in the Tennyson Research Centre at Lincoln, is inscribed 'E libris Geo Clayton Tennyson March 20th 1807 Bound by me March 1807', and has a sonorous title page: 'Manuscripts upon a great variety of subjects by George Clayton Tennyson A M Rector of Benniworth as also of Somersby and [Bag in pencil] Enderby in the County of Lincoln Louth MDCCCVII.' The book was used later by the young Tennyson at Cambridge; there are caricatures and rough drawings on the inside cover which are certainly not by George Clayton.

Thomas Hardwicke Rawnsley (1790–1861) had been educated at Eton and Oxford, and thereafter had a decent and gentlemanly career in the Church in a number of Lincolnshire parishes. Following Spilsby and then Falkingham in 1814, he was for many years rector of Halton Holgate. As his social and intellectual equal, Rawnsley was a man whom the troubled rector of Somersby could trust and whose jokes could lift his uneasy spirits.

George Clayton often felt crushed by the self-imposed task of educating his children. Lamentations about the labour that this involved crop up regularly in his letters:

Dear Rawnsley,
   In your not having come to see me for so many months, when you have little or nothing to do but warm your shins over the fire while I, unfortunately, am frozen or rather suffocated with Greek and Latin, I consider myself as not only slighted but splifflicated. You deserve that I should take no notice of your letter whatever, but I will comply with your invitation partly to be introduced to the agreeable and clever lady, but more especially to have the pleasure of seeing Mrs Rawnsley, whom, you may rest assured, I value considerably more than I do you. Mrs T. is obliged by your invitation, but the weather is too damp and hazy, Mr Noah – so I remain your patriarchship's neglected servant.[11]

Rawnsley brought out the best in George Clayton.

Meanwhile, the Rawnsley household fed the young Alfred Tennyson's imagination. Rawnsley had three children, Edward, Drummond and Sophy, and the Tennyson children were on excellent terms with all of them.[12] Later, in the 1830s, Alfred would be a little in love with Sophy Rawnsley, and she in turn would recall the young Tennyson with affection:

He was so interesting because he was so unlike other young men; and his unconventionality of manner and dress had a charm which made him more acceptable than the dapper young gentleman of the ordinary type at ball or supper party. He was a splendid dancer, for he loved music, and kept such time.

His conversation was even better than his dancing: 'we liked to talk better than to dance together at Horncastle, or Spilsby, or Halton; he always had something worth saying, and said it so quaintly'.[13]

* * *

The three eldest Tennyson boys – Frederick, Charles and Alfred – spent a few years at a school in Louth, which was chosen partly because they could live nearby at the home of their Fytche grandmother and aunt. Louth Grammar School was an Elizabethan foundation with strong traditions. It had an excellent reputation and was well regarded in the county. However, when little Alfred Tennyson was sent there (aged seven), it was suffering from a tyrannical headmaster.* The Reverend Dr John Waite was an old-fashioned, brutal man, whose preferred mode of teaching was to beat the boys into submission. In later years Tennyson said of him that he 'thrashed a boy more unmercifully for a false quantity than a modern headmaster today would thrash a boy for the worst offence of which schoolboys could be guilty'. The school took its tone from the head's violence, and there was a great deal of bullying among the boys. Alfred's spirit was broken by this, and he vividly recalled one particularly horrible day when he was sitting on the school steps, weeping from the ill-treatment he had just had from Waite. This provoked one of the school bullies, who came out of his way to punch him in the chest, crowing, 'I'll teach you to cry.'[14]

Alfred suffered from this regime for four years. There was not enough money for all the boys to go to good schools, but George Clayton's somewhat poignant sense of what was due to a gentleman's oldest son caused him to make a special case of Frederick, who was taken away and sent to Eton in 1818. Alfred, by contrast, left Louth Grammar School in 1820, aged eleven, having learnt nothing but fear.

The childhood of the Tennysons at Somersby was odd but not unhappy. Alfred's son Hallam wrote persuasively that 'Their imaginative natures gave them many sources of amusement. One of these lasted a long time: the writing of tales in letter form, to be put under the vegetable dishes at dinner, and read aloud when it was over.' Alfred was their natural leader. Hallam quoted his aunt Cecilia, Tennyson's youngest sister, who remembered that when she was a little girl:

> in the winter evenings by the firelight little Alfred would take her on his knee, with Arthur and Matilda leaning against him on either side, the baby Horatio between his legs; and how he would fascinate this group of young hero-worshippers, who listened open-eared and open-mouthed to legends of knights and heroes among untravelled forests rescuing distressed damsels, or on gigantic mountains fighting

---

*This man was in fact related to the Fytches, and therefore to the Tennyson boys, and it must have seemed an obvious choice of school.

with dragons, or to his tales about Indians, or demons, or witches. The brothers and sisters would sometimes act one of the old English plays; and the elder members of the family thought that my father, from his dramatic rendering of his parts and his musical voice, would turn out an actor.[15]

Tales, stories, legends and memories were amplified by the family's collective story-telling gift into a rich and layered tapestry of narratives that became part of the young Alfred Tennyson's nurturing experience. Lincolnshire people had savage manners, and included memorable characters such as his grandfather Old George Tennyson's coachman. When he was rebuked for having dirty harness, this man 'rushed into the drawing room' at Bayons, 'flung the whole harness on the floor and roared out "clean it yourself then"'. One of the Somersby cooks was equally hard to manage. 'Master Awlfred' (as she called him) remembered this woman, in a rage against Dr Tennyson and his wife, yelling that 'If you raäked out Hell with a smaäll-tooth coämb you weän't find their likes.' (Tennyson must have given Hallam this anecdote in his own imitation of the rural Lincolnshire accent.) Tennyson's father liked the rough villagers and was on good terms with them: the poor 'were fond of the "stern Doctor", as they called him, and would "do anything for him"'.[16] Tennyson's maternal grandmother Elizabeth Fytche contributed to this brew of memories with examples such as this, probably from the 1760s, of a rustic Lincolnshire tragedy. She remembered having seen 'a young widow, dressed in white, on her way to be strangled (her body afterwards to be burnt)'. She was a widow because she had poisoned her husband.*

The imaginative world of the Tennyson children was fed by Shakespeare and Byron. The latter was so great a hero that when news of the poet's death reached Somersby in 1824, Alfred, then fourteen, went out to carve the words 'Byron is dead' on a rock in a hollow near the church which stood opposite the family home. The children cast themselves and each other in an ongoing narrative of knights and ladies. The medievalism that they encouraged as a group took them as far as possible from the real world. Their mother adored and indulged her tall, good-looking sons and daughters. Her tenderness also extended to the whole of the animal kingdom. Her fondness

---

*Hallam Tennyson (*Memoir*, I, p. 7 and n) added a note (quoting Lecky's *England in the Eighteenth Century*) explaining that this horrible medieval punishment was not abolished until 1790. A woman convicted of murdering her husband was publicly burnt at the stake, 'but in practice the sentence was usually mitigated, and she was strangled before the fire touched her body'.

for dogs was well known – the village boys would exploit this by catching an unfortunate dog and beating it outside Somersby's windows until Mrs Tennyson gave them money to persuade them to stop. Her own pets included an owl and a monkey. The owl would perch on her head, and the monkey, her favourite, furious with jealousy, would wait its chance to attack the owl ('took him by the leg, and hurled him to the ground').[17]

Shakespeare and Marlowe stirred Tennyson to write his own play, a lively (but unfinished) drama, *The Devil and the Lady*,[18] written when he was an adolescent. The Latin quotation on the title page, *spes alit juventutem et poesin, vituperatio premit et laedit*, was ominously appropriate. It translates as 'hope nourishes youth and poesy, abuse represses and injures it'. This anticipated, at an early age, the extraordinary sensitivity that the adult Tennyson would feel over adverse criticisms of his poetry.[19] Tennyson wrote *The Devil and the Lady* in a notebook which is now at Harvard. The young writer's liveliness and energy spill chaotically over the inside cover of this book. He identified himself: 'A Tennyson Somersby In Agro Lincolniensis aet 14' and accompanied this inscription with exuberant drawings: a prone figure, a three-legged figure, and an armless figure running. There are hints of a setting – the gable end of the Tennyson house at Somersby, and what could be part of the church behind it. The running figure could simply be enjoying his own energy – Wordsworth's glad animal movement – or perhaps running away from childhood and into adolescence. This would match the play's content, which has an exuberant sense of sexual awakening about it. To accompany part of the devil's speech (fol. 10v) there is a sketch of a horned head, as though Tennyson was using drawings to give identity to the dramatic figures that he was inventing.[20] The play itself is a gifted comic pastiche, with a nod to the Faust legend as transmitted by Marlowe.[21]

A bit later, the adolescent Tennyson wrote poetry marked by a desire for death and an extreme sensitivity to suffering, elements that can be related to his very troubled relationship with his father. Dr Tennyson's depressions were all-consuming: 'the sense of his father's [i.e. Old George's] unkindness and injustice' preyed on his nerves and his health, and caused him at times to be terribly despondent. More than once, Alfred, scared by his father's fits of despondency, 'went out through the black night, and threw himself on a grave in the churchyard, praying to be beneath the sod himself'.[22]

This troubled boy, who could be driven by his father's moods to crave his own death, recognised at the same time his father's intelligence, his literary sensibility and his creativeness. When in a good frame of mind, George Clayton liked to write poetry. Among the uneventful though competent eighteenth-century odes and elegies that he left are a couple of political satires.* The best of these is a long and very comic poem, a 'Sublime Ode' about the Regent's misbehaviour with his mistresses, dating from 1806.[23]

Dr Tennyson became more prosperous after 1815, after Old George had secured a further living for him (at Grimsby). He was able to extend the house at Somersby and to live like a gentleman, keeping his own carriage. He designed a Gothic extension to the rectory as a dining room for his expanding family. His coachman, a sturdy and devoted character called Horlins, who served the family for many years, helped him with the building of this structure, and Dr Tennyson himself carved the decorative detail over the mantelpiece and the windows.[24] But his increased income from his parishes, and regular help in the form of an allowance from his father, was as nothing compared to the wealth of Matthew Russell, his sister Elizabeth's husband, who inherited a fortune in the Durham minefields in 1817. As well as owning Brancepeth Castle, he controlled, as was then the practice, two 'rotten' boroughs and had political influence in both Lincoln and Grimsby. Russell threw himself into the restoration of Brancepeth Castle, spending some £80,000 – an astonishing sum, the equivalent of many millions in today's money – on refurbishments which included newly commissioned stained-glass windows for the hall and a collection of medieval armour for display.

Charles Tennyson, George Clayton's brother, had become very close to his sister, and his attentions paid off in 1819 when he was elected MP for Grimsby. Matthew Russell bore much of the cost of Charles's election campaign, and the two families were thus increasingly closely bound together. Elizabeth wrote genially to Charles:

> Never trouble your heart on the score of obligation to Russell which your excellent head is working or has already worked out. What would he do in many emergencies without you, who extricate him so handsomely and spare his purse?[25]

Surprisingly, as an MP Charles committed himself to reform, embracing measures that were at odds with the political principles held by both his father and the brother-in-law who had so generously

---

*The age of the Prince Regent, later George IV, invited this kind of treatment.

funded him. He favoured the abolition of 'rotten boroughs' and supported the Catholic Emancipation Bill of 1829, and he introduced a liberal bill to reform the game laws. Proud though he was of his younger son, none of this was particularly welcomed by Old George.

Ill health dogged both the sons of the Old Man of the Wolds. Charles showed symptoms of stress in the form of fits. He had been called to the Bar in 1806, and thus lived in London for two years. During this period he met his wife, the heiress Frances Hutton, whom he married in 1808. The fits began in the same year. He wrote to his brother George Clayton saying that his problem was 'a bad secretion of bile & a foul state of stomach and bowels',[26] but the reality seems to be that he had a mild form of epilepsy. The families of the two brothers remained close and took holidays together on the Lincolnshire coast. Dr Tennyson favoured 'oeconomical' Mablethorpe: 'A poor parson with a house to build & furnish cannot be supposed to have any spare rhino [cash] to sport away in extravagant expeditions.'[27] In 1816, George Clayton himself also began to have fits: 'when he open'd his eyes they roled [sic] without meaning and then he spoke incoherently'.[28] The condition was known to be hereditary and was also, at that date, seen as shameful (it was thought to be linked to sexual promiscuity). George Clayton made the situation worse by excessive drinking.

In 1820, Dr Tennyson wrote his father a recklessly bitter letter. 'God judge between you & me,' he railed. 'You make and have always made a false estimate of me in every respect.' Once embarked, he could not stop. He had been 'thrown into a situation unworthy of my abilities & unbecoming either your fortune or my just pretensions'. As for his many children, he was 'kept in the dark with respect to their future prospects, with broken health & spirits'. He closed his letter as though he did not expect any further communication with his father in his lifetime: 'there is a tribunal before which you and I may speedily appear, more speedily perhaps than either of us desire or expect – there it will be seen whether you through life have treated me with that consideration & kindness which a son has a right to expect from a father'.[29] Old George Tennyson was more sensitive to his son's anguish than he was willing to show. Within a few weeks of receiving this letter, he settled a large block of capital on the children.

In 1822, George Clayton took a water cure at Cheltenham. His problem was alcoholic poisoning, but he displayed a pathetic faith in the therapeutic value of the spa water. Elizabeth and Matthew Russell were in the town as well, taking the water therapy. Despite his own poor state, George Clayton took charge. 'Eliza & I are both here,' he wrote to their mother, '& I have consulted a physician with respect to each of our cases.'[30] Within a few weeks, however, Matthew Russell died, very suddenly, probably of a thrombosis. George Clayton was tenderness itself with the stricken widow, and after he had returned to Somersby there followed a period of affectionate correspondence. The whole family came together for a while. Despite her grief, Elizabeth generously offered money to buy tuition for the Somersby children (so that the burden did not fall entirely on George Clayton).

The harmony was not to last. In a letter to his brother in January 1821, George Clayton poured out his anger on the person who least deserved it: his affectionate, generous, loyal and recently widowed sister Elizabeth Russell. He felt patronised and disadvantaged by her, and full of irrational resentment at her offer to help educate his children if he was in financial distress. This was followed by a confused account of a visit to Somersby that she had not made: 'We are three and twenty in family* & sleep five or six in a room. Truly we have great accommodation for Mrs Russell & her suite. We have not the house at Brighton nor the castle at Brancepeth.'[31]

The anger at Mrs Russell ebbed and relations were restored, but George Clayton's health was never going to recover. The fits became more frequent and the drinking made them worse. By March 1825 he was frightening his wife by spending days in bed (usually following a fit) declaring that he was about to die. However, in July of 1825 he felt well enough to travel to Cambridge with his three oldest sons in order to enter Frederick at St John's College. He was taken severely ill on his return home and was not expected to live; so serious was it that his father, Old George, wrote to Mr Burton, patron of the livings, hoping that he would not dispose of them immediately if his son died (the problem of course being that the large family of Somersby Tennysons would then be homeless).

Old George had more immediate grief of his own in the summer of 1825 when his wife, the gentle Mary Turner, who had done so much to alleviate the effect of her husband's anger over the years, died on 20 August. Mary had loved him, despite his grim, humourless, ambitious nature, and in his own way he clearly loved her. He now felt Bayons

---

*The 'three and twenty' may have been literally true. It is possible that there were as many as ten staff employed to look after Dr Tennyson, his wife and their eleven children. They kept a housekeeper, a cook, a coachman and a governess for the girls, as well as varying numbers of other indoor and outdoor servants.

Manor to be a dismal and lonely house: 'poor dank and melancholy and ever will be while I live at it; being unhappy in myself, I make all around me if not miserable, quiet and grave'.[32] The old man never recovered his former confidence and aggression, but he continued to receive claims on his money to support the Somersby children. Some of these communications from Dr Tennyson took the form of polite but urgent requests; others were truculent and abusive demands. A letter of January 1827 requesting payment of Frederick's Cambridge expenses ended by declaring that Old George's injurious and unkind manner 'absolutely precludes me from visiting you, when I know you harbour so unjust & unfavourable an opinion of me, neither can it be pleasant for you to receive me, a person, according to your description, of so despicable a character'.[33]

Much later, when he wrote *In Memoriam*, Alfred Tennyson would express relief as well as pangs of loss and nostalgia when the time came, in 1837, to take leave of his beloved Somersby ('ring out wild bells' can be taken as celebrating liberty from the ties of the past). *Maud*, written in the 1850s, when Tennyson was securely famous and well on his way to being decidedly wealthy, nevertheless comes back in an obsessional way to the young man's feelings about both his doomed father and his favoured uncle.

Tennyson struggled with the need to avoid hating and resenting his father. There was no other intelligent adult male taking a personal daily interest in him in the way that good schoolmasters or tutors would have done if his childhood had been more typical of his class and time. His father was the single most important force in his early life. Clearly the adolescent Tennyson was aware of the damage that George Clayton was doing to his family, but instead of quarrelling with him, he placed all the troubles at Somersby at the door of his uncle, Charles Tennyson d'Eyncourt, the 'oiled and curled Assyrian bull'. Alfred Tennyson deflected the blame and lived in denial of what his father had actually done.

The scholars who have worked in detail on Dr Tennyson's manuscripts and commonplace book have this to say:

> He [Alfred Tennyson] was torn between deep affection and pity for the father he saw as victim and hatred and aggression towards the uncle and grandfather he saw as all-powerful and malevolent. The effect of such intense exposure to a parent (reminiscent of the well-documented examples of the Mill and the Gosse families) is

23

evident not only in Alfred's early poetry but perhaps also in the poet's life-long search for consolation.[34]

Alfred Tennyson entered Trinity College, Cambridge, in November 1827. He and his brother Charles were already published poets (*Poems by Two Brothers*, published in Louth in 1827), which was socially helpful. Charles had joined the college months earlier, in October; their oldest brother Frederick was already a member (since 1826, having transferred himself from St John's). Tennyson liked to keep close to these two brothers, with whom as a boy he had shared the attic bedroom at Somersby rectory. After briefly sharing lodgings with them both at number 12 Rose Crescent, he and Charles moved into rooms in Trumpington Street, number 57 Corpus Buildings, now part of Corpus Christi College (where legend has it that Alfred kept a pet snake which vanished under the floorboards).

The excitement and sense of liberty that would have been natural to a young man in his position, coming to Cambridge from such a confined and troubled family, were missing. Instead he felt intensely homesick. He remembered the simple delights of a fine night in Lincolnshire, and contrasted that with similar weather in Cambridge. An undergraduate friend and contemporary, John Allen, later copied out a large number of the young Tennyson's poems into a notebook, in some cases helpfully dating them. This one is dated by Allen as from 1827, and therefore must have been written very soon after Tennyson first arrived at Trinity:

> Playfellow winds and stars, my friends of old,
>   For sure your voice was friendly, your eyes bright
>   With sympathy, what time my spirit was cold
>   And frozen at the fountain, my cheek white
> As my own hope's quenched ashes. As your memories
>   More than yourselves ye look; so overcast
>   With steam of this dull town your burning eyes:
> Nay, surely even your memories wear more light
> Than do your present selves. Ye sympathize
> As ever with me, stars, from first to last.[35]

A little poem called 'Home', written the following year, is more specific still about the homesickness:

What shall sever me
From the love of home?
Shall the weary sea,
Leagues of sounding foam?
Shall extreme distress,
Shall unknown disgrace,
Make my love the less
For my sweet birth-place?
Though my brains grow dry,
Fancy mew her wings,
And my memory
Forget all other things –
Though I could not tell
My left hand from my right, –
I should know thee well,
Home of my delight![36]

CHAPTER 2

Cambridge, 1827–1830

So when four years were wholly finishèd,
She threw her royal robes away.
'Make me a cottage in the vale,' she said,
'Where I may mourn and pray.

'Yet pull not down my palace towers, that are
So lightly, beautifully built:
Perchance I may return with others there
When I have purged my guilt.'

When Tennyson went up to Trinity College, Cambridge, he left behind in Somersby a rapidly deteriorating family situation. His mother had found it necessary to separate for a while from her husband. Tennyson and his brother Charles travelled with her to London in June 1827 to visit relations (leaving Dr Tennyson to his epilepsy, drink and depression in Somersby). That expedition to London may have been the first time that Alfred had ever travelled beyond the confines of Lincolnshire. He visited wealthy Aunt Russell at her house in Berkeley Square. She found him preoccupied with his own creative inner life to the exclusion of all else. He 'slept during the time he staid upon the drawingroom sopha. I wish he had something in Life to interest him as well as his beautiful poetry – Westminster Abbey was the only thing which particularly charmed him, it suited the *pensive* habit of his soul'.[1] George Clayton had been drinking so heavily that a friend of his wife's family, William Chaplin, warned that he was 'dangerously disposed to his wife & children; & I dread the fatal effects towards some of them, which would consign him to perpetual confinement for his life'. Elizabeth was in fear for her own life, he said, and 'a coroner's verdict would declare him under the influence of insanity, should such a horrid death be perpetrated by him'. This led to a family conference, which involved the family doctor, Dr Bousfield. Surprisingly, Dr Bousfield found Dr Tennyson perfectly normal: 'as well as I have usually seen him of late' and displaying 'acuteness of mind and playfulness of manner'.[2] But he acknowledged that the excessive drinking was a problem, and he recommended a change of scene: accordingly Dr Tennyson went to Paris for a few weeks. After his return in March 1828, there was an accident at Somersby:

The cook set fire to her dress and was so seriously injured that she died a few days later. The Doctor himself was badly burned in trying to help her. The entire burden of looking after the poor woman and arranging for her funeral and other consequences of her death fell on Dr Tennyson, for his wife had no ability to deal with such situations, and the resulting pressures were increased by malicious gossip in the neighbourhood, where the Doctor's growing eccentricity had made him a target for ridicule. Now a tale went round that he had given orders for a butt of water to be kept in future by the kitchen door, so that any cook who caught fire could jump in and extinguish herself without troubling her master. The effect on the unfortunate Dr Tennyson was disastrous. His health rapidly deteriorated and the old resentment against his father and brother flared up again.[3]

In 1829, Frederick Tennyson was rusticated from Cambridge. As the oldest son, he was accustomed to getting his own way, and he was ferociously strong-willed. He had been missing chapel (attendance at chapel was compulsory in the college) and had made matters worse by failing to write the impositions required of him as punishment. One can understand that this intelligent, passionate young man would find it intolerable to be treated as though he was still a schoolboy. He was summoned to the convention of the college to explain himself. At this meeting he was 'smilingly and satirically impertinent', and given his evident refusal to submit to any kind of authority, the convention rusticated him for three terms. For Dr Tennyson, having Frederick under his roof at Somersby, angry and at a loose end, was explosive. He drank more heavily than usual and was found to have armed himself with a knife and a loaded gun, which he threatened to fire through the kitchen window; he then threatened to kill Frederick.[4] His terrified wife reported that he cursed her and the children in terms 'such as a husband & a Father and above all a person of his sacred profession ought particularly to avoid'. Dr Tennyson called in the village constable and asked him to remove Frederick from the house. The constable took the practical and compassionate step of providing refuge for the young man in his own cottage. After three days Dr Tennyson had calmed down somewhat and sent for his son, and an agreement was patched up: Frederick would have an annual allowance (a generous one of £100) if he would now study for a career in the law. Frederick agreed to go to London and work towards becoming a barrister.[5]

Elizabeth Tennyson had been pushed to the extreme of her endurance and she wrote to Old George about her husband's 'ungovernable violence': 'I do not feel it safe either for myself or my children to remain any longer in the house with him.'[6] She moved out and took lodgings in Louth with her children. George Clayton was left at Somersby with the servants and the coachman, Horlins (the one person in the household who was able to manage him). The staunch Thomas Hardwicke Rawnsley did what he could to take care of him, and it was agreed by the family that foreign travel should be tried once more. Dr Tennyson was packed off again to Paris on his own, whence he wrote to say that he was well-treated and recovering, but bitter over his family: 'I feel that I have been treated most indecently by them,' he declared in May 1829. This was followed by a series of increasingly manic letters describing his travels in France and Italy, and intensifying reproaches of his family for neglect. His brother Charles was worried that he was suicidal.[7]

George Clayton stayed away until June 1830. When he returned to Somersby, he seemed markedly better, but Elizabeth had no doubt that if he started drinking again there would be further trouble. For his own part Dr Tennyson reported a series of colourful stories about his adventures. His son Charles, who assumed that the stories were true, repeated them to a friend, John Frere: 'My father has returned from his tour and I am much surprised to see him well after the neck-break adventures he has encountered.'[8] These adventures included being thrown down a precipice from a small carriage while crossing the Alps, and finding himself accused of a murder at a carnival in Rome. These stories were inventions, like the earlier tales of his escape from Russia: the unfortunate man was doing what he could to make his own life seem interesting.

This horribly disturbing family drama was unfolding during the first year of his life that Alfred Tennyson had spent away from home. It is not surprising that he was often wretchedly depressed and lonely. He was close to his widowed aunt, Elizabeth Russell, throughout this period. She was able to be generous to this gifted nephew, and made him an annual allowance, probably of £100, which continued throughout his young manhood (and indeed possibly after his marriage, although by the 1850s he could hardly have been said to be short of money). To this favourite aunt, known to him as 'Asile' (reversing her family name, Elisa), he wrote on 18 April 1828 to report on his experiences at Cambridge:

> I am sitting Owl-like and solitary in my rooms [. . .] the shouts of drunken Gown and drunken Town come up from below with a

sea-like murmur [. . .] I know not how it is but I feel isolated here in the midst of society. The country is so disgustingly level, the revelry of the place so monotonous, the studies of the University so uninteresting, so much matter of fact.

There is a good deal of posturing here: self-regarding, consciously clever, and above all, perhaps, distancing himself as far as possible from the problems of Somersby by creating a kind of epistolary palace of art in which he can play. The tales from the *Arabian Nights* find their way into this letter. Tennyson wanted to be an enchanted prince:

I wish to Heaven I had Prince Houssain's fairy carpet to transport me along the deeps of air to your Coterie – nay, I would even take up with his brother Aboul-something's glass for the mere pleasure of a peep. What a pity it is that the golden days of Faerie are over! What a misery not to be able to consolidate our gossamer dreams into reality! Be it so. I must take my cigar philosophically and evaporate them in smoke, twirl my thumbs rotatorily, cross one leg over the other and sink back in my chair. No – it won't do. The eternal riot of this place, the wear and tear of mind and body are a very insufficient balm to the wound of recollections.[9]

Tennyson was noted for his strikingly romantic physical presence. The actress Fanny Kemble, who visited her brother John Kemble when he was a member of Trinity, remembered that 'Alfred Tennyson was our hero, the great hero of our day.' A contemporary undergraduate, W. H. Thompson, later to be Master of Trinity, when he first saw him come into Hall, said: 'That man must be a poet.' Another contemporary described him as: 'Six feet high, broad-chested, strong-limbed, his face Shakespearian', and displaying a memorable union of 'strength with refinement'.[10] The loneliness of the new undergraduate in the unfamiliar city did not last, and soon Tennyson's magical relationship with Arthur Hallam would dissolve it completely.

Tennyson had been entered on the college books in January 1828; Arthur Hallam arrived in October of the same year. At Eton Hallam had had a reputation for brilliance and precocity, his intellectual achievements both stimulated and managed by his father, who was violently ambitious for him. By the age of sixteen he was writing poised and mature philosophical essays and composing passable sonnets in Italian, and his fellow Etonian, William Ewart Gladstone, thought him the most brilliant person he had ever met. But his father's pressure was damaging. Arthur was prone to depressions and intensely severe headaches; these continued throughout his schooldays and beyond, into his undergraduate life. Most of his Etonian friends went to Oxford, and it seems to have been in order to separate Arthur from these companions that his controlling father sent him to Cambridge.

To Alfred Tennyson, Arthur Hallam was simply dazzling – elegant, worldly, assured and rich, all the things Tennyson felt he could never be. Emotionally, however, the two young men were alike – they were both lonely at Cambridge and they both had troubling relationships with their fathers. The first surviving references to each other in their letters are from May and June 1829. They are brief and jovial: clearly an easy familiarity had already developed.[11]

Hallam's feelings for Tennyson are expressed in a sonnet about their friendship, 'To A.T.':

> Oh, last in time, but worthy to be first
> Of friends in rank, had not the father of good
> On my early spring one perfect gem bestowed,
> A friend, with whom to share the best and worst.
> Him will I shut close to my heart for aye.
> There's not a fibre quivers there, but is
> His own, his heritage for woe, or bliss.
> Thou would'st not have me such a charge betray.
> Surely, if I be knit in brotherhood
> So tender to that chief of all my love,
> With thee I shall not loyalty eschew.
> And well I ween not time with ill or good
> Shall thine affection e'er from mine remove,
> Thou yearner for all fair things, and all true.[12]

The earlier friend to whom Hallam refers here is James Milnes Gaskell (who was at Eton with him). The young Gladstone, however, then an undergraduate at Oxford, took it as a reference to himself. Hallam's friendship with this famous statesman of the future, formed while they were boys together at school, was decisively weakened by the fact that their fathers had sent them to different universities. Gladstone was a passionately emotional man, and his feeling for Hallam was strong and possessive. When Hallam proudly declared in this poem that Alfred Tennyson now had first place in his affections, Gladstone was severely hurt. There was an extraordinary exchange of letters between the two young men, the one behaving like an outraged lover racked with indecisiveness, the other responding with guilt, dignity, self-restraint and a kind of assured assertiveness. The occasion was the appearance of Arthur Hallam's volume of poems, privately printed and circulated among friends in 1830. Ostensibly, Gladstone's difficulty here was that Hallam was showing signs of free-thinking in religious matters, but the real problem is plain to see:

> I wish to thank you heartily for sending me a book in which there is so much to admire: and what is more than that, in which there is so much to instruct and to elevate. [Gladstone deleted the next sentence.] I do not speak of any points in wh. I am unable to enter into your views, for it is more pleasant to dwell upon those where I in common with many may sympathize and admire without attacking.

After this veiled barb, the letter moves to outright reproach:

> That I much regret not having heard from you it would be vain to deny: at the same time let me assure you that I do not conceive I ever was properly qualified for intercourse with you – therefore it was not my legitimate possession – therefore I have no right to desire its restitution.

Hallam replied:

> I am somewhat surprised, but more grieved, that you should consider the state of our intercourse requires the tone you have taken. I have always found you a true friend, and have always wished to prove the same to you [. . .] Circumstance, my dear Gladstone, has indeed separated our paths, but it never can do away with what has been.[13]

If one was invited to read this letter unseen and guess its provenance, the high moral tone and steely emotional control might lead one to think that its author was a senior professional figure in his fifties. Arthur Hallam was nineteen.

James Milnes Gaskell (1810–73) and Arthur Hallam were both 'in love' with a young woman called Anna Wintour, for whom they had developed strong feelings during an idyllic visit to Rome in the winter of 1827–8.[14] Anna Wintour was at least seven years older than these Etonians, who, however mature and well-presented, were hardly likely to attract her. That made no difference to the myth that developed about her, a myth that was not restricted to Hallam and Gaskell. It was said of Wintour that 'all Cambridge was set on fire by her beauty', and that the Italian polish acquired during her residence abroad 'must have made her perfectly irresistible'.[15] Hallam and Gaskell became very close through this joint infatuation, Hallam writing to Gaskell on 2 February 1829, shortly before his eighteenth birthday:

> Carissimo, I have thrown open to you my whole heart; you know all my weakness as well as all my aspirations towards good; may I never be brought to think that I have made the experiment in vain. For an experiment it surely is: it is said in the cold world that no good comes of opening out one's inmost self to the view even of him whom we have deemed our friend; that where all is known nothing is imagined, and hence mutual discontent and exhaustion – 'And thereof comes in the end despondency and madness!' [From Wordsworth's 'Resolution and Independence'] I will prove them liars, however; for I know whom I have trusted.[16]

It looks wholly laughable, but Hallam persisted in taking his own emotional life with deep seriousness: 'I do very solemnly entreat you, Gaskell, not to let distrust come between us,' he wrote a full year later to his rival in love.[17]

Arthur Hallam early became a member of the Cambridge Conversazione Society, also known as 'the Apostles'. This was a self-selecting group of twelve young men, most of them from Trinity College, which met as a discussion group behind closed doors in the rooms of one of their number every Saturday evening. In 1829 Tennyson was elected to this society. This was largely through Arthur Hallam's influence, though the person who actually proposed him was another Trinity man, Hallam's friend Robert Tennant;* Tennant had been a gifted schoolboy at Christ's Hospital and was a young man of lively literary interests who had a personal acquaintance with Coleridge. It was Tennant who had proposed Hallam himself for membership of the society in the previous year. The Apostles were to provide Tennyson's preferred model for well-conducted intellectual communities for the rest of his life.

---

*Robert Tennant (1809–42) graduated in 1831, took holy orders, and later became an Anglican minister in Florence. Following his early death his Italian widow kept a House of Mercy near Windsor to which Gladstone sent prostitutes for rehabilitation. The ideas of one of the founding Apostles, Frederick Denison Maurice (1805–72), underpinned much Apostolic thinking. He would later become a famous philanthropist and Christian socialist. Another founding Apostle, John Sterling (1806–44), was a brilliant, complex but sadly short-lived figure who would in due course write one of the most influential reviews of Tennyson's 1842 volumes.

Among the contemporary Apostles who were close friends of Tennyson were Richard Chenevix Trench (1807–86), later Archbishop of Dublin, and James Spedding (1808–81), son of a landowner in the Lake District, who would become the country's leading authority on Francis Bacon. Spedding's quiet, dry, steady personality and his excellent literary judgement would be of great service to Tennyson's growth as a poet.

An Apostle whom it was impossible to ignore or forget was Richard Monckton Milnes (1809–85), a cousin of James Milnes Gaskell. Monckton Milnes would be created Baron Houghton in 1863, and would become a poet, Liberal politician, reformer and cheerful man of affairs. He was inclined to develop romantic crushes on other young men, and he was particularly attracted to Arthur Hallam, much as Gladstone had been at Eton. Hallam himself was fully aware of this. As an undergraduate Milnes was short, fat, harmlessly boastful and exhibitionist, and he loved to perform in student theatricals. There were no women at Cambridge to take the female roles, and Monckton Milnes was remembered by his friends as a hilarious Mrs Malaprop and a striking, if overweight, Beatrice. (His Beatrice sat heavily on one of the stage furnishings and broke it.) Monckton Milnes and Tennyson had this love of theatricals in common: Tennyson often appeared in undergraduate productions, and was effective as a darkly saturnine and eloquent Malvolio.

Monckton Milnes was good-natured, self-indulgent and generous; in later life he was notably kind and encouraging to the young Swinburne. A champion and editor of Keats, he became known in literary circles for his pioneering *Life, Letters and Literary Remains of John Keats* (1848). This publication would provoke Tennyson to write an indignant poem in protest at what he saw as posthumous invasion of Keats's privacy. The distinguished American commentator and politician Henry Adams would give an affectionate transatlantic perspective on Monckton Milnes, writing of him that he was 'rich according to Yorkshire standards', and that he entered Parliament without any desire to work hard for his country: 'he was one of the numerous Englishmen who refuse office rather than make the effort of carrying it, and want power only to make it a source of indolence'.[18]

Among the other Apostles were two sober and inseparable Scots, Francis Garden (1810–84) and Robert Monteith (1812–84). Monteith, although the younger man, was in fact Garden's uncle. They both matriculated at Trinity College in the same year, 1829, and in March 1830 Arthur Hallam himself proposed the pair for election to the Apostles (presumably it was impossible to entertain the notion of having one without the other). Robert Joseph Ignatius Monteith was the grandson of the founder of the cotton trade in Scotland, and would become a calico printer at Blantyre and Barrowfield in Lanarkshire. Francis Garden would be ordained in the Anglican Church and was for a time one of the joint editors of the High Church periodical the *Christian Remembrancer*.[19] They were loyal members of the society, though what they contributed to the Apostles beyond a certain measured propriety is not clear.

John Moore Heath (1808–82) and his brother Douglas Heath (1811–97) were also both Trinity men and both Apostles. During 1832–3 John Moore Heath kept a commonplace book, which is now in the Fitzwilliam Museum in Cambridge. It contains copies of a number of Tennyson's poems (some of them – 'St Simeon Stylites', for example – annotated and corrected in Tennyson's own handwriting).[20] From Heath's manuscript scholars have been able to determine the date of composition of some of Tennyson's early poems.

A Trinity man who would later become close to Alfred Tennyson was Edward Fitzgerald (1809–83). Fitzgerald, 'Old Fitz', would in due course be famous to the literary world for his English version of the *Rubáiyát of Omar Khayyám* (1859). He and James Spedding had been schoolboys at Bury St Edmunds Grammar School before they went up to Trinity; John Kemble (1807–57) and his friend William Bodham Donne were Trinity men and Apostles who had come from the same Bury St Edmunds school. Kemble (Jack to his friends) was from the well-known theatrical family; his father was Charles Kemble and his sister was the celebrated actress Fanny Kemble. Kemble would later be an academic: he would become a distinguished philologist and historian of languages. Others whose later lives would mesh closely with Tennyson's were the great novelist William Makepeace Thackeray (1811–63) and William Henry Brookfield (1809–74).* Brookfield was a lively friend of many of the Apostles although never himself elected a member.

At the Tennyson Research Centre there is a list of the 'Acts of the Apostles' – papers given by members of the Cambridge Apostles in 1829 and 1830 – which includes reference to the paper given by Arthur Hallam on 5 December 1829: 'Whether the existence of an intelligent First Cause is deducible from the phenomena of the universe?'

---

*William Brookfield became related by marriage to Arthur Hallam's family: in 1841 he married Jane Octavia Elton, who was the youngest daughter of Arthur Hallam's uncle, Sir Charles Abraham Elton. Subsequently his daughter-in-law, Frances Brookfield, would publish a valuable memoir of the Apostles (see Bibliography).

Tennyson failed to give a paper to the society at all, and on 13 February 1830 his membership technically lapsed because he had defaulted: 'Tennyson is "Moderator"' (essayist): but 'No essay was read to the Society this evening and Tennyson resigned his seat.'[21] He had in fact prepared an essay, or at least made some attempt to do so. A fragment of a composition on 'ghosts' survives in one of his notebooks (now at Harvard): a very small leatherbound book which also contains some notes on his classical studies, a number of drawings, and bits and pieces of early poems. Twelve sheets have been cut out – Tennyson often used sheets from his own work books as spills to light his pipes – so that the essay may have been more or less complete before the book was mutilated. What remains establishes the context – the group of friends comfortably attentive to the speaker – and considers the pleasures of shared terror. The 'power of telling deep, horrible agreeable ghost stories' was certain to command an audience, he wrote. 'Every cheek is blanched, every eye fixed upon the narrator: he speaks in a simple manner of a high matter: he speaks of life & death & the things after death: he lifts the veil but the form behind it is shaded in deeper obscurity.' His audience would 'feel their hair bristle & their flesh creep with a sense of unutterable mystery'.[22] This has the makings of a good spine-tingling Gothic evening for the young men. It is a pity that Tennyson did not deliver his paper and keep a record of the discussion that he might have prompted.

Hallam was regarded by all the Apostles as the animator and the intellectual focus of the group. Did he deserve this? An historian of the society thinks he did:

Hallam seems to have inspired unqualified admiration in almost everyone who came to know him. From his earliest years he had shown remarkable intellectual gifts, and he had been brought up as a privileged being in a family headed by one of the more distinguished writers of the day. Henry Hallam had the highest hopes for his brilliant eldest son: under his cautious supervision (or perhaps despite it) Arthur developed into an impressively well-read and cosmopolitan youth, with an exceptional knowledge of modern literature and thought. In character he was reflective, earnest, rather solemn, yet he charmed his contemporaries with the openness of his manner and the sympathy with which he treated them. He was far from being merely amiable: indeed, he tended to be a demanding and critical friend, for he was as aware of his superiority as anyone else and was rather too accustomed to being idolized. But his friendship seemed immensely valuable to those around him, and they anxiously, even jealously, strove to please him and be near him.[23]

Arthur Hallam was indeed strikingly precocious. He worked out a moral philosophy for himself and his friends which profoundly influenced Alfred Tennyson and which underpinned much of Tennyson's writing. The basis of this moral philosophy was Platonic, and central to Hallam's reading of Plato was the teaching that love is the fountain-head and also the final destination of a moral education. His paper to the Apostles delivered in his rooms in Trinity on 14 May 1831 addressed this topic. The title was 'Did the Epicureans do more than the Stoics for the advancement of that portion of mental philosophy which relates to the origin of our moral sentiments?' He developed this further into an essay about Cicero, specifically asking what were 'the merits of Ciceronian philosophy'. His discussion led him to see a fatal split between Cicero the orator and Cicero the man. The orator was an unsurpassed virtuoso, while the man lacked the 'loftier powers of the imagination' and, crucially, did not grasp the central significance of friendship. Cicero did not understand 'the sublime principle of love'. 'Love' as taught by Plato (and neglected by Cicero), 'in its simplest ethical sense, as a word of the same import with sympathy, is the desire which one sentient being feels for another's gratification, and consequent aversion to another's pain', and the capacity for such desire 'is the broad and deep foundation of our moral nature'.[24] Hallam acknowledged that Plato's dialogues advocating a perfect love between men could create a problem for nineteenth-century readers: it was a 'more lively sentiment than has existed at other times between man and man', and 'misunderstanding' of this sentiment 'has repelled several from the deep tenderness and splendid imagination of the Phaedrus and the Symposium'.[25]

The society was committed to absolute freedom of thought and speech. Such freedom was intoxicating to these young men. Arthur Hallam was seen as the best mind of the group, the future philosopher and statesman, but Alfred Tennyson, their poet, was the pre-eminent figure. Frances Brookfield's account indicates how the others looked on him at the time:

> He would have been a great man though he had never written a verse. He had the nobility, the strength, the individuality and the complacency of greatness. There was nothing small about him – not even diffidence as to abilities, qualms as to results nor deference to popular opinion. He had also the presence of a great man; he was

strikingly handsome, as all the world knows, splendid of face and strong of limb.[27]

Brookfield wrote of the impact of the group on Tennyson's natural disposition to laziness and diffidence:

> The activity of these earnest young minds, their independence and eagerness to make their way in the world had a stimulating effect upon Tennyson's mind, at that time inclined to be lethargic. They gave him a sense of responsibility; for the first time in his life he began under these influences to think for himself, and to decide what his future career should be.

Tennyson was 'a man of moods', subject to swings of depression, and his friends were 'always eager to drive away the shadows from his soul'. They also tried to remedy his many small eccentricities: Douglas Heath told him that he ought to wear a clean shirt. The poet replied: 'H'm, yours would not be as clean as mine if *you* had worn it a fortnight.'[28]

One achievement set Alfred and Charles Tennyson apart from their friends. They had already published *Poems by Two Brothers*; the poems in this volume were in fact by three brothers: three or four were Frederick's work.

Alfred Tennyson had grown from childhood to adolescence in an age of conflict. Napoleon and the Duke of Wellington loomed large in the landscape of his imagination, and his excited reading of Coleridge, Byron, Shelley, Scott and Ossian provided him with a way of writing on big ambitious themes. Often his poems in this volume explicitly champion the underdog. 'The Vale of Bones' celebrates the Scottish dead slaughtered by the English at Flodden, 'The Druid's Prophecies' laments the destruction of the Druids' groves at Anglesey by the Roman conquerors. 'The Old Sword', which is very much the work of an adolescent flexing his muscles, strikes heroic attitudes without any particular adversary in mind. These poems, written when Tennyson was sixteen or seventeen, are less individual and striking than the versification of *The Devil and the Lady* written at fourteen. In his remarkable study of Tennyson's early poetry, W. D. Paden plausibly suggested: 'Alfred was growing. At about sixteen a boy changes. He makes the proper motions before a mirror, striving to do perfectly something that he may have accomplished earlier with more grace and assurance though with less thought. He retreats into conventionality whenever he is unsure.'[29]

Poems by Two Brothers attracted hardly any attention and virtually no sales, yet Thomas Jackson, the otherwise unknown Louth bookseller who had published the volume, had offered the considerable advance of £20 in books and cash.[30] Alfred and Charles Tennyson wrote very precise instructions about publication to Jackson early in 1827; among other things they insisted that there should be no initials or any other clue to their identity in the anonymous volume (perhaps to circumvent the awkwardness of the 'two brothers' of the title being in fact three brothers).[31] The question of why an obscure provincial bookseller would pay surprisingly good money to these completely unknown adolescent poets is unexplained.

Is it possible that Old George, in a secret remorseful gesture, paid Jackson for publication in order to give some recognition and hope to the unruly Somersby household? He may have done. However, Paden suggested that it could equally have been their great-uncle, brother of their grandmother Mary Turner, who had been their benefactor. This great-uncle, the comfortable, worldly and hedonistic Rev. Samuel Turner of Caistor, was fond of the boys, especially of Charles.[32] The pleasure that the young men took in the appearance of their book was wild and unbounded. On the afternoon of publication Alfred and Charles hired a carriage with some of the money that Jackson had paid as their advance, and drove over the wolds and marshes to their favourite part of the coast, Mablethorpe, where they 'shared their triumph with the winds and the waves'.[33]

The Tennyson brothers at Cambridge, then, were noted as being already published poets as well as for their remarkable presence. Frederick was big, broad and the only Tennyson to have blond hair, while Alfred was well over six feet, broad-chested, with a mysterious Spanish swarthiness and strikingly opulent dark curling hair, which he grew long. He also had magnificent eyes, deep-set and melancholy, with a distant longing in them. That he was woefully short-sighted added to the mysteriousness of his gaze and his air of looking above and beyond his immediate surroundings. His resonant bass chest voice was so melodious (despite his Lincolnshire accent) that he was constantly in demand to perform his own poetry.

As an undergraduate Tennyson had recurrent periods of illness, real or imagined; these may have been unconscious reactions to the continuously disturbing state of affairs in Somersby. In a letter to his grandfather he said that he suffered 'determination of blood to the Head', had been ordered to be 'cupped' (bled by a physician, a remedy for high blood pressure) and feared going blind because his vision was blurred by floaters and 'muscae volitantes'.[34] The symptoms he described are in fact common effects of short-sightedness and are experienced by many who use corrective lenses for myopia. For the rest of his life he would worry about his eyes. Later he wore spectacles.

Dr Tennyson believed powerfully in his third son's talent and in the summer of 1829 urged him to compete for a university prize, the Chancellor's Gold Medal for poetry. Tennyson himself was reluctant, and his son Hallam Tennyson reported that 'unwillingly he patched up an old poem on *The Battle of Armageddon*, and came out prizeman over Milnes, Hallam and others'.[35] He was not particularly pleased by this, however, and would let friends know that he had only been persuaded to compete by parental pleading. Arthur Hallam had sent a copy of his own poem on the same theme to Gladstone, who wrote appreciatively about it. Hallam replied in a letter about Tennyson which has prophetic force:

> I am glad you liked my queer piece of work about Timbuctoo. I wrote it in a sovereign vein of poetic scorn for any body's opinion, who did not value Plato, and Milton, just as much as I did. The natural consequence was that ten people out of twelve laughed [. . .] My friend Tennyson's poem, which got the prize, will be thought by the ten sober persons afore mentioned twice as absurd as mine. [Nevertheless] the splendid imaginative power that pervades it will be seen through all hindrances. I consider Tennyson as promising fair to be the greatest poet of our generation, perhaps of our century.[36]

Feeling out of sorts, Tennyson decided, despite pressure from the Vice-Chancellor, that he did not want to read the poem himself at the ceremony, and invited Charles Merivale to read it as his proxy. He and Merivale had become good friends by April 1828, when Merivale had written to his father, 'I have got the third of the Tennysons in my room, who is an immense poet, as indeed are all the tribe – was the father so?' Merivale said later that he had the honour of reciting the poem because Tennyson was 'too shy or too proud to exhibit himself on such an occasion. I fancy I spouted his verses with considerable effect.'[37]

Tennyson's prize-winning poem was received with polite bewilderment by Cambridge at large. Charles Wordsworth wrote to his brother Christopher (who had won the medal in 1827), 'if such an exercise had been sent up at Oxford, the author would have had a better chance of being rusticated, with the view of his passing a few months at a Lunatic Asylum, than of obtaining the prize'.[38]

In June 1830, Tennyson published *Poems: Chiefly Lyrical*. He was then a twenty-year-old undergraduate, yet this volume contains some of the most famous poems of the nineteenth century, including 'Mariana' and 'The Kraken'. Initially the plan had been for a joint publication. Hallam and Tennyson had not known each other long when Arthur wrote an excited letter (11 October 1829) to Monckton Milnes, saying that there was a possibility that the three of them might publish a volume together, though he felt that Tennyson might not want a three-legged joint publication: 'You have my free vote for publishing along with Tennyson, and myself,' he wrote to Milnes, 'but mine alone is not enough, and as he refused his brother [Charles] on the score of not wishing a third, some difficulty may lie in your way'.[39] The next stage of the planning was for Hallam and Tennyson to collaborate (as Wordsworth and Coleridge had collaborated on their *Lyrical Ballads*), but at a late stage Henry Hallam, Arthur's father, put a stop to that. He wrote later (in the preface to his dead son's literary *Remains*, 1834) that he thought Arthur would put himself in a vulnerable position by publishing poetry which was personal and revealed his own feelings in an unguarded way. Such a publication might be bad for his reputation in the legal profession.

The publisher whom Arthur Hallam had approached, for himself and Tennyson, was Effingham Wilson (1783–1868), a London bookseller associated with philosophical radicalism. Hallam effectively acted as literary agent and undertook all the negotiations, as well as being distributor, publicist and general factotum. He secured a contract in which Tennyson took half share of the profits and also the risk of his first volume.[40] After his father had forced him to withdraw from publication, Arthur had his own poems printed and circulated in May of 1830. Tennyson's volume was published in June. Arthur sent his own volume to friends, and at the same time energetically trumpeted Tennyson's. On 31 May 1830, for example, he wrote to their fellow Apostle William Bodham Donne:

> I incline to hope that in respect of my being an Apostle, and a friend of some of our best friends, you will pardon the liberty I take in sending you a little book which I have just committed the sin of printing, and was on the verge of committing the greater sin of

publishing. You will find in it, I believe, little or no poetry [. . .] I hope in a short time to have the much greater pleasure of sending you a volume of Lyrical poems by Alfred Tennyson, of whom you cannot but have heard [. . .] Friendship certainly plays sad pranks with one's judgement in these matters; yet I think if I hated Alfred Tennyson as much as I love him, I could not help revering his imagination with just the same reverence. The book will be small; but did not Samson slay some thousand Philistines with a jawbone? [. . .] His brother's Sonnets you have seen, I am told; and I rejoice much that you like them: but Charles, though he burns and shines, is a lesser light than Alfred.[41]

Charles Tennyson had published his own *Sonnets and Fugitive Pieces*[42] earlier in the same year, and copies had been in the hands of his friends since March 1830. Charles's sonnets received exhilarating endorsement from one of the greatest poets and critics of the day, Samuel Taylor Coleridge, who took a kindly interest[43] (he picked out 'The Lark' as 'among the best sonnets in our language').[44] Given that Coleridge admired his work, Charles Tennyson could have felt encouraged to think that both he and his brother should persist as poets. The reality, though, was that Charles had little confidence in himself and he worried that his poetry was neither original nor compelling. He continued to write, but he would not publish another volume for over thirty years.*

Hallam was becoming ever closer to Alfred Tennyson – he stayed at Somersby in April 1830, and was immediately adopted as one of the family by Tennyson's mother and all his siblings (Tennyson's father was abroad from May 1829 to July 1830, so Hallam had not met him). When *Poems: Chiefly Lyrical* came out, Hallam sent a copy together with his own privately printed poems to Tennyson's mother. In his accompanying letter he spoke movingly about his friendship with her son, and gave a muted explanation of the reasons for separate publication:

As I have at last the pleasure of sending to Alfred his long expected book, I take this opportunity of begging that you will accept from me a copy of some poems, which I originally intended to have

---

*Tennyson always loved and encouraged his brother. In 1864, Charles Tennyson Turner, as he was now known, published a volume of sonnets dedicated to Alfred, and there were two more volumes, in 1868 and 1873 (the 1873 volume was dedicated to Tennyson's niece, Agnes Weld).

published in the same volume with his. To this joint publication, as a sort of seal of our friendship, I had long looked forward with a delight which, I believe, was no way selfish. But there are reasons which have obliged me to change my intention, and withdraw my own share of the work from the press. [. . .] I have little reason to apprehend your wasting much time over that book [his own *Poems*], when I send you along with it such a treasure in your son's poetry. He is a true and thorough Poet, if ever there was one; and though I fear his book is far too good to be popular, yet I have full faith that he has thrown out sparks that will kindle.

And this immensely confident young man declared bravely: 'No labour on my part shall be wanting to bring his volume into general notice.'[45]

In 1830 Arthur Hallam and Alfred Tennyson travelled together to the Valley of Cauteretz on a famous expedition. The scheme was in part dreamed up by the headstrong and brilliant John Sterling. All the Apostles were liberal, and indeed often radical, in their politics, and Sterling was stirred by the presence in London of Spanish exiles who were involved in a heroic struggle to depose the Spanish monarchy. Thomas Carlyle* remembered seeing the Spaniards:

Daily in the cold spring air, under the skies so unlike their own, you could see a group of fifty or a hundred stately tragic figures, in proud threadbare cloaks; perambulating, mostly with closed lips, the broad pavements of Euston Square and the regions about St Pancras new Church. [. . .] Old steel-gray heads, many of them; the shaggy, thick, blue-black hair of others struck you; their brown complexion, dusky look of suppressed fire, in general their tragic condition as of caged Numidian lions.[46]

One of these figures was the courageous and colourful José María de Torrijos y Uriarte, who had some success in persuading liberal-minded English contacts in London and elsewhere to support the cause of Spanish liberation. Sterling, John Kemble, Richard Chenevix Trench, Hallam and Tennyson were all won over, with varying degrees of enthusiasm.

The adolescent Tennyson had written a number of political poems, and his 'Written During the Convulsions in Spain', a poem considered

---

*Carlyle's *Life of John Sterling* was published in 1851.

for *Poems by Two Brothers* and omitted from it 'for some forgotten reason', dates from this period:

> Roused is thy spirit now,
> Spain of the lofty brow!
>   Streams o'er thy campaign the far-flashing glaive:
> Sweetly may Freedom's rays
> Smile on thy future days,
>   Smile on the hopes of the young and the brave![47]

In his memoir of his father Hallam Tennyson recounted this adventure of 1830:

> During the summer my father joined Arthur Hallam, and both started off for the Pyrenees, with money for the insurgent allies of Torrijos – a noble, accomplished, truthful man, worthy to be a leader. He it was who had raised the standard of revolt against the Inquisition and the tyranny of Ferdinand, King of Spain. Alfred and Arthur held a secret meeting with the heads of the conspiracy on the Spanish border, and were not heard of by their friends for some weeks.

'The hopes of the young and the brave' had stirred the Apostles, and Hallam and Tennyson were given a minor role. They were to take letters and money provided by Torrijos to support a group of insurrectionaries who were holed up in the Pyrenees. The journey was successful, and very agreeable: they were disconcerted, though, when they delivered their messages and the funds to one 'Ojeda', who 'informed them that he desired "couper la gorge à tous les curés," then clapping his hand on his heart murmured "mais vous connaissez mon coeur" – "and a pretty black one it is," thought my father'.[48]

At Cauteretz, Arthur Hallam reported:

> We [. . .] recruited our strength with precipitous defiles, jagged mountain tops, forests of solemn pine, travelled by dewy clouds, and encircling lawns of the greenest freshness, waters, in all shapes, and all powers, from the clear runnel bubbling down over our mountain paths at intervals, to the blue little lake whose deep, cold waters are fed eternally from neighbouring glaciers, and the impetuous cataract, fraying its way over black, beetling rocks, which seemed as if ages had been necessary to make them yield a passage to the element now so overwhelming, and so lavish of its triumphant strength.[49]

Tennyson and Hallam returned safely, but back in England were concerned about the fate of friends who remained in Spain with the insurgents. The Kemble letters, a collection of correspondence which is now in Dunedin, New Zealand, cast further light on the adventure. From these letters we know that William Bodham Donne wrote on 10 June anxiously seeking news. 'The sense of what we have both of us to do and to suffer is too near and heavy upon me.' Trench wrote from England to Kemble in Gibraltar on 24 June, breezily declaring (twice) his readiness to face death in the Spanish cause. 'I am in high spirits at the prospect of our speedy hanging, as anything is better than to remain & rot in this country,' he declared, signing himself as Kemble's 'yokefellow in projected hanging'. Facetious though this is, neither of them was blind to the fact that the mission was dangerous. Trench went out to Gibraltar in the autumn of 1830, and the correspondence – in French and Spanish – between Kemble and Torrijos's group intensified in purpose and urgency. Later in the sequence Torrijos himself wrote to Kemble, confident that if adequately prepared the rebellion would end in victory: 'In this kind of business the days and weeks spent are deemed worth it if the desired result is achieved.' He closed with sunny fatalism: 'We will either achieve our object, or we will go together.'[50]

By November of 1830 Hallam was decidedly worried. He wrote (from Trinity College) to Donne:

> I went to France with Alfred Tennyson, bearing letters &c from Torrijos and Sterling to the Spanish patriots on the Pyrenean frontier: and this business, with the events that soon thronged in with so awful a rapidity, completely occupied me for the time. [. . .] In these days the presumption is always in favour of one's friends being far away, sucked into the race of some revolutionary Maelstroom. I doubt not but you, in common with us all, are very anxious concerning Kemble & Trench. The chances are fearfully against them. Yet if one tenth part of the favourable intelligence which Sterling used to receive from all parts of Spain had been correct, who would not have been certain of a prosperous issue? I fear much from Kemble's rashness of temper.[51]

Indeed, Tennyson had had a report that Kemble had been captured in Spain and was on trial for his life, but this proved to be untrue.[52] Kemble and Trench were reported safe and well in November, and by December they were back in England. Trench was soon regretting the adventure in Spain. By March 1831 he had come to think that the

Cambridge enthusiasts had backed what was probably an unworthy cause by comparison with other revolutionary movements in Europe: 'I c'd eat my heart to think how we have played the fools with the time, when there was a far nobler field in Poland or even in Italy.'[53]

For a young Irishman called Robert Boyd, the Spanish resistance was still a matter of passionate commitment. He effectively led a second mission to Spain, providing £5,000 of his own money to buy a ship. Torrijos was part of the mission (which was supported by Boyd's cousin John Sterling, though Sterling's precise role in the matter was unclear). Carlyle, entering excitedly into the spirit of desperation and adventure which prevailed among Torrijos and his fellow Spaniards in London, as well as his own idealistic young friends, gave a vivid account:

> It was in the months when the Torrijos enterprise was in the birth-throes; crying wildly for capital, of all things. Boyd naturally spoke of his projects to Sterling [. . .] Sterling naturally said, 'If you want an adventure of the Sea-king sort, and propose to lay your money and your life into such a game, here is Torrijos and Spain at his back; here is a golden fleece to conquer, worth twenty Eastern Archipelagos.'[54]

Boyd accompanied Torrijos and his band to Spain. Late in 1831, the project began to go badly wrong; Torrijos did not receive the support he expected in southern Spain and took refuge on Gibraltar. This was only temporary: under a treaty with the Spanish, the British governor had to order him and his party to leave. At the end of November 1831, Torrijos's men (Boyd among them) sailed for Málaga in response to what had appeared to be an invitation and a promise of safe passage from the governor there. This was a treacherous ruse; on arrival they were taken prisoner and transported in heavy irons to a Carmelite convent where a Capucin friar attended them and heard their confessions (with the exception of Boyd). Torrijos urged his companions 'to look death firmly in the face'. There was an eternity of bliss, he promised, 'for those who die innocent'. Boyd declared that he trusted 'too firmly on the mercy of God to feel unmanned at the approach of death'.[55] Boyd, Torrijos and their companions were then executed by firing squad on the beach at Málaga, and thus the Torrijos enterprise came to an end.*

* * *

---

*By this point the Torrijos force was too small to be any kind of threat. The letters refer to the number of men who sailed to Málaga variously as sixty or fifty-five; the number executed on the beach was forty-nine.

Tennyson was drawn to Spanish costume. He knew that he was thought to look Hispanic himself, and he traded on this by adopting the wide-brimmed floppy hat and long black cloak which remained his favourite outdoor wear for the rest of his life. However, although in Spain it seems he was already wearing the cloak, a friend of the Rawnsleys, a Mrs Clay, reports that he was wearing a stovepipe hat of the period. The same lady noted his Spanish appearance: 'she did not wonder that Tennyson was not thought of as being an Englishman in the Pyrenees', since 'she never saw a more Spanish-looking man in her life'.[56] Mrs Clay was a fellow passenger on the steamer (the *Leeds*) on which Hallam and Tennyson sailed from Bordeaux to Dublin at the end of their European trip:

> In the summer of 1830 my father, mother, and sister, with myself, spent the summer in the Pyrenees, and started from Bordeaux on the 8th September in the steamer 'Leeds' for Dublin. Our fellow-passengers [included . . .] Mr Tennyson and his friend Mr Hallam. The weather was fine, and we were sitting on deck. Mr Hallam was a very interesting, delicate-looking young man, and we saw nothing of him the first day; he was in the saloon. The second day was warm, and he came on deck, and kindly read to us some of Scott's novels, which had recently been published in one volume. We were all much charmed with our group of fellow-passengers. In my father's original pencil sketch Mr Tennyson had a large cape, a tall hat, and a very decided nose.[57]

Meanwhile, there was revolution on the Apostles' doorstep. On 2 December 1830, Hallam wrote excitedly to Richard Chenevix Trench about the courage of the agricultural labourers rioting against social injustice in Cambridgeshire:

> The game is lost in Spain; but how much good remains to be done here! The country is in a more awful state than you can well conceive. While I write, Madingley, or some adjoining village, is in a state of conflagration, and the sky above is coloured flame-red. This is one of a thousand such actions committed daily throughout England. The laws are almost suspended; the money of foreign factions is at work with a population exasperated into reckless fury.

Hallam seemed to be supporting both sides in this outbreak of violence. Many of his friends armed themselves to defend the fabric of the university from attack, while Hallam basked in his own credentials as a

European revolutionary: 'Alfred went, as you know, with me to the south of France, and a wild, bustling time we had of it. I played my part as conspirator in a small way, and made friends with two or three gallant men.'[58] More conservative undergraduates, including Charles Merivale, enjoyed themselves defending Cambridge from the riotous rustics:

> Out we sallied, some half-dozen, with single-sticks and such weapons, and had just reached the great gate quite ignorant of what was going on, when on turning round we saw a general red glare hanging steady and still over the Master's Lodge. In a few minutes half Cambridge was in arms (in sticks, that is) and on the road to Coton.[. . .] We had a meeting among ourselves in College this afternoon and elected six captains, of whom I am one, each of whom is to bring a troop of ten men to begin with. The system will then probably be extended. The same is going on in Trinity. Of course we are to put ourselves under the directions of the Dons, who insist very properly on no fire or steel [. . .]. Some of my friends could not go to bed last night without looking into their beds, and overhauling their trunks for fireballs and other dreadful engines.[59]

Marion Shaw's recent work on the New Zealand Kemble collection brings out the significance of the correspondence. The letters were 'obviously precious' to Kemble: they were carefully preserved and are accompanied by a list, in Kemble's hand, giving the sender and the date of each. There were 113 letters (two of them are now missing), written between 22 June 1827 and 23 October 1831. Poetry was a constant topic: Trench, Hallam, Kemble and Donne, as well as Alfred Tennyson and his brother Charles, were all seen by their friends as poets in the making. And some of the letters 'must have been kept and valued because they are a record of friendship between men'. The strong feelings that the young men had for each other were generously and regularly affirmed. William Bodham Donne wrote to John Kemble in May 1829, revelling in Kemble's 'beautiful acknowledgments of the feelings you have towards me'. Mutual love and moral education went hand in hand: it would be Donne's 'highest and most honourable ambition' to follow the good examples of Kemble and Trench. Trench in turn wrote to Kemble in March 1830, 'My heart sickens to see you again, and to tell you how dearly I love you.'[60]

The poetry that Tennyson was writing at this period was highly energised, visionary, political, and in some cases erotic. The political poetry includes a spirited sonnet about Napoleon and two fashionably radical sonnets about the oppression of Poland.*

The young poet was haunted by death. As a late adolescent at Somersby he had written this:

> A spirit haunts the year's last hours
> Dwelling amid these yellowing bowers:
>   To himself he talks;
> For at eventide, listening earnestly,
> At his work you may hear him sob and sigh
>   In the walks;
> Earthwards he boweth the heavy stalks
> Of the mouldering flowers:
> Heavily hangs the broad sunflower
>   Over its grave i' the earth so chilly;
> Heavily hangs the hollyhock,
>   Heavily hangs the tiger-lily.[61]

This first stanza of 'A spirit haunts the year's last hours' is copied out into a book he used at Cambridge, Harvard Notebook 4. In this fat and copiously used little leatherbound volume much of the handwriting is very small, as though the young poet was being careful to make the best use of his space. There are drawings of a woman in medieval dress, of Arabic figures, and architectural sketches. There are notes on Lord Shaftesbury and on Leigh Hunt, bits of Anglo-Saxon vocabulary, some drafts of 'Oriana', with Arthur Hallam's notes and amendments, and of 'The Lover's Tale'. There is also a draft of 'My Life is full of Weary Days' in which the context is the friendship with Arthur Hallam and the possibility that he, Tennyson, might die before Hallam does:

> Shake hands, my friend, across the brink
> Of that dark grave to which I go
> Shake hands once more: I cannot sink
> So far – far down but I shall know
> Thy voice, and answer from below.
>
> When in the darkness over me
> The four-handed mole shall scrape,

---

*A Polish insurrection against control by Russia in November 1830 led to a war of liberation which the Poles had no chance of winning: they were crushed and humiliated in September 1831.

> Plant thou no dusky cypress-tree,
> Nor wreathe thy cap with doleful crape,
> But pledge me in the flowing grape.[62]

There were also poems of religious doubt and of suicidal despair. 'The Two Voices' is the best known of these. The opening stanzas rephrase Hamlet's famous reflection on the possibility of self-slaughter:

> A still small voice spake unto me,
> 'Thou art so full of misery,
> Were it not better not to be?'
>
> Then to the still small voice I said;
> 'Let me not cast in endless shade
> What is so wonderfully made.'[63]

The voice continues to urge suicide; the speaker continues to debate with him. James Spedding wrote to W. H. Thompson in August 1834 about this poem, referring to it as 'Thoughts of a Suicide'. In a metaphor borrowed from Shelley's 'Ozymandias', Spedding wrote that it was 'a vast trunk on the shore – it wants both the beginning and the end [. . .] vast and costly both in design and material, but the expression in many places obscure'.[64]

A poem of urgent adolescent religious anguish, wholly appropriate to the son of a depressed clergyman, was written probably several years earlier than 'The Two Voices'. With its cumbersome title 'Supposed Confessions of a Second-Rate Sensitive Mind Not in Unity with Itself', it looks as though it could be a comic dramatic monologue, but in fact the young poet was using the mask of the 'second-rate sensitive mind' to explore his own feelings in earnest:

> O God! my God! have mercy now.
> I faint, I fall. Men say that Thou
> Didst die for me, for such as *me*,
> Patient of ill, and death, and scorn,
> And that my sin was as a thorn
> Among the thorns that girt Thy brow,
> Wounding Thy soul.[65]

And so on, for nearly two hundred melancholy lines. With this intense interest in death and despair went an equally charged involvement with sex. His late adolescent erotic poetry includes a sonnet about kissing:

> Methinks if I should kiss thee, no control
> Within the thrilling brain could keep afloat
> The subtle spirit. Even while I spoke,
> The bare word KISS hath made my inner soul
> To tremble like a lutestring, ere the note
> Hath melted in the silence that it broke.

This mood, excited and breathlessly virginal, was sustained into a poem never intended for publication which has survived because it was quoted in full in a letter from John Kemble to William Bodham Donne in 1834.

> Love's latest hour is this,
> True love from love must part,
> Yet ere I lose my bliss,
> Sweet! let me feel thine heart.
> One Kiss! one Kiss! one Kiss!
> Cling, clasp me heart to heart!⁶⁶

All adolescents have experienced this huge excitement. Very few of them have written accomplished verses on the subject. Album pieces of the period were typically addressed to a young woman who may or may not have been given a name. Tennyson's early poems on young women were different: they were not gifts to the girls, they were physical celebrations. This included the poems that he judged too slight for publication, such as 'Lisette' ('My light Lisette / Is grave and shrewd, / And half a prude, /And half coquette'), the oddly unflattering 'Marion' ('Thou art not handsome, art not plain, / And thou dost own no graceful art') and the wholly fabricated and exotic 'dark Indian maiden' named 'Anacaona'.⁶⁷ Most of his young women, as Tennyson himself said, 'were evolved, like the camel, from my own consciousness'. But some had real models. They included Sophy Rawnsley for 'Lilian' and his mother Elizabeth Tennyson for 'Isabel', who possessed:

> A courage to endure and to obey;
> A hate of gossip, parlance, and of sway,
> Crowned Isabel, through all her placid life,
> The queen of marriage, a most perfect wife.

The troubles in the marriage were calmed by her quiet strength:

> A clear stream flowing with a muddy one,
> Till in its onward current it absorbs

With swifter movement and in purer light
The vexed eddies of its wayward brother.[68]

Arthur Hallam said that 'Madeline' was also a real person. Perhaps she is a composite of the girls who had appealed to Tennyson before 1830, but her coquettish manners resemble those caught in the later poems about Rosa Baring; and indeed it is possible that 'sweet pale Margaret' and dreamy 'Adeline' with her 'dew-lit eyes' are versions of Rosa.

A cherished doctrine among the Apostles was the centrality of poetry in human affairs. This was both reflected and reinforced by Tennyson's presence and his practice, and is also the theme of some of his own poems from these years:

The poet in a golden clime was born,
    With golden stars above;
Dowered with the hate of hate, the scorn of scorn,
    The love of love.

He saw through life and death, through good and ill,
    He saw through his own soul.
The marvel of the everlasting will,
    An open scroll,

Before him lay: with echoing feet he threaded
    The secretest walks of fame:
The viewless arrows of his thoughts were headed
    And winged with flame.

Here, in 'The Poet' (published in 1830 and assigned by Tennyson to his 'juvenilia'), the 'viewless arrows' recall Keats's 'viewless wings of Poesy' from the 'Ode to a Nightingale', while the hate and scorn of the third line reflect an influential essay about the nature of poetry by F. D. Maurice in the *Athenaeum of* 8 April 1828.[69]

Maurice wrote: 'The mind of a poet of the highest order is the most perfect that can belong to man. There is no intellectual power, and no state of feeling, which may not be the instrument of poetry, and in proportion as reason, reflection, or sympathy is wanting, in the same degree is the poet restricted in his mastery over the resources of his art. The poet is the great interpreter of nature's mysteries. [. . .] He cannot be a scorner, or selfish, or luxurious and sensual.'[70] As though testing the practical applicability of this resonant essay, Arthur Hallam and other Apostles (but not Tennyson) travelled to Oxford on 28 November 1829 for a debate on the respective strengths of Byron and Shelley. Gladstone was prominent among the Oxford team. Clearly there was a joke at work, the point of which was that the Cambridge group urged the claims of the Oxford poet (Shelley), while the Oxford group pressed for the ascendancy of the Cambridge poet (Byron). Oxford's support for Byron soundly defeated Cambridge's case for Shelley; none of the Cambridge group was particularly crestfallen over this, but they did note with regret that the Oxford Union building was more handsome then their own.

In some of the poems that he was writing at Cambridge, the young Tennyson was following in the footsteps of these great radical poets, Byron and Shelley, by exploring political causes. The unpublished poem 'Hail Briton!', written some time between 1831 and 1833, refers to a range of contemporary movements for political change, and in particular to the Polish uprising against Russia and to the excitement surrounding the 1832 Reform Bill.

Among the experiments of these years Tennyson was creating beautiful and expressive verse showing other possible directions that he could have taken. 'The Dying Swan' moves from action to sound, from dramatic moment (the swan gives voice) to a musical cadence based on deliberately excessive repetition:

> anon her awful jubilant voice
> With a music strange and manifold,
> Flowed forth on a carol free and bold;
> As when a mighty people rejoice
> With shawms, and with cymbals, and harps of gold,
> And the tumult of their acclaim is rolled
> Through the open gates of the city afar,
> To the shepherd who watcheth the evening star.
> And the creeping mosses and clambering weeds,
> And the willow-branches hoar and dank,
> And the wavy swell of the soughing* reeds,
> And the wave-worn horns of the echoing bank,
> And the silvery marish-flowers that throng
> The desolate creeks and pools among,
> Were flooded over with desolate song.[71]

---

*Tennyson provided a note for 'soughing': 'Anglo-Saxon *sweg*, a sound. Modified into an onomatopoeic word for the soft sound or the deep sighing of the wind.' (Ricks, *Poems*, I, p.254n.)

Much later, in *Idylls of the King*, Tennyson's reiterative 'and' could become irritatingly mannered; here it is part of an exuberant experiment.

A strikingly ambitious early work was 'The Lover's Tale'. The first two parts of this narrative poem were written (as a complete work) during 1827–8 when Tennyson was nineteen, and they were set up in type and ready for publication when Tennyson abruptly wrote to Moxon, the publisher, to withdraw them:

> After mature consideration I have come to the conclusion of not publishing the last poem in my little volume entitled 'Lover's Tale' – it is too full of faults and though I think it might conduce towards making me popular [. . .] yet to my eye it spoils the completeness of the book and is better away.[72]

Arthur Hallam greatly admired the poem and was dismayed to hear about this drastic last-minute excision from the volume. He rallied the Apostles and tried to persuade Tennyson to change his mind: 'By all that is dear to thee – by our friendship – by sun moon & stars – by narwhales & seahorses – don't give up the *Lover's Tale*. Heath is mad to hear of your intention. I am madder. You must be pointblank mad.'[73] But Tennyson was adamant. The poem then lingered for half a century; Tennyson wrote a third part much later in his life, and the whole work was published in 1879.

Hallam's enthusiasm for Boccaccio's *Decameron* made him particularly keen on publication of 'The Lover's Tale'. There was a copy of the *Decameron* at Somersby, and Tennyson's source is the story in which a young Bolognese gentleman called Gentile falls in love with a married woman, Catalina. Hearing that she has died, he visits her in her tomb, lies down beside her, kisses her, and lays his hand on her breast. There is then a startling reversal: discovering that Catalina's heart is still beating, he carries her away from the tomb to be nursed back to health by his mother, and then restores her to her husband.

Tennyson reworked the narrative so that the lover and the young woman, Julian and Camilla, were cousins and childhood sweethearts, while Camilla's husband, Lionel, was Julian's closest friend. In its 1832 state, the poem consisted of Julian's troubled internal monologue and his anguished uncertainties, visions and dreams. He imagines that Camilla has died; then has a startling vision of her funeral procession. His friend Lionel seems to be following the bier:

> A strong sympathy
> Shook all my soul: [. . .] I told him all my love,
> How I had loved her from the first; whereat
> He shrank and howled, and from his brow drew back
> His hand to push me from him; and the face,
> The very face and form of Lionel
> Flashed through my eyes into my innermost brain,
> And at his feet I seemed to faint and fall,
> To fall and die away.

Julian's most passionate moment with Camilla is again visionary and illusory; it takes the form of a violent dream in which Camilla and Julian are looking at a painting of a ship and then find themselves within the painting itself:

> all at once
> That painted vessel, as with inner life,
> Began to heave upon that painted sea;
> An earthquake, my loud heart-beats, made the ground
> Reel under us, and all at once, soul, life
> And breath and motion, past and flowed away
> To those unreal billows: round and round
> A whirlwind caught and bore us; mighty gyres
> Rapid and vast, of hissing spray wind-driven
> Far through the dizzy dark. Aloud she shrieked;
> My heart was cloven with pain; I wound my arms
> About her: we whirled giddily; the wind
> Sung; but I clasped her without fear: her weight
> Shrunk in my grasp, and over my dim eyes,
> And parted lips which drank her breath, down-hung
> The jaws of Death: I, groaning, from me flung
> Her empty phantom: all the sway and whirl
> Of the storm dropt to windless calm, and I
> Down weltered through the dark ever and ever.[74]

When Tennyson returned to this poem nearly fifty years later, the strengths of that hallucinatory closing sequence were not maintained. 'The Lover's Tale' had become more literal-minded and more decorous. The frenzied visions and wild passion of the first two parts were to be followed by a third-person narrative in which Lionel becomes a bloodless altruist nobly surrendering his happiness to another.[75]

Arthur Hallam was clearly right to press for publication in 1832.

The early two-part poem seethes with obsession and Gothic excitement, and the drowning sequence with which it closes provides in a figurative form the sexual fulfilment which is passionately enacted by the tone and imagery of the verse and withheld by its literal narrative.

It is striking how powerfully the young Tennyson could write about sexual desperation: both in famous instances such as 'Mariana' (published in 1830 but possibly written before his residence at Cambridge) and 'The Lady of Shalott' (1832)*, and in tiny poems such as 'Fatima'. 'Fatima' arises from Tennyson's boyhood reading of the *Arabian Nights* (the 1805 edition of the Galland translation was in Dr Tennyson's collection at Somersby). Fatima shows her needs to be unambiguously sexual: 'Last night, when some one spoke his name, / From my swift blood that went and came / A thousand little shafts of flame / Were shivered in my narrow frame. / O Love, O fire! once he drew / With one long kiss my whole soul through / My lips , as sunlight drinketh dew.'

---

*The title page of this volume gives its publication date as 1833, but Moxon issued it in 1832; for convenience it is hereafter referred to as the 1832 volume.

CHAPTER 3

Somersby and Arthur Hallam, 1831–1833

O for the touch of a vanished hand,
And the sound of a voice that is still!

Dr Tennyson returned from his continental tour – or enforced exile – to find changes, including the first steps in a serious political career for his brother Charles, who had a junior ministerial appointment.* Dr Tennyson wrote to congratulate him, and on his return from France he visited him in London. There at least he felt certain of his reception. The question of whether his wife Elizabeth would accept him back at Somersby was one that he did not want to face.

There was also deep anxiety about his young son Edward (born January 1813). As a little boy Edward had been a gifted, sensitive child, and later, as a teenager, he wrote poetry, as his brothers did. A fragmentary poem which survived in a manuscript book of Mary Tennyson's gives some inner evidence of the young man's mental distress:

> Alone I rove, alone I prove
>> All human pleasure vain,
> I sigh for change, there is nothing strange
>> In this wide world of pain.[1]

At the age of nineteen Edward was sent off to Acomb, York, ostensibly to study medicine, but in fact to be placed in the care of a medical practitioner, Horace Brydges Hodgson, who had recently set up a small private lunatic asylum (which was also his own family residence). Thereafter the whole of Edward's life was to be spent in small asylums of this kind. There is barely any mention of him beyond the census returns, where he is (for example) a 'Gentleman', 'Formerly Student [Born] Lincolnshire Somersby Lunatic' and 'Patient Unm[arried . . .] Imbecile'. He died, still confined, in 1890 at the age of seventy-seven.[2]

* * *

---

*The government controlled by the Duke of Wellington had been replaced in 1830 by Earl Grey's reforming ministry, which included a number of political contacts of Charles Tennyson's. After some negotiation on Charles's part, he was taken on by Lord Grey as Clerk of the Ordnance.

In late February and early March of 1831 Frederick Tennyson was writing to his uncle Charles in Tealby about Dr Tennyson's health, without any discernible tone of constraint or hostility in his letter: 'My dear Uncle, My Father has been seriously ill for some days and Dr Bousfield thinks him in great danger. He was attacked about ten days ago with a disorder of the stomach.'

Dr Tennyson's 'disorder' was liver failure resulting from alcoholic poisoning. Frederick went on to say, calmly and accurately, that 'the next change is of vital importance. We pray that it may, but we have but little hope that it will *be for the better.*' Charles's son George Hildeyard Tennyson visited Somersby to see Dr Tennyson for himself, and sent a further sombre report on 3 March: 'My Uncle did not know me – he is sometimes perfectly sensible – at others, talks wildly and is evidently deranged for the time being. Dr B[ousfield, the family physician] says his disorder is depression of the Brain.' There are many euphemisms for alcoholism, but George Hildeyard obviously knew what the problem was, since he also wrote that Dr Tennyson 'gave way to great excess before his illness'. And this intelligent and agreeable young man was also acute about the callousness of some of his own branch of the Tennysons: 'I am sorry to observe a want of feeling in some parts of the family.'³

Old George had always been troubled by his older son, but he was very shaken by the prospect of losing him: 'I feel for you very much my dearest Father,' wrote Charles. Charles himself was deep in official duties, but was ready to leave London to comfort his father, he said. He already feared that his brother might well be on his deathbed, since in the same letter he checked carefully that he and Rawnsley were still the executors of George Clayton's will. Any doubt was removed by Dr Tennyson's massive stroke, reported in Alfred's letter of 15 March to his uncle Charles: 'All shadow of hope with respect to my poor Father's ultimate recovery has vanished. Yesterday he lost the use of one side. It is evident that he cannot last many hours longer.'⁴ Dr Tennyson died at Somersby the following day.

With his death, the precarious warmth of feeling that had grown between the two families during Dr Tennyson's illness quickly cooled. Old George was anxious that Charles should not attend the funeral, and Charles's son George Hildeyard Tennyson wrote a troubled and embarrassed letter setting this out and promising to give the reasons in full when he and his father were face to face. In fact Old George relaxed his embargo somewhat and seems to have allowed Charles to consult his own feelings, but the facts speak for themselves: neither Charles nor George Hildeyard went to the funeral, which took place at Somersby on 24 March. The grand families of Lincolnshire tended to side with the Tealby Tennysons although with some degree of pity, albeit patronising, for the dead man. Eliza Massingberd of Gunby Hall wrote to her son Francis (Mrs Massingberd had a relaxed attitude to spelling):

> As to Poor Dr Tennison I have always felt great compassion for him [. . .] I should be very glad to hear his pride of intilect was so far humbled as to induce him to pray to his mediator to interseed for him with the Almighty to pardon his sins. [. . .] His father has *indeed much* to answer for.

Mrs Massingberd gave particulars, but her information is unreliable: 'the Corpse was put into a Barn as soon as he was dead', she claims. 'I suppose that was done to prevent infection as he died at last of a Tipus Fever.'*⁵ There is a barn behind the house at Somersby (with accommodation for the coachman), but Dr Tennyson's corpse was certainly not consigned to it.

Arthur Hallam wrote to Emily Tennyson on 30 March 1831: 'Oh Emily, will it not be sad to leave Somersby?'⁶ Elizabeth Tennyson and her younger children expected to be evicted from the rectory immediately, and there were plenty of other grounds for anxiety. Old George Tennyson had been seriously worried by his Somersby Tennyson grandchildren well before their father's death. On 26 January 1829 he had written to his younger son about the bills that Frederick, Charles and Alfred were running up at Cambridge, and about the expense of the family as a whole:

> Charles and Alfred left me on Friday. They did not act *dis*respectably to me, but they are so untoward and disorderly and so unlike other people I don't know what will become of them, or what can be done with, or about them. I tried to impress them with the feeling that they and Frederick were spending or wasting half their Father's Income, and he had only half to maintain himself, his wife, and to educate 4 other Boys and 4 Girls, and that unless the money expended for their Education was to fit them for professions to get their livings, so that they might be out of the way for an expenditure on the Education of their brothers and sisters and for putting their Brothers in a way of getting their livings, they, Frederick,

---

*The fact that Dr Tennyson had died of drink was never openly acknowledged. The official version given on the doctor's certificate, typhoid fever, was a convenient fiction.

Charles, and Alfred, would be the ruin of them and act most unkindly and dishonourably. Those three boys so far from having improved in manner or manners are worse since they went to Cambridge.[7]

Dr Tennyson's brother, Charles, was now effectively in charge of the Somersby family. The other executors were Dr Tennyson's close friend Thomas Hardwicke Rawnsley, who was extremely humane in his dealings, and Eliza Tennyson's brother, John Fytche. On 18 May 1831 Charles wrote to his father giving his own sobering account of his late brother's affairs. This letter would have done nothing to reassure the Old Man of the Wolds. There were clearly considerable debts to be paid, including those of the brothers at Cambridge, and the question of how the young men were to earn their living was urgent. 'We [Charles Tennyson, John Fytche and Thomas Rawnsley] discussed what was to be done with the Children.' Alfred came under pressure to choose a profession, but his evasiveness and reluctance were clearly a match for Charles:

Alfred is at home, but wishes to return to Cambridge to take a degree. I told him it was a useless expense unless he meant to go into the Church. He said he would. I did not think he seemed much to like it. I then suggested Physic or some other Profession. He seemed to think the Church the best.

As for the others, Charles believed that Frederick would certainly be a clergyman (this was completely wrong) while his nephew Charles had already been provided for because he would be the heir of his great-uncle Samuel Turner. Samuel Turner was a 'hard-drinking, gambling, pluralistic parson' who one day 'smashed the bottom of his glass of rum and water on the dinner table as he inveighed against "this new-fangled Byron"'.[8] He was fond of Charles, and he knew enough about the Somersby family to be aware that as the oldest son Frederick Tennyson at least would inherit enough to live on; Samuel Turner owned enough properties to yield a gentlemanly income, and Charles was the next son down the line. Also Charles was well suited to the life of a country clergyman, and the incumbency of Grasby was part of Samuel Turner's legacy to him.

With his anxious administrator's mind Uncle Charles listed and tried to dispose of the other sons. Edward's mental health meant he was unemployable, so there was nothing to be done there, but Arthur he thought could be a land agent, Septimus a solicitor and Horatio a sailor. Following these neat predictions – none of which would be fulfilled except in the cases of Charles Tennyson Turner, who was already secure, and poor crazy Edward – Charles dismissed the four daughters ('the Girls of course remain at home'). In a shrewd afterthought he spotted the truth about Alfred. Even if he became a clergyman, 'I think his mind is fixed on the idea of deriving his great distinction and greatest means from the exercise of his poetic talents.'[9] Old George Tennyson was not reassured.

With the death of the head of the Somersby family, Alfred's grandfather, Old George, reverted to his customary callousness, shown all too clearly by his behaviour over his son's funeral. The fact that Dr Tennyson was buried at Somersby was a cruel snub. The family vault was at Tealby; Dr Tennyson had been the eldest son. But to keep contamination of Tealby by Somersby to a minimum, Old George insisted that he should be separated from his family in this way until the end of time. His grave is beautiful and moving, in fact – far more so than the florid Gothic revival monuments to the other Tennysons and the Tennyson d'Eyncourts in Tealby church – marked by a handsome marble memorial slab in the ancient churchyard opposite the rectory.

The death of his father was a disaster for Alfred. It cut across his Cambridge world of friends, love and learning, and left him in effect taking responsibility for his mother and siblings. The Old Man of the Wolds was meeting the Tennyson brothers' expenses at Cambridge. Frederick and Charles were allowed to stay on and graduate. Alfred was further from graduation, he was not training for any profession, and in any case he was so distressed by his father's death that his immediate instinct was to go back to Somersby and look after his family. His sisters believed that they would be both homeless and penniless, and his mother was clearly unable to cope. Alfred was distraught. The night after his father's death he slept in Dr Tennyson's cold bed, in the sheets in which he had died, seeking to evoke his father's spirit.

It is easy to blame the Old Man of the Wolds for the difficulties that overtook George Clayton. However, his great-grandson, Sir Charles Tennyson, sought to redress the balance by pointing out in his 1949 biography of Alfred Tennyson, that old Tennyson believed in frugality and justice. The three young men at Cambridge had accumulated debts to a total of £800. The individual debts were not large, though, and as Sir Charles puts it: 'the figures suggest not so much extravagance as negligence and the inevitable slow accumulation of an adverse balance against young men who had no experience in the management of money'. Dr Tennyson had also left debts of his own, but there were assets which could cover them. The old man did not insist on the sale of these assets, but he put in place funds which were under his control, the interest from which would support his son's widow and children. The Somersby Tennysons' grievance over the fact that Dr Tennyson had been 'disinherited' in the first place meant that they received the moneys made available to them with simmering resentment. Old George had a 'habitual sense of exact justice, which perhaps made what they, rightly or wrongly, considered the one great injustice, the more intolerable to those who felt themselves to be its victims'.[10]

Old George believed that he himself 'had spent his long life as a good father and a good citizen' and that his younger son 'was worthily following in his footsteps. Charles had worked hard at the Law, married money, and was now a Minister of the Crown.' By contrast there was 'poor George's widow at the Rectory, always trying to put him in the wrong, and her extraordinary children. He felt sure that those wretched boys would never earn a living.' Sir Charles concluded this defence in terms the irony of which is self-evident, and which at the same time fairly represent Old George's own view of the matter:

It was very hard that an old man of eighty-one, who was a martyr to gout, should be plagued with such anxieties. But one thing at least he could feel satisfied about. Everything that had happened showed how wise he had been about poor George. It would have been unthinkable that he or any of the Somersby boys should be head of the family.[11]

Leaving Cambridge for Lincolnshire did not mean that Alfred had to lose touch with Arthur Hallam. By 1831 Hallam had become very close to all the Tennysons, and was in love with Alfred's sister Emily, whom he had met on his first visit shortly before Christmas 1829. Hallam was highly susceptible to the beauty of young women (witness his exuberant calf-love of Anna Wintour in his seventeenth year).[12] Somersby had become a calmer place by the time Arthur and Alfred returned from their adventures in the Pyrenees in the summer of 1830, but Hallam found the death of Dr Tennyson and

Alfred's abrupt departure from Cambridge upsetting. He was forbidden by his father to be in contact with Emily; he wrote to her nonetheless, and his love letters were in effect family letters as well, full of concern for Alfred. On 17 April 1831 he wrote to her from Cambridge:

> I was very much pleased to see Alfred's handwriting: he shall hear from me very soon. His account of his eyes is most distressing: for God's sake exert your influence with him, to make him take medical advice, or rather to follow that which he has taken.

He followed this up immediately with a brief note to Alfred himself: 'I am very much distressed about the condition of your eyes. Surely you owe it to us all not to let yourself carelessly fall into the misery of blindness.' Hallam guessed that Tennyson's problems were more mental than physical. He wrote to Frederick Tennyson on 8 July:

> Poor Alfred has written to me a very melancholy letter. What can be done for him? Do you think he is really very ill *in body*? His mind certainly is in a distressing state. I wish you, or somebody, would transcribe for me some of his recent poems.

Arthur was worried about his beloved Emily as well, and Tennyson's general misery did nothing to assuage his anxiety about her: 'Alfred's account of Emily is worse than yours; but it is clear as daylight that change of place and society would do her good.' He chafed under the separation from her forced on him by his father: 'It is horrid that I should not be allowed to be at Somersby now; if nothing else, I should break the uniformity of her life.'[13]

In August 1831, Arthur Hallam's essay 'On some of the Characteristics of Modern Poetry and on the Lyrical Poems of Alfred Tennyson' was published in the *Englishman's Magazine*. Hallam was just twenty years old, and his precocious assurance was bound to irritate the established reviewers of the day, but the essay is actually remarkably acute. He boldly claimed five distinctive virtues for Tennyson's poetry. The first two are 'Luxuriance of imagination' (and control of that luxuriance) and the power of 'embodying himself' in imagined characters. The third is the most strikingly phrased, and is the best of Hallam's insights. Tennyson, he said, could imagine with intense vividness ('vivid, picturesque delineation of objects') and could then unite what he had imagined into a single intense vision '*fused*, to borrow a metaphor from science, in a medium of strong emotion'. The fourth virtue identified by Hallam was Tennyson's metrical virtuosity (never denied, even by the poet's contemporary detractors) and the fifth – the one about which any modern reader is permitted to have reservations – was Tennyson's 'elevated habits of thought'.[14]

It was natural enough that Hallam and the other Apostles should claim the moral and philosophical high ground for their poet, but to a reader of the 1830 volume it can seem misjudged. Further, Hallam's selection of poems to quote and praise in the volume seemed to miss the point to some extent. He selected for quotation or mention 'Recollections of the Arabian Nights', the 'Ballad of Oriana', the 'Ode to Memory', the 'Confessions of a second-rate, Sensitive Mind', 'The "How" and the "Why"', 'The Sea Fairies' and 'Adeline'. 'Mariana' is not discussed here, though Hallam greatly admired it: it is both one of the best poems in the volume and the most apt demonstration of the luxuriance, dramatic power, unifying imagination and metrical brilliance (and 'elevated habits of thought') that Hallam had claimed for his friend.

Early in 1832, Arthur Hallam, Frederick Tennyson and Charles Tennyson all graduated from Cambridge. Arthur wrote to Emily with the news: 'At last my odious labours are finished, & being a Bachelor of Arts I can write to you comfortably.' He had heard of Alfred's distracted condition and nervous collapse following his father's death:

> I was very, very much grieved at the account, given by Fred, of Alfred's condition of mind & body. What can be done? I do not suppose he has any real ailment beyond that of extreme nervous irritation; but there is none more productive of incessant misery, & unfortunately none which leaves the sufferer so helpless. I trust my coming will be beneficial to him: but meantime nothing should be left undone that may wean him from over-anxious thought.[15]

Since his father's death Tennyson had lived an unfocused life, oscillating between Somersby, Cambridge and his friends who were now settling in London. Arthur Hallam, by contrast, was intent on a particular object: following his twenty-first birthday in February of 1832, he took the view that his father's embargo on contact with Emily Tennyson was now lifted. Consequently he felt free to visit Somersby, which he did in March of that year, writing an exhilarated letter to the faithful William Henry Brookfield. Of Emily he reported 'the full blaze of conscious delight with which I perceive that she loves me. And I – I love her madly.' And of Tennyson he wrote: 'Alfred is, as I expected, not apparently ill; nor can I persuade myself anything real is the matter. His spirits are better; his habits more regular; his condition altogether healthier.' Tennyson had received a gift of £100 from the ever-generous Aunt Russell, and was talking of travelling in Europe. Charles, Frederick and Alfred had all 'taken to digging – one more resemblance of Somersby to Paradise.'[16]

For a whole happy month Arthur was able to linger in this paradise, and later in March wrote a revealing letter to Richard Chenevix Trench, exploring some of the odder and more diffident aspects of Alfred Tennyson's personality (now that the engagement to Emily was acknowledged at Somersby – if not by Arthur's father – the relationship with Alfred was that of brother as well as friend):

His nervous temperament and habits of solitude give an appearance of affectation to his manner which is no interpreter of the man, and wears off on further knowledge. Perhaps you could never become very intimate, for certainly your bents of mind are not the same, and at some points they intersect [in the sense of 'cut across each other']; yet I think you could hardly fail to see much for love, as well as for admiration.[17]

Tennyson wanted to get to know Richard Chenevix Trench better, but the two of them were actually very different. Trench was a solemn, patrician young man from Dublin, old before his years, pious and high-principled. He would be ordained (and married) while still very young, in 1832, and would be a reforming force in the Church, becoming a distinguished Archbishop of Dublin in 1863. It was easy for the other young men to laugh at Trench's seriousness. 'It is impossible to look upon Trench and not to love him,' Tennyson wrote to Brookfield, 'though he be, as Fred [Frederick Tennyson] says, always strung to the highest pitch, and the earnestness which burns within him so flashes through all his words and actions, that when one is not in a mood of sympathetic elevation, it is difficult to prevent a sense of one's inferiority and lack of all high, and holy feeling. Trench is a bold truehearted Idoloclast – yet have I no faith in any one of his opinions.'[18]

Tennyson's Cambridge friends were anxious not to lose touch with him; Robert Tennant and W. H. Brookfield visited Somersby early in 1832, and Garden and Monteith, those somewhat formidable Scottish kinsmen, were due as guests at Somersby in April. In a letter to another Cambridge friend, John Frere, Frederick Tennyson regarded this with some apprehension: 'Hallam has been staying here a month & we are expecting Garden & Monteith from Cambridge, who, though excellent fellows, particularly at the head of their own tables asking you to drink Champagne – & full of amiable qualities – especially Garden, are, entre nous, rather too magnificent for a little Parsonage in a remote corner of Lincolnshire.'[19]

Tennyson was upset by a review of *Poems: Chiefly Lyrical* by 'Christopher North' in *Blackwood's Edinburgh Magazine*. The reviewer was Professor John Wilson, who as 'Christopher North' adopted the character of a grumpy old man who walked with a crutch, the conceit being that he used the crutch as a weapon to assail things that irritated him in the contemporary world. As well as mocking the young poet – which it certainly did – the 'Christopher North' review mocked its own adopted persona. More importantly, though, a good half of the review was judicious praise of Tennyson's poetry.

Wilson in fact wrote two pieces on Tennyson's 1830 volume in *Blackwood's*. In February 1832 he published a brief article in which he acclaimed the young poet as showing great promise:

Though his wings are far from being full-fledged, they promise now well in the pinions – and I should not be surprised to see him yet a sky-soarer. His 'Golden Days of good Haroun Alraschid' are extremely beautiful. There is feeling – and fancy – in his Oriana. He has a fine ear for melody and harmony too – and rare and rich glimpses of imagination. He has – *genius*.

In the much longer piece, 'Tennyson's Poems', of May 1832, Wilson had been irritated by Hallam's essay in the *Englishman's Magazine*: 'The besetting sin of all periodical criticism, and now-a-days there is no other, is boundless extravagance of praise; but none splash it on like the trowelmen who have been bedaubing Mr Tennyson.' He displayed what he regarded as immaturities in the volume for the reader's mockery ('silly', 'prettyish' and not 'true poetry'), but at the same time he applauded the 'profound pathos' of 'Mariana' (the poem that Hallam had unaccountably omitted from his essay) and the review's final paragraph came down in the poet's favour: 'we may have exaggerated Mr Tennyson's not unfrequent silliness', and 'the millions who delight in Maga will, with one voice, confirm our judgment – that Alfred Tennyson is a poet.'[20]

Hallam worked hard to persuade Tennyson that Wilson's review did no harm, and was high-spirited rather than malicious: 'Professor Wilson has thought fit to have a laugh at you & your critics' (the latter being Hallam himself). Alfred, however, was too thin-skinned to recognise this, and he reacted in his 1832 *Poems* with this:

TO CHRISTOPHER NORTH
You did late review my lays,
Crusty Christopher;
You did mingle blame and praise,
Rusty Christopher.
When I learnt from whom it came
I forgave you all the blame,
Musty Christopher;
I could *not* forgive the praise,
Fusty Christopher.

In itself this was not a bad riposte: it has the 'Christopher North' spirit of contrariness and noisy knockabout. But it provided a target for J. W. Croker in his review of the 1832 volume which would appear the following year. This would be a much more directly hostile, indeed personal, engagement with Tennyson than was John Wilson's.

Tennyson was being vigorously encouraged by Arthur Hallam to get on with the publication of a second volume of poems, but depression and indolence took command of him, and he lingered at Somersby doing very little. In June 1832 he suddenly found Somersby claustrophobic, and went to London, where he caught up with a number of friends and was able to recreate to some extent the joyful society in which he had lived at Cambridge. James Spedding, John and Douglas Heath, John Allen and Charles Merivale all visited him (and Arthur Hallam) at the rooms in which he was staying with Jack Kemble, who lived in lodgings in Southampton Row where he was studying law. Kemble talked about his recent visit to Germany, and this fired in Tennyson a need to travel to the Rhine himself. He could use his aunt's money for the trip, and he persuaded Hallam to accompany him. Hallam was by this time even more in love with Emily Tennyson, and he hurriedly wrote to her the 'strange news' of this impromptu holiday: 'I am going tomorrow with Alfred up the Rhine for three weeks! He complained so of his hard lot in being forced to travel alone, that I took compassion on him, and in spite of law and relatives etc. I am going.'[21]

After sailing to Holland, they had a horrible experience in quarantine for cholera for six days before they were allowed to travel on. They jointly wrote a comic letter of complaint about this to Jack Kemble (they had recently seen his sister Fanny performing at Covent Garden in a forgettable drama called *The Hunchback*). Arthur wrote at length complaining about the dinginess, the expense, the tedious fellow passengers also caught in quarantine, and 'being bitten every night by flying and creeping vermin'. Tennyson wrote: 'I am bugbitten, flybitten, gnatbitten, and hungerbitten. I have had no sleep for the last three nights.' He concluded his remarks with this judgement: 'Damn all Dutchmen! is it not infinitely more reasonable that Dutchmen should die of cholera than that English gentlemen should be detained on board a villainous ex-steamboat?'[22]

They ran short of money, and Tennyson was disappointed by the Rhine; it seemed no more interesting than Lincolnshire. They stayed in comfortable and picturesque places, but he found the weather too cool and the food indigestible.[23]

Arthur Hallam's attributes – his energy, enterprise, business acumen, presence, confidence and address – were of priceless service to Alfred Tennyson. It was Hallam who put Tennyson in touch with the publisher Edward Moxon, who would see Tennyson's work into print until the late 1850s. Moxon was a man of excellent taste and discrimination. His was a story absolutely characteristic of the nineteenth century. Born in 1801, he was some eight years older than Tennyson. He was brought up in Wakefield, Yorkshire, the oldest of nine children of a 'cropper' in the cloth industry,*[24] and from an early age he had literary ambitions. After working for a provincial bookseller for a while, he found work with Longman, in London. He sent his own poetry to Charles Lamb, secured an introduction to the wealthy and well-connected poet Samuel Rogers, and with the encouragement of these two figures published a volume of his own poetry (with Longman) in 1826. The book attracted Wordsworth's attention; Moxon published further poetry of his own, and by the late 1820s was able to set himself up as a publisher.

He made his mark with an expensive, high-quality volume: Samuel

---

*A cropper cut off the rough surface of the cloth with large shears before the material was pressed and finished so that the nap lay evenly.

Rogers's *Italy*, with illustrations by no less an artist than J. M. W. Turner (published jointly with T. Cadell in December 1830).[25] Moxon's biographer wrote that *Italy* was the turning point: 'It is hardly possible to exaggerate the importance of the book to the new publishing house. Rogers was influential among literary people; he enjoyed a long-established reputation for taste in art and literature; he was the friend of men and women in high society. The *Italy* gave prestige to the firms [Moxon and Cadell] that put it out and attracted customers to their premises.'[26]

Tennyson's passivity in relation to his own publishing was less extraordinary than it looks. The young men around him were playing a game: he was their tame poet and genius, aligned with Shelley and Wordsworth. It was an important part of his role that he should be the visionary figure with no capacity for practicalities, while Hallam, Trench, Merivale and the other members of the circle looked after his worldly interests.

In July 1831 Hallam wrote to Moxon offering one of Tennyson's sonnets (without Tennyson's permission) and his own essay on Tennyson's 1830 volume for the *Englishman's Magazine*, of which Moxon was now the editor. It had become clear that Tennyson would not be allowed to go back to Cambridge at his grandfather's expense unless he were preparing himself for ordination (or a profession). But Arthur Hallam was good at disobeying authoritarian old men (such as his own father) and had a contrary scheme afoot. He wanted Moxon to take (and pay for) poems of Tennyson's for the new periodical. He wrote to Charles Merivale:

I may venture to ask you to take a little trouble for me in London, or rather for Alfred Tennyson, who according to custom has devolved his business on me. You may possibly have heard that a bookseller hight Moxon publishes a Magazine called the Englishman's. Further it may have come to your knowledge that in No 5 of that publication appeared a sonnet of Tennyson's, & a review of his book written by your humble servant. [. . .] What I have to say is this – Alfred, not intending to go into the Church, as the grandfather who has 'patria potestas' over him wishes and not having yet brought himself to cobble shoes for his livelihood, is desirous of putting his wits to profit, & begins to think himself a fool for kindly complying with the daily requests of Annuals without getting anything in return. Now the aforesaid Moxon is a very good sort of fellow, and knows what's what in poetry, which you know 'is as high as Metaphysic wit can fly' [from Butler's *Hudibras*] and wishes Alfred to send him [poems] for his Mag. The matter I entrust to you then is this; to call upon Mr Moxon, 64 New Bond Str., introducing yourself under shelter of my name and Alfred's, and to pop the question to him,

'What do you pay your contributors? What will you pay Alfred Tennyson for monthly contributions?' Also, while your hand is in, to ask whether if Alfred was to get a new volume, ready to be published next season, Moxon would give him anything for the copyright, & if anything, *what*. You might dexterously throw in, that I have a promise that any article I might write should be admitted either into Edinburgh or Quarterly, & that I could therefore vouch for the books being reviewed in one, or both.[27]

Hallam's assurance and precocity, and the useful contacts that flowed from being the son of Henry Hallam, meant that he could already conduct himself as a confident member of literary London. Arthur continued to press, and Tennyson continued to delay. Arthur had the manuscript of Tennyson's poems with him when he wrote, on 13 September 1832: 'Moxon is impatient to begin the volume; unless I hear before Wednesday concerning the order I shall take that upon myself.'[28] Tennyson then stirred himself to write on his own behalf to Moxon on 13 October, authorising publication (and at the same time placing responsibility for most of his own actions as author on Hallam, 'to whom I gave full powers to treat with you').[29] The appearance of Alfred Tennyson's *Poems* (published in 1832 though '1833' appeared on the title page) was a personal triumph for Arthur Hallam.

In a letter to Tennyson from Cambridge dated March 1831, Arthur Hallam had written: 'I am going up to London tomorrow, girded up for warfare. I hope to fight like a true knight, although Emily's eyes will not be there to "rain influence." Oret pro nobis. I shall write to her in a few days.'[30] Writing to Emily was in direct violation of Henry Hallam's prohibition (which Arthur had pretended to accept). Even after this was relaxed, early in 1832, when Arthur turned twenty-one and his stern father – who was also fair-minded and loving – felt that he no longer had a right to exercise absolute control, Arthur thought it prudent to keep his father in the dark about the actual extent of his contact with Somersby. Toward the end of the holiday together on the Rhine he wrote to 'Jack' Kemble:

If you are in London you will very soon have the pleasure of seeing us, as we have turned our faces homewards, & are coming with moderate swiftness by the way of Belgium. [. . .] We have, neither of us, money to stay more than a few hours in London, & then shall make the best of our way into Lincolnshire. I suppose my own family has left London by this time: at all events I shall not go home, if I can help it, before I go to Lincolnshire; so, in case you meet my father, or the like, you need not give quite so precise an account of my intended proceedings as I have given you. Our journey has not been to me unpleasant; but Alfred swears the Rhine is no more South than England, & he could make a better river himself![31]

The Rhine had yielded a piece of occasional, or light, verse which is neat, gentle and to the point. It is a tribute to the happiness that Tennyson had enjoyed in the upper room at Somersby which he had shared as a boy with his brothers Frederick and Charles. Arthur Hallam on his visits to Somersby also shared this room with Tennyson:

> O darling room, my heart's delight,
> Dear room, the apple of my sight,
> With thy two couches soft and white,
> There is no room so exquisite,
> No little room so warm and bright,
> Wherein to read, wherein to write.
>
> For I the Nonnenwerth have seen,
> And Oberwinter's vineyards green,
> Musical Lurlei; and between
> The hills to Bingen have I been,
> Bingen in Darmstadt, where the Rhene
> Curves toward Mentz, a woody scene.
>
> Yet never did there meet my sight,
> In any town, to left or right,
> A little room so exquisite,
> With two such couches, soft and white;
> Not any room so warm and bright,
> Wherein to read, wherein to write.[32]

This was an emotional young man recording a loved place and some loved people (his brothers and Arthur Hallam). These were true feelings; he wanted to express them and he saw no reason not to do so, but his 'darling room' would become the object of fierce mockery.

Arthur Hallam's visits to Somersby were never as long as he would have wished. He wrote to William Brookfield in August 1832:

I have been very miserable since I saw you: my hopes [of early marriage to Emily] grow fainter & fewer, yet I hope on, & will, until the last ray is gone, & then – . Emily, thank Heaven, is better than she has been, & I think rather more cheerful. Somersby looks glorious in full pride of leafy summer. I would I could fully enjoy it: but ghosts of the Past & wraiths of the Future are perpetually troubling me. I am a very unfortunate being; yet, when I look into Emily's eyes, I sometimes think there is happiness reserved for me.[33]

Like much that Hallam wrote, this seems disconcertingly mannered and self-regarding, but there can be no doubt that his love for Emily was genuine. Emily herself was often ill and depressed during this period, and the family were in constant unhappy anticipation that they would be forced to leave the rectory at Somersby.

Arthur's letter to her just before his Christmas visit in 1832 addresses precisely this unhappiness:

Be visible – that's a good girl – when I arrive. Every hour of you will be precious, since I cannot stay longer than I did last time. I fear the shadow of the coming event [moving out of the Rectory] will be on your spirit; but really you must try to pluck up a bit, & make me properly merry for the Eve. If you set up a 'reg'lar good cry' because it is your *last* Eve at Somersby, how shall I remember it is my *first?*[34]

It was not, of course, Emily's last Christmas in the house – the family was not obliged to move until 1837. But 'be visible' was a request with a point to it. When depressed, Emily would go to her room and stay there, and so she did, again, over this brief Christmas holiday. She and Arthur barely saw each other during these three days – instead they sent each other painstaking letters in Italian. Arthur Hallam had studied deeply in both the literature and the language of Italy. He taught the language to Emily Tennyson and they exchanged love letters in (somewhat inaccurate) Italian in order to keep their correspondence confidential. There was a certain amount of vanity in this. Arthur's Italian was better than Emily's, and some of his instructions to her about learning the language are surprisingly sharp in tone; not quite bullying, but certainly dominating. His work in Italian, like his enthusiasm for literature, took time away from his legal studies, and contributed to his father's vexation with him.

* * *

Henry Hallam was angry to discover that his son had been in regular correspondence with Emily Tennyson throughout the period of the prohibition. He was further vexed when he learnt that Arthur had actually been visiting Somersby without his knowledge. On 22 August 1832 he wrote an immensely pained letter to Thomas Hardwick Rawnsley (as one of Dr Tennyson's executors) complaining with commendable dignity about being deceived both by his son and by the Tennyson family.* In it he refers to his correspondence with 'the late Dr Tennyson' ('which is doubtless in the possession of Mrs T.'). These exchanges had taken place early in 1831 – shortly before Alfred's father's death, therefore. Dr Tennyson was by then in a wretched state. Yet over the matter of his daughter Emily's attachment to Arthur Hallam he had appeared reasonable and balanced in his dealings with Henry Hallam:

> Dr Tennyson's answer to my letter was an excellent one; & he appeared to coincide altogether in the views I had taken of the subject [these letters seem not to have survived]. It was certainly my hope, & was intimated by me as delicately as I could, that the young lady would have released a promise made by a boy of 19, who had neither his father's consent, nor any reasonable prospect of fulfilling the engagement. I stipulated with my son that he should not go to Somersby *during his minority*; & Dr Tennyson felt that, on his own & his daughter's account, he could not think of inviting him.
>
> The lamented death of Dr T. took place not long after this; & nothing passed between my son & myself on the subject till last spring, when, having come of age, he expressed his wish to go to Somersby. I could not object to this, having limited my prohibition to his minority; & it came out about this time, that correspondence had been kept up all along with the young lady. If this was done with Mrs Tennyson's approbation, I must say that, making every allowance for a mother's feelings, under distressing circumstances, she had done all in her power to frustrate not only my intentions, but those of her husband, as signified to me.[35]

Following this stiff but not unjustifiable observation, Henry Hallam went on to say that he would not make his son an allowance of more than £600 per annum. This was actually a reasonable

---

*This letter survives because the Rawnsleys were careful to keep an archive of their correspondence about and with the Tennysons. Their collection is now in the Houghton Library at Harvard.

income for a young married couple at that date, but Henry also expected that Emily's grandfather would settle a capital amount on her. The old man resisted, as was to be expected, and Arthur Hallam himself then wrote bold – indeed extraordinary – letters to members of Emily's family, asking Charles Tennyson d'Eyncourt to extract a good capital sum from the Old Man of the Wolds, and suggesting to Frederick that the aunts, Mrs Bourne or the wealthy Mrs Russell, should be persuaded to settle £4,000 on Emily in expectation of a handsome inheritance for her on Old George's death. His anger with the Old Man of the Wolds was spirited and fiery: 'A negotiation has been going on between my father and the old man whose only good quality is his relationship to the person I love best in the world,' he wrote to his old Etonian friend James Milnes Gaskell on 8 September 1832. 'The wretch [Emily's grandfather] makes most shabby, beggarly offers, which my father considers inadequate.' Unlike his friend Alfred Tennyson, Arthur Hallam was willing to earn his own living. But the law felt increasingly like a dead end. He was a writer and critic first and foremost. Making a living by his pen would be precarious, as he knew, but he felt, reasonably enough, that struggling on in something to which he was unsuited would not bring in much money either: 'Bookmaking is a worse trade than ever; the law, besides being a profession which I hate, could not repay me for many a long year, and then only in case I succeeded in it.'[36]

Consciously or not, by insisting on the legal profession, Henry Hallam was punishing his wayward son. In a letter to Tennyson of 10 October 1832, Arthur complained of the 'overwhelming of law business which is now on my hands' and which was getting in the way of his work on Tennyson's proofs. His restless mind kept turning back to his pleasure in literature. Since June of 1832, or earlier, he had been steadily working towards the publication of Tennyson's second volume of poetry. On 20 June he had written to Emily: 'I don't doubt that Moxon would publish any volume Alfred might make up for him free of expense. It is worth considering: a 2nd book just now would set Alfred high in public notice, & afford him the means of putting money in his pocket.'[37] He was seeing Tennyson in London from time to time during this month. Tennyson had plans to travel abroad seeking 'colour' for more poems, but by 23 June Arthur reported to Emily that her brother was still in London, unable to make up his mind about travelling, and entertaining his friends in inconsequential ways. Edward Spedding described such an evening: Alfred 'enacted 1stly a Teutonic Deity – 2ndly the Sun Coming out from behind a Cloud – 3rdly a man on a close stool – and lastly put a pipestopper in his mouth by way of beak, and appeared as a great bird.'[38]

The two volumes of poetry, 1830 and 1832, can be read as part of a single rapidly unfolding creative process. Many of the poems had been written well before the dates of publication; some of them were by a teenager who had not yet experienced the maturing influence of Cambridge. But the impact of Cambridge, of the classics, and of Arthur Hallam is felt poignantly in the 1832 collection. Some of the poems are addressed directly to Hallam. Two sonnets, for example, explore progressive stages in Tennyson's feelings for his friend:

> If I were loved, as I desire to be,
> What is there in the great sphere of the earth,
> And range of evil between death and birth,
> That I should fear, – if I were loved by thee?
> All the inner, all the outer world of pain
> Clear Love would pierce and cleave, if thou wert mine,
> As I have heard that, somewhere in the main,
> Fresh-water springs come up through bitter brine.
> 'Twere joy, not fear, claspt hand-in-hand with thee,
> To wait for death – mute – careless of all ills,
> Apart upon a mountain, though the surge
> Of some new deluge from a thousand hills
> Flung leagues of roaring foam into the gorge
> Below us, as far on as eye could see.[39]

In the second sonnet, the relationship seems less strenuous and more domestic. The speaker recalls the first meeting of the two friends:

> As when with downcast eyes we muse and brood,
> And ebb into a former life, or seem
> To lapse back in some confusèd dream
> To states of mystical similitude;
> If one but speaks or hems or stirs his chair,
> Ever the wonder waxeth more and more,
> So that we say, 'All this hath been before,
> All this hath been, I know not when or where.'
> So, friend, when first I looked upon your face,
> Our thought gave answer each to each, so true –
> Opposèd mirrors each reflecting each –

That though I knew not in what time or place,
Methought that I had often met with you,
And either lived in either's heart and speech.[40]

The 1832 volume closed with 'To J.S.', a poem addressed to James Spedding, saluting the memory of his brother Edward, who had died very young on 24 August 1832. The close of the poem is delicately poised:

Sleep sweetly, tender heart, in peace:
    Sleep, holy spirit, blessèd soul,
While the stars burn, the moons increase,
    And the great ages onward roll.

Sleep till the end, true soul and sweet.
    Nothing comes to thee new or strange.
Sleep full of rest from head to feet;
    Lie still, dry dust, secure of change.[41]

Among the major poems of the 1832 volume were 'The Lady of Shalott', 'The Palace of Art' and 'The Lotos-Eaters', although not in their most familiar versions. All three were to reappear, much revised, when Tennyson published two volumes of poetry ten years later, in 1842. The three poems in their original state were part of the mood of undergraduate experience at Trinity; 'The Lotos-Eaters' in particular expressed the languor and pleasure that these young men at Cambridge enjoyed. Laziness was to be relished. The poem starts with its least lazy word: from that point it is downhill all the way.

'Courage!' he said, and pointed toward the land,
'This mounting wave will roll us shoreward soon.'
In the afternoon they came unto a land
In which it seemèd always afternoon.

Tennyson worked hard, if one may put it that way, at the effect of laziness: 'The "strand" was, I think, my first reading,' he explained, many years later, 'but the no rhyme of "land" and "land" seemed lazier.'[42] It is a delicious form of escape. The poem in its first state closes with a preference for eternal leisure: 'Oh! islanders of Ithaca, we will not wander more. / Surely, surely slumber is more sweet than toil, the shore / Than labour in the ocean, and rowing with the oar.'[43]

J. W. Croker's review of the 1832 volume in *Quarterly Review* (April 1833) was savage. Croker's method was to display sections of the poetry in a spirit of crude mockery. He had slow and ruthless sport with 'O Darling Room', saying that he had himself visited the scenes on the Rhine that are described in the poem and 'did not see in any of them anything like *this little room so exqui*SITE.'[44] 'O Darling Room' had been an honest expression by Tennyson of an urgent need for a refuge and a secure work space now that his father had died and the family would have to leave Somersby. Insecurity and anguish about where he would live, and disproportionate distress when his arrangements miscarried, would in fact haunt him for much of his life.

In the summer of 1833, Henry Hallam required Arthur to accompany him on a European tour. Arthur felt somewhat oppressed throughout this excursion, for excellent reasons: enforced absence from Somersby, his father's constant vigilant and somewhat forbidding company, and the fact that no part of the tour was under his control. But such pleasure as the trip gave him he wanted to share, and his letters are full of consciously detailed descriptions of cities and landscapes so that the Somersby family could vicariously enjoy his experiences on this journey. He greatly preferred Italy to Austria and Hungary, and thus felt the tug of his favourite country just beyond the Alps but unattainable because of his father's schedule. Salzburg felt Italian, so he enjoyed it more than the other places; and the valley of the Saal reminded him of his trip to the Pyrenees with Tennyson in 1830.

> Is not this a jewel of a place? I have sworn in my secret soul that I will come here [agai]n some day, God willing, & not alone, Nem [his nickname for Emily]; nor am I quite clear that ten years hence we may not have made a home of Salzburg. Is Alfred mad meanwhile that he does not employ his annual hundred in instantly coming to this place, & staying as long as he possibly can?[45]

After the pleasures of Salzburg, it was a shock to be made by his father to go to Vienna. He found it attractive to look at, as he wrote to Tennyson on 6 September, but it compared badly with Salzburg and the mountains. 'This is the dull time of the year [. . .] the Prater the great public drive is perfectly empty and I never saw a more insipid place.' But he admired the paintings, Veronese and Titian especially, and commended Titian's Danaë and the shower of gold* as a subject for a poem: 'Do you write just as perfect a Danaë!'[46] Tennyson's 'Now sleeps the crimson petal, now the white' includes an erotic metaphor – concluding with the meteor's silent furrow – based on the legend of Danaë; perhaps he was recalling Arthur's suggestion:

> Now lies the Earth all Danaë to the stars,
> And all thy heart lies open unto me.
> Now slides the silent meteor on, and leaves
> A shining furrow, as thy thoughts in me.

Arthur's letter to Emily on 11 September marked an escape from Vienna to Budapest, which refreshed and excited him, and he wrote a detailed and lively description so that she should continue to share his experiences. He also mentioned that he would return to Vienna the following day.

The editor of his letters took up the thread:

Henry [Hallam] and his son returned to Vienna on 13 September, with Arthur complaining of fever and chills. It was apparently a recurrence of the ague he had suffered earlier that year, and, though it would delay their departure for Prague [the next destination that Henry Hallam had planned], there seemed to be little cause for alarm. Quinine and a few days rest were prescribed. By the fifteenth, Arthur felt better; and in the evening, after a short walk with his father, ordered some sack and lay down. Leaving his son reading, Henry went out again. He returned to find Arthur still on the sofa, apparently asleep. Only after a short time did Henry notice the odd position of the head. He called to his son. There was no response. All efforts to rouse him were in vain: Arthur Henry Hallam was dead at age twenty-two.[47]

News of this tragedy did not reach Somersby until October. Because of the slow progress of the mail to that part of Lincolnshire, it is possible that Tennyson did not hear of Arthur's death until as late as 6 October, when a letter dated 1 October 1833 arrived from Henry Elton, Arthur Hallam's uncle.

---

*In Greek mythology, Danaë was one of the women beloved of Zeus – she was shut up in a tower to protect her, but Zeus consummated his love for her by descending in the form of a shower of golden stars.

At the desire of a most afflicted family, I write to you, because they are unequal, from the Abyss of grief into which they have fallen, to do it themselves.

Your friend Sir, and my much loved Nephew, Arthur Hallam, is no more – it has pleased God to remove him from this his first scene of Existence, to that better World, for which he was Created.

He died at Vienna on his return from Buda, by Apoplexy, and I believe his Remains come by Sea from Trieste.

Before they received Henry Elton's letter, the Tennysons had what they later came to believe was a supernatural message about this catastrophe. Alfred's sisters, Mary and Matilda, had been out walking in the lanes near Somersby in late September 1833 when Matilda witnessed what she thought at first was 'a white goat walking on its hind legs' but it 'disappeared through a gap in a hedge where no gap was'. She was so 'awed' by this that she burst into tears.[48]

Arthur seems to have died from an aneurysm in the brain. It is likely that he had been showing symptoms of abnormal blood vessels in his brain for some years – he often had appalling headaches, he was very red in the face at times, and he had inexplicable illnesses and periods of tiredness.

The shock to the Somersby family was that of a personal bereavement: they all loved Arthur. Emily was plunged into a kind of widowhood which for the moment seemed permanent.

To the Cambridge friends as a group, this sudden death was a horrible violation of the natural order of things. The Apostles all wrote to each other about the death of Hallam: it was as though his brilliance had been so intense that they had feared, some of them at least, that he might flare and burn out. John Kemble wrote to his sister Fanny saying that 'this was always feared by us as likely to occur'. It was a collective bereavement.

The shock has been a bitter one to bear: and most of all so to the Tennysons, whose sister Emily he was to have married. I have not yet had the courage to write to Alfred. This is a loss which will most assuredly be felt by this age, for if ever man was born for great things he was. Never was a more powerful intellect joined to a purer and holier heart; and the whole illuminated with the richest imagination, with the most sparkling yet the kindest wit.[49]

Henry Hallam kept in close touch with the Tennyson family, and wrote to Alfred at the end of December telling him about the arrangements for Arthur's funeral at Clevedon, in Somerset.[50] Tennyson did not attend the funeral.*

Tennyson's reaction to Arthur Hallam's death was not straightforward, but there was a remarkable outpouring of poetry. It was during the months immediately after this tragedy that he wrote 'Ulysses', 'Tiresias', the first state of 'Tithonus' and the 'Morte d'Arthur'.

Of 'Ulysses' Tennyson would say, many years later, that it was 'more written with the feeling of his loss upon me than many poems in *In Memoriam*'. This was because 'Ulysses' is the story of a survivor, in which 'life must be fought out to the end'.[51] Technically and dramatically it was an extraordinary achievement. In this intimately personal poem Tennyson, aged twenty-four, played the role of an old man preparing for death and summoning the will to confront it courageously. Figured as a final voyage, 'Ulysses' sums up the life of its speaker:

> I am a part of all that I have met;
> Yet all experience is an arch wherethrough
> Gleams that untravelled world, whose margin fades
> For ever and for ever when I move.
> How dull it is to pause, to make an end,
> To rust unburnished, not to shine in use!
> As though to breathe were life. Life piled on life
> Were all too little, and of one to me
> Little remains: but every hour is saved
> From that eternal silence, something more,
> A bringer of new things.

Saving life from the eternal silence would be one of the functions of Tennyson's art at its best right to the end of his life. 'Ulysses' ends with courageous defiance and stoical acceptance:

> Though much is taken, much abides; and though
> We are not now that strength which in old days

---

*Richard Monckton Milnes, by contrast, did make the journey down to Clevedon. In the Lincolnshire circle there was one surprising reaction to Hallam's death: John Rashdall, a young and well-connected clergyman who had got to know the Tennysons at Cambridge, wrote: 'Hallam is dead! – such is life: the accomplished-vain philosophic Hallam, dead, suddenly – at 23.' (Rashdall's Journal, fols. 13, 14v, 21v; also quoted in part in Rader, p.12.)

Moved earth and heaven; that which we are, we are;
One equal temper of heroic hearts,
Made weak by time and fate, but strong in will
To strive, to seek, to find, and not to yield.

Early in 1834, Tennyson wrote the most haunting of all his short lyrics of bereavement, set on his favourite part of the Lincolnshire coast, Mablethorpe. This epitomises the virtuosity with which he could capture intense feeling with the sparest of linguistic resources. The verses are deceptively simple-looking, but they deal with a fundamental problem. How is one to find words to express the inexpressible?

Break, break, break,
    On thy cold gray stones, O Sea!
And I would that my tongue could utter
    The thoughts that arise in me.

O well for the fisherman's boy,
    That he shouts with his sister at play!
O well for the sailor lad,
    That he sings in his boat on the bay!

And the stately ships go on
    To their haven under the hill;
But O for the touch of a vanished hand,
    And the sound of a voice that is still!

Break, break, break,
    At the foot of thy crags, O Sea!
But the tender grace of a day that is dead
    Will never come back to me.[52]

The carefree cries of the child followed by the young man's song are piercing reminders of what has been lost; Arthur has died on the threshold of adulthood, his loved childhood and gifted adolescence preparations for nothing but blank emptiness. The voices of the young and the movement of the ships force home the cruelty of bereavement. Life goes on, sunlit, buoyant, intent on its own purposes, in stark juxtaposition with the unalterable fact of this one death.

The need to hear Arthur Hallam's voice and to recover the touch of his hand would become recurrent preoccupations of Tennyson's elegy for his dead friend, *In Memoriam*. Lyric LVI cries out, 'O for thy voice to soothe and bless!', lyric VII speaks of the 'Doors, where my heart was used to beat / So quickly, waiting for a hand, / A hand that can be clasped no more', and lyric XIV presents a consoling but impossible vision, the whole resting upon a conditional:

> If one should bring me this report,
>   That thou hadst touched the land today,
>   And I went down unto the quay,
> And found thee lying in the port;

The passengers disembark from the ship:

> And if along with these should come
>   The man I held as half-divine;
>   Should strike a sudden hand in mine,
> And ask a thousand things of home;
>
> And I should tell him all my pain,
>   And how my life had drooped of late,
>   And he should sorrow o'er my state
> And marvel what possessed my brain;
>
> And I perceived no touch of change,
>   No hint of death in all his frame,
>   But found him all in all the same,
> I should not feel it to be strange.

Perhaps Tennyson in reality had such a dream. If so, his mind was subjecting him to a refinement of psychological torture, one of the cruel tricks that bereavement can play, just as painful as the experience of the husband who dreams about his dead wife:

> Tears of the widower, when he sees
>   A late-lost form that sleep reveals,
>   And moves his doubtful arms, and feels
> Her place is empty, fall like these.[53]

'Break, break, break' takes the emotional centre of such a dream and strips it of dramatic context. 'The touch of a vanished hand' leaves a great deal unsaid, just as in the first line's 'break, break, break' each of the commas represents a gap in which the grief over Arthur was choked back and unspoken. 'I would that my tongue could utter' invites us, if we have not already noticed it, to attend to the ache of wretchedness in the spaces between the words in this extraordinarily spare and economical lyric.

CHAPTER 4

Wandering, tribulation and lost love, 1833–1845

I stood like one that had received a blow:
I found a hard friend in his loose accounts,
A loose one in the hard grip of his hand,
A curse in his God-bless-you: then my eyes
Pursued him down the street, and far away,
Among the honest shoulders of the crowd,
Read rascal in the motions of his back
And scoundrel in the supple-sliding knee.

Tennyson was a rootless and suffering figure following Hallam's death in 1833. There had of course been two shattering bereavements; the first shaking of the foundations of his security had been the loss of his father in 1831. Two deaths within two years caused Tennyson to feel as though the whole universe was against him, and the rational order of things horribly upset. Robert Bernard Martin has written thoughtfully about the period following those bereavements, saying that Tennyson was in a wilderness, personally and emotionally, for some eighteen years, 'almost homeless, wandering from friend to friend, settling briefly with his family, then pulling up stakes and going off unexpectedly'.[1] The problems were social and economic as well as emotional. Arthur Hallam had been the one person in the world whom Tennyson could love and trust absolutely. He had also become an indispensable support for him in his writing and in his early dealings with publishers. The disastrous history of the Somersby household had done nothing to give Tennyson confidence in the notion that marriage and a family might bring personal happiness, and for most of the 1830s and 1840s he was short of money. There was epilepsy in the family, and during these two decades he also had intermittent very severe anxieties about his health.

From this perspective Tennyson can be seen to have chosen a life of irresponsible drifting, like a confused adolescent, displaying 'refusal or inability to take on the normal responsibilities of a man'.[2] But he nevertheless showed self-possession and tenacity when negotiating with publishers over money, and careful self-preservation in prioritising the writing of his own poetry above everything else.

Since the day he left Cambridge he had resisted all attempts to persuade him to find paid employment of any kind, and even the publishing of his own poetry – which did bring some money – was something over which he lingered, showing such reluctance that friends – Hallam, Fitzgerald, Spedding, Merivale and the Lushingtons – successively found it their duty to bring him up to the pitch of committing his work to the public. The nomadic, chaotic Alfred Tennyson of legend, a legend built up and lovingly transmitted for posterity by his many friends in these vagrant years, was in fact displaying an inner resolution. He was a *poet*, nothing else, and he claimed no other identity, role or mode of existence. Many of those who loved him would encounter a locked door of inner coldness and self-possession in Alfred Tennyson, and even with Arthur Hallam it can often seem that what Tennyson loved was not Arthur himself, but Arthur's love of Tennyson: his own image and his own genius as reflected in Arthur's loyal admiration. Perhaps in the outpouring of *In Memoriam* Tennyson was mourning above all the sense of being unconditionally and unequivocally venerated, promoted and admired.

Tennyson's wanderings in the 1830s and 1840s present a problem. The magnificent poetry that resulted from his experiences in these years did not reach fruition and publication until much later. This creates a kind of double chronology. Arthur Hallam died in 1833. Tennyson grieved over this, then internalised it, then made it into the material for art, which eventually bore fruit in *In Memoriam*, the great poem that would make him world famous. But *In Memoriam* was not published until 1850, so for seventeen years the poet carried with him everywhere the steadily growing manuscripts of his 'elegies', as he called them, to his dead friend. He took them to odd hotels and boarding houses by the sea, to the several homes in which his mother and his younger siblings lived after they left Somersby in 1837, to the many homes and rooms of his male friends in London where he sought conversation and stimulus and relief from his own depressions and hypochondria. He read them aloud to friends, he lent them to be copied out into other friends' notebooks; sometimes he lost them and they were rescued for him.

In parallel with the steady growth of the 'elegies', he had other developing projects, which would in due course become *The Princess*, *Maud* and *Idylls of the King*. Early poems like 'The Lady of Shalott' foreshadowed his great Arthurian poems. The possibility of creating a major Arthurian work was drafted in his private notes when he was at Cambridge aged twenty, but *Idylls of the King* was not completed until 1885. 'The Lady of Shalott' looks as though it belongs directly to his poems based on Malory. In fact, when he wrote it, Tennyson was unaware, as he said later, of the story of Elaine in Malory; his source for 'The Lady of Shalott' was a fourteenth-century Italian novella relating 'How the Damsel of Scalot died for love of Lancelot de Lac'.[3] The first four *Idylls*, the long poems based on the stories of King Arthur, made their appearance in 1859, and the development and publication of the Arthurian poems continued into the 1880s, so the gestation period here was forty years or longer.

Tennyson's relationships with young women (in the 1830s) were to be reflected in major poetry which was delayed and meditated upon until the 1850s and beyond.

Part of his misery as a young man was his belief that he could never marry a girl of his own social rank. 'Mariana' and 'The Lady of Shalott' are intensely successful realisations of a kind of low-level frenzy of frustration which inhabited Tennyson's imagination over a whole range of verse, major and minor, in his Cambridge years and in the strange period after Hallam's death, in which he was in social and emotional limbo. An immediate target for his powerful emotions was a young woman called Rosa Baring.*

In terms of the upper-class marriage market of the day, Rosa Baring would have been a very considerable catch for any ambitious young man. Her grandfather, Sir Francis Baring, Bt, was chairman of the East India Company and founder of what was until very recently one of the greatest British private banks. 'The first merchant in Europe; first in knowledge and talents, and first in character and opulence', as the *Gentleman's Magazine* characterised him. Rosa's father, William Baring, was the fourth son of Sir Francis. He was not a partner in the family business but was nevertheless decidedly wealthy following his father's death in 1810. He died young in a boating accident, and in 1824 his widow, Frances, married Arthur Eden, a member of another wealthy and well-established family. From 1825 Arthur Eden leased Harrington Hall, a magnificent red-brick house within two miles of Somersby rectory, with the result that the young Tennysons and the

---

*Rosa Baring was omitted from Hallam Tennyson's *Memoir* of 1897, introduced into the narrative by the poet's grandson's biography of 1949, and more closely integrated into the records of Tennyson's personal and emotional wanderings in the 1830s by R. W. Rader's pioneering study of *Maud* published in 1963.

young Rawnsleys became friends of Rosa Baring and of Arthur Eden's children.

Arthur Hallam had been Tennyson's point of entry into the upper class. Like Hallam, Rosa Baring stood for money, privilege and social assurance. She was intellectually commonplace but she was physically attractive, and she belonged to the world of entitlement from which the Somersby Tennysons felt they had been brutally exiled. Harrington Hall was an appropriate setting for a poetic genius who also needed the status of a gentleman. Tennyson made many references in his poetry to Harrington, its garden and its little church, as though these were touchstones for the perfect life in the perfect place. As late as 1886, when he was seventy-seven years old, he recalled Harrington for 'Locksley Hall Sixty Years After':

> Yonder in that chapel, slowly sinking now into the ground,
> Lies the warrior, my forefather, with his feet upon the hound.

> Crossed! for once he sailed the sea to crush the Moslem in his
>   pride;
> Dead the warrior, dead his glory, dead the cause in which he
>   died.[4]

This very well-preserved crusader tomb is a striking feature of the little church at Harrington, the legs crossed with one foot resting on a faithful dog, and the shield covering the knight's breast. Originally it was immediately next to the altar. The church was extended at a later date so that the crusader, who has never been moved, now lies in a seemingly arbitrary position halfway along the right-hand wall. The rose garden at Harrington which was made famous by *Maud* no longer has its roses, but the wall surrounding it is still there. It was a handsome enclosed space, the perfect private setting for a lovers' assignation.

Rosa Baring fully understood that Tennyson's feeling for her was three parts social ambition to one part sexual passion. She was rich and Tennyson desperately needed money; she was not stupid, and it must have been obvious to her from the outset that Tennyson was looking for personal advancement. The gulf between them was part of his appeal. In his invaluable *Memories of the Tennysons*, H. D. (Drummond) Rawnsley wrote that in her old age Rosa Baring remembered the young Tennyson vividly:

> Alfred, as we all called him, was so quaint and so chivalrous, such
> a real knight among men, at least I always fancied so; and though

we joked with one another about his quaint, taciturn ways, which were mingled strangely with boisterous fits of fun, we were proud as peacocks to have been worthy of notice by him, and treasured any message he might send or any word of admiration he let fall.

Rawnsley also reported that:

She and her companions round Somersby, who were not too frightened of him, hung upon the words of the quaint, shy, long-haired young man, who had in his boyhood's day made an impression of being more learned and more thoughtful than was common, and of being wise beyond his years. She would tell of how she and one of her girl friends, in admiration of the young poet, would ride over to Somersby, just to have the pleasure of pleasing him or teasing him as the case might be. From time to time he would write a verse or two for one or other of the girls who had been with him at a picnic in the woods, or send some little verse of reconciliation after a tiff at a dance; and although she confessed that all poetry in those days seemed to her mere 'jangledom,' yet it was always delightful to her to believe that the 'rose of the rosebud garden of girls,' had reference to her.[5]

Rosa's indirectly reported phrasing is interesting. She enjoyed 'pleasing him or teasing him'. The verses and tiffs and flurries of excitement are expressions of sexual interest between these young people as vivid as one was likely to encounter among the gentry of rural Lincolnshire in the 1830s. A poem to Rosa, written in 1834, displays the rich sensuality of this girl and the young man's excited response to her:

> Rose of roses, bliss of blisses,
> Were not thine the kiss of kisses?
> Ah! for such a kiss as that!
> Ah! for such a rose as this is![6]

At the same time, Tennyson was completing the ambitious narrative poem 'The Gardener's Daughter', most of which was written before Hallam's death. It reflects rather transparently Tennyson's feelings both for Arthur Hallam and for Rosa Baring. The *donnée* of the poem is the intensely close friendship between two young men, the speaker and his friend Eustace, which is in some tension with the attachment that the speaker forms with 'Rose', who is the 'gardener's daughter' of the title. Tennyson is reversing the social status of the models – in the poem, an upper-class man is drawn to a woman very much his social inferior. From the perspective of Rosa Baring's mother and stepfather, the actual relationship between Tennyson and Rosa must have looked like the opposite of that.

Things were placid enough in the earlier phase of Tennyson's romantic attachment to Rosa; witness this adoring 1834 lyric:

> . . . oh, be sure
> That if I had not loved, I had not blamed;
> For my whole heart is vassal at thy feet.

The relationship quite soon developed rough edges, though, and became the more interesting for them. 'A tiff at a dance' yielded a reproachful poem ('To Rosa', 1836) brimming with energy. The form of the poem is striking – it is a double sonnet, highly accomplished and controlled – and the content is full of contrition for an unspecified offence:

> Sole rose of beauty, loveliness complete,
> If those few words were bitter or unjust,
> Yet is thy gentle nature so discreet
> That they will pass thee like an idle gust.

What had the young Tennyson said to upset her? It is safe to assume that he had been rough and unmannerly in the urgency of his demands on her. He here took an oath of good behaviour, but it is highly compromised good behaviour, since it invokes Rosa's own conspicuous physical attractiveness – rather than, for example, the Bible or the stars – as sanction and authority:

> By that Madonna grace of parted hair
>   And dewy sister eyelids drooping chaste,
>   By each dear foot, so light on field, or floor,
>   By that full form and slender moulded waist,
>   And that all perfect smile of thine, I swear,
>   That these rash lips shall blame thee, Rose, no more.[7]

This poem was written following a quarrel at a Spilsby ball in 1836. (It is a mark of Tennyson's drifting condition at this time that he appears to have had a very similar quarrel with Sophy Rawnsley at the same ball.)

By 1836, the two-year understanding with Rosa Baring had run its course. Tennyson's feelings modulated sharply. First came a rational appraisal of the social and economic reality – Rosa could not marry a poor man. She was a 'jewel', as a sonnet of late in 1836 tells us, but an unattainable one:

> Why did I linger? I myself condemn,
> For ah! 'tis far too costly to be mine,
> And nature never dropt a human tear
> In those chill dews whereof she froze the gem.

What appears to be the last poem in this sequence is contemptuous and angry:

> How thought you that this thing could captivate?
> What are those graces that could make her dear,
> Who is not worth the notice of a sneer
> To rouse the vapid devil of her hate?
> A speech conventional, so void of weight
> That after it has buzzed about one's ear
> 'Twere rich refreshment for a week to hear
> The dentist babble or the barber prate [. . .]
> A perfect-featured face, expressionless,
> Insipid, as the Queen upon a card.[8]

Did Rosa ever read this one? If she had seen it when she was a young woman, she had forgotten it in her old age; otherwise her recollections of Tennyson would scarcely have been as affectionate as they were. Professor Rader was surely right to see Tennyson's feelings for Rosa as serious: 'the feeling' in his love poems to Rosa 'is obviously not brotherly affection but infatuation manifestly sincere and fervent'. He was no longer an ardent teenager 'but a man of twenty-six who only two years before had been shattered by the death of Arthur Hallam' and was 'seeking to redirect the emotional energies which, once absorbed in Hallam, were now without a living object'.[9] In other words, Tennyson believed himself to be seriously in love, but at the same time he felt bruised, tormented and oversensitive. Three angry sonnets 'to a coquette' (Rosa again)[10] – vividly express this:

> A nobler yearning never broke her rest
> Than but to dance and sing, be gaily drest,
> And win all eyes with all accomplishment.

The judgement with which this sonnet ends is decidedly harsh:

> For ah! the slight coquette, she cannot love,
> And if you kissed her feet a thousand years,
> She still would take the praise, and care no more.

Concurrently with his passion for Rosa Baring, Tennyson had a gentle, much more familial and domestic flirtation going with Sophy Rawnsley, daughter of his father's close friend T. H. Rawnsley. The flirtation was familial in that he had known Sophy since she was a baby (she was born in 1818) and since Dr Tennyson's death in 1831 T. H. Rawnsley had become one of the guardians of the Somersby Tennysons. So Sophy was like a close cousin. 'Airy, fairy Lilian' was written for her when she was a child and in 1834 Tennyson wrote a tender little love poem to her:

> Sweet, ask me not why I am sad,
> But, when sad thoughts arise,
> Look on me, make my spirit glad
> To gaze upon thine eyes.
> For how can sorrow dwell in mine
> If they might always gaze on thine?[11]

Did the two girls know that they were rivals for his affection, and did this emotional triangle reach crisis point at the Spilsby ball in 1836? Certainly Tennyson had to write a poem of apology not only to Rosa (quoted above) but also to Sophy Rawnsley. The apology to Sophy is far less intense (and shorter) than the one to Rosa, decorously apologetic but not passionate:

> My coldness was mistimed like summer-snow;
> Cold words I spoke, yet loved thee warm and well.
> Was I so harsh?

Tellingly, this poem reminds Sophy that their relationship is like that of siblings, not lovers:

> What madness moved my blood
> To make me thus belie my constant heart
> That watch't with love thine earliest infancy,
> Slow-ripening to the grace of womanhood,
> Through every change that made thee what thou art.[12]

These lines addressed to Sophy have an endearing tenderness and friendliness, contrasting sharply with the frustration and anger of the Rosa poems. Sophy belonged to Tennyson's social level; Rosa emphatically did not.

Rosa's rejection of Tennyson clearly bit very deep. He was still writing out his hurt, anger and humiliation many years later. 'Locksley Hall' was published in 1842 and 'Locksley Hall Sixty Years After' in 1886, yet the first draft of the original poem (the MS is now at Yale)* is on paper watermarked 1835 and could have been written as early as this same year, though probably the best guess for its date of composition is 1837. Edmund Lushington thought he remembered that it was read to him in 1837 or 1838.[13] It certainly reflects Tennyson's extraordinarily powerful feelings about Rosa.[14]

The early state of 'Locksley Hall' – a poem about a weary soldier returning to his childhood home – is angrier than the published version. It reveals surprisingly raw hatred for 'Amy' – the Rosa figure, who marries somebody else – after she has committed herself to an oafish husband. The punctuation is jagged and percussive, and this contributes to the unbuttoned rage of the poem in manuscript:

> O my cousin, shallow-hearted! O my Amy! Mine no more
> O the dreary, dreary moorland! O the barren, barren shore!
>
> Falser than all fancy fathoms, falser than all songs have sung
> Puppet to a father's threat, and servile to a shrewish tongue!
>
> Is it well to wish thee happy? – now that thou has[t] dared
> decline
> On a range of lower feelings and a lesser heart than mine!

The variations are small but telling: the published state is:

---

*Tennyson gave this manuscript to a young American admirer, Frederick Goddard Tuckerman, in 1855. Tuckerman wrote an enraptured letter to his brother about this event: 'Since my return to England I have been visiting Alfred Tennyson, passed four or five days at his house, in the Isle of Wight, most delightfully as you may suppose, Mr and Mrs Tennyson treating me with utmost courtesy and kindness [. . .] I should tell you that at parting Mr Tennyson gave me the original Ms of "Locksley Hall", a favour of which I may be justly proud as he says he never did such a thing in his life before, for anybody.'

Is it well to wish thee happy? – having known me – to decline
On a range of lower feelings and a narrower heart than mine![15]

A couple of unpublished lines towards the end of the manuscript dismiss the whole of the opposite sex in a spurt of rage:

Woman is the lesser being: all her pleasure & her pain
Is a feebler blinder motion bounded by a shallower brain.

There's no sign, though, that the speaker wants to turn away in disgust to look for another male friend – another Hallam. Instead he 'will take some savage woman, she shall rear my dusky race'.[16] The rootless young man who wrote these lines already had a vehemently held sense of entitlement. Amy's marriage will be a disaster: 'As the husband is, the wife is: thou art mated with a clown, /And the grossness of his nature will have weight to drag thee down.'[17]

So who was this unfortunate 'clown'? In sober reality he was Rosa's choice of husband, Robert* Duncombe Shafto, a perfectly decent, intelligent and – above all – wealthy young cousin of Arthur Eden, Rosa's stepfather. He married Rosa on 22 October 1838 and clearly from the viewpoints of both families, it was an excellent match into which Rosa was happy to enter. She had known Duncombe Shafto since she was a child, he would provide material comforts of the kind she was used to, and she would live among people she knew and trusted for the rest of her uneventful life. However, it was not a love match. Lady Brougham, a relation of Rosa's, wrote in her diary for 2 January 1838 about a visit that Shafto had paid to her in London, and about the Eden family's urgent desire for the marriage to be agreed: 'I saw plainly he had not made up his mind to marry Rosa Baring as they wished & did not wish to bring the matter to a conclusion.'[18] This was a dynastic marriage, undertaken after due deliberation and circumspection.

Duncombe Shafto was far from being the brutal drunken materialist and coarse country squire of Tennyson's bilious imagination. He was a justice of the peace, a member of Parliament, a rich landowner and a wholly suitable husband for Rosa. Alfred Tennyson never stood a chance, and anyone less blinkered by his own imperatives would have recognised that long before he did.

If 'Locksley Hall' were only about Alfred Tennyson's frustration

---

*The 'Robert' was a long-established family name, since he was from the family of 'Bobby Shafto' of the famous song, a County Durham shipping family.

with Rosa Baring, it would not be of great interest. As it stands, the poem may lament the fate of the underdog, but it also celebrates his strength; it displays a mature man's memory of his younger self at a time when he was driven by ambition and talent. The narrative is of the kind explored by Dickens in *Oliver Twist* at the same date (and in *David Copperfield* some twelve years later), in which a disadvantaged young man makes good. Indeed, the poem is at its most Dickensian when it brings its hero through the darkness to the great capital:

> Make me feel the wild pulsation that I felt before the strife,
> When I heard my days before me, and the tumult of my life;
>
> Yearning for the large excitement that the coming years would
>   yield,
> Eager-hearted as a boy when first he leaves his father's field,
>
> And at night along the dusky highway near and nearer drawn,
> Sees in heaven the light of London flaring like a dreary dawn;
>
> And his spirit leaps within him to be gone before him then,
> Underneath the light he looks at, in among the throngs of
>   men.[19]

The metre is itself propulsive, as though enacting the young man's drive, and the dramatic content is closely related to Tennyson's own emergence from Lincolnshire. This remembered younger self is the kind of hero who appealed to a working-class audience.[20] The thrusting youngster looking to further his ambitions in London imagines a future for his country, in which landscapes of the 1830s are radicalised out of all recognition:

> Men, my brothers, men the workers, ever reaping something
>   new:
> That which they have done but earnest of the things that they
>   shall do:
>
> For I dipt into the future, far as human eye could see,
> Saw the Vision of the world, and all the wonder that would be;
>
> Saw the heavens fill with commerce, argosies of magic sails,
> Pilots of the purple twilight, dropping down with costly bales;

Heard the heavens fill with shouting, and there rained a ghastly
  dew
From the nations' airy navies grappling in the central blue.[21]

Commentators on the First World War often admire H. G. Wells's
The War in the Air (1907) as a work which had accurately anticipated the aerial conflicts of 1914–18; but in 'Locksley Hall' Tennyson
had imagined battles between 'the nations' airy navies' seventy years
earlier. Further, he had imagined that this coming war would be
followed by permanent world peace: 'the battle-flags were furled/ In
the Parliament of man, the Federation of the World'. The dramatic
situation in the poem does not permit us to read it as a Chartist or
radical manifesto for England, though, given that the speaker is a
disillusioned older man remembering the idealism of his own youth.
At the same time this mature speaker is still excited by the thought
of the future:

Not in vain the distance beckons. Forward, forward let us
  range,
Let the great world spin for ever down the ringing grooves of
  change.*

The mature man's politics are distinctly early Victorian. (Victoria
succeeded to the throne in 1837, therefore probably while the poem
was in composition.) The future as this older man imagines it will be
one of material progress, and the young idealist's 'Federation of the
World' is here replaced by an unlovely triumphalist ascendancy for
Europe:

Through the shadow of the globe we sweep into the younger
  day:
Better fifty years of Europe than a cycle of Cathay.†

---

*'Not in vain the distance beckons' is misquoted (as 'distance beacons') in Ricks, *Poems*.
The detail about 'Locksley Hall' remembered by all its readers is the mistake that
Tennyson made here, which he himself explained in a note: 'When I went by the first
train from Liverpool to Manchester (1830) I thought that the wheels ran in a groove.
It was a black night, and there was such a vast crowd round the train at the station
that we could not see the wheels. Then I made this line.'
†In the twenty-first century it is hard not to note the historical irony of that reference
to 'Cathay', China, as an immobile and moribund country with no significance in the
modern world.

The poem ends with a curse on Locksley Hall, which is to be punished for the blocking of the young man's ambitions earlier in his life. A thunderbolt approaches:

Let it fall on Locksley Hall, with rain or hail, or fire or snow;
For the mighty wind arises, roaring seaward, and I go.[22]

Tennyson's rage and humiliation over Rosa Baring were not confined to 'Locksley Hall', and nor did they subside in 1842. She also features in *Maud*, which was not published until 1855. By that date he was famous, settled, affluent, married and a father; but the anguish was not forgotten. The unattainable love object in *Maud* is the speaker's social and economic superior; she is attracted to him, but cannot act on it because of the interdiction imposed by her rich family. The Hall is an old house tainted by new money – much as the Edens, with their new money, had taken over Harrington Hall and smartened it up:

I am sick of the Hall and the hill, I am sick of the moor and
  the main.
Why should I stay? can a sweeter chance ever come to me
  here?
[. . .]

Workmen up at the Hall! – they are coming back from abroad;
The dark old place will be gilt by the touch of a millionaire:

In a cancelled draft, the memory of poor Rosa stirred violent contempt, reviving the resentment over having been 'not good enough' all those years before:

Well, I was half-afraid but I shall not die for her sake,
Not be her 'savage' and 'O the monster'! their delicate ways!
Their finical interlarding of French and the giggle and shrug!
Taken with Maud – not so – for what could she prove but a
  curse.
Being so hard, she has hardly a decent regard for her pug.

In the published poem, Bayons Manor, seat of the usurping Tennyson d'Eyncourts, was condemned for being a 'gewgaw castle' (property of the young coal baron who is preferred to the poet as Maud's suitor). There was another gewgaw castle in the family, and Tennyson may also have been glancing at this one, despite the fact that it was the home of the most generous of his relations, his aunt Elisa Russell. The castle in question here was the Russells' country seat, Brancepeth Castle in County Durham, now lavishly restored. Aunt Russell certainly believed that her late husband's way of life was coming under attack in the poem. Tennyson stoutly denied this in a long letter of 16 July 1856 (a letter which has been torn – perhaps in vexation by Elisa Russell). 'What must you think of me,' he asked, 'if you think me capable of such gratuitous and unmeaning personality and hostility? I am as sensitive a man as exists and sooner than wound another in such a spiteful fashion would consent never to write a line again.'[23] But it is easy to conclude that he was indeed thinking of Brancepeth. His recall of his own depression and anger in the frustrating 1830s had caused him at this point to abdicate from literary tact:

> Seeing him gewgaw castle shine,
> New as his title, built last year,
> There amid perky larches and pine,
> And over the sullen-purple moor
> (Look at it) pricking a cockney ear.[24]

This theme in *Maud* could be said to gather up and recapitulate all the anger, resentment and frustration that the young man had felt, and deploy it in a narrative poem which placed and distanced the pain and humiliation of that young relationship. Tennyson thus finally put Rosa securely into his emotional past.

At a deep inner level, while working at his hopeless suit with Rosa Baring and at the same time flirting with Sophy Rawnsley and enjoying Lincolnshire society, Tennyson was writing his steadily growing sequence of poems mourning his dead friend. Once he had adopted the ABBA stanza, he consciously reserved it for the 'elegies' for Hallam. We identify it intimately now with *In Memoriam*, and much discriminating praise has been heaped on it. But it was not Tennyson's first choice of stanza form. One of the Harvard notebooks has a very early version of what later became lyric III in ABAB stanza form:

> A cloud was drawn across the sky,
>   The stars their courses blindly run.
> Out of waste places came a cry
>   And murmurs from the dying sun.

In every form the sense receives
  A something hitherto unmet,
In every motion of the leaves
  The shadow of a vain regret.

The whole house shaken to its fall,
  This travelled mind a foreign land,
Love mixt with all – love lord of all,
  Thought drifting like the hills of sand.[25]

This and the ABBA stanza were alternatives in his mind at this stage of the composition (October 1833), very shortly after he had heard about Hallam's death.

In its draft state lyric IX, 'Fair ship, that from the Italian shore', is in both Harvard Notebook 16 and Trinity College Notebook 17; both are dated 1833, but the Harvard notebook is clearly the one in which he first composed the poem. Harvard Notebook 16 is a very small black leather book, with 'Album' stamped in gold on the spine. In Tennyson's hand inside the front cover is written 'Alfred Tennyson' and then, in Hallam Tennyson's hand, 'St Agnes Cophetua Ulysses' and the dates – 1831–1833 – when Tennyson used this book. Folio 19 is the sheet on which he wrote when he first heard about Hallam's death in October 1833. The deletions and corrections were made immediately, so that looking at this page we are witnessing the act of creation and overhearing the poet's thoughts:

Fair ship, that from the Italian shore
  Sailest the ['glassy', deleted] placid ocean plains,
  With my lost Arthur's loved remains,
Spread thy full wings & waft him o'er.

['Convey thy charge', deleted, 'Draw this dear freight', deleted]
So draw him home to those that mourn
  In vain. ['for him', deleted] A ['happy', deleted] favourable
    speed
  ['All day strain all thy cords, be tight', deleted] Ruffle thy
    mirrored masts & lead
Thro prosperous floods his holy urn!

He fixed on the final version of these stanzas almost immediately, and they have reappeared in all published editions unchanged:

Fair ship, that from the Italian shore
   Sailest the placid ocean-plains
   With my lost Arthur's loved remains,
Spread thy full wings, and waft him o'er.

So draw him home to those that mourn
   In vain; a favourable speed
   Ruffle thy mirrored mast, and lead
Through prosperous floods his holy urn.

Once he had established these first two stanzas, the rest of the poem came to him with absolute assurance, though the changes from manuscript to printed text, small though they are, are significant:

All night no ruder air perplex
   Thy sliding keel, till Phosphor, bright
   As our pure love, through early light
Shall glimmer on the dewy decks.

There was no full stop after 'decks' in the original, so that 'Phosphor' governed the verb 'Sphere' in the following verse ('Sphere all your light', light in the singular being the object in the MS).

Sphere all your lights around, above;
   Sleep, gentle heavens, before the prow;
   Sleep, gentle winds [waves in the MS], as he sleeps now,
My friend, the brother of my love;

My Arthur, whom I shall not see
   Till all my widowed race be run;
   Dear as the mother to the son,
More than my brothers are to me.[26]

In the manuscript, 'Phosphor' provided all the light in both verses two and three, but the plural 'lights' opens the sky to a whole galaxy of stars. In *In Memoriam* as a whole Arthur was named rarely, and the changed punctuation lowered the emotional intensity of the mention of his name in the last stanza here. In the manuscript, 'My Arthur' was an aposiopesis within dashes, the punctuation giving the words the immediacy of a speaking voice, with a catch in the breath and a sob of spontaneous grief: 'My friend, the brother of my love – / My Arthur – , whom I shall not see / Till all my widowed race be run – / Dear as the mother [etc.]'.

'More than my brothers' could have been a hurtful phrase, and Tennyson later added lyric LXXIX, which offered an apology to his closest brother, Charles Tennyson Turner:

'More than my brothers are to me,' –
Let not this vex thee, noble heart!
I know thee of what force thou art
To hold the costliest love in fee.

This urges the argument that while the familial closeness of Charles ('thou and I are one in kind') had been a source of strength since their childhoods, Arthur Hallam's distinctive differences from the Tennysons made him the more valuable to Alfred Tennyson: 'He supplied my want the more / As his unlikeness fitted mine.'[27] Tennyson was writing the emotional truth as he felt it: among the men that he loved, Hallam took first place. It helped that all his brothers were fond of Arthur Hallam. Frederick wrote to a friend (February 1833) that 'the number of a man's friends can never be great, but since he who was more than Brother to us has been taken away out of humanity, methinks indeed we have marvellous few remaining'.[28]

The Tennysons had lived in limbo at Somersby since Dr Tennyson's death in 1831, and Frederick had been particularly restless and unplaced. Rebellious and troublesome during his undergraduate years, he had done one good thing for himself: he had made friends with his cousin, George Hildeyard Tennyson, his uncle Charles's son. When George Hildeyard secured an appointment for himself in the residency at Corfu, Frederick went to join him (uninvited) in the hope of finding some employment for himself. As a result he was abroad in 1835, a year when the fortunes of the Somersby Tennysons were changed by two further deaths.

In March 1835, their great-uncle Samuel Turner died, and his estates at Grasby and Caistor were left to Charles Tennyson, second of the Somersby sons, who now changed his name to Charles Tennyson Turner: 'He was nominated to the Grasby living and straightway moved from Tealby to Caistor. There he took up his abode in the fine old house in the market place, in which his grandfather had courted Mary Turner sixty years before.'[29] The second death was that of their grandfather, the Old Man of the Wolds, in July.

Had the old man relented, towards the end of his life, and left a significant part of his wealth to the helpless widow of his older son, George Clayton? Of course not. Property at Grimsby was left to

Frederick, the oldest son. A property at Grasby worth £3,000 was left to Alfred Tennyson. Funds to the same amount were left for the support of Edward (whose insanity was already obvious) and other properties worth in the region of £20,000 were left to be sold for the benefit of the remaining Somersby children. All the rest of Old George's estates and property in Lincolnshire went to his younger son, Charles, and his family.[30] The Somersby Tennysons felt considerable bitterness. The Tealby Tennysons, by contrast, exulted in their cousins' disappointment in a thoroughly unlovely manner. Edwin Tennyson d'Eyncourt wrote to his brother George Hildeyard Tennyson d'Eyncourt in August 1835: 'I suppose by this time that you have received my Father's letter announcing my poor Grand Father's death.' The snobbish addition of 'd'Eyncourt' was looming large in the young man's mind. 'I am very glad we have changed our name, as it gives us a good position, and if we had not my Father would always have been Mr Charles Tennyson. Besides which it will keep us in a great measure clear of the Somersby Family who really are quite hogs. Not one of them came to the Funeral.'[31]

The calumnies continue in a letter from Frances Tennyson d'Eyncourt, Charles's wife, to her son George Hildeyard Tennyson d'Eyncourt:

> I hear the family at Somersby are one and all much disappointed at their *handsome* increase of Property, but they expected more and the girls very handsome fortunes besides. Some people are never satisfied!! They also say that Frederick ought to have taken the name of d'Eyncourt, as being the eldest son of the eldest son; you will probably have heard that not one of that family attended the funeral, nor has one been here to call.[32]

In September, Charles Tennyson d'Eyncourt wrote to his son George:

> I know no reason why any of that family should be dissatisfied. My Father has done what he always said he would do, and this was well known to them all and is the same as he would have done if my Brother had lived except that he has been *a Father* to George's Children. Alfred I find has been so violent (though he gets the Manor of Grasby and an estate there) that Mr and Mrs Bourne sent him away from Margate where he was with them.[33]

Alfred's 'violence' was surpassed by Frederick's volcanic sense of grievance. He reacted angrily and unguardedly over the legacies, and later added to this a bizarre bit of behaviour which remains unaccountable from any rational viewpoint. In May 1836 he wrote proposing marriage to his cousin Julia, Charles Tennyson d'Eyncourt's daughter.[34] Did he think thus to recover by marriage some of the Tennyson d'Eyncourt fortune that he regarded as his by right?

In May 1835, Alfred Tennyson and Edward Fitzgerald stayed with James Spedding at his family home, Mirehouse, a beautiful Jacobean house near Keswick. Mirehouse sits placidly in its own sunlit grounds with a fine prospect of Bassenthwaite. It is still much as Tennyson knew it, and furniture and manuscripts associated with the poet are on display in the house. James Spedding made a fine sketch of Tennyson smoking his pipe in a favourite chair near a fireplace, and this sketch, together with the chair itself, are there to bring Tennyson's physical presence alive for visitors. Spedding also made some engaging sketches of Tennyson's party tricks, such as the way he could turn himself into the sun appearing from between the clouds.

Spedding made his guests very welcome, and the three young Cambridge friends excitedly talked poetry and engaged in earnest Apostolic debate, while at the same time exploring the countryside and making boating expeditions on the lake.

This visit to Mirehouse was of great significance to Fitzgerald because it was his first opportunity to get to know Tennyson. Fitzgerald was a diffident man, disinclined to assert himself; he had been on the fringes of Tennyson's circle at Trinity but they had barely known each other then. As a result of the visit to Mirehouse, and perhaps flushed and excited by the close proximity to genius that he now enjoyed, Fitzgerald wrote to Tennyson* offering money:

Dear Tennyson, though I am no Rothschild, my wants are fewer than my monies: and I have usually ten or twelve pounds sitting very loosely in my breeches pocket – To what doth this tend? – Marry, to this – I have heard you sometimes say you are bound by the want of such a sum: and I vow to the Lord that I could not have a greatest pleasure than transferring it to you on such occasions. I should not dare to say such a thing to a small man: but you are not a small man assuredly; and even if you do not make use of my offer, you will not be offended, but put it to the right account. It is very difficult to persuade people in this world that one can part with a Bank note without a pang – It is one of the most simple things I have ever done to talk thus to you, I believe: but here is an end: and be charitable to me –[35]

---

*This very important letter – badly damaged – is at Yale.

Accounts of the consequence of this offer vary, but Carlyle, at least, believed that Fitzgerald paid Tennyson an allowance of £300 a year for much of the 1830s and 1840s. Tennyson was clearly very grateful – yet later he was to be distant and somewhat callous towards Fitzgerald, and at the same time he was so often depressed and withdrawn that almost all his friends at various times expressed frustration with his moods. Sadly, the fact that for Fitzgerald to part with money was easy, while for Tennyson money was an intense and urgent need, must itself have been galling.

The Sellwoods and the Tennysons had known each other since Tennyson and Emily were children,* but Hallam Tennyson reported that Alfred Tennyson had first noticed her beauty in 1830:

> The Sellwoods had driven over one spring day from Horncastle, to call at Somersby Rectory. Arthur Hallam was then staying with the Tennysons; and asked Emily Sellwood to walk with him in the Fairy Wood [near Somersby]. At a turn of the path they came upon my father, who, at sight of the slender, beautiful girl of seventeen in her simple gray dress, moving 'like a light across those woodland ways,' suddenly said to her: 'Are you a Dryad or an Oread wandering here?'[36]

On 24 May 1836, Alfred Tennyson's older brother Charles, now a man of independent means following old Samuel Turner's death, married Louisa Sellwood. Tennyson stood as his brother's best man, and Emily was her sister's bridesmaid. Tennyson had been aware of Emily since his magical vision of her as a woodland spirit, which was now six years in the past. He had got over his infatuation with Rosa Baring and its attendant frustrations; and it was at this wedding that he first felt powerfully drawn to Emily:

> Love lighted down between them full of glee,
> And over his left shoulder laughed at thee,
> 'O happy bridesmaid, make a happy bride.'

Emily Sellwood belonged to the same social world as the Rawnsleys. She was the eldest of the three daughters of Henry Sellwood, a lawyer

---

*Agnes Weld, daughter of Anne Sellwood and thus Louisa and Emily Sellwood's niece, recorded of the Tennysons and Sellwoods: 'The young people were constantly riding and driving over to spend the day with each other, for Horncastle, the busy Lincolnshire town where the Sellwoods resided, was only seven miles from Somersby.' (Weld, p.2.)

who had based himself in the attractive Lincolnshire market town of Horncastle. In some ways Henry Sellwood resembled Tennyson's grandfather: he too was ambitious, intelligent and restless. In 1812 he had married Sarah Franklin, one of the ten children of a local man, Willingham Franklin who had worked as a grocer and draper in Lincoln, but had subsequently moved with his family to Spilsby, where he flourished and added a banking business to his retail concerns.[37]

Emily was born the year following the marriage of Henry Sellwood into the Franklin family. In the same year Henry Sellwood was establishing himself as a manager of estates and general man of affairs. By 1823 he had become sufficiently established in Horncastle to be asked to respond to the toast 'to the prosperity of Horncastle' at a local event, the Dispensary Ball. In a letter written many years later, Emily would recall that she first saw Alfred Tennyson when she was about nine years old:

I *saw* him first in his Father's carriage at my Father's door [his father was visiting Henry Sellwood in Horncastle] when I was a little child and he about thirteen. Even then he was pale with the same very refined features. These he had when I saw him again when he was twenty one – though then he had the hue of southern France in his complexion as he had always after, when I saw him which I did at long intervals.[38]

The first of these encounters must have been in 1822 or 1823, and the second in the late summer of 1830 after Tennyson had returned from his expedition to the Pyrenees with Arthur Hallam.

In 1837, the Tennysons as a family had to confront the long-feared, long-postponed departure from Somersby. By this time the elder brothers, Frederick and Charles, had both left home, and Alfred found that he was in charge of the move, taking all the decisions and dealing with the numerous practicalities. His sweet, pious, animal-loving mother was herself quite unable to face the problem of finding a new home. Early in 1837, Tennyson visited a number of possible houses; the one he settled on had the obvious appeal – for Tennyson himself if not for his mother and siblings – of being within twelve miles of London and thus within reach of many of his old Cambridge friends. It was in Epping Forest: Beech Hill House at High Beech, Epping. Tennyson had successfully moved his family there by the early summer and then spent much time in London, staying often with James Spedding, and for a period taking rooms of his own at 12 Mornington Crescent.

Leaving Somersby after nearly thirty years was inevitably very

painful. Other children would grow up in this loved house, knowing
nothing of the troubled family who had been forced to leave. Part of
lyric CI of *In Memoriam* reads:

> Unwatched, the garden bough shall sway,
> The tender blossom flutter down,
> Unloved, that beech will gather brown,
> This maple burn itself away;
>
> Unloved, the sun-flower, shining fair,
> Ray round with flames her disk of seed,
> And many a rose-carnation feed
> With summer spice the humming air;
> [. . .]
> Till from the garden and the wild
> A fresh association blow,
> And year by year the landscape grow
> Familiar to the stranger's child;
>
> As year by year the labourer tills
> His wonted glebe, or lops the glades;
> And year by year our memory fades
> From all the circle of the hills.[39]

By 1837, Tennyson was sufficiently well-known to be in demand in
London literary circles. One really helpful contact was the elderly,
charming, wealthy bachelor poet Samuel Rogers. Rogers clearly took
to Tennyson's exotic good looks as well as his talent, and Tennyson
was regularly to be found at the older man's legendary breakfast parties
in the grandeur of his rooms in St James's Place. Tennyson had also
called on William Ewart Gladstone in Carlton Gardens in 1837
(Gladstone referred to this as 'an unexpected honour, for I had no
other tie with him than having been in earlier life the friend of his
friend'). At one of his breakfasts in 1839, Rogers brought the two men
together for a more cordial and productive meeting. Thereafter
Tennyson and Gladstone remained in touch. They would always have
Hallam's friendship as a strong, though uneasy, common bond.[40]

Early in 1837, Richard Monckton Milnes, Tennyson's old Cambridge
friend, asked him to contribute a poem to *The Tribute*. He would
be among friends; Chenevix Trench and Milnes himself would be in the
volume. A grumpy exchange followed. Milnes wrote inviting Alfred to
his home in Yorkshire, Fryston ('Freezetown' to his Cambridge friends).

We will have Freezetown all to ourselves and you may smoke while I play the organ. Now be a good boy and do as you're told. Lord Northampton is getting up a charity book of poetry for the destitute family of a man of letters, born in the dead letter office, and he earnestly prays you to contribute not your mite but your might to it.[41]

Milnes's breeziness struck Tennyson as tactless, and his lightness of tone and air of entitlement in this letter didn't work. Alfred Tennyson took his poetry seriously, and he disliked elegant 'annuals' of verse (very popular publications of the day, often exchanged as Christmas gifts). Nor was he pleased by the fact that Milnes had already promised Northampton that he would contribute to the volume. 'Three summers back,' he replied, 'provokt by the incivility of editors, I swore an oath, that I would never again have to do with their vapid books.'[42] Milnes was angry with what he saw as Tennyson's 'insulting irony', and Tennyson had to write back temperately to say that he had had no intention of calling anything in which Milnes or Chenevix Trench were willing to publish 'vapid'. This second letter was appropriately pitched, and he promised a poem: 'I will either bring or send you something for your Annual.'[43]

Accordingly, Tennyson's lyric 'Oh! that 'twere possible', in its first state, under the title 'Stanzas', was published in *The Tribute* for 1837.* The contributors were not 'vapid', given that they included Wordsworth, William Whewell (the Master of Trinity, not otherwise known as a poet), Alfred Tennyson's brother Charles Tennyson Turner, Milnes himself, Chenevix Trench, Aubrey de Vere and another Trinity man, John Frere. There is no doubt, though, that in giving the volume his haunting little masterpiece Tennyson was raising *The Tribute* to unaccustomed heights:

> Oh! that 'twere possible,
> After long grief and pain,
> To find the arms of my true-love
> Round me once again!

---

*The Tennyson Research Centre in Lincoln has Charles Tennyson's copy of this publication: *The Tribute: a collection of Miscellaneous Unpublished Poems by Various Authors*. The beneficiary of Milnes's good intentions was now dead, as the preface says: 'this work was projected as early as Spring, 1836, while the late Reverend Edward Smedley was still living, and its original object was to spare him the necessity for those arduous literary labours which at the time threatened his sight or his life. His hearing he had already lost, and disorder in his eyes was to all appearance sapping a sense still more precious.' (Northampton, p. iii.)

When I was wont to meet her
  In the silent woody places
    Of the land that gave me birth,
  We stood tranced in long embraces,
Mixt with kisses sweeter, sweeter,
    Than any thing on earth.

A shadow flits before me –
  Not thou, but like to thee
Ah God! that it were possible
  For one short hour to see
The souls we loved, that they might tell us
  What and where they be.[44]

This lyric, first written in 1834, shortly after the death of Hallam, would later be the node around which the whole of the monodrama *Maud* would be composed between 1854 and the final revised version in 1856.

In January 1838, Tennyson wrote to Mrs T. H. Rawnsley, wife of his father's old friend. He longed to see a 'Lincolnshire face', and he complained of the pretensions of life nearer London. He spoke warmly of the Arabins, the good-natured people from whom he was renting High Beech, but had little to say for the other neighbours. 'The people are sufficiently hospitable but it is not in a good old fashioned way so as to do one's feelings any good. Large set dinners with store of venison and champagne are good things of their kind', but in general the society was 'artificial, frozen, cold and lifeless'.[45]

During this period Tennyson saw his Cambridge friends regularly but kept Emily Sellwood at a distance. This was very strange, as they were regarded by both the Tennyson and the Sellwood families as having entered into a long-term engagement. Tennyson's income from his legacies, plus the allowance he was receiving from Fitzgerald, would in fact have been enough to support a wife, but he used poverty as an excuse. In December 1837 he wrote:

> I have been at this place (High Beech in Epping Forest) all the year, with nothing but that muddy pond in prospect, and those two little sharp-barking dogs. Perhaps I am coming to the Lincolnshire coast, but I scarcely know. The journey is so expensive and I am so poor.[46]

Since he had no difficulty finding the money to see his friends in London or Cambridge when he wanted to visit them, it is hard to resist the suggestion that he was unable to make up his mind about Emily. A tantalising line written from Barmouth, in Wales, in July 1839 hints that communication was going wrong: 'In *letters*, words too often prove a bar of hindrance instead of a bond of union.'[47] 'A bar of hindrance': was he pushing her away? Emily came to stay with the family in Beech Hill, and Tennyson visited her in Horncastle, but the possibility of marriage was kept on hold. Emily's sister Louisa, who had married Charles Tennyson in 1837, gave intermittent reports of Emily's poor health; as a young man needing to make his way in the world, it could be that Tennyson was hesitant to take on a sick wife as his life companion.

Another relationship went badly wrong in the course of 1837. John Heath, a loyal Cambridge friend who had advised in detail on Tennyson's poems (and whose copies of the early poems in his notebook are a reliable guide to the dates of some of them), had been engaged to marry one of Tennyson's sisters, the beautiful Mary, but now he broke it off. Mary had become obsessively religious, and it could well be that Heath was worried about her state of mind. Among the other Tennysons, Arthur, Horatio and Septimus all showed signs of poor mental health (and possibly of epilepsy), while Edward had been in a private asylum since 1832. Mary now became part of the High Beech household, and therefore Tennyson's responsibility; he also knew that he was likely to be permanently responsible for his sister Matilda. (Family tradition was that Matilda had been dropped on her head in a coal-scuttle as a child and since then had been unable to live a normal life.)[48]

It was as a direct result of the move to High Beech that Tennyson became acquainted with Dr Matthew Allen,* a relationship that was to have fateful consequences.

---

*Matthew Allen's medical skills were based on informal apprenticeship rather than formal training: he had been apprenticed to one of his brothers, Oswald, who was an apothecary. With a small legacy from another relative, he visited existing institutions for the insane in the north of England and Scotland, to study the methods used. He set himself up in business as an apothecary in Princes Street, Edinburgh, from 1811, and continued to work with the insane, but it was not long before his first serious financial problems began to dog him. The business failed and he was imprisoned for debt; his brother Oswald loyally secured his release and discharge from bankruptcy. Oswald set him up in a small business making soda-water (one of the items in which an apothecary of the period would typically trade), but that also failed. Allen was imprisoned again, rescued again by his brother, and found a post as apothecary at York Asylum. Here he learned enlightened modern methods of managing the insane, and being an intelligent and enterprising man he established a good reputation for himself in the field. His doctor's qualification was awarded by the Marischal College in Aberdeen in 1821.

Dr Allen was a Scot: an intelligent and able man, who was developing radically new ways of caring for the insane. In 1837, the year in which the Tennysons moved to High Beech, he published his *Essay on the Classification of the Insane*.[49] Allen's purpose in writing this essay was to champion his own regime, which was indeed liberal and enlightened, and to stress that earlier treatments had been cruel, 'treating them [the insane] and *all who have the care of them as criminals*'.[50]

In his book, Allen described his own institution at Epping, where he cared for the insane in three separate and well-appointed houses: Fair Mead for male patients, Springfield for women, and Leopard's Hill Lodge for the most severe cases of either sex. Visitors to the institution – relations of the patients, for example – were impressed by the attractive normality of the public rooms; the patients were not restrained, but were encouraged to take long walks, to engage in manual labour and exercise, and to be physically healthy. Allen urged that humane treatment would yield good results, and he wrote of the success with which he had got people who had entered the asylum as little more than animals to associate with other patients and establish relationships. He spoke of two imbeciles walking arm in arm and at least getting to know each other.[51]

Edward Tennyson was beyond help, but Alfred's brother Septimus was a voluntary patient of Allen's several times between 1837 and 1840, and Tennyson himself sometimes stayed in one of Allen's houses as well. No stigma attached to an arrangement of this kind, and this was important to Tennyson. The friendship flourished. Tennyson responded to the sensitivity, tact and understanding that he encountered in the doctor. The personal warmth between the two men grew rapidly.

A little later Matthew Allen would give medical treatment to the poet John Clare; he also tried to establish a fund for Clare to help him to live independently. All this was going on while the Tennysons lived nearby. The scene in an insane asylum in Part II of *Maud* is based on Tennyson's knowledge of Dr Allen's establishments. It is not known whether Alfred Tennyson met Clare while he was in Matthew Allen's care, but it seems possible that he would have done.

Tennyson's friend J. H. Blakesley gives us a memorable picture of the poet among his Cambridge friends:

Alfred Tennyson has been with us for the last week. He is looking well and in good spirits, but complains of nervousness. How should he do otherwise, seeing that he smokes the strongest and most stinking tobacco out of a small blackened clay pipe on an average nine hours every day? He went off today by the Wisbeach [coach] to Epping, where he complains there are no sounds of Nature and no society; equally a want of birds and men.[52]

In April 1838, Fitzgerald wrote to Bernard Barton: 'we have had Alfred Tennyson here; very droll, and very wayward: and much sitting up of nights till two and three in the morning with pipes in our mouths: at which good hour we would get Alfred to give us some of his magic music, which he does between growling and smoking; and so to bed'.[53] And in November 1839 Fitzgerald wrote:

> I have got Alfred Tennyson up with me here, and to-day I give a dinner to him and two or three others. It is just ordered: soles, two boiled fowls, and an Apple Tart – cheese, etc. After this plenty of smoking [. . .] I could not finish my letter on Saturday, and here I sit down to it again – still more smoke dried and two-o'clock-in-the-morning-fuddled than before. I want A.T. to publish another volume: as all his friends do: especially Moxon, who has been calling on him for the last two years for a new edition of his old volume: but he is too lazy and wayward to put his hand to the business. He has got fine things in a large Butcher's Account book that now lies in my room: but I don't know if any would take you much.[54]

It must have been during this year that Fitzgerald commissioned a portrait of Tennyson by Samuel Laurence (1812–84).* The portrait was first exhibited in 1840, and shows the young poet with flowing hair, magnificent eyes and a strong and somewhat imperious manner about him. It is the earliest portrait of Tennyson, and therefore of indispensable significance, as well as being a beautiful image in itself. After Tennyson's death, his widow and his son Hallam arranged to have the Laurence portrait retouched by Burne-Jones, with the result that it looks sweeter and more gentle than when it was first painted; the greater strength and resolution of the original can be seen in a contemporary engraving now held at the Tennyson Research Centre.[55]

Despite such outbursts of sociability with old friends, Tennyson was at this time fundamentally lonely; his walks were sometimes in the company of his brother Horatio, but were more often solitary. High

---

*Fitzgerald had become a friend of Laurence through James Spedding, who had briefly studied art in London after taking his degree at Cambridge.

Beech had in its grounds a pond large enough for skating when it froze in the winter. 'He would swoop around it on his Lincolnshire skates, his blue cloak billowing out behind him as he cut endless lonely figures. Often he walked up and down the house reciting poetry to himself, shaping it to copy down later in his red-curtained, bay-windowed study above the dining-room.'[56]

By 1840, the prevarication and procrastination had come to an end, and Tennyson decided not to marry Emily Sellwood. On 9 January he wrote her a letter which, like most of the other items in their early correspondence, survives as a fragment but is nevertheless clear in its import (the second-person 'thee' and 'thou' were still often used between intimates at that date in Lincolnshire):

> I send thee all the sweetest and tenderest wishes for thy happiness here and hereafter, and if my wishes could make thee happy thou shouldst leap all day long like a lamb new to the field and the world; but though my wishes have little power on thy constant wellbeing yet let me wish thee a happy new year from January to December: may thy sisters and thy Father and thy Father which is in Heaven love thee more and more until thou rest satisfied in their love. I am sometimes killed with sadness when I think of thee, but I always hope that thou keepest within thee a clear faith in good things, which shall come to thee in time or out of time – it makes little difference, so that the result be good. Bless thee therefore as thou wilt be blessed. I bless thee [who] am not worthy to bless thee, for I know thy worth.[57]

This, as Ann Thwaite has said, 'must have chilled her heart': 'Was Emily really now to rest satisfied only in the love of her sisters, her father and her Father in Heaven?'[58]

Tennyson and Emily had been effectively engaged to marry from 1837 onwards. His brother Charles writing many years later to the Tennysons' older son, Hallam, gave this explanation for the long uncertainty and delay that followed:

> His monetary position did not improve as he expected, and he got into low and desponding spirits as to his future prospects; and from a sense of honour, though sorely against the grain, came to think that under the circumstances it was unjust and unfair in him to hold your mother bound.[59]

This was not the only reason. Tennyson was moving steadily ahead with the 'elegies' and was at last bringing himself to publication of the poems which would appear in 1842 (in two volumes). His strongest instinct was to protect the writing of his poetry from distractions and constraints.

There was also opposition to the marriage from the Sellwood side. Emily and her family were strong orthodox Christians, and it was obvious to them that Tennyson was speculative and free-thinking in his attitude to religious questions. In addition, Charles, Alfred's brother, had by the late 1830s become so gripped by opium addiction that he had caused terrible grief to Louisa, whose health broke down under the strain (the couple were now living apart). There was also an interfering Sellwood aunt ('Aunt Betsy'), who probably prompted a reference from Tennyson to certain old 'crones in or about Horncastle' who were 'causelessly bitter against me and mine'.[60]

For Emily, probably the most distressing passage in any of the letters that she received from Tennyson was a long, contorted paragraph full of hesitancies and references to Christian faith, hinting at secret aspects of Tennyson himself which would prompt revulsion in her if she had full access to them. The tangle of feeling in this anguished letter is plain to see, but the sense remains painfully obscure. He was separating himself from her, he seemed to say, for her benefit and for his, and despite the fact that he loved her and felt that his happiness was dependent on her well-being:

> How should this dependence on thy state coexist with my flying from thee? ask not, believe that it does. 'tis true, I fly thee for my good, perhaps for thine, at any rate for thine if mine is thine. If thou knewest why I fly thee there is nothing thou wouldst more wish for than that I should fly thee.

What was it in Tennyson that might cause Emily to be repelled by him? Religious doubt, his unstable family, his own uncertain prospects? It is not clear. The letter continued:

> Sayest thou 'are we to meet no more?' I answer I know not the word nor will know it. I neither know it nor believe it. The immortality of man disdains and rejects it. The immortality of man to which the cycles and the eons are as hours and days.

He urged her to find comfort in her faith, while conceding that the same comfort was not available to him: 'Fine is it, that I should preach to thee, so much stronger and holier than I am. Thou knowest it is my vice of old, however much the "Physician heal thyself" may apply to me.'⁶¹

Shortly after this, Henry Sellwood imposed a ban on correspondence between them; perhaps he did so because of the distress caused to Emily by this kind of letter from the man she loved. His younger daughter Louisa had already suffered horribly from marriage to a Tennyson. Ann Thwaite has suggested that he may have heard Emily weeping in her room at night. 'It is easy to sympathise with the father's resolve to put an end to the arrival of such letters, though it seemed the letters were themselves putting an end to a good deal, including the thought of a shared fireside.'⁶²

'Love and Duty', which was to be published in 1842, is an intensely personal poem which is clearly about the break from Emily.⁶³ With most of his poetry Tennyson would be happy to linger, hoard, revise and polish, sometimes for many years, but with this poem it was probably important to him that Emily should see in print a permanent demonstration of the pain that he had felt in parting from her:

> Could Love part thus? was it not well to speak,
> To have spoken once? It could not but be well.
> The slow sweet hours that bring us all things good,
> The slow sad hours that bring us all things ill,
> And all good things from evil, brought the night
> In which we sat together and alone,
> And to the want, that hollowed all the heart,
> Gave utterance by the yearning of an eye,
> That burned upon its object through such tears
> As flow but once a life.
>   The trance gave way
> To those caresses, when a hundred times
> In that last kiss, which never was the last,
> Farewell, like endless welcome, lived and died.
> Then followed counsel, comfort, and the words
> That make a man feel strong in speaking truth;
> Till now the dark was worn, and overhead
> The lights of sunset and of sunrise mixed
> In that brief night; the summer night, that paused
> Among her stars to hear us; stars that hung
> Love-charmed to listen: all the wheels of Time
> Spun round in station, but the end had come.
>
> O then like those, who clench their nerves to rush
> Upon their dissolution, we two rose,

> There – closing like an individual life –
> In one blind cry of passion and of pain,
> Like bitter accusation even to death,
> Caught up the whole of love and uttered it,
> And bade adieu for ever.[64]

In truth, Tennyson was not unhappy in his continuing bachelor state. He had plenty of opportunities to divert himself. Hallam Tennyson recalled in the *Memoir* how vividly his father relished London:

From time to time he stayed in town and mingled with all sorts and conditions of men. He always delighted in the 'central roar' of London. Whenever he and I went to London, one of the first things we did was to walk to the Strand and Fleet Street. 'Instead of the stuccoed houses in the West End, this is the place where I should like to live,' he would say. He was also fond of looking at London from the bridges over the Thames, and of going into St Paul's and into the Abbey. One day in 1842 Fitzgerald records a visit to St Paul's with him when he said, 'Merely as an inclosed space in a huge city this is very fine,' and when they got out into the open, in the midst of the 'central roar,' 'This is the mind; that is a mood of it.'

He writes, 'My lodgings are the last house, Norfolk Street, Strand, at the bottom of the street on the left; the name is Edwards which you will see projecting from the door on a brass plate.' Generally he would stay at the Temple or in Lincoln's Inn Fields; dining with his friends at The Cock, and other taverns. A perfect dinner was a beef-steak, a potato, a cut of cheese, a pint of port, and afterwards a pipe (never a cigar). When joked with by his friends about his liking for cold salt beef and new potatoes, he would answer humorously, 'All fine-natured men know what is good to eat.'[65]

Friendship with Thomas Carlyle was part of this London life in the 1840s. Carlyle, according to Edward Fitzgerald, was 'naturally prejudiced against one whom everyone was praising, and praising for a sort of poetry which he despised. But directly he saw and heard the Man, he knew there was a man to deal with and took pains to cultivate him; assiduous in exhorting him to leave Verse and Rhyme, and to apply his genius to Prose and Work.' Fitzgerald quoted Carlyle as saying that Tennyson was 'a life-guardsman spoilt by making poetry'.[66]

*   *   *

Meanwhile, another Emily, Tennyson's sister, who had long given the impression of being Arthur Hallam's grieving widow, had surprised her family with a decision about her own future. She embarked on a new life by becoming engaged to Richard Jesse, a lieutenant in the navy.

It may well have been while Emily was a guest of the Hallams in 1834 that she met Jesse at a dinner party. Arthur Hallam's cousin Jane Elton felt that it was a disappointing match and that the contrast between the brilliant Hallam and the run-of-the-mill Richard Jesse was very sharp: Emily Tennyson, she wrote, 'is actually going to be married – and to whom after such a man as Arthur Hallam [. . .] to a boy in the Navy, *supposed* to be a Midshipman'.

Since Hallam's death, Emily had received an income from Arthur's father Henry Hallam, made to her partly out of the contrition he felt over his obstructive treatment of the young lovers while his son was still alive. She had remained close to the Hallam family, was often a guest in their house, and in particular kept up a lively and very affectionate correspondence with Ellen, Arthur's sister. Jane Elton's view was that the allowance from Henry Hallam brought with it the implicit agreement that Emily would never marry: 'I feel so distressed about this, really it quite *hurts* me, I had such a romantic adoration for her, looked at her with such pity, and now all my feeling about her is bouleversé – and Alfred Tennyson falls headlong into the abyss with her – but I cannot think he would like her to marry.'[67]

This woefully unfair view of the matter was not shared by Henry Hallam himself: he generously agreed to continue his allowance of £300 a year to Emily. Tennyson had assumed, as a stanza of *In Memoriam* shows,* that his grieving sister was in effect Hallam's widow, and that she would never marry; but in the event he wholeheartedly supported her. Richard Jesse was not Arthur Hallam; still, Tennyson gave the bride away at the ceremony in 1842, and his other sisters were also there to wish her well and to see her at last married to a man she loved. Richard Jesse was a straightforward brother-in-law, brave and good-looking, with an excellent reputation in the navy, and he and Alfred remained close.

In 1842, Moxon at last published Tennyson's *Poems*, in two volumes, his first book-length publication of poetry since the *Poems* of 1832. The

---

*Lyric VI of *In Memoriam* predicts that Emily Tennyson will live in 'perpetual maidenhood'. This was probably written at Christmas 1841. Within a month, Emily Tennyson and Richard Jesse were married.

first of the 1842 volumes was assembled by selection (and revision) from his earlier volumes of 1830 and 1832, while the second comprised new poems which he had been writing in the intervening period. Few of these works in the second volume were new in the sense of recent – he had been tinkering with some of them for ten years or more. It is sobering to note how young Tennyson was when he wrote works which have become permanent features of the literary canon: 'The Kraken', that astonishingly rich apocalyptic masterpiece, retained its mysterious force untouched by revisions, and 'Mariana' had few changes, all minor.

One of the oddest of Tennyson's poems, the dramatic monologue 'St Simeon Stylites', about a member of the early Christian Church who spent his life sitting on top of a pillar, had been written in 1833. It may have been inspired in part by the colourful Cambridge clergyman called Simeon (vicar of the church of the Holy Trinity), known for his Low Church evangelical Christianity, rhetorical flourishes and excessive enthusiasm. The Apostles enjoyed the joke. W. H. Thompson took the poem to be 'a wonderful disclosure' of 'self-complacence and self-sacrifice.' [68]

'St Simeon Stylites' was being circulated and discussed by the Apostles in November 1833. Was it a new poem at that date? Its theme and style fit very oddly with Tennyson's grief for his friend so recently dead, but then jocular letters to him from fellow Apostles also seem at odds with bereavement. Stephen Spring Rice and John Kemble both wrote to him in November about the annual Apostles' dinner, wishing that he could come from Somersby to join them. Spring Rice listed the expected company and added, 'If your health is proposed I shall oppose it on the ground of your having been an unworthy member of the Society!!', while Kemble wrote: 'There is little stirring here save that we all look with interest for news from you', and that 'St Simeon Stylites' was said by 'the mathematicians Spring Rice and Heath' to be 'not "the watcher on the pillar to the end," but to the *nth*'.[69] It could be that the poem had been written before Hallam's death but had been passed around the Cambridge friends, in Heath's copy perhaps, during this autumn term. Tennyson is on record as having enjoyed reading it aloud, stressing its macabre and preposterous features and tricking out the performance with groans at the appropriate places:

> In hungers and in thirsts, fevers and cold,
> In coughs, aches, stitches, ulcerous throes and cramps,
> A sign betwixt the meadow and the cloud,
> Patient on this tall pillar I have borne
> Rain, wind, frost, heat, hail, damp, and sleet, and snow.[70]

Fitzgerald remembered that Tennyson recited the poem with 'grotesque Grimness, especially at such passages as "Coughs, Aches, Stitches, etc."'.[71] The young Tennyson's skills enabled him to enter persuasively into the mind of an old man close to death and engaging with his own mortality:

> Now I am feeble grown; my end draws nigh;
> I hope my end draws nigh: half deaf I am,
> So that I scarce can hear the people hum
> About the column's base, and almost blind,
> And scarce can recognise the fields I know;
> And both my thighs are rotted with the dew;
> Yet cease I not to clamour and to cry,
> While my stiff spine can hold my weary head,
> Till all my limbs drop piecemeal from the stone,
> Have mercy, mercy: take away my sin.[72]

Part of the joke is that its author was himself, in Apostolic terms, figuratively dead. In the following year, 1834, R. J. Tennant wrote to him about another Apostles' dinner:

Last Saturday, we had an Apostolic dinner, when we had the honour among other things of drinking your health, as having *once been* one of us.[. . .] most of them stayed till past two: John Heath volunteered a song, Kemble got into a passion about nothing but quickly jumped out again, Blakesley was afraid the Proctors might come in, and Thompson poured huge quantities of salt upon Douglas Heath's head.[73]

'The Lady of Shalott' owes its fame in part to its remarkable technical skill, in part to the beautiful inventiveness of its content. The rhyme scheme, AAAABCCCB, required the mastery of a virtuoso to bring it off. When we read the poem, or better still hear it performed by a reader with a strong sense of its music, it seems effortless. The metre and the rhyme scheme work together to an effect which is incantatory and hypnotic; the narrative is a story of enchantment, and the performance itself an act of enchantment.

Tennyson departed freely from his Italian source; 'the web, mirror, island etc., were my own'.[74] The web was a favoured metaphor for the act of writing; the isolation of an island conferred freedom from responsibility but brought with it the penalty of exile from the normal consolations of human society (as in 'The Lotos-Eaters'); the mirror both reverses and displays the delightful physical world from which the lady has been secluded by her enchantment. When Sir Lancelot appears, the lady hears him, as well as seeing him in her mirror; furthermore, she sees him in a doubled reflection. The sexual promise of a strong male voice chanting nonsensical words for the sheer pleasure of singing in the sun on a fine day, together with the physical splendour, assurance, audacity and beauty of this figure, brings to bear a pressure which is irresistible.

> All in the blue unclouded weather
> Thick-jewelled shone the saddle-leather,
> The helmet and the helmet-feather
> Burned like one burning flame together,
>   As he rode down to Camelot.
> As often through the purple night,
> Below the starry clusters bright,
> Some bearded meteor, trailing light,
>   Moves over still Shalott.
>
> His broad clear brow in sunlight glowed;
> On burnished hooves his war-horse trode;
> From underneath his helmet flowed
> His coal-black curls as he rode,
>   As he rode down to Camelot.
> From the bank and from the river
> He flashed into the crystal mirror,
> 'Tirra lirra,' by the river
>   Sang Sir Lancelot.[75]

Elaine Jordan's comment on this is apt and engaging: 'All this artistry in the real world appeals to the Lady who is already "half sick of shadows" at the sight of the young lovers; these shadows are the reflections of which she weaves an image. To match this doubling with her room Lancelot's image, catching the light of the sun, is reflected both directly and from the river. It's all too much.'[76] Too much, indeed. The Lady's excitement is expressed in the intensifying sequence of monosyllable verbs which leads to the poem's crisis, 'she left', 'she made', 'she saw', 'she looked'. To *look* – this conscious and deliberate act of disobedience – directly violates the terms of the spell under which she lives:

> She left the web, she left the loom,
> She made three paces through the room,

> She saw the water-lily bloom,
> She saw the helmet and the plume,
> She looked down to Camelot.
> Out flew the web and floated wide;
> The mirror cracked from side to side;
> 'The curse is come upon me', cried
> The Lady of Shalott.[77]

'The Lady of Shalott' was first published in 1832. For its re-publication in 1842, Tennyson pruned some of the conceits which impeded reading and made a key alteration to the final lines. The new ending closed the poem with Lancelot's words, not with the Lady's written epitaph.* This altered the whole weight of the story, which now became the drama of a doomed erotic awakening, a one-sided sexual infatuation going nowhere. In the new ending Lancelot betrays some slight compassion, perhaps, but it is of a decidedly detached kind (given that this is a woman who has died of love for him):

> He said, 'She has a lovely face;
> God in his mercy lend her grace,
> The Lady of Shalott.'[78]

Tennyson's young life had been one of enclosure within Somersby, followed by liberation into the sunlit world of friendship and adulation at Cambridge, and then back into the sequestration of Somersby after his father's death. His hypnotic early poems reflected this pattern: to engage with the world outside the enclosed space was a potentially fatal risk. 'The Kraken'† is a violent symbolic poem epitomising the problem in its central metaphor. Like Yeats's 'The Second Coming' or Shelley's 'Ozymandias', it is a visionary poem of overwhelming force

---

*The first ending functioned well as a musical coda but added nothing to the narrative: 'The web was woven curiously / The charm is broken utterly, / Draw near and fear not – this is I, / the Lady of Shalott.' [Tennyson's italics, 1832]

†Tennyson knew of a sea-monster called the Kraken from the work of Erik Pontoppidan, an eighteenth-century Norwegian bishop; Pontoppidan's account was summarised in an article in the English Encyclopedia (1802), of which the Tennysons had a copy at Somersby. Tennyson had also recently read Falkland, by Bulwer Lytton (published in 1827), which contains a striking account of a dream. The dreamer is 'a thousand fathoms beneath the sea', where he sees 'coral banks, which it requires a thousand ages to form, rise slowly' and 'the sea-serpent, the huge chimera of the north, made its resting place by his side, glaring upon him with a livid and death-like eye, wan, yet burning as an expiring sun'. (Quoted in Ricks, Poems, I, p. 269n.)

and impact, the strongest poem of this kind that Tennyson would ever write. The tight verse form, a kind of adapted sonnet of fifteen lines, gives it a formidable concentrated power:

> Below the thunders of the upper deep;
> Far, far beneath in the abysmal sea,
> His ancient, dreamless, uninvaded sleep
> The Kraken sleepeth: faintest sunlights flee
> About his shadowy sides: above him swell
> Huge sponges of millennial growth and height;
> And far away into the sickly light,
> From many a wondrous grot and secret cell
> Unnumbered and enormous polypi
> Winnow with giant arms the slumbering green.
> There hath he lain for ages and will lie
> Battening upon huge seaworms in his sleep,
> Until the latter fire shall heat the deep;
> Then once by man and angels to be seen,
> In roaring he shall rise and on the surface die.[79]

The pleasure of drug use celebrated in 'The Lotos-Eaters' and the visionary violence of 'The Kraken' appealed to impressionable undergraduates like William Henry Brookfield, who wrote to Hallam on 15 January 1831 about the delights awaiting them in the new term:

> In a fortnight we will all up & crow once more in Trinity
>   Blow up the fire Gyp Haggis,
>   Bring brandywine for three;
>   Bard Alfred, Bird William, and Clerk Arthur
>   This night shall merry be.*

Brookfield had been experimenting with drugs – quite seriously, it seems – and reported their effect to Hallam:

> I took opium last night and I suppose the C. History [Henry Hallam's study *Constitutional History*] brought you to my dreams. Methought that I gazed as of you closely [into your] blue eye. Me-further-thought it changed into the calm sea: – there was a dark haired dreamy

---

*A 'gyp' was a college servant; the 'Bard' is Tennyson, the 'Bird' is William Brookfield himself (his nickname was Owl) and Arthur Hallam is the 'Clerk' or scholar of the triad.

looking lady in white, sailing about delicately steering a huge college
cap – then came Alfred & became a great Kraken – the female sailed
by him in safety, which made me think it was somebody he had a
respect for – then the sea became your eye again & the lady a mote
which your Father bid you pluck out.[80]

'The Kraken' was a hot topic; it had made a considerable stir among
the Apostles. Brookfield also touches here on Tennyson's sexual allure
('the female sailed by him in safety'). Alfred was famous for his good
looks; Brookfield may have had reason to think that he had been
having some success with the young women of the town.

The Kraken's fate is the universal fate of any living thing that seeks
to fulfil its own needs, it seems. The stories of Mariana and the Lady
of Shalott are instances of that fate. Mariana's lover will never arrive:
she has no escape from enclosure in a 'moated Grange' which stood
in what was clearly Lincolnshire, rather than the notional Vienna of
Measure for Measure that had given Tennyson his source. The moated
grange's neglected garden is intensely reminiscent of Lincolnshire on
a damp late summer afternoon:

> With blackest moss the flower-pots
>   Were thickly crusted, one and all:
> The rusted nails fell from the knots
>   That held the pear to the gable-wall.
> The broken sheds looked sad and strange:
>   Unlifted was the clinking latch;
>   Weeded and worn the ancient thatch
> Upon the lonely moated grange.

In the lines ending 'strange' 'latch' 'thatch' 'grange' the ABBA stanza
form appears briefly. The music of this rhyme scheme beautifully
expresses stagnation, helplessness and entrapment. Those same moods
would be conveyed by the ABBA scheme in parts of the great elegy
for Hallam (though these lines were written well before Hallam's death
and pre-date the first drafts of *In Memoriam*). Psychological disturbance
and sexual frustration build to the internalised nightmare of stanza
six of 'Mariana', where:

> The blue fly sung in the pane; the mouse
>   Behind the mouldering wainscot shrieked,

> Or from the crevice peered about.
> Old faces glimmered through the doors
> Old footsteps trod the upper floors,
> Old voices called her from without.[81]

There can be no release for Mariana other than the death for which she longs in the poem's refrain. And in 'The Lady of Shalott', the Lady will destroy herself because she cannot escape the lure of Lancelot, whose masculinity is fabulously itemised: his broad clear brow, his coal-black curls, his 'helmet and the helmet-feather' which 'burned like one burning flame together'.[82] With their colours, their high nominal content and their careful particularity, these stanzas operate dramatically as well as descriptively, forcing the reader to participate in the Lady's fatal need to look at Lancelot's physical beauty.

Tennyson also revised his young man's vision in 'The Lotos-Eaters'. The irresponsibility enjoyed by Ulysses' companions in the first, luxuriant version of this poem was replaced by a rather more sober state of mind, appropriate to an older man but losing the playfulness and freshness of the original undergraduate vision. In the 1832 version, the poem closed with the men's minds dissolving into a musical and rhythmical sensual paradise:

> Men of Ithaca, this is meeter,
> In the hollow rosy vale to tarry,
> Like a dreamy Lotos-eater, a delirious Lotos-eater!
> [. . .]
> Surely, surely slumber is more sweet than toil, the shore
> Than labour in the ocean, and rowing with the oar.
> Oh! islanders of Ithaca, we will return no more.

In 1842 the men have an Olympian, or God-like, perspective (surprisingly, Tennyson capitalised 'God' here, though these are clearly classical rather than Christian gods). They can see the human condition that they have left behind and they make a judgement, namely that it is better to leave it. In place of sensual drowning they have a conceptualising Olympian calm. A certain amount was gained by this mature decision-making, but much was lost. Tennyson had forced his imagination to grow up prematurely.[83]

'The Palace of Art' was among the most undergraduate of Tennyson's early poems. He claimed that he was provoked to write it by his friend and fellow Apostle Richard Chenevix Trench, who had said: 'Tennyson, we cannot live in Art.'[84] Richard Cronin has made an attractive case for reinstatement of the 1832 version of the poem as against its 1842 revised state. He argues that 1832 brought out the experience of being a Trinity College undergraduate, free, pleasure-loving, often chaotic, brilliant and self-regarding, but forced at the end of the period of study – three or four years – to go out into the fallen world. The Palace then is itself the college, and it remains standing when the Soul leaves it, and the Soul hopes that some day it may visit it again.

Tennyson's fellow undergraduates loved this poem: 'Merivale reports that the poem was "read successively to each man as he came up from the vacation", and the pitch of the man's enthusiasm was reckoned to mark the degree of his good taste. "Only think of an 'Apostolic' dinner next Friday," wrote James Spedding. "Only think of the 'Palace of Art'".' In this student view the poem is about play and pleasure:

> In both versions [1832 and 1842] the Soul is invited to 'make merry and carouse', but in 1842 she does not take the invitation up, or perhaps it is the case that only intellectual or aesthetic feasting come within her purview. In 1832 her tastes had not been so monotonously elevated. Then, she delighted in sucking luscious nectars with the dainty greed of a humming-bird, and she gorged on fruit and wine, 'ambrosial pulps and juices.' It is birthday party food, food through which the teeth can sink without the need for tedious chewing, a child's midnight feast glimpsed through a literary haze, and it is hard to strike a moral pose in the face of such innocent, Keatsian greed.[85]

As many undergraduates do, Tennyson at times had mixed feelings about his university. Byronic scorn, not inappropriate in a Trinity man, animated this sonnet, 'Lines on Cambridge of 1830':

> Your doctors, and your proctors, and your deans,
> Shall not avail you, when the Day-beam sports
> New-risen o'er awakend Albion. No!
> Nor yet your solemn organ-pipes that blow
> Melodious thunder through your vacant courts
> At noon and eve, because your manner sorts
> Not with this age wherefrom ye stand apart,
> Because the lips of little children preach
> Against you, you that do profess to teach
> And teach us nothing, feeding not the heart.

Tennyson kept this out of sight for forty years: it was printed in *Tennysoniana* in the 1870s.[86] Many Cambridge graduates will be familiar with that black perspective from which the stony grandeur of the institution looks hopelessly out of touch with the needs and moods of its young transitory residents. There is radical energy in the sonnet as well as criticism, as Richard Cronin points out, of the religious tests still operating in the university. Only those who had taken an oath affirming their membership of the Church of England were permitted to graduate; this directly affected some of Tennyson's friends, such as William Bodham Donne, who would not take the oath, and F. D. Maurice and John Sterling, both of whom took it very reluctantly.

The balance of Tennyson's sympathies, though, was with his college, not against it: at the end of 'The Palace of Art', the Soul has to leave the Palace and live in a cottage. But she decrees: 'pull not down my palace towers, that are / So lightly, beautifully built'; and she leaves open the possibility that she will return, as the Apostles after their undergraduate years would enjoy returning to Trinity for their Apostolic dinners.[87] As Richard Cronin has said:

> If we accept Tennyson's palace as an idealised Cambridge, it becomes less surprising that the Soul does not want the building pulled down, that she even contemplates the possibility that she will 'return', and it gives much sharper point to her wish that she might 'return with others'. *The Palace of Art* was written soon after the foundation of the University of London, the first direct challenge to the Church of England monopoly over higher education. The new university was welcomed by Maurice and Sterling, who launched a campaign in the *Athenaeum* for a wholesale reform of Cambridge, including the abolition of the religious test.[88]

The 1842 volumes reminded the English reading public that here was a major poet, still young and still active, who had been silent for a number of years and who now, with this substantial publication, was securing a place for himself as the foremost poet of the day. The two volumes were helpfully reviewed by men of Tennyson's own age, including close friends among the Apostles: Richard Monckton Milnes in the *Westminster Review* and James Spedding in the *Edinburgh Review*. Spedding had in effect replaced Hallam in Tennyson's life as a close, sympathetic and constructive reader of work in progress. His important review (April 1843) made explicit the judgement that was already implicit in the general reception of the volumes, namely that 'the decade during which Mr Tennyson has remained silent has wrought a great improvement'.[89]

The other reviews were mixed, as they were always to be for Tennyson, but that conservative publication the *Quarterly Review* (where the 1832 *Poems* had been ferociously attacked by Croker) now carried a long review by John Sterling. Sterling's review was favourable, though he voiced important reservations about the 'Morte d'Arthur', which may have contributed to the many delays in the development of Tennyson's huge Arthurian enterprise, *Idylls of the King*. Tennyson was notoriously thin-skinned about criticism, and this added to his reluctance to publish and explains the very long gestations of certain poems.

While his work prospered and his public identity quietly became more secure, Tennyson's private circumstances continued in flux. High Beech was expensive and thought to be bad for his mother's health, with the consequence that he again found himself responsible for enabling the whole family to move house. The move this time was to Tunbridge Wells, which he immediately disliked. In February 1840 he wrote an exasperated letter to Emily Sellwood about the emotional drain that it had been:

> So much to do and so much to feel in parting from the house. Such a scene of sobbing and weeping was there on Monday morning among the servants at Beech Hill, and cottagers' daughters, as that cockney residence has seldom witnessed. [. . .] Finding we had human hearts, though we lived in a big house, they thought it all the harder that they were to lose us so soon.[90]

It would never suit him to stay for prolonged periods with his mother and siblings, and in mid February he was in London invading Edward Fitzgerald's rooms in Charlotte Street. Fitzgerald was generous and kind to him – as was his invariable habit – and reported to his friend Bernard Barton that Tennyson was in a very low state, full of lamentation and self-pity. Fitzgerald was acute about the things that were wrong with him:

> When I got to my lodgings, I found A. Tennyson installed in them: he has been here ever since in a very uneasy state: being really ill, in a nervous way: what with an hereditary tendency to nerve, and having spoiled what strength he had by incessant smoking, etc. I have also made him very out of sorts by desiring a truce from complaints and complainings. Poor fellow: he is quite magnanimous,

and noble natured, with no meanness or vanity or affectation of any kind whatsoever – but very perverse, according to the nature of his illness. So much for Poets, who, one must allow, are many of them a somewhat tetchy race.[91]

In the late spring Tennyson was in Lincolnshire, visiting Horncastle, where he had a cool reception from some of Emily's relations, and by May he was again in his favourite part of the Lincolnshire coast, Mablethorpe, from where he wrote Emily an odd, very self-conscious account of his own sense of the passage of time: 'I am not so able as in old days to commune *alone* with Nature.'[92] On the way south he caught sight of Fitzgerald just outside Leamington: 'I stopt the coach and he got up and we drove to the George here [in Warwick], and had an evening together.' They visited Warwick Castle and 'tumbled about the ruins' of Kenilworth. They then made the necessary pilgrimage to Stratford-upon-Avon in order to visit Shakespeare's monument (the bust in the parish church), and then his birthplace where Tennyson behaved like the kind of tourist he would later learn passionately to despise: 'We went also into the room where they say he was born. Every part of it is scribbled over with names. I was seized with a sort of enthusiasm and wrote mine, though I was a little ashamed of it afterwards.'[93]

This letter is among the last that Tennyson would write to Emily before the cluster of circumstances – his decision, and that of Emily's father – that would bring the correspondence to a close for ten years. The early letters to Emily were mostly destroyed after his death by their son Hallam (on his mother's orders), but among the survivals is a remarkable phrase. Tennyson wrote to Emily in 1839 from Aberystwyth, one of his destinations on his first visit to Wales, a country which he described in these terms: 'I cannot say I have seen much worth the trouble of the journey, always excepting the Welsh-women's hats which look very comical to an English eye, being in truth men's hats, beavers, with the brim a little broad, and tied under the chin with a black ribband. Some faces look very pretty in them. It is remarkable how fluently the little boys and girls can speak Welsh.' After reflecting thus on the oddity of children speaking their native language in their native land, he disparaged the Welsh coast by comparison with that of Lincolnshire: 'O for a good Mablethorpe breaker!' On a separate piece of paper which is probably part of the same letter, he wrote: 'I require quiet, and myself to myself, more than any man when I write.'[94] *I require quiet, and myself to myself*: there is a steely determination (and self-confidence) in the verb here. Was he making it clear how important it was that the girl on whom he had set his heart should understand that he would always put his own writing first? Tennyson was still a man who above all needed solitude, 'myself to myself'.

The Tennysons as a family – and Alfred Tennyson especially – could not settle in Tunbridge Wells, and in July 1841 they moved house again, to Boxley Hall, near Park House, the Lushingtons' family house near Maidstone. The close proximity of the Lushingtons was an attractive prospect; two of the Lushingtons, Edmund and Henry, had been Apostles and close fellow spirits of Alfred Tennyson. Much light is thrown on the years at Park House by the diary of George Stovin Venables, another Apostle and a very close friend of Henry Lushington, for whom he cherished deep feelings which were not reciprocated.

Edmund and Henry were both close to Tennyson in age; Edmund was born in 1811, Henry in 1812. Their youngest brother Franklin Lushington also became a close and trusted friend in later years. Edmund was a seriously scholarly classicist who had been a Fellow of Trinity in the early 1830s. After a few years of teaching at the college, he had been appointed Professor of Greek at the University of Glasgow, which meant that from 1838 onwards he spent half of each year in Scotland. When his father died in March 1839, Edmund inherited Park House and the other Lushington properties, though 'not until thirty-six years later would the new master of Park House reside there the year round'.[95]

Henry had chambers in London which he shared with Venables, and these rooms also became a favourite haunt. Venables' journal recalls many visits from Tennyson, some of which he clearly found unwelcome. Together the young friends 'read over more of the poems, principally the Hallam series, which are exquisitely true & touching, though perhaps few men, at least middleaged men will be able to feel their peculiar truth'. His comment on the elegies for Hallam is striking: the kind of love Tennyson wrote about in them would be recognised by young men but would be opaque or puzzling to anyone older. Many contemporary male readers of the elegies may have felt that their emotional force was essentially adolescent, but few said so as clearly as Venables.[96]

In Memoriam certainly expressed love for another man; this was legitimised for Tennyson by the fact that he wrote it partly according to his literary models, especially Shakespeare's sonnets, and partly according to the customary discourse of the young men at Trinity in the 1820s, who addressed each other with intimate affection and often spoke of their love for each other, as the Kemble letters show. Tennyson obviously had a very strong attachment to Hallam, but it was never recognised by either of them as sexual; the complete innocence with which *In Memoriam* celebrates his feeling for his friend makes that certain. He saw the friendship as heroic and ennobling.

Hallam was more aware of the alternative possibility. Any upper-class young man of the period who had been to a public school would know what homosexual behaviour was, and Hallam quite enjoyed the fact that Gladstone and Monckton Milnes were both attracted to him. Tennyson's schooling had ended when he was eleven. The all-male society of Cambridge was completely new to him, and was an emotional release as well as an emotional hothouse. The intensity with which he formed the friendship with Hallam is not at all surprising. He and Hallam certainly found in each other satisfaction, pleasure, comfort, delighted companionship and unfailing mutual support. Tennyson's word 'love' does as well as anything else to express what the relationship was.

As for his relationships with women, there is an obvious problem, which is that, after his death, his widow and his son destroyed masses of his early papers. Anything that might have hinted at sexual experience before his marriage has vanished. More is known about the previous generations; as an undergraduate in 1775, Tennyson's great-uncle Samuel Turner had a lively correspondence with a Cambridge contemporary about where best to buy 'cundums' and where to find the easy houses in London.[97] The excesses of the Regency were a very recent memory when Tennyson was at Trinity, and the moral climate of fashionable society was worldly and relaxed. It is unlikely that his contemporaries at Cambridge would have denied themselves the sexual opportunities afforded by their wealth and status. Did Tennyson behave in the same way? There is absolutely no evidence. He had a strong sense of entitlement and did not deny himself other pleasures, such as drink and tobacco, so maybe he experimented sexually in the same way as many of them did. It is likely. Again, did he have sexual relations with women during his nomadic years after 1837? Probably, although they would have been infrequent: during those years he was often drained by drink and depression.

On 12 June 1841, Venables and Henry went down together to Park House, where Tennyson was already staying as a guest of the Lushingtons. Tennyson read his own poetry to the gathering in the evenings. Venables noted in his diary that some of the poems were 'admirable', and added, sourly, 'Not that these things are by any means unmixed pleasure.' He wanted more unshared time with Henry and the other Lushingtons, and resented the fact that even his thirty-first birthday, 1 June, was given over to Tennyson's poetry reading. Venables' diaries became increasingly caustic. Tennyson was constantly present in the company of the Lushingtons and of James Spedding.[98]

On 7 November Venables wrote: 'called on Alfred Tennyson [probably in Spedding's chambers], & sat with him a long time, talking mostly about Lushington matters, a kind of conversation of which one cannot tire'. On 8 April 1842, Venables 'called on Alfred Tennyson at Spedding's rooms, & found proof sheets lying about. Read several things, most of Morte d'Arthur, Locksley Hall, Talking Oak , &c He thinks they do not look so well in print.' Venables became tired of supporting Tennyson: on 15 April he 'looked over the new version of the Miller's Daughter, the Lady of Shalott, Mariana, & one or two others which are on the whole improved. I do little good by this looking at his things, & it is burdensome for fear of being a burden.'[99]

The poems were published by Moxon and the speed of his operation is astonishing: Tennyson was still going through his proofs with Venables on 5 May; the two volumes were published on the 14th.

On 6 July 1842, Edmund Lushington opened the grounds of his house for the annual festival of the Maidstone Mechanics' Institution, a philanthropic organisation designed by followers of Robert Owen and other socialist thinkers of the period for the education (and 'moral improvement') of the working class. It was quite an event, as reported in the *Maidstone and Kentish Advertiser*. There were two bands, one for quadrille and one for country dancing; there were games including cricket and trap bat, a steam engine turning a circular saw with great rapidity and a steam boat plying round a lighthouse, and an exhibition of philosophical instruments such as telescopes, microscopes and the like. A 'capacious booth erected for the occasion' seated 800 persons for tea, and afterwards 'a large fire balloon ascended'. Finally the entire assembly gathered in front of the house to make a vote of thanks to Edmund for his hospitality.[100] This philanthropic and socially responsible event in a country house setting gave Tennyson his frame for *The Princess,* his extraordinary narrative poem of the late 1840s in which he explores women's rights and education, and the possibility of establishing a university for women.

In parallel with all this literary activity a personal drama was unfolding. Shy, charming, introverted Edmund Lushington was increasingly in love with the beautiful Cecilia Tennyson, the youngest of Alfred's sisters. The strong familial sense of the Apostolic community of young men had clearly helped the relationship along. By 9 May 1842 Edmund and Cecilia were engaged to be married, and the marriage itself took place in Boxley church on 14 October. Cecilia was twenty-five, Edmund was thirty-three.

Alfred Tennyson's involvement with Matthew Allen was already well advanced. Allen had come up with a scheme for a 'patented process of carving wood' (manufacturing decorative furniture) 'by machinery'. He coined the word 'Pyroglyph' for this mechanical wood-carving venture, and urged the Tennyson family to invest. To outsiders it was clear that the venture was unreliable from the beginning. But Tennyson invested the whole of his inheritance – and his hopes – in the scheme, and persuaded his mother and his sisters to invest as well. His oldest brother Frederick, who had a more substantial legacy than his siblings, kept his distance. On 6 November 1841, Allen wrote Frederick a letter which is full of what are obviously bare-faced and desperate lies:

> [. . .] Another [party] who is intimately acquainted with all my private affairs has generously come forward to assist me without any reward, so that I shall get through without making any sacrifice of a further share or even that of selling a share in this establishment, or even my coal mine, all of which you know I contemplated, so that if you do not choose, or you choose to allow your uncles to prevent you from having this share, *tell me so at once.* The concern will soon realize enough of money and credit for all I shall want. Yesterday it was the decided opinion of my Bankers and Solicitors that in twelve months your share would be worth Ten thousand Pounds, and that in five years it ought to give you that yearly, and really I feel that if you cannot put an end to this painful state of things *I must.*[101]

The consequences of his friendship with Dr Matthew Allen would hit Tennyson very hard indeed. Allen was complex, intelligent and charming as well as being fundamentally dishonest. He formed a genuine personal attachment to Tennyson, warming to the poet's remarkable physical presence and his burgeoning reputation. However, he also saw Tennyson's inheritance from his grandfather, together with all the other legacies that the Somersby Tennysons had received, as potentially very useful to his scheme. Tennyson in turn saw a possible source of greatly enhanced wealth which would secure his social position and enable him not only to marry Emily but also to live as a gentleman, in an appropriate and fitting style. Why should he not aspire to these things? His two older brothers had enough capital to live on, his cousins were independently wealthy, even his sisters were reasonably provided for so long as they stayed with their mother until they were able to find suitable husbands (three out of the four of them did).

When we examine the approach to money displayed by Alfred Tennyson and his siblings, we are back in a world where late-eighteenth-century attitudes were still current. In this view, a well-born young man's range of options was narrow: he could be a politician, a civil servant (appointments to which, until the Northcote-Trevelyan reforms of the 1850s, were through personal connections and private patronage), a clergyman (where the better livings were again found through patronage), a lawyer, a professor, or an officer in the services. Outside that economic group he was likely to be a socially inadmissible adventurer, like the outrageous Wickham in *Pride and Prejudice*. Alfred Tennyson declined the chance of any kind of profession other than that of poet. Dr Allen's scheme therefore looked like an excellent prospect. Allen's letters to him seemed genuinely affectionate, sensitive and caring: 'I have been very sad since we parted, and I can hardly tell why, unless it were because you were so out of spirits. I hope by this time that your family circle has taken them all away and that you are now as happy as I can wish you to be.'[102]

Tennyson's restlessness took him in February 1841 to Mablethorpe, from where he wrote to Fitzgerald urging him to have faith in the wood-carving scheme. But Fitzgerald, who was wealthy and understood investments, could recognise the behaviour of a rogue and opportunist. 'Curse not anything till you see what it brings forth – not even pyroglyphs,' Tennyson wrote. Tennyson was isolated at Mablethorpe – from choice – but loneliness was making him susceptible to Allen's blandishments. 'I am in great haste waiting for the muffinman, my only communication with the world, who comes once a week, bringing the produce of his art, and also what letters may be stagnating in the Alford post – waits five minutes and then returns.'[103] His letters to Allen himself (and to Allen's wife) are jokey, intimate and show no sense of boundaries: he was making himself vulnerable. Allen's communications to him were all lies, and Tennyson innocently passed them on to his father's old friend T. H. Rawnsley, who as one of his father's executors was obviously concerned about what the young

Tennysons were getting into. The wood scheme was going on 'very well' and 'there are as many orders as can be executed', he wrote vaguely (but in his own view reassuringly) to Rawnsley. He encouraged his sisters to write to their uncle and trustee Charles (Tennyson d'Eyncourt, as he was now called) to reproach him for preventing them from investing the whole of their capital in Allen's scheme. Part of their astonishing letter of 14 November 1841 reads: 'Surely if you wish to prove yourself what you profess to be, *a kind Uncle*, there can now be no further obstacle'. Not surprisingly, Charles Tennyson d'Eyncourt wrote to their mother to say: 'I retain every proper and kind feeling toward my nieces consistent with what is due to myself, but I cannot permit any one to write offensive Letters to me.'[104]

By early in 1842, it had become obvious to Tennyson that he had lost his capital. A lawyer whom he consulted in July (rather late in the day) wrote to him to confirm all his fears: 'I perfectly agree with you as to the view you take of the position your Mother and Sisters are placed in with regard to the wood carving concern.' He declared himself 'disgusted with the affair', which was a fraudulent tangle of arrangements designed to lock the Tennysons' money into the business.[105] Tennyson then wrote a passionate and distraught letter to Allen, but appears not to have sent it: the MS in the Tennyson Research Centre is an incomplete fair copy. The handwriting is careful, and the text just stops: it is not signed, and there are one and a half blank sheets following the last word of text.

In the letter, Tennyson not only laid bare his suspicion of Allen but also expressed his deep personal hurt over Allen's treachery:

> you seem to me for a long time to have made yourself as strange to me as possible; and I cannot help feeling and feeling deeply that it was not so before I lent you all I had in the world. [. . .] I am very very unwilling to think any ill of a man whom I have regarded with affection & admiration for the valuable qualities of his head & his heart & what seemed to me his clear religious feeling. My faith in you has been strong – most strong.

With the loss of this faith, he now saw Allen as 'One of the herd, a mere commonplace man, ready, like all worldlings, after a thousand promises, at the first glimpse of prosperity, to kick down the ladder by which he mounted.' It is remarkable how the personal hurt and outrage seemed to outweigh the obvious and serious financial loss: 'Your unkindness will afflict & oppress me more than any apprehension of worldly risk or loss.'[106] He was in a wretched state of mind when he wrote in July 1842 to the loyal Fitzgerald: 'If you had known how much I have gone through since I saw you, you would pardon perhaps my ungracious silence in return for so many kind letters: if you had known – , but then I don't mean to tell you: you will very likely know soon enough.'

His misery over the money was reinforced by misery over his recently published poems: 'don't abuse my book: you can't hate it more than I do, but it does me no good to hear it abused; if it is bad, you and others are to blame who continually urged me to publish'.[107]

Mary Tennyson was now on dangerously friendly terms with Allen's wife; indeed, it is clear that Allen's strategy was to work the situation so that he and his wife built on warm personal friendship with the whole Tennyson family. Alfred wrote to Mrs Allen asking her to prevent her husband from borrowing money from Septimus. 'Dr Allen has already at different times received from our family about £8000':[108] a statement which would obviously be passed on to Allen himself and could have indicated to him that there might be more where that sum had come from.

The story of the pyroglyphs had a better outcome than Tennyson's headlong folly over the matter merited. He could not recover his money, but Edmund Lushington with great generosity took out an insurance policy on Allen's life for Tennyson's benefit. In January 1845, when Allen died of a heart attack, Fitzgerald contacted Tennyson, who replied: 'I *had* heard the news. No gladness crossed my heart but sorrow and pity: that's not theatrical but the truth.' Fitzgerald then wrote triumphantly to Frederick Tennyson:

> Dr Allen is dead! Did you know this? He died of disease in the heart. Let no man say henceforth that anything is made in vain. Alfred came up to London, smitten with some sorrow. But he took no steps concerning the matter, and I left him in London – smoking, as when first I saw him. The water business would do him good if he gave it fair chance – but he smokes, and drinks a bottle of wine a day. He looks however twice as well as he did a year ago; and is certainly in better spirits.[109]

The anguish in Tennyson's mind comprised a toxic mix: loss of social status, frustration over the slow sales of his work (despite the excellent service that he had throughout their relationship from his publisher Moxon), and the personal loss of a man he had come to trust and regard as a friend. Something of the pain of Allen's treachery is still felt in part of the otherwise unexciting narrative poem ('Sea Dreams: An Idyll') that he made out of the experience seventeen years after it was all over. Allen appears as the pious, affable figure whose treachery has become all too manifest. A husband describes to his wife how he has been defrauded by an erstwhile friend, who when they met by chance in the street:

> [. . .] began to bloat himself, and ooze
> All over with the fat affectionate smile
> That makes the widow lean. 'My dearest friend,
> Have faith, have faith! We live by faith,' said he;
> 'And all things work together for the good
> Of those' – it makes me sick to quote him – last
> Gript my hand hard, and with a God-bless-you went.
> I stood like one that had received a blow:
> I found a hard friend in his loose accounts,
> A loose one in the hard grip of his hand,
> A curse in his God-bless-you: then my eyes
> Pursued him down the street, and far away,
> Among the honest shoulders of the crowd,
> Read rascal in the motions of his back
> And scoundrel in the supple-sliding knee. [110]

CHAPTER 5

Growing reputation and
The Princess, 1845–1850

Tears, idle tears, I know not what they mean,
Tears from the depth of some divine despair
Rise in the heart, and gather to the eyes,
In looking on the happy Autumn-fields,
And thinking of the days that are no more.

Between 1839 and 1845, Tennyson was subject to several periods of debilitating depression as he cast about for a decent source of income. Obviously the disastrous investment in Matthew Allen's wood-carving scheme had been an expression of his desperation in these years.

By 1845 his fame was spreading and his circumstances were clearly improving. The reviews of the 1842 volumes had established him as a major literary figure, whether he himself was willing to believe this or not. Lushington's policy on Matthew Allen's life paid out £2,000 to Tennyson; in addition he had now earned £746/8/1 from sales of *Poems* (four editions). In the same year he began to receive a pension from Robert Peel's administration.[1] Thomas Carlyle had been instrumental here; he had kept in close touch with Tennyson during the whole miserable affair of being cheated by Allen, and in 1840 suggested to Fitzgerald that Tennyson ought to be a strong candidate for a Civil List pension. Henry Hallam, Arthur's father, committed himself to the cause and wrote to Robert Peel, strongly backing Tennyson's claim by praising him 'as the very first among the younger class of living poets'. Peel read some of Tennyson's poems, was duly impressed, and the offer of a pension of £200 a year followed in September 1845.[2]

Tennyson was squeamish about accepting patronage, and as a consequence he slightly delayed his reply to Peel's offer. On 29 September when he wrote to Peel accepting the pension he said simply, 'I was from home and my family not aware of my direction', but his clear reluctance to be seen as the object of charity can be inferred from a reassuring letter from Henry Hallam himself a few days later:

Your scruples about the pension need not molest you much [. . .].
Peel, as I told him, will be applauded on all sides for such a

distribution of patronage. It is not the habit of any one to find fault with the disposal of public money in regard of literary merit.

Hallam went on to tell Tennyson that he was 'a great favourite with the young ladies – however like Orpheus you may be in other respects you will never be torn to pieces with sharp female claws'.[3] Henry Hallam was seldom other than serious; this cumbersome joke is very much out of character. Tennyson was restless and uncomfortable in Cheltenham, where his mother had now decided to live – the society 'en masse' in the town was decidedly undistinguished, as he wrote to Aunt Russell in October – and his continuing 'scruples about the pension' were part of the restlessness.

The pension was the occasion of a spat which Tennyson would later regret. Edward Bulwer Lytton bitterly attacked the fourth edition of Tennyson's *Poems*, published in 1846, with a squib called 'The New Timon' printed in *Punch*:

> Let School-Miss Alfred vent her chaste delight
> On 'darling little rooms so warm and bright!'
> Chaunt, 'I'm aweary,' in infectious strain,
> And catch her 'blue fly singing i' the pane.'

Lytton added a note to the effect that Tennyson was 'in the prime of life, belonging to a wealthy family, without, I believe, wife or children', yet was now because of the Peel pension 'quartered on the public purse'. Tennyson's response, 'The New Timon and the Poets', also published in *Punch*, was itself personal, arrogant and offensive (Lytton was both a literary 'subaltern' and a superficial dandy who wore a corset):

> I *thought* we knew him: What, it's you,
> The padded man – that wears the stays –
>
> Who killed the girls and thrilled the boys,
> With dandy pathos when you wrote,
> A Lion, you, that made a noise,
> And shook a mane en papillotes.
>
> And once you tried the Muses too;
> You failed, Sir: therefore now you turn,
> You fall on those who are to you,
> As Captain is to Subaltern.[4]

Lytton had been a Trinity undergraduate a few years earlier than Tennyson. As a literary man and a political careerist he made a large number of enemies, but he also had good friends, including Dickens and Disraeli. As member of Parliament for Lincoln, he supported Alfred's cousin, Tennyson d'Eyncourt, in the House of Commons. Lytton was a prolific novelist: his long list of successful historical romances included *Harold, the last of the Saxons* (1848; this novel would have a bearing, years later, on Tennyson's own work). His first publication was a novel, *Falkland* (1827), which Tennyson had read as an undergraduate: interestingly it had provided hints for some of Tennyson's Cambridge poems, notably 'The Kraken', 'The Palace of Art', 'Mariana' and 'Mariana in the South'.[5]

Tennyson disliked Lytton's friendship with the d'Eyncourt cousins, and he already saw him as a literary enemy: he suspected (almost certainly rightly) that Lytton had been the author of an anonymous hostile review of his 1832 volume (in *The New Monthly*). This review had dismissed Tennyson's lyricism as borrowed and imitative, 'the worst conceits of the poets of the time of Charles II, and the most coxcombical euphuisms of the contemporaries of Elizabeth.'[6] The fires were already stoked, then, for an outbreak of bad temper.

The fact that Bulwer Lytton had talked hypocritically about Tennyson to the d'Eyncourt cousins added to Tennyson's fury. Lytton was staying with the d'Eyncourts at Bayons (and working on his historical romance, *Harold*, which he would dedicate to Charles d'Eyncourt) at the time that 'The New Timon' appeared. Tennyson wrote a brief reminiscence of this quarrel which his son Hallam published in the *Memoir*:

> I never wrote a line against anyone but Sir Edward Lytton Bulwer. His lines did not move me to do so. But at the very time he was writing or had written these he was visiting my cousins, the d'Eyncourts, and said to them, 'How much I should like to know your cousin Alfred.'

The canard about his circumstances had stung as much as Lytton's verses: 'he stated in a note that I belonged to a very rich family. The younger son, his friend, who had inherited was rich enough, but the elder branch was shut out in the cold, and at that time I had scarce anything'.[7]

Tennyson's squib had been sent to *Punch* by his friend John Forster, and he began regretting its appearance immediately. He followed it with a second contribution to *Punch*, a balanced little rhyme about literary quarrels in which he acknowledged that he would have done better to keep quiet: 'Surely, after all, / The noblest answer unto such / Is perfect stillness when they brawl.'[8] Still, his display of anger countered the charge that he was a 'school-miss' who was only interested in dimity interiors like his 'darling room'. It did his reputation no harm to show that he could defend himself robustly.

Had Tennyson and Bulwer Lytton managed to become friends instead of enemies, they might well have found that they had a good deal in common. They were both tall, impressive, very good-looking and attractive to women; they were both intensely proud and sensitive to adverse criticism; they both saw themselves as of high descent but unfairly disinherited; and they both made very substantial fortunes from the success of their writings.

Many years after the initial quarrel, Tennyson and Lytton came to respect each other. Lytton died in 1873, and in 1876 Tennyson managed a graceful gesture to his memory: he dedicated his historical drama, *Harold*, to Lytton's son (the second Lord Lytton, who was at that date Viceroy of India). In this dedication he acknowledged Bulwer Lytton's novel as one of his sources, and added: 'Your father dedicated his "Harold" to my father's brother; allow me to dedicate my "Harold" to yourself.'[9]

The Rawnsley family would always exert a very strong pull on Tennyson. The clergyman Thomas Rawnsley had been an important and very necessary stabilising force during his childhood. He had been the only person locally who could help Dr Tennyson to forget his grievances and enjoy a normal sociable life. Thomas Rawnsley's son, Drummond Rawnsley, another clergyman and stable family man, was Tennyson's closest Lincolnshire friend. In a long letter written in October 1845 to Thomas Rawnsley, Tennyson protested that 'however appearances are against me I *have* a love for old Lincolnshire faces and things which will stick by me as long as I live'.[10] He was restless in Cheltenham, and would have preferred to spend some of the winter months with his Lincolnshire circle rather than with Henry Hallam, to whom he had pledged himself. He knew that he could not in decency decline the hospitality of the man who had engineered his pension and was also Arthur Hallam's father, but he would have been more comfortable with the Rawnsleys.

He did not enjoy feeling beholden, and he was worried about the way some of Lincolnshire would take the news of his good fortune over the pension. 'I doubt not that I shall meet with all manner of livor [malignity], scandal, and heart-burning, small literary men whose letters perhaps I have never answered, bustling up and indignant that they are past by – they!'[11] He encouraged Rawnsley to visit Cheltenham, but in decidedly mixed terms (it was 'a handsome town' in 'one of the prettiest counties' but 'a Polka-parson-worshipping place').[12] Tennyson was careful not to disparage Lincolnshire by an implied comparison with the liveliness of Cheltenham. In reality, though, he was ambivalent about Lincolnshire. The Somersby Tennysons had suffered slights from Lincolnshire society, and there was a certain consolation now in being able to look on that society as provincial and restricted. Notwithstanding his Lincolnshire accent and his untidy appearance and 'coarseness', Tennyson was by this time a London poet and a national figure.

Tennyson visited Henry Hallam and his family in November. Hallam was markedly kind to him, and wrote afterwards praising his character, genius and fame, and reminding him of the 'sacred recollections' of his dead son.[13] But Tennyson was in a distressed and unstable state, and in January he was said by Elizabeth Barrett Browning to be 'seriously ill with an internal complaint and confined to bed' (the news came from the Lushingtons, and she had heard it from her brother who was a friend of George Stovin Venables). It was in this same letter that she famously expressed her astonishment over the proposed theme of what would become *The Princess*. 'Isn't the world too old and fond of steam, for blank verse poems, in ever so many books, to be written on the fairies?'[14]

All Tennyson's friends knew that 'The University for Women' (that is, *The Princess: A Medley*) was brewing. His writing had suffered severe setbacks while he struggled with his emotional problems and financial crises, but throughout these *The Princess* was never out of his mind. When it was published in 1847, he made it clear to its readers – from its subtitle – that it did not wish to take itself seriously. It was not attempting to be an epic. Nor was Clough's *Bothie* of 1848, which is in a sense a similar work, an undergraduate plaything. Clough's poem had a particularising title followed by a disavowing subtitle: *The Bothie of Toper-na-fuosich: A Long-Vacation Pastoral*. Clough had inadvertently used a dialect obscenity in the title (suggested to him by 'some very unscrupulous Gaelic wit').* This boyish mishap is part of the undergraduate feel of the poem, which is reinforced further by its dedication. 'My long vacation pupils will I hope allow me to inscribe this trifle to them, and will not, I trust, be displeased if in a fiction, purely fiction, they are here and there reminded of times we enjoyed

---

*Hence the change to the title by which it is now known, *The Bothie of Tober-na-Vuolich*.

together.'[15] As the 'long-vacation pastoral' firmly indicates, what these works have in common with Tennyson's 'The Epic' (which prefaced his 'Morte d'Arthur' of 1842) is that they are grounded in undergraduate experience.

In both *The Princess* and *The Bothie*, the narrative leads a young man from the world of friendship to fulfilment with the perfect woman. The Prince marries his Princess Ida, and Philip, the Oxford undergraduate, marries his Scottish peasant girl, Elspie. The Prince and Ida will live royal lives in a place and time which feel vaguely medieval (though the frame of the poem, with its references to modern science and engineering – and powered flight – gestures firmly towards the future) while the destination of the lovers in the Clough poem is, in nineteenth-century terms, modern but equally remote. They emigrate to New Zealand:*

There he hewed, and dug; subdued the earth and his spirit;
There he built him a home; there Elspie bare him his children,
David and Bella; perhaps ere this too an Elspie or Adam;
There hath he farmstead and land, and fields of corn and flax
    fields;
And the Antipodes too have a Bothie of Tober-na-Vuolich.[16]

The Princess belonged to the world of the Lushingtons. Henry Lushington heard Tennyson read some of the poem in April 1845, and commented in detail on what had been written so far. His brother Edmund, the most attentive of the family, remembered hearing parts of it read while Tennyson was visiting Park House in the years 1845, 1846 and 1847.[17] There was a summer house in the grounds where Tennyson could find privacy when he wanted it, and the family tradition has it that much of *The Princess* was written there in these three consecutive summers. The poem was first published late in 1847 without a dedication, but the second edition, published early in 1848, was dedicated to Henry Lushington as a kind of belated acknowledgement of the help that he had given.

The Princess was a comic and oblique treatment of a serious subject: much of it sounded like a joke, but it contained passages of major poetry which in effect compelled the audience to take the work seriously. Tennyson substantially reworked and revised, as though he himself was baffled by it: he knew that it was important but did not

---

*Many of the early European settlers in New Zealand were Scots, like Clough's Elspie, and the oldest European building in New Zealand dates from the 1830s.

quite know how to shape it. *The Princess* is a milestone in his quest for the significant long poem, a quest which he had pursued through previous long works in sharply contrasting verse forms (his schoolboy drama *The Devil and the Lady* as well as 'The Palace of Art'). The rights and education of women were serious topics on which he had been brooding for some years. He had brilliant sisters at home and he was aware of young women in Cambridge who could not enrol as undergraduates, but would perhaps like to play a role in the institution. A little *jeu d'esprit* called 'The Doctor's Daughter' dresses one of these irresistible girls as a 'Proctor', in other words a (mature, and male) university law enforcer. This was written in 1830 when he was twenty-one, and was a Cambridge joke:

> Sweet Kitty Sandilands,
>   The daughter of the doctor,
> We drest her in the Proctor's bands,
>   And past her for the Proctor.
>
> All the men ran from her
>   That would have hastened to her,
> All the men ran from her
>   That would have come to woo her.
>
> Up the street we took her
>   As far as to the Castle,
> Jauntily sat the Proctor's cap
>   And from it hung the tassel.[18]

Did this actually happen? It is unlikely, but it is fun to think of Alfred Tennyson, Arthur Hallam, Richard Monckton Milnes and other wags persuading a lively girl to impersonate one of the grumpy old terrors of the place. Several of the cartoons that Tennyson drew in his undergraduate notebooks show proctors rebuking the young men – the proctors are always fat, with squat, commonplace features, prodigious sideburns, tasselled caps and long gowns, and in one case an ominous and conspicuous genital bulge. Kitty Sandilands would have been hard pressed to manage all that, even with Monckton Milnes's help. But the geography is specific – she would have walked with her gang of male friends, giggling, all the way down Trinity Street, past St John's, past the medieval shops and public houses until she crossed the Cam at Magdalene Bridge and then up the hill to the old Castle Mound, at the top of which she would have been ceremoniously enthroned.

And the joke contained a serious point. Why was Kitty Sandilands barred from aspiring to the dignity of a proctor? Within the imaginative world of *The Princess*, Tennyson made such a thing possible.

Lilia, the strong-minded sister in the poem, could well be based on Louy, Edmund Lushington's vivacious and independent sister. Sir Walter Vivian, though, the bluff elderly family man and squire who hosted the feast for the Mechanics' Institute[19] in the poem, was the opposite of Edmund, who at that date was very young, not yet married, and much happier with one or two intelligent friends than with a large gathering. At Glasgow he was far too scholarly to be an inspiring teacher; his students liked him as a personality but got little out of his lectures.

The setting of *The Princess* is imagined as a female Cambridge, and therefore vaguely medieval, but the young women in it are not only modern but belong to the future. One of the Prince's young friends points this up:

> 'Pretty were the sight
> If our old halls could change their sex, and flaunt
> With prudes for proctors [though Kitty Sandilands was no
> prude], dowagers for deans,
> And sweet girl-graduates in their golden hair.'[20]

At an early stage of the poem's composition there was more preoccupation with the future than there is in the final published text. Harvard Notebook 22 has this intriguing section of futuristic romance (composed in the late 1830s):

> We crost into a land where mile-high towers
> Pufft out a night of smoke that drowsed the sun;
> Huge pistons rose and fell, and everywhere
> We heard the clank of chains, the creak of cranes,
> Ringing of blocks and throb of hammers mixt
> With water split and spilt on groaning wheels
> Until we reacht the court.[21]

This is a future for industrial Britain as imagined by the great engineer Isambard Kingdom Brunel, or perhaps William Armstrong, the formidable Tyneside weapons manufacturer, or even – at a level which is in all senses more fundamental – Sir John Bazalgette, the cloacal genius who created Victorian London's sewage system.

It is hard to get a 'handle' on *The Princess*. Its subtitle, a 'medley',

is one of those teasing words like 'idyll' which leaves one at a loss –
what kind of work of art are we looking at? After the elaborate and
ornate experiment – the beauty of all these young women playing at
men's roles in a building designed for men – the fierce old King, the
Prince's father, roughly articulates the traditional viewpoint with which
mature males feel comfortable. This is how the young Prince needs to
treat his Princess:

> Man for the field and woman for the hearth:
> Man for the sword and for the needle she:
> Man with the head and woman with the heart:
> Man to command and woman to obey;
> All else confusion. Look you! the gray mare
> Is ill to live with, when her whinny shrills
> From tile to scullery, and her small goodman
> Shrinks in his arm-chair while the fires of Hell
> Mix with his hearth: but you – she's yet a colt –
> Take, break her: strongly groomed and straitly curbed
> She might not rank with those detestable
> That let the bantling scald at home, and brawl
> Their rights or wrongs like potherbs in the street.
> They say she's comely; there's the fairer chance:
> *I* like her none the less for ranting at her!
> Besides, the woman wed is not as we,
> But suffers change of frame. A lusty brace
> Of twins may weed her of her folly. Boy,
> The bearing and the raising of a child
> Is woman's wisdom.[22]

At a literal level the poem's narrative seems to endorse this. At the
same time the distanced, comic, ornate manner of the whole invites
us to think that none of the opinions or attitudes expressed are to be
taken seriously. It is as though Tennyson built an elaborate defence
strategy designed to distance himself from whatever doubts or scruples
about his treatment of the theme may be lurking beneath the poem's
highly polished surface. The several 'weird seizures' from which the
Prince suffers – all introduced into the poem in 1851 – are a further
distancing device. None of this is real:

> [. . .] like a flash the weird affection came:
> King, camp and college turned to hollow shows;
> I seemed to move in old memorial tilts,

And doing battle with forgotten ghosts,
To dream myself the shadow of a dream. [23]

The notion that life is a dream is a Shakespearean one, embedded in
much of *A Midsummer Night's Dream*, *Hamlet* and *The Tempest*.

Dreamlike lyrical delight characterises the verses in *The Princess*
that are loved and quoted:

> Tears, idle tears, I know not what they mean,
> Tears from the depth of some divine despair
> Rise in the heart, and gather to the eyes,
> In looking on the happy Autumn-fields,
> And thinking of the days that are no more.

This song was written near Tintern Abbey, 'full for me of its bygone
memories', as Tennyson said of it. 'It is the sense of abiding in the
transient.' Tintern Abbey is not very far from Clevedon, where Arthur
Hallam was interred in the church. Of the immediate trigger for the
tears, Frederick Locker Lampson quoted Tennyson as saying that it was
not 'real woe' but 'the yearning that young people occasionally experience for that which seems to have passed away from them for ever'.[24]

'Tears, idle tears' was part of the original 1847 text, but some of
the songs were added later. These are not imagined as literally sung
within the text; they are rather lyrics which stand at a tangent to the
main narrative. A beautiful sunset in the main narrative prompted this
song (added in 1850):

> The splendour falls on castle walls
>   And snowy summits old in story;
> The long light shakes across the lakes,
>   And the wild cataract leaps in glory.
> Blow, bugle, blow, set the wild echoes flying,
> Blow, bugle; answer, echoes, dying, dying, dying.*

The songs were 'the best interpreters of the poem', and were designed
to enable the reader to see that 'the child [Lady Psyche's child] is the
link through the parts'. One of them is a lullaby for this child:

> Sweet and low, sweet and low,
>   Wind of the western sea,

---

*Magnificently set for Peter Pears in Benjamin Britten's *Serenade for Tenor, Horn and Strings*.

Low, low, breathe and blow,
   Wind of the western sea!
Over the rolling waters go,
Come from the dying moon, and blow,
   Blow him again to me;
While my little one, while my pretty one, sleeps.[25]

As a part-song set in 1863 by Joseph Barnby this soon joined the standard repertoire of Victorian choral societies.

The Princess closed by commenting on its own strategies. It has many styles – the young men have been using 'mock-heroic gigantesque' while the women have used a quite different register. The poem's narrator refers to it as a 'strange diagonal',[26] a compromise between satire and realism. But behind these distancing devices, and the teasing and bantering tone, there is a serious argument at work, one which was continuous with the daring and generosity of spirit of the Cambridge poems. As an undergraduate Tennyson had written a celebration of great women throughout history in 'A Dream of Fair Women', in which he had been explicit about the need to change the power relationship between the sexes:

In every land I thought that, more or less,
   The strongest sterner nature overbore
The softer, uncontrolled by gentleness
   And selfish evermore:

And whether there were any means whereby,
   In some far aftertime, the gentler mind
Might reassume its just and full degree
   Of rule among mankind.[27]

The twin ideals – of equality and of the right of women to a university education – are expressed so eloquently and at such length in *The Princess* that the poem's equivocating close does not erase them.

Despite the fact that she herself will later benefit from a man's brute strength (she is saved from drowning by Cyril, the Prince who loves her), Princess Ida's first speech to the three young men (disguised as women) is compelling in itself, and is not invalidated by subsequent events:

O lift your natures up:
Embrace our aims: work out your freedom. Girls,

> Knowledge is now no more a fountain sealed:*
> Drink deep, until the habits of the slave,
> The sins of emptiness, gossip and spite
> And slander, die.[28]

The Prince, Cyril, is the last of the 'medley's' several narrators. His name is an anagram of 'lyric', as though he is in fact the authoritative voice of poetry itself. His argument is that marriage between them will complete the identity of both:

> For woman is not undevelopt man,
> But diverse: could we make her as the man,
> Sweet Love were slain: his dearest bond is this,
> Not like to like but like in difference.
> Yet in the long years liker must they grow;
> The man be more of woman, she of man;
> He gain in sweetness and in moral height,
> Nor lose the wrestling thews that throw the world;
> She mental breadth, nor fail in childward care,
> Nor lose the childlike in the larger mind;
> Till at the last she set herself to man,
> Like perfect music unto noble words.

Cyril – 'Lyric' – finds the perfect music to accompany him in Ida's mind and in her beauty, and as the two become 'liker' so they will become 'The single pure and perfect animal, / The two-celled heart beating, with one full stroke, / Life.'[29]

In both *The Princess* and 'Morte d'Arthur', the frame shows high-spirited young men engaged in learned fooling – itself a strong tradition in English writing (*Tristram Shandy* is a major example). And there is a love story in each poem.[30] 'Morte d'Arthur' and 'The Lady of Shalott' are among the poems in which Tennyson can clearly be seen to be responding to the same influences and preferences that stirred the Pre-Raphaelite Brotherhood. Inspired by prophetic phrases from *Modern Painters*, the first volume of which had been published by the twenty-four-year-old John Ruskin in 1843, this group, of whom the most conspicuous were Dante Gabriel Rossetti, John Everett Millais, William Holman Hunt and Thomas Woolner, set themselves to challenge the Royal Academy and the academy

---

*'Knowledge is now no more a fountain sealed' became an inspiration for nineteenth-century women educators, and is the motto of the Girls' Public Day School Trust.

schools, and to claim the authority of nature itself as the basis of their art.

Unlike Rossetti and Millais, the sculptor Thomas Woolner was a rough provincial (from Hadleigh in Suffolk), the son of a minor post office official. He was outspoken, courageous, capable of being bearish and brusque in manner, and violently ambitious. In 1849, when he was twenty-five, a reward for his ambition came in the form of an introduction to Tennyson. This was fortuitous timing – Tennyson was forty-one, a well-established poet on the way to the immense recognition which would come his way in 1850. But he liked rough-hewn and ready young men, and agreed to sit for a medallion in December 1849. It was hard for Woolner to establish continuity, however, because so many changes were taking place in Tennyson's life in the spring and summer of 1850.

When he was not on one of his extended visits to Park House, Tennyson's home was now the house that his mother rented in Cheltenham. He had a sustained period of work there early in 1845, in 'a little room at the top of the house in St James' Square' remembered by Dr Buchanan Ker, brother of Mary Tennyson's husband, as 'not kept in very orderly fashion', with books and papers 'quite as much on the floor and the chairs as upon the table', where Tennyson, 'pipe in mouth, discoursed to his friends more unconstrainedly than anywhere else on men and things and what death means'. George Stovin Venables visited him there in March 1845. Venables recalled that he 'went up to A.T.'s room, & sat a good while, he reading out passages from Pericles & Love's Labours Lost. He is a very fine critic.'[31] Tennyson was clearly reading Shakespeare's late romance, *Pericles*, and the comedy, *Love's Labour's Lost*, while brooding upon his own comedy-romance. In *Love's Labour's Lost* a group of scholarly young men renounced the company of women; in Tennyson's 'medley' that position was reversed, the scholarly young women renouncing men.

Tennyson's social life was increasingly active. He had met Wordsworth some years earlier, but it was during this year that he got to know the great poet; several of his friends recorded Tennyson's delighted account of a supper party, where Wordsworth had said 'come brother bard, to dinner'. Tennyson had been tongue-tied and awkward, but at last he had summoned the will to pour out his admiration to the old man, who took his hand 'and replied with some expressions equally kind and complimentary. Tennyson was evidently much pleased with the old man, and glad of having learned to know him.'[32]

Part of the social circle was 'the Sterling Club'. This society, named after the controversial Apostle John Sterling, who had died young, was in effect a London continuation of the Cambridge Apostles, and a dinner on 29 April 1845 was correspondingly a matter of grand young men who had known each other at Cambridge: 'Two Spring Rices, Lord Ebrington, Spedding, Law, Alfred Tennyson, Venables, Merivale, T. F. Ellis, Trench'.[33]

Tennyson also needed calmer companionship than this, and one of his restful friends was Aubrey de Vere (1814–1902), the charming, gentle and aristocratic Irish poet, who had come up to Cambridge some ten years after Tennyson. Stephen Spring Rice, de Vere's cousin, was an Apostle and acquaintance of Tennyson's; through Spring Rice, de Vere became friendly with Monckton Milnes and James Spedding. He had first met Tennyson, again through Spring Rice, in 1842. De Vere himself was a mystical and solitary soul, a man who would find his spiritual home in the Roman Catholic Church. Like those other loyal friends, Spedding and Henry Lushington, de Vere was an excellent and supportive critic of Tennyson's work in progress. On 17 April he called on Tennyson 'and found him much out of spirits. He cheered up soon, and read me some beautiful elegies' (drafts of *In Memoriam*), and on the 18th he heard Tennyson read his 'University of Women' (*The Princess*).[34]

In August of 1846, Tennyson took a holiday in Switzerland with his now indispensable publisher, Moxon. In the course of his holiday he wrote the lyric 'Come down, O maid, from yonder mountain height', which would find its place as one of the most memorable and resonant passages in *The Princess*. He and Moxon travelled down the Rhine – Tennyson was stirred by memories of his visit to the area with Arthur Hallam in 1832 ('Nonnenwerth and Drachenfels, sad recollections' – Nonnenwerth had been particularly recalled in Tennyson's ill-starred poem about his 'darling room').

They reached Lucerne and took a steamer over the lake to Weggis, where he found that he was expected to share a room ('fleabitten') with Moxon. The hotel was noisy with other guests ('infernal chatter of innumerous apes'). They saw essential sights such as the Rhigi, the 'far off Jungfrau looking as if delicately pencilled', and visited Küssnacht, Flüelen, and William Tell's chapel. The minor vexations of travel continued unabated: 'bad beer – sour ill looking maid – go into church – two rouged harridans in flounce and furbelows for Virgins'. A night in Lungern, charming place though it is, was spoilt by 'infamous beds swarming with fleas'.[35]

Towards the end of this holiday the two men visited Charles Dickens in Lausanne. Dickens was puzzled by the fact that Tennyson had brought Moxon with him, noting that Moxon was 'an odd companion for a man of genius', and 'snobbish' but good-natured. It soon became clear to him that Moxon was in effect looking after Tennyson, and that without Moxon's help the practicalities of the holiday would have been hard for Tennyson to manage.[36]

Tennyson reported to his friend Fitzgerald that the Swiss were 'greedy, goitred, miserable-looking poor devils'.[37] For most of his long life he would behave as though the refreshment and stimulus of travel were rewarding for him, while at the same time his actual expeditions were all too often accompanied by a steady litany of complaints.

Henry Lushington had become an indispensable friend to Tennyson and a sharply intelligent reader of his poetry. There was an unwelcome separation from him early in the following year, when Henry had 'received a letter from Lord Grey, colonial secretary in the new Whig government of Lord John Russell, offering him the chief secretaryship of the British government on the island of Malta. [. . .] The position ranked second only to the governor's in the civilian administration of the island, and under Lord Grey's plans to liberalize the Maltese government, gave promise of acquiring additional importance.'[38] This was a great loss. Tennyson determined to make the most of Henry Lushington's sensitivity and insight before he left.

The Tennysons as a family continued to treat Edmund and Cecilia's home as their own, particularly when the owners themselves were away in Glasgow. George Stovin Venables, who regarded himself as Henry Lushington's closest friend, was by 1847 increasingly irritated by this. Venables had the generosity of spirit, though, to help Tennyson with poems, proofs and publicity. Henry was plunged into depression by the prospect of going to Malta, despite the fact that he had no other career, and Venables was anxious to have some time with his dear friend, on his own. He arrived at Park House by invitation on 11 February 1847, but the place was already full of unwelcome Tennysons: 'Mary Tennyson and Miss Hamilton, a Scotch old maid [. . .] also of course Horatio & Matilda Tennyson, which is a great nuisance.' The next day Venables 'found no opportunity of speaking to H[enry], all day from the crowd in the house'. Later Venables again visited Park House to find his beloved Henry taken up by Tennyson: Henry was reading the newly completed *Princess*. Despite himself Venables took an interest, borrowed the MS of the poem, and on a railway journey to Hereford 'read the greater part of the New University with pleasure and admiration'. By 16 February Tennyson had returned, intending, as he wrote to T. H. Rawnsley, to 'see the last' of his 'brother-in-law's brother', who would soon be off to Malta and, 'being a man of feeble stamina', was 'afraid of the climate and altogether down in the mouth about it'. Tennyson would 'do my best to set him up, though I am very unwell myself'. Tennyson again found himself apologising to Lincolnshire friends: because of Henry Lushington's imminent departure and his own illness, 'a journey into Lincolnshire so as to catch all your "clan" in full conclave is quite impossible'. 'My old friendships are as dear as ever,' he declared, and he asked Rawnsley to 'not be hard of faith but believing'.[39]

Tennyson's illness led him to take a water cure at Umberslade Hall near Birmingham, where he read proofs of *The Princess* and remained for a month or more. It is not clear what his illness was, but it was certainly a nervous disorder of some kind. Anxiety about whether to resume contact with Emily may have contributed to it, and there is also a sense in which he was in conflict with himself over his own emerging success. He was increasingly lauded and feted: his friends now included Carlyle, Wordsworth and Browning, and he had become the leading author of the best poetry publisher in London. The obscure, vagrant identity that he had cherished since his 1830 volume no longer fitted the reality of his situation.

Thomas Carlyle, now settled in Chelsea, was captivated by Tennyson's physical magnificence and the sense of being in the presence of a kind of wild creature or noble savage, and the two men became good friends in the course of the 1840s. Carlyle recalled his first meeting with Tennyson in 1840: 'A fine large-featured, dim-eyed, bronze-coloured, shaggy-headed man inwardly, with great composure in an inarticulate element as of tranquil chaos and tobacco smoke; great now and then when he does emerge: a most restful, brotherly, solidhearted man.'[40] 'Restful' at that date Tennyson certainly was not; his inner life was one of anxiety and anguish. As he got to know him Carlyle saw him more accurately, and in a letter of 1844 he wrote of Tennyson's physical beauty, his 'rough dusty-dark hair; bright-laughing hazel eyes; massive acquiline face, most massive yet most delicate', and of the marks of suffering on him: 'a man solitary and sad, as certain men are, dwelling in an element of gloom, – carrying a bit of Chaos about him, in short, which he is manufacturing into Cosmos!' He noted that Tennyson smoked 'infinite tobacco' and was often unwell.[41]

Once Tennyson called at Chelsea, looking for Thomas, and found his wife instead. He was acutely awkward with a woman on her own, and Jane's solution was to entertain him as Carlyle would have done, with pipes, tobacco, brandy and water. Relaxing somewhat, he smoked for three hours on end, and talked to her 'exactly as if he were talking with a clever *man*'.[42] James Spedding's rooms in Lincoln's Inn Fields, Edward Fitzgerald's rooms in Charlotte Street and the top-floor rooms in 1 Mitre Court Buildings shared by Henry Lushington and George Venables, were always open to him. If he saw lights he would go up and find a group, usually of former Cambridge men, who would enable him to renew the old easy sense of companionship.

Early in the 1840s Carlyle introduced him to a new friend, Sir John Simeon. It was on this occasion that Carlyle memorably described Tennyson as 'sitting on a dung-heap among innumerable dead dogs' (by which he meant simply that Tennyson was preoccupied by the past – this was certainly true).[43] The meeting was at Bath House, the London residence of Lord and Lady Ashburton. The Ashburtons were related to Rosa Baring (and their son, William Baring, had become another of Tennyson's friends). Lady Ashburton, intelligent, vulgar, lion-hunting and famously ugly, enjoyed surrounding herself with geniuses, and Tennyson regularly found himself invited to Bath House as his reputation grew.

Meanwhile, nervous distress and irritability caused him to seek out further water cures, at Cheltenham in 1846, at Birmingham with a well-regarded practitioner, Dr Edward Johnson in 1847, and then later in 1847 for a longer and more fruitful period – during which he was writing some of the songs for the revised and expanded *Princess* – at Dr Gully's water-cure establishment in Malvern. One of the attractions was that the vicar of Malvern was the Rev. John Rashdall, whom Tennyson had known at Cambridge and in Lincolnshire, and who had married Rosa Baring's sister. (This was the same Rashdall who had been disconcertingly sharp in his diary about Arthur Hallam's death in 1833.) Tennyson stayed in Rashdall's vicarage rather than in one of the attractive properties that Dr Gully had acquired to accommodate his patients. Gully had treated Henry Hallam, which must have given Tennyson confidence in him.

Dr Gully and Dr Wilson, his partner in the practice, held that 'all chronic disease was caused by a faulty supply of blood to the viscera; either the blood was poor in quality or owing to defective circulation it was not carried off and the viscera became engorged with it. The application of cold water to the skin by various methods: compresses, or packing in sheets wrung out of cold water, or sitz baths or jets or douches was used to animate the circulation and get it working normally.'[44]

Tennyson's friends were puzzled by his need for these water cures. Fitzgerald saw it as a discouraging sign:

> Tennyson is emerged half-cured, or half-destroyed, from a water establishment: has gone to a new Doctor who gives him iron pills; and altogether this really great man thinks more about his bowels and nerves than about the Laureate wreath* he was born to inherit. Not but he meditates new poems; and now the Princess is done, he turns to King Arthur – a worthy subject indeed – and has consulted some histories of him, and spent some time in visiting his traditionary haunts in Cornwall. But I believe the trumpet can wake Tennyson no longer to do *great* deeds; I may mistake and prove myself an owl; which I hope may be the case. But how are we to expect heroic poems from a valetudinary? I have told him he should fly from England and go among savages.[45]

Like his father (and his brother Charles), Tennyson had a self-indulgent and addictive personality, and he needed periods in which the stimulants – alcohol, especially, but also tobacco, late nights and urban excitement – were replaced by what were in effect spiritual retreats.

After the publication of the first version of *The Princess* late in 1847, Tennyson's friends were struck by his restlessness. This had to do with the need to take further the big Arthurian project which had begun with the 'Morte d'Arthur' published in 1842. He projected a visit to Arthurian sites in Cornwall but was persuaded by Aubrey de Vere to be his guest in Ireland first (de Vere argued that the waves and the cliffs were even more romantic in Ireland than they were in Cornwall). He accompanied de Vere to his family seat, Curragh Chase in County Limerick, where he was entertained handsomely but struck his host as restive and ill at ease. De Vere was anxious about him:

> I hope we shall make this visit pleasant to him. I wonder why he came, and whether he is fond of me, I fear not much so. Yesterday,

---

*Fitzgerald's observation about the Laureate wreath was apposite; early in 1847 Tennyson had been asked by William Whewell, now Master of Trinity, to write an ode for the installation of the Prince Consort as Chancellor of Cambridge later in the year. Tennyson was pleased by the invitation but found that he could not write anything that satisfied him ('the work does not seem to prosper in my hands', Lang and Shannon, I, pp. 272–3) so he declined, and the request was passed on to the incumbent Laureate, Wordsworth.

when I looked up at dinner and saw him sitting between my sister-in-law and her sister, in this remote land, strange to him, I felt all at once such an affection for him as made his noble face look very dim and misty. He has indeed a most noble countenance, so full of power, passion and intellect – so strong, dark and impressive.

Tennyson was an awkward guest: he read aloud a good deal to his hosts, his regular strategy for coping with sticky situations, but he was reluctant to join in other entertainments. He was supercilious and resistant when a dance was held at the house, but here the Irish were a match for him. The mother of one of the young unmarried girls who were guests at the dance turned on him and rebuked him: 'How would the world get on if others went around growling at its amusements in a voice as deep as a lion's? I request that you will go upstairs, put on an evening coat and ask my daughter to dance.'[46] Since Tennyson was an excellent dancer, he was then able to enjoy the evening, and he began to engage rather better with the characteristic Irish enjoyment of revelries of this kind. From Curragh he went to Killarney, where the light on its celebrated castle prompted one of the songs for *The Princess*, 'The Splendour Falls on Castle Walls'.*

Edward Fitzgerald, hitherto one of Tennyson's most devoted disciples, was feeling disillusioned. He was unable to see the point of *The Princess* and he confessed this to Tennyson's brother, Frederick (whom he always addressed as 'Frederic') in May 1848:

I had a note from Alfred three months ago. He was then in London: but is now in Ireland, I think, adding to his new poem, the Princess. Have you seen it? I am considered a great heretic for abusing it; it seems to me a wretched waste of power at a time of life when a man ought to be doing his best; and I almost feel hopeless about Alfred now. I mean, about his doing what he was born to do.

In the same letter, Fitzgerald wrote that he had heard Jenny Lind. Frederick was passionate about music – indeed it was a major part of

---

*There is an alternative tradition that this famous song was in fact either composed or revised during Tennyson's visit to Malvern in September 1848. He gave a copy to Dr Gully's sister, Anne, who wrote at the bottom, 'Given to me by the poet in the drawing room of the Priory House, Great Malvern' (Dr Gully's private residence). (Lang and Shannon, I, p.28on.) The text of this copy has now disappeared, but it had a variation from the published state. The colouring of a Malvern sunset contributed 'the red light shakes across the lakes' in place of 'the long light shakes across the lakes' in the printed text. (Jenkins, *Tennyson and Dr Gully*, p. 8.)

his life – and in his generous way Fitzgerald liked to keep him informed about current performances in London. Fitzgerald also loved gossip about their mutual Cambridge friends. James Spedding, for example, was respected by all of them but they also liked to laugh gently at his solemnity, self-sufficiency and austere celibacy. Fitzgerald had decided that Spedding was in love with Jenny Lind: 'Night after night is that bald head seen in one particular position in the Opera house, in a stall; the miserable man has forgot Bacon and philosophy, and goes after strange women.'[47]

In May 1848, Tennyson finally went to Cornwall in search of Arthurian legends.His arrival at the inn in Bude was marked by a mishap. 'Arrived at Bude in dark, askt girl way to sea, she opens the back door . . . I go out and in a moment go sheer down, upward of six feet, over wall on fanged cobbles.' He gashed his leg so badly that it did not heal for six weeks.

He stayed in simple places, with grocers and shopkeepers as well as in small inns, and found to his surprise that many of the Cornish people whom he met (including a miner who hid behind a wall to have a close view of him) knew his poetry well.[48]

He made friends with Robert Stephen Hawker (1803–75), the learned, celebrated and highly eccentric vicar of Morwenstow. Hawker was himself a poet, as well as an antiquarian and a genuine scholar of all matters Cornish. He was a generous-minded and compassionate pastor; he suffered agonies of grief over the casualties caused by shipwreck along the particularly dangerous section of coast which was part of his parish. Tennyson and Hawker were alike in some ways: they were both big men; they enjoyed wild landscapes and the company of simple people; they both cultivated a distinctive personal appearance. Tennyson's Spanish cloak and hat had already become part of his personality, and Hawker was a flamboyant dandy. He refused to wear black clothes or a clerical collar; his preferred outfit was an expensive but dirty velvet-trimmed brown cassock, worn at all times (even when scrambling over rocks on the coast, with all his skirts tucked up and a pair of sturdy grey trousers beneath them). This was set off by a soft black velvet cap or a kind of pink fez without a tassel. On occasions he liked to dress as a mermaid and sit out on a rock in the bay near his vicarage. Later in life he became addicted to opium and his personality began to disintegrate (among other things he became a compulsive fantasist), but, at the time Tennyson met him, he was scholarly, interested and helpful. At first he was disconcertingly cold, but as he came to understand the nature of Tennyson's quest he became voluble and friendly. He talked to him at length about his Arthurian project and lent him a great many books and manuscripts to read while he visited the places associated by legend with King Arthur's Camelot: Tintagel, Camelford, Kynance, St Ives, Land's End and the Lizard.[49]

The stories of King Arthur had preoccupied Tennyson since his adolescence. 'Sir Launcelot and Queen Guinevere' was completed in his twenty-first year in 1830, though not published until 1842. 'The Lady of Shalott' was written by 1831 (he corresponded with Arthur Hallam about it in October of that year) and published in 1832 (revised in 1842). 'Morte d'Arthur' was written in reaction to the shock of Arthur Hallam's death (thus in 1833–4) and published in 1842, and 'Sir Galahad' also was written by 1834 (and published in 1842).

In 1848 Tennyson's foe Bulwer Lytton pre-empted him with a twelve-book narrative poem, *King Arthur*, the story of a Welsh king willing to die rather than surrender his kingdom. Bulwer's poem nodded acknowledgement to Malory but strayed a good distance from the sources and was essentially a colourful episodic invention with some degree of energy and talent about it. His prose preface to his epic reads as though written in conscious rivalry with Tennyson.

> Whatever the defects of this Poem, it has not been hastily conceived or lightly undertaken. From my earliest youth, the subject I have selected has haunted my ambition – for twenty years it has rested steadily on my mind, in spite of other undertakings, for the most part not wholly ungenial [preparing for a poem which . . .] seeks to construct from the elements of national romance, something approaching to the completeness of epic narrative.

Bulwer Lytton's poem venerated male friendship and valour, and his Arthur was physically magnificent, and enjoyed an ideal friendship with his Lancelot:

> O'er the light limb, and o'er the shoulders broad,
> The steel flowed pliant as a silken vest;
> Strength was so supple that like grace it showed,
> And force was only by its ease confest [. . .]
>
> And if the friendship scarce in each the same,
> The soul has rivals where the heart has not;

So Lancelot loved his Arthur more than fame,
And Arthur more than life his Lancelot.
Lost here Art's mean distinctions! knightly troth,
Frank youth, high thoughts, crown'd Nature's kings in both.[50]

A mark of Tennyson's capacity for what Carlyle called his 'chaos' was his ability to lose his own manuscripts. One of the most startling of his letters (now in the Beinecke Library, Yale) shows that a manuscript book containing the most complete state of what would become *In Memoriam* was almost lost and destroyed in 1849, the year before it was published. In February Tennyson was staying with friends at Bonchurch, on the Isle of Wight, and had left the book in London. From there he wrote to Coventry Patmore:*

I went up to my room yesterday to get my book of elegies – you know what I mean – a long butcher-ledger-like book. I was going to read one or two to an artist here. I could not find it? I have some obscure remembrance of having lent it to you. If so, all is well. If not will you go to my old chambers and institute a rigorous inquiry. I was coming up to-day on purpose to look after it, but the weather is so ferocious I have yielded to the wishes of my friends here to stop till tomorrow. I shall be, I expect in town tomorrow at 25 M.P. [25 Mornington Place, the rooms in which Tennyson was staying in London] where I shall be glad to see you: at 9.10 P.M. the train in which I come gets into London. I suppose I shall be in Mornington Place about 10 o'clock. Perhaps you would in your walk Museum-ward call on Mrs Lloyd and tell her to prepare for me. With best remembrances to Mrs Patmore, believe me Ever yours A

A 'rigorous inquiry' is a comic usage echoing newspaper reports of police investigations of the day. (Tennyson's published *Letters* have 'vigorous', which is a misreading.[51]) Patmore liked to tell the story of how he had rescued the elegies. Somewhat hugging himself with

---

*Coventry Patmore (1823–96) was at this time in his twenties and working in the printed books department of the British Museum. He was ambitious, wrote poetry, and consciously modelled himself on Tennyson, whose acquaintance he sought out; Tennyson warmed to him and saw a good deal of him during 1846–7 while they were both bachelors about town. The friendship changed somewhat after Patmore's marriage in 1847, which became the basis of Patmore's later commercial success; his long verse sequence in praise of marriage, *The Angel of the House*, brought him a reputation and strong sales which freed him from his work at the British Museum.

self-importance, he later said to William Allingham (who recorded it in his diary):

> I have in this room perhaps the greatest literary treasure in England – the manuscript of Tennyson's *next poem*. It is written in a thing like a butcher's account-book. He left it behind him in his lodging when he was up in London and wrote to me to go and look for it. He had no other copy, and he never remembers his verses. I found it by chance in a drawer; if I had been a little later it would probably have been sold to a butter-shop [for wrapping butter – the editors of Tennyson's *Letters* quote this in a footnote but give 'butcher-shop' (by association, presumably, with the 'butcher-ledger-like' book) instead of 'butter-shop'].[52]

Patmore heightened the effect here in three different ways: in fact Tennyson had an excellent memory for his own poetry; there were many drafts of individual elegies in his multiple notebooks; and there were two 'butcher's book' manuscripts of the elegies in existence by this date.[53] But it is still a good tale.

Recalling Tennyson for a memoir published in 1900, Willingham Franklin Rawnsley wrote:

> My earliest remembrance of him is of his visiting my parents at Shiplake, before 1850, when I was turned out of my little room in order that he might have a place of his own to smoke in. He was then still working on 'In Memoriam,' and it was in this little room of mine that he wrote the 'Hesper Phosphor' canto (no. CXX). It was on 7th of February, in or about 1850, that Tennyson and my father drove to Reading, and on their return they were quoting some verses to one another with much amusement. Tennyson said to me, 'And oh, far worse than all beside, he whipped his Mary till she cried.' 'What is that?' I asked. 'Oh, you'll know tomorrow,' was all the answer I could get; and it puzzled me greatly.

The mystery was cleared up the following day, Willingham Rawnsley's birthday, when he was given a copy of *Struwel-Peter* (in which the verse about Mary being whipped appeared).

These memories are indispensable, because they are so sharp:

It was at Shiplake that he said to my mother, after reading Matthew Arnold's 'Merman,' 'I should like to have written that.'* And it was then too that on his casting about as he often did, for a new subject to write on, my mother, as she herself told me, suggested his enlarging his lovely little fragment, published some years before in 'The Tribute,' than which she told him he had never written anything better, and which, for he acted on the suggestion, is now imbedded in 'Maud.' The lines were:

> Oh that 'twere possible
> After long grief and pain
> To find the arms of my true love
> Round me once again.

I have the whole canto as it then stood, written out at the time for my mother.[54]

The 1842 volumes and *The Princess* enhanced Tennyson's reputation so that by the late 1840s this brilliant, drifting man, who in 1845 had seemed almost a vagrant, was becoming more established and more secure. Socially, though, he was still regarded as something of an outsider. It puts Tennyson's attitudes to Lincolnshire into perspective to be reminded of the way in which the wealthy and the grand of the county continued to regard him. Harrington Hall, for example, the scene of Tennyson's doomed attachment to Rosa Baring, had been leased by the Barings from its owner, one Weston Cracroft (1815–83). Cracroft was a friend of Thomas Rawnsley, whom he visited late in 1849, writing in his diary some reflections which displayed the fixed attitudes of this typical Lincolnshire gentleman. In his tone there is innocent surprise over the fact that Rawnsley, 'a poor country parson', had seriously grand contacts among the gentry ('Sir Gilbert Heathcote, Lord Willoughby d'Eresby and heaps of other "nobiles" its very remarkable'). At the Rawnsleys' dinner party on 18 November the misfit among the guests, in Cracroft's view, was 'Alfred Tennyson the poet'. Cracroft took some interest in Tennyson (he was becoming indisputably famous), but his appearance and bad manners were marked against

---

*In general Tennyson and Arnold were seldom cordial about one another's work, but they regarded each other with a good deal of respect. In November 1856 Arnold would be surprised and pleased to learn that Tennyson had said that if something should happen to him, Matthew Arnold ought to be his successor as Laureate. (Lang, *Letters of Matthew Arnold*, I, p. 347.)

him: 'When he lights up his face is almost fine, but his expression coarse when unexcited. On the whole his features coarse, and complexion dirty and sallow – he wears spectacles – conversation agreeable.' When Tennyson put his feet up on the sofa, his hostess 'all of a sudden quietly warned him off'. [55] (Sofia Rawnsley, wife of Thomas Rawnsley since 1815, had known Tennyson as a little boy and as a dreamy and unkempt young man.) The following day, lunching with Edward Rawnsley (one of Thomas's sons) at Raithby, Cracroft encountered Tennyson again: 'a scrubby looking fellow by daylight – dress no way neat – in short a poet'.[56]

The Lushingtons had facilitated the writing and publishing of *The Princess*, and, later, they played a key role in Tennyson's rapprochement with Emily Sellwood. Arriving at Park House from Wales on a Friday in September 1847, Venables found among several visitors 'Miss Sellwood and A.T.'. On the following Monday, having given very little notice, Tennyson went off to London in the afternoon, and Venables noted that Emily Sellwood left Park House the following Saturday. A few days later Venables reported that 'A.T. appeared, to me most unexpectedly', and he and Venables left Park House on Monday, 4 October. When Venables was next at Park House, 10 October, Emily was there but Tennyson was not – Emily left two days later, on the 12th. The possibility of 'accidentally' meeting at Park House, however briefly, must have been tantalizing for them both, but Alfred and Emily were doing what they could to avoid awkwardness – and, in particular, any discussion of their relationship amongst their friends – by taking care not to be under the same roof for any length of time. [57]

Early in 1849, Emily saw the manuscripts of the memorial poems for Arthur Hallam which would become *In Memoriam*. They had been lent to her by her cousin, Catherine Franklin, who in 1842 had married Drummond Rawnsley. It was as a consequence of reading these verses that Emily wrote a remarkable letter (known only because it was quoted in full by Willingham Franklin Rawnsley in *Memories of the Tennysons*; the original seems not to have survived). The letter is often dated 1 April 1850, but it seems likely, as Ann Thwaite suggests, that it was actually written a year earlier, in April 1849.[58]

Emily was encouraged by Catherine to send a message about the elegies to Tennyson. She found in *In Memoriam* comforting assurance that Tennyson was a man of deep feeling and, crucially, that he was fundamentally a Christian believer. To communicate with him directly was a momentous step, given the breaking-off of their engagement back in 1840, and, here in her letter to Catherine, Emily was understandably very cautious about it:

> My dearest Katie . . . Do you really think I should write a line with the Elegies, that is in a separate note, to say I have returned them? I am almost afraid, but since you say I am to do so I will, only I cannot say what I feel . . . You and Drummond are among the best and kindest friends I have in the world, and let me not be ungrateful, I have some very good and very kind. The longer I live the more I feel how blessed I am in this way. Now I must say good bye – Thy loving sister. Emily.

> I thought I would write my note before the others came. Here it is, no beginning nor end, not a note at all, a sort of label only. 'Katie told me the poems might be kept until Saturday. I hope I shall not have occasioned any inconvenience by keeping them to the limit of time; and if I have I must be forgiven, for I cannot willingly part from what is so precious. The thanks I would say for them and for the faith in me which has trusted them to me must be thought for me, I cannot write them.'

Within this letter to Catherine Rawnsley Emily quoted an enthusiastic letter about the memorial poems that she had herself received from Charles Kingsley (1819–75), the clergyman, writer and Christian socialist who was a close friend of Drummond Rawnsley and a warm admirer of Tennyson's work. Kingsley had written:

> I have read the poems through and through and through and to me they were and they are ever more and more a spirit monument grand and beautiful, in whose presence I feel admiration and delight, not unmixed with awe. The happiest possible end to this labour of love! But think not its fruits shall so soon perish, for they are life in life, and they shall live, and as years go on be only the more fully known and loved and reverenced for what they are.

Emily then added her own comments to this: 'So said a true seer. Can anyone guess the name of this seer?' She expected Catherine to guess that the 'seer' who had written this was Kingsley. She followed this with a brief paraphrase of a letter that she had herself written to Tennyson, in which she had said 'that I am the happier for having seen these poems and that I hope I shall be the better too'.[59]

Since 1844, Kingsley, 'the true seer', had been rector of Eversley, which was close to Shiplake, Rawnsley's own parish. Kingsley was to review *In Memoriam* in *Fraser's Magazine* in September 1850. This in many ways remarkable review responded with great warmth to the central relationship in the poem. Kingsley was celebrated for his 'muscular Christianity', and his review gave full measure both to muscles and to Christian enthusiasm. He commended equally the 'spiritual experiences' and the mutual bond between the poet and his dead friend:

> Blessed, thrice blessed, to find that hero-worship is not yet passed away; that the heart of man still beats young and fresh; that the old tales of David and Jonathan, Damon and Pythias, Socrates and Alcibiades, Shakespeare and his nameless friend, of 'love passing the love of woman,' ennobled by his own humility, deeper than death, and mightier than the grave, can still blossom out if it be but in one heart here and there to show men still how sooner or later 'he that loveth knoweth God, for God is Love!'.[60]

In Memoriam was crucial in bringing the lovers together after their long estrangement and detachment. It was not the only factor; Tennyson felt confident, more prosperous, more socially secure, and had put the depressions and crises of the 1840s behind him. The sequence of events following Emily's reading of the poem makes it clear that she saw in it enough elements endorsing Tennyson's basic piety for her to relax her strictly orthodox Christian scruples. By Christmas of 1849 it seems clear, as Ann Thwaite has argued, that they had agreed to marry, but they had decided to keep this secret. Tennyson wrote to Catherine Rawnsley on Christmas Day 1849: 'I have made up my mind to marry in a month. I have much to do and settle in the mean time. Pray keep this thing secret. I do not mean even my own family to know.'[61] The marriage did not take place 'in a month', of course, and it is not known whether Tennyson panicked and backtracked or whether further difficulties developed between the lovers. Ann Thwaite suggests that an outside event may have caused them both to agree to postpone their plans. Emily's aunt Elizabeth (the 'Aunt Betsy' whom Tennyson had found tiresome in the past) died in January 1850, which meant that Emily went into a period of mourning.[62]

Because so few people were invited to this marriage, it is especially interesting to have the young Willingham Franklin Rawnsley's eye-witness account of it:

> It was at Shiplake that the poet, described in the Marriage License as 'Alfred Tennyson of Lincoln Inn Fields,' and his bride, who was

put down as 'Emily Sarah Sellwood of East Bourne in the county of Sussex,' in reality two Lincolnshire people, were married by another Lincolnshire person, my father, Drummond Rawnsley, very quietly on June 13th 1850.[63]

H. D. Rawnsley recorded his mother's patience with the wayward poet: 'At the time of the wedding, over which he had given a great deal of trouble to my mother [i.e. Emily Sellwood's cousin Catherine Rawnsley] by his inability to make up his mind, so that the marriage license was dated May 15, though the wedding did not take place til June 13, she had endless trouble to get not only the cake and the bride's wedding dress ready, but also his own essential wedding garments.' About these garments he wrote Catherine Rawnsley a strikingly brief and abrupt note (in early June 1850): 'It is settled for the 13th, so the shirts may be got on with.'

Tennyson's sister Mary identified closely with the diffidence, indecisiveness and fear of commitment that he was displaying, although she did also protest at his thoughtless and hurtful behaviour towards his siblings: 'Alfred maintains silence [as late as May 1850] about the engagement, which I think is not fair towards his family, especially as the Rawnsleys know it. [. . .] Poor thing, I daresay he is miserable enough at times, thinking of what he is about to do.' Of the wedding itself – although in fact she was relying on inaccurate hearsay for both the day and the weather – Mary wrote: 'Well, all is over. Alfred was married to Emily Sellwood last Friday – *Friday, and raining* [neither was true], about which I feel very superstitious. I hope they will be happy, but I feel very doubtful about it.'[64] Tennyson's brother Charles Tennyson Turner, whose wife Louisa was one of the bride's sisters, wrote a quirky letter of congratulation:

Oh, what a queer world it is! I hope however it has done a brace of amiable and remarkable people some genuine good, whirligig as it is. This time at least – well! The thing is to come off on the 13th, daddy [Mr Sellwood, Louisa and Emily's father] says. Good wishes in crowds from me. I despatch a dove's wing to you. I am going to keep pigeons, would they were carrier pigeons! then would I trouble their wings with missives of congratulation to arrive more swiftly than the railroad. coo! coo! coo! Your affectionate brother Charles[65]

The guests included old Mr Sellwood (Emily's father), Cecilia (Tennyson's sister) and her husband Edmund Lushington, Charles Weld (who was married to Anne, another of Emily's sisters) and two

Rawnsley children. Emily remembered the scrambled preparations for her great day: 'Neither the cake nor the dresses arrived in time, and the white gloves were lost, but the wedding notwithstanding took place.'[66] Tennyson was laconic and comical about the whole affair. To Sophy – now Mrs Elmhirst, but still in his own mind one of his sweethearts – he wrote about his new wife, 'We seem to get on very well together. I have not beaten her yet'. In poetry, though, he gave his real feelings. 'To the Vicar of Shiplake' acknowledged the blessing of his marriage:

> Good she is, and pure and just.
>   Being conquered by her sweetness
> I shall come through her, I trust,
>   Into fuller-orbed completeness;
> Though but made of erring dust.[67]

Only loving intimates would have put up with Tennyson's behaviour over Emily Sellwood. There were mitigating circumstances – his fame was burgeoning, the very long engagement had been deliberately kept secret from most of his friends so that the general astonishment which would now greet the news was something he was temperamentally unable to deal with, and he was clearly intensely apprehensive, indeed panicked, once the prospect of losing his liberty and uniting himself for life to another person became a reality. He was, after all, over forty and in recent years had lived a life of complete freedom (if not complete independence) and – it is fair to say – wholehearted self-indulgence. Still, his behaviour is puzzling. He was a Lincolnshire man, marrying a Lincolnshire girl, from the home of Lincolnshire friends, albeit friends who had moved to Oxfordshire. Why did the marriage have to be kept away from his native county, and why were none of his own immediate family told that it was taking place? Why were none of them invited? He doted on his mother – all the Tennysons did – so how could he bring himself to keep her in the dark about the most important personal event of his life?

Perhaps the explanation is simply that he did not know how to cope with the fact that he was now well known, and felt in danger of being torn in pieces by the mindless curiosity of a mob. Some of the boon companions of his bachelor years were indignant about the secrecy. 'Come Forster, don't be angry with me,' he wrote to the well-known journalist and man-about-town John Forster, who was later to be Dickens's first biographer. 'If I had told others and left you alone in the dark, I grant you might with justice feel some indignation. I told nobody, not even her who had most right to be told, my own mother. She was not angry, why should you be? It is nothing but the shyness of my nature in everything that regards myself. I never kept my birthday yet, nor mentioned it, till it was over.' All of his friends must have felt that they had equal right to such explanation. Perhaps in retrospect Tennyson was feeling that his secretiveness had not been such a good idea, but he had to make the best of it now that the thing was done. 'Doubt not my regard for you,' he begged Forster, 'and make allowance for my idiosyncracies however strange they may seem.'

Robert Monteith, the Apostle and Trinity man, sent a much more conventional and acceptable letter of congratulation. The tone of Tennyson's response to him is one of relief; here was at least one friend who showed no sign of feeling offended:

> I thank you and Mrs Monteith very heartily for your kind messages. There is even some chance that soon I may thank you in person; for I have left the whole eastern coast of Scotland unvisited and last year when I left you it was my intention to return and complete my tour. [. . .] I have married a lady only four years younger than myself who has loved me and prayed for my earthly and spiritual welfare for fourteen years. God grant that we may get on well together. I am sure if we do not the fault will be mine.

This is not false humility – he was genuinely worried about the married state: 'I have lived so long unmarried that I may have crystallized into batchelorhood [*sic*] beyond redemption: then I hope that I have yet some plasticity left.'[68]

Edmund Peel, a poet and a cousin of Robert Peel, had been a friend of Tennyson's since the mid 1840s, and a warm supporter of the pension awarded by his cousin to Tennyson in 1845. From June 1846 there survives a remarkable 'Extempore Sonnet' written jointly by Tennyson, Edmund Peel and a play-writing clergyman called White, following a visit that Tennyson made to the Isle of Wight. Tennyson's opening lines to this confection refer to the three of them as 'Two poets and a mighty dramatist' who 'threaded the Needles on a day in June'; in other words they took a rowing boat round the somewhat perilous west point of the island. Tennyson's health had been poor ('ricketty', in Fitzgerald's phrase) and Moxon had arranged for him to take this holiday. It was a kind of post-Apostolic holiday, three men behaving like undergraduates taking a break.[69] This same Edmund Peel saw Tennyson immediately before his marriage, but was told nothing about the impending event. When the news reached him, he sent a slightly malicious letter about it to a friend:

> Alfred is married!!! The lady, who is described to me as a very nice person, not handsome nor the reverse – and not with money nor absolutely without, is the Sister of his brother Charles' wife, her name Silwood. Charles Weld, the Secretary of the Royal Society, married another Sister. Alfred's wife has had indifferent health, and indeed (like the lady Browning married) has passed half her life hitherto on the sofa – but marriage is often a restorer.

Peel went on to quote Edmund Lushington, who as a guest at the wedding obviously knew the situation better than he did: 'The only anecdote told, in connection with any public announcement of the affair, was mentioned to me on Sunday by Lushington, who says that Alfred will gladly give 7/6 out of his limited income (for a married man) to every penny-a-liner who will keep it *out of the papers*.'[70]

Tennyson had clearly understood the appeal of his earlier image – long-haired, Spanish-looking, Cambridge-educated penniless romantic vagrant. Leaving Lincolnshire would never be a complete process: during the period in the 1830s when he and Emily were still exchanging love letters, he wrote an extraordinarily evocative letter to her about his feelings for the county. The letter probably dates from 1838:

> I have dim mystic sympathies with tree and hill reaching far back into childhood. A known landskip is to me an old friend, that continually talks to me of my own youth and half-forgotten things, and does more for me than many an old friend that I know. An old park is my delight and I could tumble about in it for ever.[71]

The Lincolnshire self was now put behind him, despite the fact that central relationships that lasted the whole of his life – with Emily and with the Rawnsleys – had begun there. Lincolnshire was provincial, and Tennyson in the 1850s was now embarked on an upward trajectory through the Victorian social system, which meant in practice that his ambitions would be centred in London (though he never made his main home there). From 1850 onwards he was clearly a 'gentleman', and he reinforced and entrenched this status for the next thirty years.

* * *

The masterpiece of 1850, *In Memoriam*, was a Lincolnshire poem which said goodbye to Lincolnshire. It put Tennyson's provincial self into a national and historical perspective. Section XI – a poem of prodigious technical skill, comprising a single sentence extending over five stanzas in which the word 'calm' expressed both the peace of the natural world and the stillness of death – displayed the familiar landscape:

> Calm and deep peace on this high wold,
>> And on these dews that drench the furze,
>> And all the silvery gossamers
> That twinkle into green and gold:
>
> Calm and still light on yon great plain
>> That sweeps with all its autumn bowers,
>> And crowded farms and lessening towers,
> To mingle with the bounding main.[72]

The three Christmases that provided the chronological frame for the elegy for Hallam also marked the retreat from Lincolnshire. The first two, XXVII and LXXVIII, were set in the Somersby rectory, where Tennyson's sister Emily grieved for her lost lover and Tennyson himself grieved for his lost friend. The third, CIV and CV, is set in High Beech, Epping, the home to which the Tennysons had moved when they had to leave Somersby in 1837. This was 'new unhallowed ground'; unhallowed both because there were no memories of Arthur in this setting, and also, poignantly, because Dr Tennyson lay in his grave in Somersby outside the church where he had served, and immediately opposite his former rectory. While they still lived there, his wife and children could see his simple memorial every day. Now, in Epping:

> We live within the stranger's land,
> And strangely falls our Christmas-eve.
>
> Our father's dust is left alone
>> And silent under other snows:
>> There in due time the woodbine blows,
> The violet comes, but we are gone.[73]

Poems C to CIII of *In Memoriam* recorded the deep sadness that was stirred in Tennyson when the day came to leave Somersby in 1837. The whole landscape recalled Arthur Hallam to him:

> I climb the hill: from end to end
> Of all the landscape underneath,
> I find no place that does not breathe
> Some gracious memory of my friend.

Leaving this physical landscape brought back with sharp immediacy the fact of Hallam's death ('I think once more he seems to die'). On the last night that they slept in the old home, Tennyson had a dream, a very vivid one, which he recorded in CIII. The figure of Arthur Hallam appeared to him as a giant figure on a ceremonial ship, surrounded by female mourners. (The whole scene seemed to anticipate the elaborate visual accounts of King Arthur's funeral ship in 'Morte d'Arthur' and *Idylls of the King*.) Tennyson embraced Arthur, 'fell in silence on his neck', and the ship with its mourners and its reunited friends set slowly out to sea. Since poem IX, the agonising fact of Arthur's death had been associated with ships, so that it was appropriate that a kind of resolution of the physical grief for him should take this form. The grief is for Somersby as well, for the leaving of Somersby and for the loss of the old Lincolnshire family life. Now that the Tennysons had to leave, the garden, the brook, the surrounding woods and the whole landscape would be 'unloved' and 'uncared for'. This group of poems marked Tennyson's reconciliation with change. The familiar garden would become 'Familiar to the stranger's child', and the whole landscape would continue to renew itself as the natural world inevitably must. In these poems there was pleasure and relief, as well as pain, in the recollection of the day that he left Lincolnshire.[74]

The middle year of Tennyson's life, 1850, was also the midpoint of a two-part story. Part one could be called 'local boy makes good'; the lad from Lincolnshire published *In Memoriam* in May, he was married in June, he was appointed Laureate at the end of the year. In short, he had arrived. Part two could be called 'consolidation and decline'; in the big ambitious Laureate enterprises, *Idylls of the King* and his Shakespeare-like history plays, he bought into the identity of the 'national poet' and tailored his works to fit that identity and the market that came with it. Still, there can be no doubt that in these works he also remained substantially true to himself. As a child and adolescent he had established a body of literary interests, rooted in his reading of Shakespeare and Malory, to which he would constantly return to nourish his later writing. This imaginative reservoir never failed him. It helped him to use his prodigious fluency as a bulwark against the undoubted fact that from 1870 onwards the tide of opinion would turn against him. Younger minds, in league with figures in literary London who had become enemies for commercial reasons, worked to demolish the monument that Tennyson had become. They would fail because his central core was unassailable.

CHAPTER 6

In Memoriam, marriage and the Laureateship, 1850–1854

My heart, though widowed, may not rest
Quite in the love of what is gone,
But seeks to beat in time with one
That warms another living breast.

The writing of *In Memoriam* had taken a total of seventeen years. Between 1833 and 1849 Tennyson had been itinerant, restless and financially anxious, often depressed, sometimes physically as well as mentally ill, and seen by some of his friends as wasting his talent. But throughout this period the elegiac verses for Hallam had been steadily accumulating.

The great poem that resulted from this bereavement was as much about the poet as it was about the ostensible subject of the poem. This is true of many elegies: it is certainly true of two of Tennyson's models, Milton's *Lycidas* and Shelley's *Adonais*. Tennyson's working titles were 'fragments of an elegy' and 'the way of the soul'; the latter phrase is closer to the poem's central preoccupation. Tennyson the clergyman's son, although neither a devout Christian nor a regular churchgoer, was stirred to the depth of his soul by this intolerable loss. Sir Charles Tennyson summarised the questions raised by Hallam's death: 'Could it really be that all this great spiritual treasure was annihilated: that all human love and all man's spiritual effort are but a momentary ripple on the ocean of eternity? Was the world wholly without purpose and man an irresponsible toy for the gigantic forces of Nature? If so, what value could there be in life? What was left but to curse God and die?'[1] These are questions about Tennyson himself, not just about his dead friend.

The major manuscripts of *In Memoriam* are in 'butcher's books', one now in Trinity College, Cambridge, and the other in the Tennyson Research Centre at Lincoln. They are both dated 1842, but it seems certain that Trinity precedes Lincoln (or as Christopher Ricks puts it, that it was in 1842 that the Lincoln MS took over from the Trinity MS).[2] The Lincoln book duplicates much of the Trinity book but seems to incorporate also a draft of the poem as it existed in 1848.

The manuscripts show that lyric number IX, beginning 'fair ship', was the first part of the elegy to be written down. In John Heath's commonplace book in the Fitzwilliam Museum in Cambridge, there is a copy of it dated '6 Oct 1833', almost certainly the actual day on which news of Arthur's death reached the rectory at Somersby. The poem was written out among other poems, drafts of Arthurian romance, related lyrics, comic items drawn from the *Arabian Nights* – these notebooks are not organised, they are an engaging young man's muddle, with a good deal of daydreaming and doodling in among the poetry. There are a great many drawings, especially sketches – seemingly inconsequential, and made for no particular purpose – of hands and feet. Some of these are on pages facing the most poignant lyrics from the elegy, as though Tennyson needed to take his mind off the painful task, to stop focusing for a while and engage in restful play.

'On a mourner', a poem which was clearly part of his original intense grief in 1833, is not in the *In Memoriam* ABBA stanza form, despite the fact that it appears in this draft of the elegy. A fair copy of it also appears in the Heath MS at Cambridge (and is a slightly revised draft). It is personal and exposed in its expression of feeling, and Tennyson was wary of showing it to anyone. It remained unknown for over thirty years, and was finally published in 1865. Even then, its most personal expressions of grief – two stanzas – remained suppressed. Nature is the imagined figure, the poem records her actions in response to the poet's bereavement. In the two cancelled stanzas she speaks to the mourner:

> 'Come, beat a little quicker now,
>   When all things own my quickening breath:
> Thy friend is mute: his brows are low:
>   But I am with thee till thy death.'
> Some such kind words to me she saith.
>
> Yet is she mortal even as I,
>   Or as that friend I loved in vain:
> She only whispering low or high,
>   Through this vast cloud of grief and pain
>   I had not found my peace again.[3]

It might be thought that, in the nineteenth-century world of Christian piety, Tennyson would find comfort in faith and a belief in the Christian afterlife. Alternatively, he might have been driven by anger and grief further into the realms of intellectual doubt that were opening up as scientific discoveries, notably in geology, challenged traditional Christian belief. *In Memoriam* veers between the two – between Christian values and the exciting new thinking associated with the natural world. Famously, in lyric XCVI, Tennyson wrote a line that can be seen as a heading for his own state of mind as a young man and, equally, as the state of mind of many intelligent and scrupulous figures who felt battered by the storms of religious controversy. The poet, himself deeply troubled, consults his recollection of his dead friend to imagine what Arthur would have said, and this is the reply: 'There lives more faith in honest doubt / Believe me, than in half the creeds.' There is a cancelled lyric* which could well have been intended to follow XCVI, since it develops the theme of Hallam's 'doubts':

> He was too good and kind and sweet,
> 　Even when I knew him in his hour
> 　Of darkest doubt, and in his power,
> To fling his doubts into the street.
>
> Our modern authors young and vain
> 　Must print or preach their doubts aloud
> 　And blurt to every passing crowd
> Those indigestions of the brain.

This lyric has further stanzas, rebuking the popular press and the open scepticism and cynicism of an unheeding public: 'we that are not kind or just / We scatter seeds that spring in flame, / Or bear their fruit in London's shame – / The Sabbath journal mixt with lust.'[4]

　The Trinity College butcher's book was annotated by James Spedding. This MS is partially mutilated: Hallam Tennyson, when working on his *Memoir* of his father in the 1890s, deliberately cut away many of Spedding's comments. It is not at all clear what principle of selection was operating, since the comments that survive are unexceptionable, intelligent and very helpful – and Tennyson acted on several of them. On lyric LVII, Hallam left the whole of Spedding's annotation on the lower half of the sheet. This lyric, 'Peace; come away: the song of woe / Is after all an earthly song', had five stanzas in the MS whereas in the published state it has four. Spedding's note in the Trinity MS reads:

---

*There are a number of lyrics that Tennyson decided not to use in the final version. This one is not in the *In Memoriam* MSS at all, but is part of a MS of *The Princess* (Cambridge University Library), and dates from about 1849.

It seems to me that the 3d stanza is not wanted, and would be better cut. The second does not quite please me. I would like it better if it contained a simple expression of fear that these songs are too perishable to preserve the memory of their subject – Something in this way – 'The songs in which I build a shrine for his memory will soon die away in men's ears. They cannot perpetuate his name – yet in these ears &c' With this exception I think it beautiful.

Tennyson therefore cut the stanza, which had read as follows:

> So might it last and guard thy dust
> For ever! would indeed for this,
> My skill were greater than it is!
> But let it be. The years are just.

This lyric, LVII, seems to have been intended as the closing lyric of the poem as it stood in the Trinity manuscript. How would we feel about the whole elegy if it ended here with 'peace, come away'? One obvious answer is that we would be left with a sense of stoic grieving in the face of irreversible and irredeemable loss. The poem functions as elegy traditionally does, but with a variant. There are fitting memorials for the dead friend, but the poet cannot claim that his own poem will be one of them:

> Methinks my friend is richly shrined;
> But I shall pass; my work will fail.

The lines also refer to Christian mourning – the tolling of a church bell – but then abruptly replace that with the Roman phrase for farewell to the dead:

> Yet in these ears, till hearing dies,
> One set slow bell will seem to toll
> The passing of the sweetest soul
> That ever looked with human eyes.
>
> I hear it now, and o'er and o'er,
> Eternal greetings to the dead;
> And 'Ave, Ave, Ave,' said,
> 'Adieu, adieu' for evermore.

With this ending we would have experienced a clean, swift, decisive close to this young life. At one level that would be invigorating, like a cold plunge into the sea. After telling the story of his first four years of mourning, 1833 to 1837, this seems to have been Tennyson's provisional conclusion: the past is past, put it away and move on. Instead, though, he clung to the poem, revisiting, embellishing, amplifying and reconsidering. The action – the movement – embodied in 'peace, come away' was rejected as an option, and replaced by the eddying and circling of the mind round its central pain. The poet moved from writing about the dead and his own grief and chose consciously to make loss and mourning into the occasion of a meditation on the universal theme of undeserved suffering and unexplained early death.

Tennyson's two early lyrics about Lazarus, XXXI and XXXII, were originally one long one, probably written in 1833. 'He was dead, and there he sits': the poem aches with its wish that Arthur could be raised from the dead, like Lazarus; that Arthur would suddenly be there looking normal and sitting quietly in an unremarkable domestic setting, as he had so often sat and talked with Tennyson.* Leonée Ormond has pointed out that Tennyson was almost certainly thinking of a large painting in the National Gallery which he knew well and greatly admired: Sebastiano del Piombo's *The Raising of Lazarus*. Hallam Tennyson remembered that he and Lionel were taken on regular summer visits to the National Gallery by their father, who 'always led the way first of all to the "Raising of Lazarus"';[5] and the Tennysons had a reproduction of this painting over the mantelpiece at Farringford.[6] The painter's subject is 'the borderline between living and dead, and between human and divine'. Tennyson's familiarity with the painting contributes to the imaginative creation of XXXI, 'where he tries to evoke the experience of Lazarus, recalled from the grave among a mass of his fellow townsmen':[7]

> 'Where wert thou, brother, those four days?'
>   There lives no record of reply,

---

*Robert Browning also wrote about the raising of Lazarus in his dramatic monologue of 1855, 'An Epistle Containing the Strange Medical Experience of Karshish, the Arab Physician'. Like Tennyson, Browning brings out the blank wonder and the pressing questions raised by this miracle: 'the man's own firm conviction rests / That he was dead (in fact they buried him) / -That he was dead and then restored to life / By a Nazarene physician of his tribe: / – 'Sayeth, the same bade "Rise" and he did rise.' (Ian Jack and Robert Inglesfield, eds, *The Poetical Works of Robert Browning: Vol. 5, Men and Women*, Oxford: Clarendon Press, 1995, p. 93.) J. R. Watson has pointed out to me that in the Lazarus lyrics Tennyson put his finger on a sensitive place in Victorian religious thought: *what happens* after death? Will we see our loved ones again? Is there a heaven? Biblical criticism and geology had thrown doubt on these things. Lazarus must have known the answers, but he did not report what he saw; or, if he did report it, what he said was not written down by St John and has been lost.

> Which telling what it is to die
> Had surely added praise to praise.
>
> From every house the neighbours met,
>   The streets were filled with joyful sound,
>   A solemn gladness even crowned
> The purple brows of Olivet.
>
> Behold a man raised up by Christ!
>   The rest remaineth unrevealed;
>   He told it not; or something sealed
> The lips of that Evangelist.[8]

The violent sense of loss was tempered in lyric LXXXV, also drafted soon after Arthur's death (thus 1833–4) but later much revised and extended. The earliest stanzas express the shock of absolute bleak loss:

> My blood an even tenor kept,
>   Till on mine ear this message falls,
>   That in Vienna's fatal walls[9]
> God's finger touched him, and he slept.

Most of the revisions are from 1842, the year of Edmund Lushington's marriage to Tennyson's sister Cecilia. This lyric can be taken as a model or template for the whole long elegy, and is remarkable for its reflectiveness on the impact of grief, the mourning process and the possible modes of recovery. One such mode has to do with finding another friend who could come close to occupying Arthur's place in Tennyson's feelings. The earliest state of the poem – 1834 – said nothing about a friend to replace the dead, but as the poem expanded, so Edmund Lushington came to occupy that space. It is Lushington who is addressed in the second stanza of LXXXV:

> O true in word, and tried in deed,
>   Demanding, so to bring relief
>   To this which is our common grief,
> What kind of life is that I lead.

And it is Lushington whose friendship is giving the poet a revival of feeling and a sense of new hope as the long lyric approaches its close:

My pulses therefore beat again
    For other friends that once I met;
    Nor can it suit me to forget
The mighty hopes that make us men.

I woo your love: I count it crime
    To mourn for any overmuch;
    I, the divided half of such
A friendship as had mastered Time.

Majestic though that friendship was, the lyric acknowledged the poet's
need to move on, emotionally.

My heart, though widowed, may not rest
    Quite in the love of what is gone,
    But seeks to beat in time with one
That warms another living breast.

Ah, take the imperfect gift I bring,
    Knowing the primrose yet is dear,
    The primrose of the later year,
As not unlike to that of Spring.[10]

The grieving process and the gradual acceptance of loss have never
been better described.

The epilogue is an epithalamion, a marriage poem, celebrating this
same friend's – Lushington's – marriage to Cecilia Tennyson.

In a piece published after Tennyson's death in *Nineteenth Century*
(1893), the architect and writer James Knowles recalled a conversation
with the poet following a reading of *In Memoriam*. Tennyson had said
of the poem:

> It is rather the cry of the whole human race than mine. In the poem
> altogether private grief swells out into thought of, and hope for, the
> whole world. It begins with a funeral and ends with a marriage – begins
> with death and ends in promise of a new life – a sort of *Divine Comedy*,
> cheerful at the close. It is a very impersonal poem as well as personal.[11]

Tennyson was speaking some forty years after the poem's first
publication, and with the benefit of this long retrospect was giving it
a shape rather more tidy than the sum of all the individual lyrics actually warrants. Still, there is no doubt that as a description of the poem's

large structure, rather than of its finely grained detail, this is true to the reader's experience. The terrible grief and anguish of the first part, leading to the first of the poem's three Christmases (the first Christmas following Hallam's death, that of 1833; lyric XXVIII), moves on to rage with the whole order of things (and with whatever deity may be held responsible for that order) in lyrics L to LVI, and to the numbed resignation of the second Christmas (lyric LXXVIII).

Between the second and third Christmases the poem works at the therapeutic task of recovering specific memories of Hallam in particular places (Somersby and Cambridge especially). Lyric XCI beautifully associates Hallam's memory with the cycle of the seasons:

> When rosy plumelets tuft the larch,
>   And rarely pipes the mounted thrush;
>   Or underneath the barren bush
> Flits by the sea blue bird of March;*
>
> Come, wear the form by which I know
>   Thy spirit in time among thy peers;
>   The hope of unaccomplished years
> Be large and lucid round thy brow.
>
> When summer's hourly-mellowing change
>   May breathe, with many roses sweet,
>   Upon the thousand waves of wheat,
> That ripple round the lonely grange;
>
> Come: not in watches of the night,
>   But where the sunbeam broodeth warm,
>   Come, beauteous in thine after form,
> And like a finer light in light.[12]

Hallam's spirit, formerly figured as a dream, a troubling vision, or a vanished hand, is now evoked as a happy memory of how the young man looked in life. He has become part of the spring and summer sunshine. The mourner is coming to terms with his grief.

The third Christmas, in lyric CIV, is the first winter following the family's move away from Somersby; and a lyric succeeding it, CVI, presenting the New Year of 1838, marks a turning-point in which the mourner looks forward, not back:

---

*Tennyson: 'The Kingfisher. I used to see him in our brook first in March.'

> Ring out the old, ring in the new,
>> Ring, happy bells, across the snow:
>> The year is going, let him go;
> Ring out the false, ring in the true.

The Christian festival of the birth of Christ is juxtaposed with a wholly secular treatment of the birth of Arthur Hallam, which follows in lyric CVII.

> It is the day when he was born,
>> A bitter day that early sank
>> Behind a purple-frosty bank
> Of vapour, leaving night forlorn.

The natural world is leaden and frozen while his friends remember him:

> We keep the day. With festal cheer,
>> With books and music, surely we
>> Will drink to him, whate'er he be,
> And sing the songs he loved to hear.[13]

This process has been necessarily slow and deliberate, which is one reason for *In Memoriam*'s length. The coldest day of this imagined year, 1 February 1811, Hallam's birthday, is balanced by the magical warmth that pervades Lyric CXV ('Now fades the last long streak of snow'). Life renews itself. This fact is now part of the mourner's felt experience:

> Now dance the lights on lawn and lea,
>> The flocks are whiter down the vale,
>> And milkier every milky sail
> On winding stream or distant sea;

> Where now the seamew pipes, or dives
>> In yonder greening gleam, and fly
>> The happy birds, that change their sky
> To build and brood; that live their lives

> From land to land; and in my breast
>> Spring wakens too; and my regret
>> Becomes an April violet,
> And buds and blossoms like the rest.[14]

This sequence is pulled together into the concluding poem, the Epithalamion, which buoyantly affirms a sense of renewal. The whole poem is addressed to Edmund Lushington. In the absence of their dead father, Alfred Tennyson's role at this wedding was to give away the bride, his little sister. The sense of recovery and of the cycle of life is expressed starkly here; at the moment of her marriage, the young bride is standing on a medieval gravestone:

> For I that danced her on my knee,
> That watched her on her nurse's arm,
> That shielded all her life from harm
> At last must part with her to thee;
>
> Now waiting to be made a wife,
> Her feet, my darling, on the dead;
> Their pensive tablets round her head,
> And the most living words of life
>
> Breathed in her ear [. . .] [15]

As all readers of *In Memoriam* know, one conspicuous feature of the poem is its attempt to reconcile orthodox Christianity with geology. The 'evolutionary' sections of the poem, LI to LVI, have been much discussed, and have been related to Tennyson's knowledge of recent findings about the history of the earth. The Scottish geologist Charles Lyell had published *Principles of Geology* in 1830–3; its subtitle made clear that it addressed the present day, it was 'an attempt to explain the former changes of the earth's surface, by reference to causes now in operation'. In this bold project Lyell was at odds both with those rival geologists who argued for ancient catastrophic events determining the appearance of the earth, and with the clergy who still controlled learning in the ancient universities, Oxford and Cambridge, and who sought to accommodate the new findings with the story of creation given in the Bible.

William Buckland, Professor of Geology at Oxford and also a canon of Christ Church, was among the clergy whose control of learning Lyell opposed. As an undergraduate, Lyell had venerated Buckland. Despite the fact that his degree was in the classics and his first career was in law, he had listened eagerly to Buckland's lectures on geology. Later, when Lyell had moved from his career as a lawyer to become a leading geologist, his work effectively challenged Buckland and any other clergy who worked in geology.

Geology in the 1830s was the most exciting of the sciences, and Lyell's work was part of the excitement. He proclaimed the centrality of geology, 'intimately related to almost all the physical sciences, as history to the moral'.[16] He dismissed the belief (held by Buckland) that the earth could yield fossil evidence of the Flood. Lyell wanted 'to free the science from Moses'.[17] He argued persuasively that the earth's present features were the consequences of a steady accumulation of small changes, and that the 'catastrophe' was a myth.

An intensely sensitive point of disagreement between the Christian creationists and the radical geologists was this: did the fossil evidence indicate the succession of species or the mutation of species (could man be descended from the apes)? Charles Lyell's reading of the fossil record was that the species succeeded each other; as one became extinct, another would emerge to fill its niche in the natural order. He left open the question of whether change could take place within a 'type' or species of creature. In Tennyson's verses it is never clear that he had absorbed or was reflecting the daring notion that species could *mutate.**

The famous jagged lyrics in *In Memoriam* which displayed the conflict between religion and science at its sharpest coexisted uneasily with the more settled lyrics which tried to smooth over the differences between the secular and the Christian readings of the nature of the earth. Thus the lyric in which the ape and the tiger and the sensual feast were left behind by increasingly civilised and cultivated mankind had based itself on reconciliation of what in the 1830s were opposites. Lyric CXVIII is not in the Trinity MS of the poem so can be assumed to belong to the period of composition after 1842.

Tennyson was still working on these sections of *In Memoriam* when he read an even more combative geological work by another Scot, the brilliant journalist Robert Chambers's *Vestiges of the Natural History of Creation*, published anonymously in 1844 (it remained anonymous until his authorship was finally acknowledged in the 1884 edition).[18] This work was sensational in its challenge to Christianity. The harsh scepticism of some of Tennyson's lyrics is consonant with the tone of the gauntlet thrown down by Chambers.

---

*It is possible that N. A. Rupke, in an influential study of nineteenth-century science (see Bibliography), was right to say that Tennyson was more orthodox than he appeared, and that in some ways he had not progressed far beyond the writings of William Paley that he had been required to read as an undergraduate. In Paley's *Natural Theology* (1802), the natural world and fossil record rapidly being unearthed at that date were evidence of a grand design, and were therefore consonant with the notion of an omnipotent creator.

Robert Chambers (1802–71), brother of the William Chambers who founded *Chambers' Edinburgh Journal* in 1832, was a journalist and publisher rather than a scientist by training; nevertheless his *Vestiges of the Natural History of Creation* was a learned work which argued that the Christian notion of a single divine act of creation was irrelevant, since both the development of all life forms and the origin of life itself could be explained by scientific laws. It was vigorously attacked by geologists and by the clergy; Adam Sedgwick, both a geologist and a clergyman, declared in a review that 'unmitigated contempt, scorn and ridicule are the weapons to be used'[19] against this dangerous book. There was wide speculation about its authorship; Pauline, Lady Trevelyan,[20] Harriet Martineau and Prince Albert were all considered as possible secret authors of this work.

The centrepiece of the revolutionary theory, that species must mutate by natural selection, which already existed in Darwin's notebooks in 1832, was of course not published by Darwin until 1859. But the daring possibility that man might be the product of mutation (and therefore obviously not created by God in God's image) was already being excitedly discussed by geologists in the 1830s, and is the liberating idea tentatively explored in Chambers's anonymous book of 1844. While not wholly excluding the notion of a creator, Chambers was clear that man belonged to a line of primates who had developed 'sociality, vocality or the use of voice, a prehensive use of the extremities, imitativeness, drollery, sagacity, all from characteristics generally applicable to this line of animals'.[21] He wrote of climate change permitting the development of new species which 'branched off' from a small group into the huge diversity that so fascinated geologists and naturalists of the period.

In his *Memoir*, Hallam Tennyson stated that the evolutionary lyrics in the elegy all pre-dated Chambers: he was eager to guard his father's claims to originality.[22] In lyric L, Time was 'a maniac scattering dust', and in LV and LVI Nature had become God's adversary, but here Time and Nature – both still capitalised in an eighteenth-century manner – are tamed:

> Contemplate all this work of Time,
> The giant labouring in his youth;
> Nor dream of human love and truth,
> As dying Nature's earth and lime;

[. . .]   They say,
The solid earth whereon we tread

In tracts of fluent heat began,
    And grew to seeming-random forms,
    The seeming prey of cyclic storms,
Till at the last arose the man;

Who throve and branched from clime to clime,
    The herald of a higher race,
    And of himself in higher place [. . .][23]

    It was Arthur himself, of course, who was this herald, and thus an embodiment of the future of creation. This future would also represent the moral salvation of the race. Tennyson made this even more explicit in his epilogue, which was a more extended response to Chambers. Here Tennyson constructed a narrative of the emergence of a perfect man, of whom Arthur himself was the forerunner. The whole activity of the universe existed for this one end. Its mechanisms will, in the future, produce a soul, which will,

[. . .] moved through life of lower phase,
    Result in man, be born and think,
    And act and love, a closer link
Betwixt us and the crowning race

[. . .] No longer half-akin to brute,
    For all we thought and loved and did,
    And hoped, and suffered, is but seed
Of what in them is flower and fruit;

Whereof the man, that with me trod
    This planet, was a noble type,
    Appearing ere the times were ripe,
That friend of mine who lives in God.[24]

The grandeur of this, and its high ecclesiastical tone, may well leave us scurrying back through the text of the elegy looking for tension, conflict and personality. The 'Epilogue' is in no sense a conclusion to the whole poem. Its function, taken together with the loudly Christian 'Prologue' ('Strong son of God, immortal Love', and so on), is to provide a decorous frame for this troubled and turbulent series of texts, full of cares and problems, but rising at times to moments of great poignancy and beauty.

Arthur's many letters to Tennyson became the centrepiece of lyric XCV, set in the garden of Somersby probably in 1836, in very hot weather. Tennyson and his family and friends remembered Arthur. The rest of the company then went to bed, but Tennyson stayed out alone in the hot night, and decided to re-read Arthur's letters:

> So, word by word, and line by line,
>   The dead man touched me from the past,
>   And all at once it seemed at last
> His living soul was flashed on mine,
>
> And mine in his was wound, and whirled
>   About empyreal heights of thought,
>   And came on that which is, and caught
> The deep pulsations of the world.

Recalling Somersby as it was in the year before the family left it, Tennyson wrote this passage in 1841. For the 1872 edition of the poem he changed it, slightly but significantly. 'His living soul was flashed on mine' became 'The living soul', while 'And mine in his was wound' became 'And mine in this'. The second state is obviously less charged. The first longs for a physical embrace (though an embrace between two souls).[25] Tennyson changed it 'as perhaps giving a wrong impression'. He may have been recalling Arthur Hallam's anxiety about the Apostles possibly 'misunderstanding' love between men as set out as an ideal in Plato's *Phaedrus* and *Symposium*. We can see him avoiding similar 'misunderstanding' in the changes to XCIII, where 'Stoop soul & touch me: wed me: hear / The wish too strong for words to name' was changed to 'Descend, and touch and enter; hear / The wish' etc.. In lyric LXXXIX 'some Platonic dream' was changed to 'Socratic dream' (presumably because 'Platonic' in itself could signify homosexual). He would have been sensitive to the anxiety that Arthur's father felt about what he saw as the excessive tenderness towards another man expressed in Shakespeare's sonnets (which his dead son had so loved and admired).[26]

As it stood, lyric LVII closed off the most sceptical sections of the poem (those on evolution as it was understood in the 1830s – that is, poems L to LVI). The revisions and meditations yielded much more writing that had to do with Tennyson's anxiety and embarrassment over the extent to which it was permissible for him to acknowledge his own 'honest doubt'. In other words, he revised partly in order to bring Christianity and science into some kind of alignment with each other. I am referring here to a struggle which occupies many of the famous lyrics in the poem. The most openly sceptical of the lyrics, LV and LVI, were not in the Trinity MS but are known to have been written in response to Tennyson 's reading of Charles Lyell (in 1836). So if we assume that he was writing in the late 1830s, we have a situation in which God and Nature were at loggerheads:

> Are God and Nature then at strife,
>   That Nature lends such evil dreams?
>   So careful of the type she seems,
> So careless of the single life;

In lyric LVI, Nature, as revealed by the geologists of the period, was a heartless, ruthless machine. Man would become extinct, like the dinosaurs, and there was no help for it.

> And he, shall he,

> Man, her [that is, Nature's] last work, who seemed so fair,
>   Such splendid purpose in his eyes,
>   Who rolled the psalm to wintry skies,
> Who built him fanes of fruitless prayer,

> Who trusted God was love indeed
>   And love Creation's final law –
>   Though Nature, red in tooth and claw
> With ravine, shrieked against his creed –

> Who loved, who suffered countless ills,
>   Who battled for the True, the Just,
>   Be blown about the desert dust,
> Or sealed within the iron hills?

> No more? A monster then, a dream,
>   A discord. Dragons of the prime,
>   That tare each other in their slime,
> Were mellow music matched with him.

Tennyson was worried about lyric LVI. It is violent and startling, and it represents the boldest of the whole elegy's challenges to organised religion. It was omitted from the trial printing of the poem early in 1850. We can assume that when Emily first read the poem in manuscript, she did not read this lyric. And indeed it could have troubled her, though she is not on record as saying so.

Lyell's book had included alarming phrases, which are clearly echoed here:

> The inhabitants of the globe, like all the other parts of it, are subject to change. It is not only the individual that perishes, but the whole species [. . .] Species cannot be immortal, but must perish, one after the other, like the individuals which compose them.[27]

Tennyson responded to, and indeed with a kind of sombre grandeur enjoyed, this cold observation of the natural world's deadliness and impersonality. The poem reflected, meditated, circled, and in the final sequence revisited this problem. In lyric CXVIII, it wanted to see Nature and Christianity as moving hand in hand towards a higher state of creation which would involve denying the animal in the self:

> Arise and fly
> The reeling Faun, the sensual feast;
> Move upward, working out the beast,
> And let the ape and tiger die.

It was a noble hope. It was less exciting, though, less engaging and less meaty (in all senses), than the celebrated violence of Nature 'red in tooth and claw'.

One model for Tennyson's great elegy was Milton's *Lycidas*, but Tennyson chose to write strikingly little of his poem in the pastoral mode, except for one section dating from the 1830s (on sheets which have become detached from the Trinity MS):

> I sing to him that rests below,
> And, since the grasses round me wave,
> I take the grasses of the grave,
> And make them pipes whereon to blow.

Figured as a shepherd here, the poet claims the privilege of innocence: 'I do but sing because I must, / And pipe but as the linnets sing' (XXI).

The convention had been appropriate to Milton's formal elegy, which was for a man he barely knew. In Tennyson, it sits oddly with the intense personal feeling that the poet was experiencing. The memory of the friendship with Hallam is translated briefly and awkwardly into classical pastoral: 'all the lavish hills would hum / The murmur of a happy Pan' in the days when 'many an old philosophy / On Argive heights divinely sang, / And round us all the thicket rang / To many a flute of Arcady.'[28]

Why does *In Memoriam* work as well it does? There is no clear chronology or narrative sequence to the poem; there is no sense of a large planned shape or firm structural control. Retrospectively Tennyson provided the poem with a scheme, but the reality is that this is partly irrelevant: the organising principle in this masterpiece is to be found neither in elegy for the dead friend, nor in the spiritual development of the sorrowing poet, nor in the sequence of three Christmases, nor in the many developing senses of the word 'Nature', but in the essential building block of the poem, the ABBA stanza form. Tennyson displayed astonishing versatility within the restrictions of this form.

Lyric V, a three-stanza lyric, tells us that language of mourning can never be more than approximate because words simultaneously convey and obstruct feeling. To declare the limitations of his own chosen method at such an early point in his elegy was a remarkably bold move.

> I sometimes hold it half a sin
> To put in words the grief I feel;
> For words, like Nature, half reveal
> And half conceal the soul within.

The tight patterning required by verse, though, can discipline and contain the anguish:

> But, for the unquiet heart and brain,
> A use in measured language lies;
> The sad mechanic exercise,
> Like dull narcotics, numbing pain.

Language surrounds feeling as the conventional dark dress worn by a mourner surrounds the human body:

> In words, like weeds, I'll wrap me o'er,
>   Like coarsest clothes against the cold:
>   But that large grief which these enfold
> Is given in outline, and no more.

The discursive anxiety of lyric V contrasts vividly with the bleak little narrative in lyric VII. This was written late in the process of composition, between 1848 and 1850, and in it Tennyson imagines himself visiting the Hallam family home, 67 Wimpole Street, where Henry Hallam was still living in the late 1840s.

> Dark house, by which once more I stand
>   Here in the long unlovely street,
>   Doors, where my heart was used to beat
> So quickly, waiting for a hand,
>
> A hand that can be clasped no more –
>   Behold me, for I cannot sleep,
>   And like a guilty thing I creep
> At earliest morning to the door.
>
> He is not here: but far away
>   The noise of life begins again,
>   And ghastly through the drizzling rain
> On the bald street breaks the blank day.[29]

The speaker himself is momentarily dead, a ghost ('a guilty thing' like the ghost of Hamlet's father). The monosyllables in the last line give it a weight and mass well beyond its actual metrical length (when read aloud, the line has to be delivered slowly), and the alliteration and onomatopoeia enact for the reader the drained emotional emptiness felt by the mourner. The massive emotional impact of this lyric is the fruit of its perfect technical control; the hand that cannot be touched recalls 'O for the touch of a vanished hand' in 'Break, break, break' (that poignantly direct response to Arthur's death, from the spring of 1834).[30]

The Apostolic years and the years of the close friendship inevitably take up a large part of the poem, and the language and thinking of the Apostles are everywhere in *In Memoriam*. The poem both meditates deeply on the nature of identity – that of the elegist, that of the dead friend, and that of the human species and its descent – and can be said to enact, in its eddying and ruminating stanza form, the process

of maturing from boy to man and discovering a sense of self. The
sense of immediate loss is agonising up until the first Christmas (lyrics
XXVII and XXVIII), when it broadens out into radical questioning of
the universe that has allowed such a disaster to happen; this despairing
phase closes with the second Christmas (LXXVIII). From that point
the mood becomes somewhat tempered, and in the third section the
elegist recovers precious memories of his dead friend and meditates
on these. After the third Christmas (CIV and CV) the elegy reconsiders
the anguished scepticism of the second section. The whole poem closes
with a compromise (a very uneasy one) between that state of mind
and orthodox Christianity.

In lyric LXXXVII, as part of the elaborate process of recovering
actual memories of Arthur Hallam (in what I have called the third
section), Tennyson revisited New Court at Trinity College and stood
outside Arthur Hallam's former rooms.

> Another name was on the door:
>   I lingered; all within was noise
>   Of songs, and clapping hands, and boys
> That crashed the glass and beat the floor;
>
> Where once we held debate, a band
>   Of youthful friends, on mind and art,
>   And labour, and the changing mart,
> And all the framework of the land.

The Apostles met on Saturday nights in the rooms of the 'moderator'
elected for the evening. Alcohol was strictly forbidden: for refreshment they drank tea and ate anchovies on toast ('whales'). The
moderator acted as host and also read out a short paper on a question or theme for the meeting. The meeting in Arthur's former rooms
that Tennyson recalls here must have been hosted by Arthur himself.
(Had Tennyson ever finished his paper on 'Ghosts', he might have
based lyric LXXXVII on a meeting in his own rooms rather than
Arthur Hallam's.)

Arthur's ascendancy among the group was seemingly effortless:

> And last the master-bowman, he,
>   Would cleave the mark. A willing ear
>   We lent him. Who, but hung to hear
> The rapt oration flowing free

From point to point, with power and grace
 And music in the bounds of law,
 To those conclusions when we saw
The God within him light his face,

And seem to lift the form, and glow
 In azure orbits heavenly-wise;
 And over those ethereal eyes
The bar of Michael Angelo.[31]

The last line refers to a feature to which Arthur liked to draw attention, with a kind of innocent vanity: a 'weighty bar, ridge-like, above
the eyebrows'. It was a feature of Michelangelo's statue of David – itself
in turn thought to be a self-portrait of the sculptor, and a physical
marker indicating genius.

A large number of lines from *In Memoriam* are immediately familiar:
'"Tis better to have loved and lost / Than never to have loved at all'
(lyric XXVII), 'Are God and Nature then at strife, / That Nature lends
such evil dreams?' (lyric LV), 'Nature, red in tooth and claw / With
ravine, shrieked against his creed' (lyric LVI), 'There lives more faith
in honest doubt, / Believe me, than in half the creeds' (lyric XCVI),
'Ring out, wild bells, to the wild sky, / The flying cloud, the frosty
light' (lyric CVI). These famous phrases reflect the elegy's major themes,
the story of personal bereavement and the linked story of the collision
between religion and science. The trigger was sheer outrage: what kind
of universe could have permitted Hallam's death to take place? Is belief
in a benevolent deity a comforting illusion, was it an error to trust
that 'God was love indeed', will man become like the dinosaurs an
extinct species, 'blown about the desert dust, / Or sealed within the
iron hills?' (lyric LVI).

The contemporary success of the poem was phenomenal but not
unaccountable. What did middle-class Victorians idealise and desire in
the 1850s? Fulfilment for them was closely aligned with the basics of
the Protestant ethic: prosperity, self-command, social standing (all that
was meant by the crucial word 'gentleman'), a degree of creativity and
recognition of creativity (the consequences of 'self-help', another crucial
phrase of the period), happiness in work (as Ruskin rightly said), and
other markers of esteem, well-being and security. A good family could
be at the heart of this, and, clearly, good sex was often at the heart
of the good family, but that obvious fact – despite the very large

number of children born to some Victorians, from the Queen down-wards – remained inexplicit. Fulfilment, for Tennyson, had to do with understanding the nature of the universe in which he lived and with being persuaded that the immortality of the individual soul was a practical fact rather than a comforting traditional doctrine. Both of these themes are of great importance in the elegy for Hallam. Is the beloved friend immortal? Is this belief tenable? Can one, by reiteration and by circling round the idea, make it feel true?

What Tennyson actually believed is hard to identify. It was certainly less straightforward than his wife's strong and grounded piety. If one thinks about three great autobiographical works published in 1850 – Wordsworth's *Prelude,* Dickens's *David Copperfield* and Tennyson's *In Memoriam* – one is struck by the coincidence of concerns in this *annus mirabilis* of English literature. Tennyson's 'honest doubt' coexisted with his troubled recognition that 'Nature, red in tooth and claw' does not endorse any orthodox Christian view of the creation of the world; Dickens's deep anxieties about his hero's moral and social orientation were reflected in a field of dramatic invention which contained people as weak and generous as Micawber and as wicked and sexually driven as Uriah Heep (David himself incorporated parts of both these men); Wordsworth's recognition that nature, the foster-mother, had reared him through both beauty and fear left little space for received Christian teaching within his poem. These three works are not explicitly Christian,* though *In Memoriam* has Christian 'bookends'. The Prologue and the Epilogue offer a Christian world-view which is questioned, with varying degrees of urgency, by the 131 lyrics that lie within this frame.

In Memoriam was published on 1 June 1850, and Tennyson was married to Emily Sellwood on the 13th. There is a sense in which both of these events were secretive: *In Memoriam* was published anony-mously, and although the poet's identity was an open secret from the day of publication, Tennyson always required that subsequent editions would not have his name on the title page. His marriage to Emily took place so secretly, with so much withholding of information from his friends and family, that it feels as though he was seeking to shield this personal event from the public gaze as he had sought to shield his own identity as the author of this intensely personal poem. And at the same time, of course, June 1850 marked a massive and decisive change

---

The Prelude in the state known to the Victorians – the 1850 text – was more Christian than is the version of the poem most read today, given that the work of scholars, editors and biographers now privileges the 1805 state as against that of 1850.

in his life in two ways: he became the most famous poet of the day, and he had finally committed himself to a lifelong relationship with the woman whom he had loved since 1834. It had taken him seventeen years to bring *In Memoriam* to publication and sixteen years to bring his courtship of Emily Sellwood to fruition. The vagrant and exotic poet, famous among his acquaintance for his inconsequential detachment from normal life, had dropped anchor.

The small volume was plain and understated in appearance, no author was named, and the title *In Memoriam A.H.H.* was cryptic; there was no note of explanation to identify the person commemorated or to explain his claim on posterity. However, Mudie's Select Library had announced on 29 May that fifty copies of Tennyson's new poem would be available on 1 June, and several of the reviewers commented on the fact that the author's identity was known in advance of the reviews being written. (The *Literary Gazette*'s reviewer, publishing on 15 June, *had* missed this advance information, since this very favourable review of the poem assumed that the writer was a woman.)[32] Sales took off strongly: 60,000 copies were sold by the end of the year.

The reviewers were largely unanimous in their support for this new work. As always, some of them were friends who could be relied upon to treat Tennyson's publications with close attention and a high level of respect. Franklin Lushington in *Tait's Edinburgh Magazine* and Coventry Patmore in the *Palladium* were both lavish with their praise, and G. H. Lewes, the partner of George Eliot, in his review in *The Leader* spoke of Tennyson as 'the greatest living poet', and praised the poem for its feeling and its deep expression of sorrow. In *The Examiner* another friend, John Forster, put the poem in extraordinarily exalted company (*Lycidas* and Shakespeare's sonnets). Surprisingly, he believed that *In Memoriam* would not become popular, while at the same time he accurately identified precisely those of its features that would soon speak personally to its many thousands of readers: it was 'a pathetic tale of real human sorrow' written with passion 'deep-felt throughout'.[33] The effect of the steadily unfolding praise over the summer was a double consolidation of Tennyson's position: he was both the major poet of the day and a writer who was at last fulfilling the intermittent indications of great promise that his previous publications had given. His hesitancy over publication between 1832 and 1842, and the tantalising absence since then of a major work other than *The Princess* in 1847, had created a hunger for his work. There was both timeliness and narrative appropriateness in the massive success that this great poem now enjoyed, in the middle year of the most powerful century that Britain had ever known.

* * *

Coventry Patmore, never one to be self-effacing, had visited Tennyson and Emily when they were on their honeymoon holiday. He stayed for some time and talked a great deal with Tennyson. Tennyson was willing to open up about the question of his religious beliefs in *In Memoriam*, but the version that he gave Patmore sounds as though it was carefully tailored to the listener. In August 1850 Patmore wrote to his wife about Tennyson:

> The more I talk with him the more I discover that I was right in thinking that he has given a defective notion of his faith in 'In Memoriam.' He is far above all the pantheistic 'religious faculty' humbug that taints so many half-geniuses in this day; and I am sure he would be horrified if he knew that any such men had been led by 'In Memoriam' to count him as a fellow-heathen.

Did Tennyson like Patmore's particular style of abject hero-worship? Presumably he did, though one cannot imagine that the kind of flattery that was laid on by Patmore – and would be laid on by many others over the years – was ever good for him. Patmore grovelled with obsequiousness. 'It is a great good to me to find that I have my superior, which I have never found in the company of anyone else,' he wrote. 'But in Tennyson I perceive a *nature* higher and wider than my own; at the foot of which I can sit happily and with love.'[34]

In March 1850, the Park House circle had been actively involved in the preparation of the elegy for publication: George Venables, continuing his devoted service to Tennyson, read and corrected the proof sheets between 5 and 13 March in London, and would have been sensitive to the considerable stretches of the poem which involved the Lushingtons. The two longest sections, lyric LXXXV and the epilogue, were addressed to Edmund Lushington: in LXXXV he is the friend who receives the poem 'O true in word and tried in deed', and in the epilogue he appears with virtually the same phrasing, 'O true and tried, so well and long'. There is a slight mystery here: Tennyson had written a note for publication confirming that lyric LXXXV was addressed to Edmund Lushington, but Hallam Tennyson would in due course suppress this note because some of the poem's manuscripts pre-dated the Lushington friendship. However, it seems certain that when the whole of LXXXV was assembled, Lushington was the addressee.

Within the poem the addressee, a tactful friend who is earnestly but gracefully concerned with Tennyson's welfare, resembles the Edmund

Lushington of numerous later letters to the poet. He questions Tennyson: 'Demanding, so to bring relief / To this which is our common grief, / What kind of life is that I lead.' Was Tennyson's 'trust in things above / [. . .] dimmed of sorrow, or sustained'? Had his love for Hallam 'drained' his 'capabilities of love'? The interrogator's words, lightly reproachful, 'half exprest', had 'virtue such as draws / a faithful answer from the breast'. Reassuringly, Tennyson replies that his pulses 'beat again' for 'other friends' and for the 'mighty hopes that make us men'. The 'widowed' heart 'may not rest / Quite in the love of what is gone, / But seeks to beat in time with one / That warms another living breast.' That other heartbeat could have belonged to any or all of several intimate friends in the Lushington circle. Tennyson's period of closest friendship, with Edmund, post-dated the broken engagement with Emily, but before the poem was finally published the engagement had been resumed.

This long poem, LXXXV, as finally patched together, is one of the least satisfactory of the sequence, barely achieving coherence. In the total argument of *In Memoriam*, though, it marks an important turning from despair toward regeneration. If Edmund is the primary person addressed, then Tennyson was deliberately associating him with the hope of a happier life, as he would certainly do in the Epilogue, which takes Edmund's marriage as its occasion.[35]

After their marriage, the Tennysons honeymooned at Tent Lodge, Coniston, home of the Marshalls (Jane Marshall was a sister of Tennyson's Cambridge friend Stephen Spring Rice), and Tennyson kept up constant correspondence with Lushington about the delight that he and Emily were taking in newly married life. Tennyson's friends, of course, discussed his marriage from their various perspectives. Carlyle, never lost for a pungent or memorable phrase, wrote to his wife early in October 1850:

The Tennysons are lodged in what they call 'the Cottage,' a plan similar to a Factor's House or Minister's Manse as I judged; one of the several little Properties which Marshall has bought as they fell in, 'to keep them out of bad hands.' There Alfred lives with his new better half, for the present; does not mean to stay above 'a couple of weeks' more: indeed I should judge it much more charming for the Marshalls than for him: 'Sir, we keeps a Poet!' Softest of soft sowder *plus* a vacant Cottage and to dinner as often as you like '*magna est pecunia et prevalebit.*' For the rest, Alfred looks really improved, I should say; cheerful in what he talks, and looking forward to a future less 'detached' than the past has been. Poor fellow, a *good* soul, find him where or how situated you may! Mrs T. also pleased me; the first glance of her is the least favourable. A freckly *round*-faced woman, rather tallish and without shape, a slight lisp too: something very *kleinstädtisch* [small town, provincial] and unpromising at first glance; but she lights up bright glittering blue eyes when you speak to her; has wit, has sense, and, were it not that she seems to be very delicate in health, 'sick *without* a disorder,' I should augur really well of Tennyson's adventure.[36]

Aubrey de Vere, shortly to be received into the Roman Catholic Church, saw Emily as a strong, supportive wife ('She thinks always of what is *good for him*') whose faith would be calming and transforming: 'piety like hers is infectious, especially where there is an atmosphere of affection to serve as a conducting medium. Indeed I already observe a great improvement in Alfred. His nature is a religious one, and he is remarkably free from vanity and sciolism.' Development of his religious nature had been impeded by Tennyson's friends: 'He has been surrounded, however, from his youth up, by young men, many of them with high aspirations, who believe no more in Christianity than in the Feudal system, and this no doubt has been a great hindrance to one with his strong sympathies.' But at the same time Emily was unlikely to become very close to de Vere, given her 'great horror of Rome'. Rome was a topic he barely felt able to discuss with her: 'only just enough to let her see that my views were different'.[37] If she had got to know him better, Emily would have agreed with de Vere about some of Tennyson's friends. She was never wholly comfortable with those who were open-minded about religious matters; sadly this included James Spedding, who was among the most loyal and steadfast of Tennyson's friends, as well as more relaxed and worldly men such as John Kemble or Monckton Milnes.

Tennyson and Emily left Coniston on 14 October. On this journey he had his first meeting with the young Matthew Arnold, who was their travelling companion as far as Crewe (as Emily recorded in her Journal).[38] Tennyson went on to visit his mother in Cheltenham, and by the end of October they were back at Park House for a stay of nearly three months, using the Lushingtons' house as the base for their own house-hunting.

Momentous recognition of Tennyson came to Park House on 9 November 1850, when he received a letter from Windsor Castle inviting him to succeed Wordsworth as Poet Laureate. He hesitated and brooded over this for four days, finally accepting on the 13th. In December of 1850 he was still at Park House, busily making revisions and corrections for new editions of *In Memoriam, The Princess* and the 1842 *Poems*. Henry Lushington had returned from Malta for the holiday season, and Tennyson may well have consulted him about these revisions.[39]

One striking aspect of the comparisons to be made between Tennyson's life and the lives of these friends is that he was focused, intensely focused, and continued to write his poetry while disaster affected everyone around him. Once married, he had a wife who devoted all her very considerable intelligence and energy to creating an environment in which his single-minded writing could continue uninterrupted. There is a very sad contrast to be made here between his marriage and that of his friend Edmund, whose wife – Tennyson's sister Cecilia – was a constant drain and anxiety throughout their many years together.

Finding a suitable place for himself as a married man was a struggle for Tennyson. He was never stoical about where he lived, and in January 1851 (from the Castle Hotel, Twickenham) he wrote to Emily in a tone of authentic anguish over missing a house that he had liked. This was a man who cared intensely about his surroundings and the right kind of space in which to write (the poet who wrote 'O Darling Room'):

O dear how grieved I am that I did not look at Chapel House when I was here before. The most lovely house with a beautiful view in every room at top and all over the rooms are so high that you may put up your beds. A large staircase with great statues and carved and all rooms splendidly papered – with a kind *gentlemanly* old man as proprietor – and all in for 50 guineas. A lady has taken it. I cursed my stars!

[. . . and after the signature:] O dear how I groan over Chapel house – *every* room bright and light and lofty and gay. Quite a joy to look at and the proprietor certainly an educated gentleman – no *fat knave* [a reference to one Edward Stanford, owner of another house they had considered] and all for 50 guineas [. . .] O dear! O dear! O dear![40]

The irony of this letter is that the unnamed lady who had taken it changed her mind and passed up the house, and the Tennysons were able to move into Chapel House, Twickenham, in March of 1851.

In the meantime, a much more serious setback was Emily's fall down a step in Reigate, and the pain that she suffered thereafter. The direct consequence of this was that the child she was carrying was stillborn, in April, as Tennyson told a number of friends in letters of that month. He was less distressed by the loss of this son than one might have expected, and found consolation in looking at the dead child and recognising what a fine boy he could have become: 'He was a grand, massive, manchild,' wrote Tennyson to Forster on 22 April 1851, with a 'noble brow, and hands, which he had clenched as in his determination to be born'.[41]

Tennyson and Emily needed a holiday together away from distressing associations. Emily was enthusiastic about Italy. Many years later Benjamin Jowett wrote that Tennyson 'had always had a living vision of Italy, Greece and the Mediterranean',[42] and this tour would go some of the way to translate that into reality.* The whole of Italy had been in political ferment since the uprising of a number of major Italian cities against Austrian rule in 1848, so it was an odd time to go, but other distinguished Britons were undeterred. Robert and Elizabeth Browning lived in Florence, and John Ruskin, with his wife Effie, spent much of the year in Venice pursuing his work on *The Stones of Venice*.

The Tennysons' first stop was in Paris, where Edmund and Cecilia Lushington were staying; it so happened that the Brownings were in Paris as well. They entertained Tennyson and Emily and advised them about what to see in Italy. The contact between the two poets and their wives was warm and sympathetic, and Tennyson and Robert Browning would regard each other with mutual affection and respect throughout their lives, although Browning said later that 'We [he and Tennyson] look at the object of art in poetry so differently!'

Browning had a small public and would wait many years for recognition as a major poet; at this date his poetry was seen as rough and difficult in contrast with Tennyson's smooth accessibility. Further, Browning held that a poet who accepted public honours was betraying the independence and freedom of his vocation. In 'The Lost Leader' he had attacked Wordsworth (though not by name) for receiving support from the state and abandoning his followers:

---

*Benjamin Jowett (1817–93) was one of the best classicists of the age and a Fellow, later Master, of Balliol. Tennyson and Jowett first met in 1852 and in later years would be firm friends.

We that had loved him so, followed him, honoured him,
   Lived in his mild and magnificent eye,
Learned his great language, caught his clear accents,
   Made him our pattern to live and to die!
Shakespeare was of us, Milton was for us,
   Burns, Shelley, were with us, – they watch from their
     graves!
He alone breaks from the van and the freemen,
   – He alone sinks to the rear and the slaves![43]

The poem was first published in 1845 (Wordsworth's Civil List pension was awarded in 1842 and he accepted the Laureateship in 1843). Browning later relented: Wordsworth was 'a great and venerable personality', though his 'defection' had still been 'an event to deplore'.[44] The fact remains that Wordsworth had accepted a Civil List pension and the Laureateship, and so did Tennyson.

The Tennysons travelled slowly, spending time at Bagni di Lucca with another friend, Francis Garden, the wealthy Scottish Apostle, who was staying there partly for his wife's health (she suffered from tuberculosis).[45] Venice and Rome would have been on their itinerary, but anxiety about political unrest in Rome and an epidemic of fever in Venice prevented them from visiting either city, and after Milan and then Florence they saw the Brownings again (in Splügen) on their way back. The holiday yielded one of the most graceful of Tennyson's poems for Emily, 'The Daisy', in which the best memories of the journey were lovingly recorded:

O love, what hours were thine and mine,
In lands of palm and southern pine;
   In lands of palm, of orange-blossom,
Of olive, aloe, and maize and vine.
[. . .]
At Florence too what golden hours,
In those long galleries, were ours;
   What drives about the fresh Cascinè,
Or walks in Boboli's ducal bowers.
[. . .]
O Milan, O the chanting quires,
The giant windows' blazoned fires,
   The height, the space, the gloom, the glory!
A mount of marble, a hundred spires![46]

*   *   *

Twickenham was within easy reach of London, and literary men found their way to Tennyson's new home. Francis Palgrave* had met Tennyson in 1849 and the first contact had been reasonably propitious: Tennyson said, 'I like what I see of you: you do not seem to have the distant air (superiority) which Oxford men show.'⁴⁷ Two days later Palgrave called on him in his rooms in Hampstead and Tennyson read him some of the 'elegies' for Hallam. When the Tennysons moved to Twickenham, Palgrave felt free to seek them out. He had a gruff greeting from Tennyson, who said, 'So you have found me out.' Emily hastened to put things right: 'You need not take Ally literally: he is glad to see you; but we came here to escape from the too frequent interruptions of London.'⁴⁸

Other young writers who made contact included George Meredith and William Allingham, the Irish poet. Allingham was an engaging young man of considerable literary talent. He had sent his *Poems* of 1850 to Tennyson. Coventry Patmore, who was by this time friendly with both Tennyson and Allingham, smoothed the way, and Allingham was invited to visit the Tennysons. Twickenham was then a rural village, and Allingham gave a vignette of the secluded spot in which the Tennysons were living. Chapel House was the last house in a handsome eighteenth-century terrace, 'a single row of about a dozen moderate-sized houses, that seemed dropped by accident among quiet fields and large trees'. ('Moderate' is a relative term: the house had a big handsome drawing room, a grand oak staircase, and a long garden separating the house from the small chapel that gave it its name.)⁴⁹ 'From his bulk, his short-sight, stooping shoulders, and loose careless dress' Tennyson was an impressive figure, looking a lot older than his forty-one years. He and Emily invited the young man to stay for dinner, and Tennyson then took Allingham up to his study overlooking the garden and read aloud the poems that he liked best from Allingham's 1850s volume; Allingham was dazzled by this flattering treatment, and would remain star-struck by Tennyson for the rest of his life.†⁵⁰

---

*Francis Turner Palgrave (1824–97), poet, critic, and a constant courtier of the Laureate, is remembered as editor of the anthology *The Golden Treasury*, one of the most important collections that the Victorian age was to produce. It gives valuable evidence of Tennyson's own preferences and critical judgements; Palgrave's selection was made in close consultation with Tennyson, and it was in practice a joint publication (1861). Palgrave was also a trenchant art critic for the *Saturday Review* and was Professor of Poetry at Oxford, 1885–95.

†Allingham's *Diary* is a rich source of anecdotes about writers and artists of the period, including Browning, George Eliot, Swinburne, Ruskin, Burne-Jones and William Morris. He was trapped for much of his life in uncongenial work as a customs officer, but as a result of a posting to Lymington in the early 1860s he became a regular guest of the Tennysons in the Isle of Wight. (Allingham, Introduction.)

By the winter of 1851, Emily was expecting another child (Hallam Tennyson, the elder of their two sons, was born on 11 August 1852). During this anxious winter, there was growing tension between the British and the French following Louis Napoleon's successful *coup d'état* and his subsequent installation as Emperor Napoleon III of France. Some of Tennyson's friends – notably Coventry Patmore – persuaded Tennyson to write poems encouraging the British to prepare themselves for military action. Tennyson duly sat down and wrote a group of militaristic patriotic lyrics with which to threaten the French. Robert Bernard Martin remarked that this is 'a series of seven poems' (including 'Rifle Clubs!!!' and 'Hands all Round!') 'that any admirer would wish had never seen light'.[51]

By February 1852, Tennyson's friends were noting his extraordinary restlessness: Franklin Lushington reported a 'state of mind which impels him to quit Twickenham and get a house in some remote part of the country, from which of course he would be equally anxious to return again into the neighbourhood of London'. He suggested that the ending of the Italian holiday had been a matter of last-minute impulsiveness:

> The chief motive of his return [to England] appears to have been the want of English tobacco, but the immediate cause of his starting northwards from Florence was his having made up his mind to go southward to Rome or Naples on a particular day and packed his trunks accordingly. When the day came it happened to blow too hard for them to go by the Leghorn steamer southward, so instead of waiting with Christian patience till the weather was better, they immediately started northwards.[52]

On 14 September 1852, the Duke of Wellington, the heroic old warrior who had become legendary in his own lifetime as an embodiment of British strength and resilience, died. Tennyson was inspired by this to write a major public poem, his 'Ode on the Death of the Duke of Wellington' (a welcome signal that 'Riflemen Form!' and the like were not the only things that Tennyson could rise to in the way of patriotic poetry). It was not technically a 'Laureate' poem since it had not been specifically requested by the Queen, but Tennyson told his aunt Elizabeth Russell that 'I wrote it because it was expected of me.' Aunt Russell had always concerned herself with his finances and continued to be generous to him, so he felt free to tell her how good a deal he had made with the publisher, Moxon, over the poem: £200 for the first 10,000 copies 'and at that rate for more, if more are wanted'.[53] It was published on 16 November by Moxon, and has rightly entered into the canon of Tennyson's major achievements.

As Cecil Y. Lang has pointed out, the poem was a success partly because its theme was close to some of Tennyson's strongest personal feelings about heroism. Arthur Hallam and Malory's King Arthur were the forerunners, and now the death of a third Arthur, Arthur Wesley Wellesley, stirred feelings of patriotism and veneration. The 'Ode on the Death of the Duke of Wellington' was his second 'Morte d'Arthur', indicating the continuing 'diffusive power' of the memory of Arthur Hallam.[54]

The Twickenham house that Alfred had so desperately desired in 1850 no longer suited the Tennysons (the drains were unsatisfactory and the locality was damp), and he again wanted to move. He would spend a good deal of 1852 sporadically house-hunting. Meanwhile little Hallam Tennyson was christened at Twickenham on 5 October 1852 with Henry Hallam and F. D. Maurice as his godfathers. Other guests included Browning, Palgrave, Jane Carlyle, the Brookfields, Henry Taylor, Thackeray, Venables, and Louisa and Charles Tennyson Turner.

James Spedding, who might well have expected to be invited to stand as one of the godfathers, was not there. Emily Tennyson saw him as unsuitable because of his independence of mind on religious matters, and Spedding himself wrote her an oblique but slightly hurt letter about this: he had been looking in the 'list of the arrivals in the Times regularly for a fortnight' but found that 'I had begun a week too late'. In somewhat double-edged phrasing he congratulated Emily on the christening of the baby as 'the accomplishment of the great event of what will be yesterday when you receive it; though you will not suspect me to think that so much depends upon it as many people believe. Whatever may be my own unfortunate deficiencies [his religious scepticism] I please myself with thinking that *he* has already all the immortal longings in him which he has a right to from both his parents.'[55]

Among the many friends who were invited to the christening but were unable to get there was Edward Lear (1812–88). Lear wrote to Emily on the day of the christening to say that the invitation had miscarried ('I only received your note 5 minutes ago') and then with characteristic enthusiasm sketched out for her his plans to make a series of landscape paintings illustrating Tennyson's poems. Edward Lear was a painter, composer, pianist, writer, wit and eccentric, and a masterly writer of nonsense stories and verses for children. He was also, as his friends knew well, a writer of dazzlingly strange and beguiling letters, usually decorated with his own drawings. He was a shy, awkward-looking, bespectacled and bearded figure of great personal charm, tormented by hidden homosexual desire, and agonisingly aware of his own ungainliness. He also suffered from epilepsy. The Tennysons had epilepsy in the family and Tennyson as a young man had always feared that he suffered from it himself. Edward Lear was a genuine sufferer, experiencing incidents of it every three or four days.

Edward Lear was a guest at Park House when he first met Tennyson. He had become close to another Trinity man, Franklin Lushington, the youngest brother of Edmund and Henry, whom he had met earlier in the year while travelling in the Mediterranean between Malta and Patras. (Lear was a constant, indeed compulsive, traveller: the travelling was to seek subjects for his paintings but was also, clearly, a way of distracting himself from the aspects of his life that troubled him.) Frank, as he was known, had been visiting Malta because by this date his brother Henry was working there as Chief Secretary to the government of the island. Lear's feelings for Frank developed into an intense passion which was not reciprocated and which was to cause him much pain over the years. Emily recognised this attachment for what it was, and did what she could to ease Lear's anguish. She wrote him a number of sensitive and affectionate letters about his relationship with Lushington, and as a consequence Lear came to think of the Tennysons as a possible refuge from his emotional storms.

Frank was offered, and accepted, an appointment as Judge to the Supreme Court of Justice in the Ionian Islands and was due to take up the post at the end of 1855. Under pressure of this impending loss, Lear wrote an idiosyncratic letter to Tennyson from 65 Oxford Terrace, Hyde Park. He called himself 'a spectator, – all through my life – of what goes on amongst those I know – very little an actor', and added:

Do you think there is a Pharmouse or a Nin somewhere near you, where there would be a big room looking to the North? – So that I could paint in it quietly, & come and see you & Mrs Tennyson promiscuously? – I know what you will say, or are saying – 'come to us' – but that *wouldn't* do: – the botherations of 6 feet paintings & all the combotherations of artist's ways *do not, & will not* dovetail with country houses in Anglosaxnland; – I have tried the matter well – & know it to be so. Utter idleness gets possession of me body and soul in that atmosphere: – afterwards, remorse.

Emotional emptiness was the problem: 'Besides, now that there is & can be no more of Frank, I have no interest, as I had when he used to be so constantly here, in sticking to work. If one were a chimney pot, or a pipkin, or a mackrel, or anything respectable & consistent there would be some comfort; but the years go by without making the use of one's faculties one ought to do, & so I feel disgusted I do.'[56]

Emily continued to be kind to Lear. She had him to stay with Frank as a fellow guest. Lear enjoyed three days of happiness, but when he wrote to thank her he again dwelt on his solitariness. He projected his lonely future: 'I wish sometimes I could settle near Park House. Then I might have a room near Boxley, & moon cripply, cripply about those hills, & sometimes see by turn Hallam & Lionel's children, & Frank's grandchildren, & so slide peacefully out of life.'[57]

Still clinging desperately to Frank, Lear travelled with him to Corfu in November. But Frank was understandably too busy with the new appointment to give much time to his friend, and in the event Lear spent two somewhat aimless years on his own, wandering and painting in the Greek islands.[58]

Tennyson, increasingly famous and prosperous and now a happy father, nevertheless remained disturbed and unsettled. Fitzgerald, always an interesting Tennyson-watcher, spent time with him at Chapel House in Twickenham in late December 1852, and was struck by his disappointment over the reception of the Ode (on the Duke of Wellington) and his fears that the country was about to be invaded by the French – fears with which Fitzgerald agreed, though less strongly:

> We had two long talks and smokes over the Ode: which he has altered and enlarged quite successfully, I think. He is disappointed that people in general care so little for it – but I tell him they will learn to understand it by degrees: and that it will outlive all ignorance. He is full of *Invasions*; and I believe truly is more wise and grave about it than any of our Ministers. He also wrote some very fine songs on the Subject – but he says nobody listens or cares.[59]

Tennyson was now miserable in the Twickenham house, and the house-hunting continued for much of 1853. Failure to suit himself over this interrupted his writing, and he found consolation in drink. In February he had to have some teeth extracted and was fitted with false ones, which gave him trouble thereafter: 'Saw Barrett and since have been eating dinner with new teeth. Queer – seems as if I never could get accustomed to it.'[60] The new teeth distorted the shape of his mouth; it was partly to overcome this that he grew the beard and moustache that became part of his image from 1855 onwards.

He made sporadic visits to London, where the old bachelor habit of casually using his friends' houses as places to doss down for the night persisted: in June he was writing cheerily to Monckton Milnes arranging to dine with him (he would stay overnight with Spedding, where he could get 'his own way' over 'the matter of smoke'). At the same time he pretended that as a sober married man his habits had now changed: 'I have given up dining out and am about to retire in utter solitude in some country house but if you feel yourself aggrieved at sending one invitation after another to me, unaccepted, I will come.'[61]

The genial William Allingham, who had made an excellent impression on Tennyson at their first meeting, was again invited to the poet's 'much-longed-for presence'. He made his second visit to Twickenham early in 1853, during one of his too infrequent escapes from his native Ballyshannon. When he arrived at Chapel House, he found little Hallam in Tennyson's arms. The dinner guests included Tennyson's elder brother Frederick, and his old friend Edward Fitzgerald (now famous for his translation and adaptation of *Omar Khayyám*). Allingham had a small accident and spilt wine on the tablecloth; Tennyson 'with his imperturbability spread salt on it, remarking as he did so, "I believe it never comes out!"' After dinner the men settled in Tennyson's study to smoke and exchange stories. Tennyson was relaxed about bawdy jokes in male company, and some of the tales were 'of an ammoniacal saltness'.[62]

In July 1853, Tennyson and Emily took a holiday with little Hallam in the north of England – they were particularly attracted to Whitby – with Francis Palgrave as their travelling companion. The plan had been for the family to travel on into Scotland, but in the event Tennyson went with Palgrave while Emily returned to Twickenham because the child was ill, 'the cold of Whitby having been too much for Hallam'.[63] Tennyson's dependence on Palgrave can seem unaccountable. Palgrave was clinging, and seemed to admire Tennyson far more than Tennyson warmed to him. But he was useful, and for that reason Tennyson put up with inadequacies and personal quirks which others would have found intolerable.

Tennyson spent some time in Edinburgh (he had been invited to stay with an acquaintance there whom he had met in the 1840s while taking the water cure with Dr Gully). While in Edinburgh he wrote

'The Daisy', his loving celebration of the Italian holiday with Emily. The Scottish itinerary then took him to visit his good Cambridge friend and fellow Apostle Robert Monteith at Carstairs, Lanark. He had decided to leave Palgrave in Edinburgh; clearly Palgrave's clinging ways were becoming an irritant to him.

Monteith and his wife warmly welcomed Tennyson, and were 'so grieved not to see you [Emily] that I am grieved you did not come even if you had made three days of the journey. Such large lofty rooms for the babe and sweet outlooks through trees of the Clyde would have charmed you.' Tennyson added that when he left Palgrave behind, 'he accused me at parting of a Goethe like coldness and indifference to friends and I told him that this would apply to him rather than me, but I really believe that he has a liking for me which he thinks is not fully returned'.[64]

He went on to see Iona and Staffa, which provoked a characteristic complaint to Emily: 'Thou canst not conceive the stew and bore of this little hotel crammed to suffocation, dinners, teas, suppers going on altogether which makes it impossible to write.' Fingal's Cave would later yield one of the best lines in *Idylls of the King* (from 'Merlin and Vivien'). Merlin's mind wanders while Vivien seeks to seduce him:

> So dark a forethought rolled about his brain,
> As on a dull day in an Ocean eve
> The blind wave feeling round his long sea-hall
> In silence.[65]

But the actual visit to the cave was spoilt for him by the realities of being a tourist: 'The cave is very remarkable not so grand as I expected, and Iona as interesting as it could be with people chatting and 40 minutes to see it in.'[66]

The need to find a satisfactory house was still pressing. Near London would obviously suit them both, and somewhere close to Farnham, in Surrey, had been a general objective, but nothing presented itself. In October, Tennyson paid a visit to Bonchurch, in the Isle of Wight; his friend and host there was the clergyman and playwright, James White, who spent most of his life contentedly on the island. He had heard that Farringford, in Freshwater, owned by the Rev. George Turner Seymour, would be available to rent. Tennyson went to see it. Emily reported that he:

found it looking rather wretched with wet leaves trampled into the downs. However we thought it worth while to go and look at it together. The railway did not go further than Brockenhurst then and the steamer, when there was one from Lymington, felt itself in no way bound to wait for the omnibus which brought as many of the passengers as it could from the train. We crossed in a rowing boat. It was a still November evening.

They spent the night in Plumbley's Hotel in Freshwater, and went to look at Farringford the following day. Looking out of the big generous window of the Farringford drawing room, Emily recalled thinking, '"I must have that view" and I said so to him when alone.'[67] Accordingly they agreed with Seymour to rent the house with a later option to purchase it.

Sir Charles Tennyson, their grandson, who had loved the place since his own earliest memories of it as a child in the 1880s, described how magical its setting must have been when Tennyson and Emily first saw it in the early 1850s:

The house, which then contained about fifteen rooms, stands on a little eminence where there had once been a signalling station, and, however still and hot the day, there is generally a breeze about it, either from the valley which runs between two ridges of down westward to Alum Bay, or from the east, where the country opens out to north and south. In 1853 there was a fine view northward to the Solent and the English coast, beyond, now obscured by the growth of trees. But what made Alfred and Emily decide that the house must be theirs, was the view to the east from the drawing-room windows, which look down over the gentle slope of the park, across Freshwater Bay to a succession of small inlets and rosy headlands, backed by the fine curve of St Catherine's down ten miles away and flanked by the noble mass of Afton down in the middle distance.

And, with all this spaciousness of outlook, the house was excellently secluded. Dense copses of pine, elm, holly and laurel, carpeted with wild flowers in continual succession from snowdrop to foxglove, sheltered it from north and south. At the back there was a belt of elm, behind which a homely walled garden of flowers and vegetables sloped down towards the west; and southward between the house and the sea, a bare mile distant, rose the High Down with its sheer face of white chalk five hundred feet high, a haunt of peregrines, kestrels, ravens, jackdaws, cormorants and sea birds past numbering.

Indeed, the whole countryside was a paradise of birds, flowers and butterflies, and the hand of man as yet lay very lightly on it. There were a few small houses and a little white hotel down by the bay; a few more huddled round the old church, which stands proudly above the tiny river Yar, and about the narrow winding lanes were scattered small stone cottages and 17th-century farms with roofs of thatch or stone tiling.[68]

When Tennyson and Emily moved into Farringford in 1853, it was by the standards of the day a relatively small country house. He adopted a little attic room as his study (it was comfortably reminiscent of the 'darling room' at Somersby) and privileged male guests would be invited up there after dinner to smoke and talk poetry, or listen to him read. Later in the 1860s this little room became his dressing room, and he adopted a ground-floor room next to the conservatory as his study. The beautiful swelling green slope to the south of the house was ideal, once one had climbed to its ridge, for walks high above the sea along the top of a precipitous chalk cliff. This extended from Freshwater Bay to the Needles, the chalk pillars at the extreme western tip of the Isle of Wight; it was then known as High Down (and is now called Tennyson Down). The house itself was Georgian and had been built engagingly with a lot of carved Gothic decorative detail which would certainly have reminded Tennyson of the eccentric dining room that his father had added to Somersby; his grandson referred to the 'absurd, but oddly pleasing, fancy which decorated all the windows and the interior panelling with imitations in wood of Gothic stone traceries, and crowned the then quite modest little Georgian house with the most inappropriate battlements'. The whole estate, which Tennyson rented, and would later own, dated from the fourteenth century and was associated with a family called de Ferringford. There had been a monastic foundation nearby, which was commemorated by the names of the fields that went with the house: Maiden's Croft (dedicated to the Virgin), the Clerk's Hill (where the clerk of the monastery lived), St George, and Abraham's Mead.[69]

Tennyson had not had a home that suited him since 1837, the year in which the Tennysons had all been obliged to leave Somersby. The events of 1850 had transformed his life, and within the space of a few months he had become famous, honoured, recognised and of course married; this did not mean, however, that he was now suddenly emotionally secure. From 1831 to the late 1840s his life had been unsettled and often turbulent, marked by his father's death, Arthur

Hallam's death, the blocked courtship of Emily Sellwood, the disastrous loss of his inheritance in 1842 and his resort to drink, tobacco and water cures in order to recover some equilibrium. Farringford in 1853 met his needs perfectly. There were no immediate neighbours, yet the house was only three and a half miles from the charming little town of Yarmouth, where visitors from Lymington on the mainland would disembark, and a short walk from Freshwater, with its church and cluster of houses and its small comfortable hotel where overflow guests could stay. It was sweet, safe, gentle, mild and secluded.[70] When they moved in, 'Two of the servants,' Emily recalled, 'burst into tears saying they could never live in such a lonely place.'[71]

The decision to rent with the firm intention to buy was risky. The income that Tennyson could rely on at this date was in the region of £500 a year, and he could reasonably expect that to rise with future royalties, but he was still getting used to the fact of being a family man with responsibilities. He wrote to Alan Ker, now married to Mary Tennyson, to say, 'I rather shake under the fear of being ruined.' He had by this time been making some prudent financial decisions (no more wood-carving schemes); he had good investments in East Lincolnshire railways and could anticipate steady earnings from his poetry. He also had his pension that had been awarded by Peel in 1845, and Aunt Russell continued to be generous.

He never shook off his resentment over having been dispossessed by the Old Man of the Wolds. The senior branch of the Tennysons was entitled to wealth and security, things that had been cruelly snatched away by the 'disinheriting' of his father in favour of his uncle. Added to this was the genuine instability of the markets and the self-evident fact, illustrated by the fall of figures such as 'Hudson the railway king' (and reflected in the disgraced capitalists of Dickens's and Trollope's novels), that fortunes could be quickly made and easily lost. Tennyson's fears about poverty were partly the reasonable anxiety of any successful self-made mid-Victorian, and partly the irrational legacy of that early family injustice.

The house in Twickenham was still Tennyson's responsibility; he solved it by persuading his mother, brothers and sister that they would be happy living there (despite the damp and the drains). He transferred the remainder of the lease to his mother.

Lionel Tennyson, Alfred and Emily's younger son, was born on 16 March 1854, and the usual flood of letters of congratulation came in. A second child intensified Tennyson's anxiety about money. 'Many thanks for your congratulations if the birth of babes to poor men are matters of congratulation,' he wrote in reponse to Coventry Patmore.[72]

Franklin Lushington stood godfather to Lionel. Aunt Russell sent a welcome cheque when she heard about the new baby. Tennyson always trusted his aunt completely over financial matters. At the same time, he suspected that his brother-in-law, Emily's husband Richard Jesse, known to be given to gossip (a 'cackling fellow', as Tennyson called him), had been telling Aunt Russell that Tennyson was now financially well off. He hastened to put this in perspective:

> If I were to die tomorrow I could only leave my wife and now two sons £150 per ann. in railways shares: that is surely no great matter: meantime my books make money but who can guarantee that they will continue to do so. A new name, and such must arise sooner or later, may throw me out of the market.

He also referred to the current stormy international complication with Russia – soon to blow up into full-scale war – and noted that that 'may go far to knock my profits on the head'.[73] To what extent was his anxiety about money based in the realities of the situation? He was already notably canny financially in his dealings with Moxon, and as the years passed and he became wealthier, his attitude to money became tough to the point of ruthlessness. It was noted (with surprise and some hostility) that he showed no sign of surrendering the annual pension that he received.

The core of Tennyson's life had not changed. Unless ill or distracted, he liked to write every day. Typically he composed poetry in his head during long daily walks. When he was young, these walks had been in the Lincolnshire wolds or by the sea at Mablethorpe; now, in the 1850s, they were on High Down near Farringford, and were central to his creative process. The poems came into being in his mind's eye, or rather his mind's ear, until they were stored in his memory. In November 1850, Patmore told W. M. Rossetti that Tennyson 'has in his memory, and on occasion recites, an immense quantity of poetry which he never intends to commit to paper'.[74]

Early in 1854, Edward Moxon proposed an illustrated edition of Tennyson's poems; this would be a protracted, expensive and troublesome project, although Moxon went about it with excellent intentions and recruited the most noted artists of the day. Tennyson was lukewarm from the outset; he felt that the realisations of what he saw in his mind's eye were so vivid that a woodcut equivalent by Millais or Rossetti could never be as effective in its impact. His letters of 1854 are full of anxiety about that, with continuing worries about money and also about his eyesight. Tennyson had been myopic from an early age, and in April he wrote to Aunt Russell that he believed he was actually losing the sight in his right eye. The reality was that like many myopic people, he suffered a good deal of eye-strain: he needed to wear spectacles for distance. His perception of distant objects like the sea or mountains or the night sky was often impressionistic and filled with colour and light rather than sharp outline, while close objects, like the flowers and leaves that delighted him with as much intensity as they delighted the Pre-Raphaelite painters and Ruskin, remained vivid and sharp.

Meanwhile, Tennyson started a friendship with Sir John Simeon, of Swainston, a substantial country house on the Isle of Wight some fifteen miles from Farringford. Simeon was a Roman Catholic and master of the Isle of Wight Foxhounds, while Tennyson adhered to Anglicanism (though he was far less devout than Emily) and disliked blood sports. But Tennyson had a lifelong interest in mysticism and a natural fellow feeling with the certainties of Roman Catholics, especially if they had a strong sense of the supernatural; Aubrey de Vere said that 'his nature is a religious one'.[75] (De Vere's own reception into the Roman Catholic Church did not dilute that friendship.) Sir John Simeon, solidly Catholic from birth, will be a recurrent name in the continuing story of Tennyson.

The major event of 1855 was the publication of *Maud*, that violent, bloodstained, sonorous dramatic monologue which distressed and mystified Tennyson's public. Social and sexual anguish haunt *Maud*, and R. W. Rader's work has shown most ably that Tennyson's feelings about Rosa Baring continue into the speaker's feelings for the unattainable Maud. She lives in a Hall – she is very much the speaker's social and economic superior – she is attracted to him, but cannot act on it because of the clear interdiction imposed by her rich family. The Hall, Maud's prison, is much hated in the poem. It is an old house tainted by new money – much as the Edens, with their new money, had taken over Harrington Hall and smartened it up.

Tennyson's troubled feelings about women, about sex, about money and about social status – all intense issues for him in the 1830s – seem to have been brought back into full consciousness, and to have been bearing on him with heavy pressure, in the years *after* he had settled himself with Emily. *Maud* gathered up and recapitulated the resentment and frustration that the young man had felt, and organised it into a narrative which placed it and distanced it. The writing of the poem was an act of exorcism, but as such it was a failure; it exorcised nothing. He was famous and financially secure, and he had fathered two sons, yet his anxieties over social status and his anger over slights, real or imagined, continued unabated.

Maud also has emotional roots in the disastrous loss of Arthur Hallam when Tennyson was twenty-four and his dead friend twenty-two (at the time of *Maud*'s publication Tennyson was forty-six). Readers of Tennyson understood elegiac restraint, they understood lyric grace, they understood his passion for the past and the way in which his refrains and his preferred stanza forms cycled back to points of memory: 'Break, break, break', or ''Tis better to have loved and lost / Than never to have loved at all.' Alert readers might have been expected to recognise the emotions of 'Oh, that 'twere possible', *Maud* II, poem IV. The male subject who inspired the first state of the poem back in the 1830s, Hallam, has become a woman for the dramatic purpose of the poem – but the most visionary stanzas display a figure who could be of either gender: 'Ah Christ, that it were possible / For one short hour to see / The souls we loved, that they might tell us / What and where they be.' The ghost remains ambiguous and elusive. In its early state, or states (there are several in the manuscripts),* this poem belongs to 1833–4. The young poet experimented here with an alternating rhyme scheme and a hint of the ABBA form, as he did in early drafts of *In Memoriam*:

> And I wake, my dream is fled;
> In the glimmering grey, behold
> By the curtains of my bed
> Without knowledge, without pity
> That abiding phantom cold.[76]

These verses belong to the same outpouring of grief for Hallam which generated 'Break, break, break', 'Ulysses', 'Morte d'Arthur', 'Tithon' (later 'Tithonus') and *In Memoriam*, and the connections are often tangible. Maud has been hugely attractive sexually to the speaker, and for that reason in itself she has at times filled him with horror. Now that she is dead she has become, in a sense, more manageable. As with Hallam, if her spirit were to return, the speaker would be able to conduct rational and remorseful dialogue with her, and thus

---

*John Heath copied two unadopted versions of it into his commonplace book, and it exists in a very early form in Harvard Notebook 13. See also Ricks, *Poems*, II, p. 571n.

George Clayton Tennyson (1778–1831),
the poet's father.

Elizabeth Fytche (1781–1865),
the poet's mother.

Somersby Rectory, the poet's birthplace, 1847.

George Tennyson, 'The Old Man of the Wolds' (1750–1835), the poet's grandfather.

Charles Tennyson, later Charles Tennyson d'Eyncourt (1784–1861), the poet's uncle.

The Old Grammar School, Louth, where Tennyson was an unhappy pupil between the ages of 7 and 11, 1816–1820.

Horncastle: the house in the market square where Emily Sellwood was brought up.

Tennyson in 1840, engraving
of the portrait by Samuel
Laurence commissioned
by Edward Fitzgerald.

Arthur Hallam (1811–33)
in about 1830.

Rosa Baring, whom Tennyson loved
briefly but intensely 1834–5.

Harrington Hall, home of the Barings, where Tennyson met Rosa Baring probably in 1832.

New Court, Trinity College, Cambridge, where Arthur Hallam
kept his rooms as an undergraduate.

Chapel House, Twickenham,
the Tennysons' married home 1851–2.

Tennyson with his two
young sons in the 1850s.

Lionel (left) and
Hallam Tennyson as small boys.

Medallion of Tennyson (1856)
by his life-long friend the sculptor and
poet Thomas Woolner, who, with the
painters Millais and Rossetti, had been
one of the founding 'Pre-Raphaelites'.

Alfred and Emily
at Farringford in
the 1850s with
their two sons.

Benjamin Jowett (1817–93),
eminent classicist and Master of Balliol.

Drawing of Farringford by Edward Lear, friend and welcome guest
of the Tennysons in the 1850s.

Charles Tennyson,
later Charles Tennyson Turner (1808–79),
the poet's favourite brother.

Frederick Tennyson (1807-98),
the poet's oldest brother, in 1865.

Farringford,
Isle of Wight,
1860.

The bust of Tennyson (1857) by Thomas Woolner; one of his most successful male portrait sculptures. It was bought by subscription for Trinity College where it stands outside the entrance to the Wren Library.

Holman Hunt's illustration for the crisis of 'The Lady of Shalott', from Edward Moxon's ill-fated illustrated edition of Tennyson's poems published in 1857.

Photograph of Tennyson in 1857
wearing his Spanish-style hat.

Emily Tennyson in 1865.

Thomas Carlyle (1795–1881)
photographed in 1867.

Tennyson as a 'dirty monk'.

Lionel Tennyson (1854–86), the Tennysons' lively and gifted younger son who caught a fatal infection in India in 1885 and died on the voyage home.

Bayons Manor, home of the Tennyson d'Eyncourts.

The summer house at Farringford that Tennyson built for Emily following an illness in 1858. Tennyson later used it for writing; the dog is watching him at work.

Letter from Edward Lear to Hallam Tennyson, September 1885.
Lear's earlier close friendship with Tennyson had by this time cooled, but he remained fond of Emily Tennyson and of Tennyson's sons.

Designs for Aldworth by Alfred and Emily Tennyson, sketched rapidly as
preliminary working ideas for the architect, James Knowles.

Aldworth, the ambitious country house built for Tennyson by James Knowles:
an engraving from 1874.

Tennyson's friend from Trinity,
James Spedding (1808–81) with one
of the founders of the 'Apostles',
Frederick Denison Maurice
(1805–72), photographed in 1859.

William Henry Brookfield
(1809–98), contemporary of
Tennyson at Trinity and
friend of the Apostles.

William Ewart Gladstone (1809–98)
in about 1870.

Horatio Tennyson (1819–99) in 1867.

Matilda Tennyson (1816–1913), the longest
lived of Tennyson's ten siblings.

Hallam Tennyson (1852–1928)
as a young man.

Monumental memorial sculpture by George Frederick Watts outside Lincoln Cathedral, unveiled in 1905.

expiate his guilt. In the published *Maud* of 1855, this passage is less mysterious and less painful: 'And I wake, my dream is fled; / In the shuddering dawn, behold, / Without knowledge, without pity, / By the curtains of my bed / That abiding phantom cold.'

Maud is technically remarkable as a dramatic monologue which displays the mental disturbance and violent mood swings of the speaker by giving him a wide variation of verse forms. The story embedded in the poem has clear lines at the literal level: Maud and the speaker were childhood sweethearts, and the speaker had heard their two fathers promise that he and Maud would be wedded when they grew up. But that has all changed: Maud's father has defrauded the speaker's father, who has killed himself, and Maud is now engaged to a young man whose wealth derives from coal. A dinner is due to take place at the Hall, and Maud has promised to leave the party for a secret meeting with her erstwhile sweetheart. Her brother, who favours the match with the coal heir, follows her and strikes the speaker, and in the ensuing fight the speaker kills the brother, and takes refuge overseas. Maud dies (presumably of grief), the speaker returns to England and endures a period in an insane asylum. The poem closes with the speaker restored to sanity and released from the asylum, but now facing almost certain death because he has volunteered to fight in the Crimean War.

Sexual rage, liberating violence and the belief that Britain had become a debased civilisation which would need bloody battle to cleanse it complicate the lines of this plot. The poem opens with the speaker's fevered recollection of his father's suicide. 'I hate the dreadful hollow behind the little wood' is both literal – the hollow is where the suicide took place – and metaphorical, rich with sexual threat and neurosis: 'Its lips in the field above are dabbled with blood-red heath.' The speaker feels 'disinherited' (as Tennyson felt he had been by his grandfather) and any chance of his making a suitable marriage has been wrecked (as Tennyson had also felt). The first part of the poem touches on the militarism that the poem expresses at its close: 'Is it peace or war? better war! loud war by land and by sea, / War with a thousand battles, and shaking a hundred thrones.' Why? Because the stasis of peace has corrupted the whole organic world visible to the speaker. Nature itself is now evil: 'For nature is one with rapine, a harm no preacher can heal; / The Mayfly is torn by the swallow, the sparrow speared by the shrike, / And the whole little wood where I sit is a world of plunder and prey.'[77]

The brilliant formal song, 'Come into the garden, Maud', with its vivid colouring, tight metrical organisation, intricate rhyme scheme

and hallucinatory high nominal content, demonstrates the speaker's
mental disintegration under the pressure of his excitement:

> There has fallen a splendid tear
>   From the passion-flower at the gate.
> She is coming, my dove, my dear;
>   She is coming, my life, my fate;
> The red rose cries, 'She is near, she is near;'
>   And the white rose weeps, 'She is late;'
> The larkspur listens, 'I hear, I hear;'
>   And the lily whispers, 'I wait.'*[78]

The high sensory excitement of this song at the end of Part I of *Maud*
is followed immediately by an extreme contrast of mood and tone.
The crisis in the story has taken place in the space between the two
parts, and the first poem in Part II is in almost incoherent blank verse.
The speaker's derangement now takes the form of numbed alienation
from his own violence.

> Why am I sitting here so stunned and still,
> Plucking the harmless wild-flower on the hill? –
> It is this guilty hand! –
> And there rises ever a passionate cry
> From underneath in the darkening land –
> What is it, that has been done?

The poem has a double ending. The first was completed in June
1855 (Emily recorded: 'We reach home again. "Maud" was finished
which added to the delight of returning'),[79] and was unequivocal in
its militarism: 'now by the side of the Black and the Baltic deep, / And
deathful-grinning mouths of the fortress, flames / The blood-red
blossom of war with a heart of fire.' In terms of patterning, this catches
up the 'red-ribbed ledges' which 'drip with a silent horror of blood'
in the first stanza of the whole poem, and neatly shows the speaker's
aggression now turned outwards, his emotional turmoil harnessed to
the promise of simple violent action (with the assumption that he will
not survive). The revised ending, published in 1856, is far less effective,

---

*This would be parodied by 'Lewis Carroll' – Charles Dodgson – in 'The Garden of
Live Flowers' (*Through the Looking-Glass and What Alice Found There*): '"She is
coming !" cried the Larkspur. "I hear her footstep, thump, thump, along the gravel-
walk!"' (Carroll, p. 141.)

with a startlingly inappropriate formulaic piety which relates neither to the poem's story nor to its dominant imagery. 'I embrace the purpose of God, and the doom assigned.'[80] It is not clear what God has to do with the main action of *Maud*.

CHAPTER 7

The reception of *Maud* and the problems
of fame, 1855–1862

I hate the dreadful hollow behind the little wood,
Its lips in the field above are dabbled with blood-red heath,
The red-ribbed ledges drip with a silent horror of blood,
And Echo there, whatever is asked her, answers 'Death.'

In 1855, Tennyson agreed to be honoured by Oxford University with
the degree of DCL (Doctor of Civil Law) and he went up to Oxford
for the ceremony. He was so celebrated that there was great excitement
among the undergraduates. Hallam Tennyson described the occasion:

My parents stayed at Balliol; and my father said, as he sat in the
Balliol gardens, 'The shouts of the Undergraduates from the theatre
were like the shouts of the Roman crowd, "Christiani ad Leones!"'
[. . .] The sea of upturned faces was very striking, and my father
had a 'tremendous ovation' when he received his degree.[1]

The DCL would appear on the title pages of Tennyson's works thereafter. His fame was such that he did not need the status conferred by
Oxford, any more than he would need (in the 1880s) the status of
becoming Lord Tennyson. The eagerness with which both these distinctions would in due course be blazoned in all his publications tells us
something about his continuing personal insecurity. When relaxed,
though, Tennyson could joke against himself. He was aware of the
effect of his long-haired, Spanish-looking image. At Oxford an undergraduate shouted from the gallery: 'Did your mother call you early,
Mr Tennyson?'[2] The young man was making a cheeky reference to
Tennyson's 'The May Queen'. But Tennyson may not have heard it,
since a few years later he told a friend that 'The only impertinence the
young fellows uttered, was "*Cut your hair.*"'[3]

Tennyson's distinguished Oxford friend Benjamin Jowett had been
instrumental in seeing the proposal for Tennyson's DCL through
Congregation, the governing body of the university. Brilliant dons were
not obviously to Tennyson's taste, and he had been somewhat nervous
of Jowett, but they quickly became good friends: so much so that

Jowett, who was a bachelor, was invited for Christmas with the Tennysons at Farringford. He was so tactful and such good company that his Christmas visits became an annual feature.

To Jowett, close friendship with a man like Tennyson was important. He needed the support of distinguished people who had no connection with the university. Despite his undisputed scholarly distinction, his own position at Oxford was insecure. The reason was that Jowett was liberal in theology. He published what were seen as radical commentaries on two books of the Bible in 1855, and in 1860 he would publish a deliberately provocative essay, 'On the interpretation of scripture'. He was persecuted in the university in a very practical way. His stipend when he was appointed Professor of Greek was an extraordinarily low £40 annually. It remained fixed at that figure until 1865, when Dean Liddell* of Christ Church intervened, and the salary was raised to £500 annually. It was not until 1870 that Jowett's ambition at Oxford was realised when he was finally elected Master of Balliol.

Tennyson's friend the Duke of Argyll wrote a number of geological papers, and Tennyson read these with enthusiasm.[4] The Duke and Duchess invited him to Argyll House in London several times with gratifying requests to recite his poetry. In March and April of 1859 he would be with the Argylls regularly, and the Duchess wrote excited letters to Emily about the pleasure of listening to him read *Maud*, or *Guinevere*, or *The Miller's Daughter*. It is hard to escape the feeling that with his shaggy, unkempt appearance and awkward manners, Tennyson was seen by these grandees as a kind of pet, a noble savage or a lumbering beast of untamed genius, though he did in fact also have deep and serious conversations with Argyll about geology.[5]

Argyll's lecture on geology to the Glasgow Athenaeum in January 1859 was dedicated to Tennyson: 'Geology: Its Past and Present. A lecture delivered to the members of the Glasgow Athenaeum, January 13, 1859. By The Duke of Argyll George John Douglas Campbell, 8ᵗʰ Duke.' The Duke was an old-fashioned creationist. Geology supported the 'argument from design' for the existence of God, as it had for Paley at the end of the eighteenth century. If the Duke noticed the urgent religious questioning in parts of *In Memoriam* (and it is hard to see how he could miss it), this was clearly not allowed to become an issue between the two men.

For Tennyson's long-standing friends, his growing fame had led to shifts and undercurrents of feeling. Carlyle was generous about his

---

*Whose daughter was the original Alice in Wonderland.

success, and pleased by his marriage (as he said in a letter to Fitzgerald): 'Mrs Alfred is a very nice creature, cheerful, good-mannered, intelligent, sincere-looking.'[6] Fitzgerald, though, was feeling hurt. 'Alfred himself never writes,' he told Frederick Tennyson on 31 December 1850:

> nor indeed cares a halfpenny about one, though he is very well satisfied to see one when one falls in his way. You will think I have a spite against him for some neglect, when I say this, and say beside that I cannot care for his In Memoriam. Not so, if I know myself: I always thought the same of him, and am just as well satisfied with it as now. His poem I never did greatly affect: nor can I learn to do so: it is full of finest things, but it is monotonous, and has that air of being evolved by a Poetical Machine of the highest order. So it seems to be with him now, at least to me, the Impetus, the Lyrical oestrus, is gone . . . It is the cursed inactivity (very pleasant to me who am no hero) of this 19th century which has spoiled Alfred, I mean spoiled him for the great work he ought now to be entering upon; the lovely and noble things he has done must remain.[7]

This would become a fixed position in Fitzgerald's mind. By April 1874 he had also developed reservations about Tennyson's marriage, as he showed rather plainly in a letter to Richard Monckton Milnes, now Lord Houghton:

> I used to tell Tennyson thirty years ago that he should be a Dragoon, or in some active Employment that would keep his Soul stirring, instead of revolving in itself in idleness and Tobacco smoke. And now he has sunk into Coterie-worship, and (I tremble to say it) in the sympathy of his most Ladylike, gentle, Wife. An old Housekeeper like Molière's would have been far better for him, *I* think. I can care nothing for his Poems since his two Volumes in 1842 – except for the dramatic element in *Maud*, and a few little bits in it. But I am told this is because I have shut up my mind, etc. So it may be. But surely he has become more Artist than Poet ever since: and if the Artist have not wherewithal to work on? I mourn over him as a Great Man lost – that is, not risen to the Greatness that was in him – for he has done enough to out-last all others of his time, I think – up to 1842. As to the Princesses, King's Idylls, etc., they seem to me to fail utterly in the one thing wanted – Invention, to make a new and better thing of old Legends, which, without it, are best left alone.[8]

A strikingly different view had been expressed in 1855 by a complete stranger, Gerald Massey, a genuine working-class voice and a fiery political radical. Basing his piece on *The Princess* and *In Memoriam* (he had not yet read *Maud*), Massey aligned Tennyson with the poets who had emerged from the political convulsions of late-eighteenth-century Europe, seeing him as a successor to Wordsworth, Coleridge, Byron and Keats. Tennyson, in this view, was 'one of the brood of giants who stepped into life through the rent of Revolution, although he is in the second generation'.[9] Massey's point here was that mid-Victorian society was oppressive and its poetry had become cautious, while Tennyson's poetry retained some of the explosive energy of the great romantics. 'Poetry in our time is a continual protest against the pressure of tendencies adverse to the full and free human development. [. . .] The force of circumstances which we have thrown up around us is fast crushing all spiritual force out of ourselves.' Tennyson's poetry, in this argument, 'comprehends the best elements of his predecessors, together with an added strength, grace, and beauty. His genius pours itself, as it were, like oil upon their troubled waters.'[10]

Massey was right about Tennyson's strength, but wrong about its nature: the strength was literary, not political. He was endlessly inventive technically; he worked hard to avoid repeating his own verse forms and took pride also in resisting forms that had been used successfully by earlier poets. He was at all times at his best in his own personal stronghold, the power of his own versification and of his literary voice.

Tennyson always claimed that *Maud* was not personal. He denied that the militarism of the speaker reflected his own views, and in his defence of the poem over the years he repeatedly and indignantly insisted on the fictional nature of the dramatisation. From Robert Browning such an argument readily found acceptance. In his monologues Browning displayed extraordinary dramatic virtuosity, so that when he created his devious egotistical Roman Catholic bishops – the Renaissance Italian bishop in 'The Bishop orders his Tomb at St Praxed's' and the Victorian contemporary figure in 'Bishop Blougram's Apology' (based on Cardinal Wiseman) – readers had no difficulty in recognising the poet's creative skill for what it was: these men were not Browning. *Maud* is a different case. Tennyson liked to point to its dramatic methods by calling it his 'little *Hamlet*, the history of a morbid, poetic soul, under the blighting influence of a recklessly speculative age',[11] but this and similar disclaimers did not silence those who saw the speaker of *Maud* as a version of Tennyson himself. This was fair, given that Tennyson was by now a dramatic production himself. Since young manhood he had assiduously attended to his own image as poet. The flowing hair, exuberant beard and moustache, myopic gaze, Spanish hat and cloak, magnificent speaking voice and distracted bardic manner were all part of an identity which, as he grew older, became increasingly indistinguishable from his private self. Now that he was famous, Tennyson was always, as it were, on stage, and *Maud* was part of his performance. Browning's dramatic monologues were masterpieces of concealment and disguise. *Maud* was a masterpiece of the opposite kind, an emotionally explicit poem laying bare the pain of Tennyson's younger life.

Tennyson's exotic presence set him apart from the kind of gossiping and cheerful men, such as Monckton Milnes, who were fully at home in the worldly society of literary and political London. While he loved the adulation, Tennyson found conversation with these admiring and wealthy people hard to sustain. His way of dealing with the situation was to offer to read his own poems. *Maud* was increasingly the centrepiece of these performances. It was as though he was bludgeoning those with whom he had personal contact to compel them to repudiate the adverse comments that had appeared in print. So strong was his will that this became an established pattern, one that the hostesses did not attempt to break.

It is not at all surprising that Tennyson had been upset by the poem's reception. For the *Edinburgh Evening Courant*, *Maud* was 'a thing to be blotted, if possible, from the memory', and to the *Athenaeum* the poem was 'not worthy of its author'. The *Press* found it 'a strain of puling incoherent sentiment and disordered fantasy such as might flit through the brain of a love-sick youth in the measles'. (Why *measles*, one may ask?) *Blackwood's* found it 'ill considered, crude, tawdry, and objectionable' and *The Times* complained that 'Mr Tennyson has never yet presented to the public anything so crude, so shapeless, and so common-place.' The *Morning Post* offered a somewhat laboured joke to the effect that there was an extra letter in '*Maud*', and that the title should have been either 'Mad' or 'Mud'.[12]

Crude, tawdry, commonplace: such phrases carried the implication that Tennyson was of low social status, and this was bound to sting. Another recurrent charge – that his work was derivative – made him equally angry. He received an anonymous letter which particularly rankled: 'Sir, I used to worship you, but now I hate you. I loathe and detest you. You beast! So you've taken to imitating Longfellow. Yours in aversion ---.'[13] He told John Forster that he believed this to be from a clergyman and poet called Archer Thompson Gurney. Gurney had recently complained that Tennyson ignored his poetry; it is unlikely, though, that Gurney wrote the letter, given that he was on friendly terms with some of Tennyson's friends (notably F. D. Maurice). But this anonymous attack became for a while a bee in Tennyson's bonnet.

Later in 1855, Tennyson changed his mind. He wrote to Gurney saying that he had misjudged him, and setting out carefully the way he wanted *Maud* to be seen in relation to his own identity as poet:

> Strictly speaking I do not see how from the poem I could be pronounced with certainty either peace man or war man. I wonder that you and others did not find out that all along the man was intended to have an hereditary vein of insanity, and that he falls foul on the swindling, on the times, because he feels that his father has been killed by the work of the lie, and that all through he fears the coming madness. How could you or anyone suppose that if I had had to speak in my own person my own opinion of this war or war generally I should have spoken with so little moderation. I took a man constitutionally diseased and dipt him into the circumstances of the time and took him out on fire.[14]

Actually, Gurney *had* attacked *Maud* (at least implicitly). He had referred slightingly to Tennyson's influence in a work (in verse) called *A Satire for the Age: The Transcendentalists* (revised in 1855). There he blamed Tennyson's example for the 'glut of nonsense, this sad lack of brains, / This mystical parade, insane pretence, / That never, never deviates into sense.' The effect of this was to align Tennyson with the 'Spasmodic' school (not with Longfellow, as did the 'yours in aversion' anonymous letter).[15] Tennyson may not have been aware of *A Satire for the Age*, and in any case a number of other commentators compared *Maud* with the work of Alexander Smith and the Spasmodics.*

Acquaintances of Tennyson had mixed responses to *Maud*. A few days after its publication on 28 July 1855, Matthew Arnold had written (in a private letter to his friend Arthur Hugh Clough) that he had read 'extracts' from the poem. He declared that the whole of Tennyson's

---

*The Spasmodic school, of whom Sydney Dobell (1824–74) and Alexander Smith (1830–67) were the best known, had a brief success in the early 1850s. Dobell's *Balder* (1854) is a particularly striking example of the Spasmodics' preference for psychological drama and lonely disillusioned heroes. Such work could invite comparisons with *Maud*.

1855 volume, *Maud: and Other Poems*, was 'a lamentable production, and like so much of our literature thoroughly and intensely *provincial*, not European'.[16] (The volume included 'The Charge of the Light Brigade' and the 'Ode on the Death of the Duke of Wellington'; Arnold's 'provincial' may be targeting occasional verses of this kind rather than *Maud* itself.) Coventry Patmore – who had been a friend of Tennyson's for some ten years – wrote in the *Edinburgh Review* an account of the poem which included the statement that 'no man reflects our age more truly than Mr Tennyson does, when he is not thinking of doing so'.[17] This, when one thinks about it, is a statement replete with latent hostility. Tennyson, it seems, was not in control of his own poem, and as a consequence the chaos of the age is faithfully reflected in the moral disorder of the work.

The relationship with Gladstone was competitive and guarded, although ostensibly friendly, throughout the long lives of these two great men. Gladstone reviewed *Maud* long after its publication, in 1859, and quoted the warmongering passages from the poem, including the lines: 'Is it peace or war? better war! loud war by land and by sea, / War with a thousand battles, and shaking a hundred thrones.' 'Our divining-rod,' Gladstone complained, 'does not enable us to say whether the poet intends to be in any and what degree sponsor to these sentiments, or whether he has put them forth in the exercise of his undoubted right to make vivid and suggestive representations of even the partial and narrow aspects of some endangered truth. [. . .] We do not recollect that 1855 [the height of the Crimean War] was a season of serious danger from a mania for peace and its pursuits; and even if it had been so, we fear that the passages we have quoted far overpass all the bounds of moderation and good sense.' Heavily sententious though this is, it is not wrong. It needs to be remembered, also, that this essay was full of praise for most of the poetry that Tennyson had published by that date. *In Memoriam*, which stirred such personal feelings of ancient rivalry between the two men, was in Gladstone's generous phrase 'perhaps the richest oblation ever offered by the affection of friendship at the tomb of the departed'.[18]

Had he been less thin-skinned, Tennyson could have consoled himself with the fact that some of the reviews of *Maud* were positive and discriminating. The *Spectator*'s reviewer found that the poet had scaled new heights. The poem was 'perfectly intelligible in its action, the character of the autobiographic hero is well marked, and the changes of passion are indicated with a dramatic force and singleness of aim which Mr Tennyson has never before reached'.[19] And in the *Saturday Review*, Goldwin Smith, a man whom Tennyson encountered later at

Lady Ashburton's house party at the Grange in the new year of 1856, was perceptive about *Maud*'s dramatic method. Its protagonist relied 'on external sensations instead of internal efforts' and was 'a man of high intellect and exquisite sensibility, keenly alive to all impressions, dependent on the world without him for happiness, and cynical because it is not afforded'.[20]

There were heartening private messages which went some way to ease the pain. The sculptor Thomas Woolner* wrote loyally (8 October 1855) from 27 Rutland Street, Hampstead Road, one of his characteristically noisy and exuberant letters to Emily for her to pass on to Tennyson. He wanted Tennyson to know that 'The poem has been more delight to me than anything I have known for a long long time, and it never tires, but I feel towards it as at first with a more ample comprehension of its delicate and minute beauties. Mrs Browning told me she thought it much the finest work he had ever done.'[21]

Ruskin also wrote: 'I hear of so many stupid and feelingless misunderstandings of *Maud* that I think it may perhaps give you some little pleasure to know my sincere admiration of it throughout.' It dampened the praise, somewhat, to learn that Ruskin assumed the speaker's opinions to be Tennyson's own: 'I think with you in *all* things about the war.'[22]

The Crimean War (1853–6), like many other major international conflicts, had started as a petty squabble. France and Russia had rival claims to territory in what had been the Ottoman Empire. Russia issued an ultimatum to Turkey in March 1853 and then occupied the Ottoman Danubian province (modern Romania). Britain joined France to resist what was seen as an aggressive expansionist policy on the part of the Russians. The war became 'the Crimean' war because it resolved into a campaign on the part of the British and the French to take the Russian naval base of Sebastopol. The British were badly equipped for a winter campaign on the Crimean peninsula and were famously poorly led; the whole British army became a contemporary byword for incompetence. The war ended not with the fall of Sebastopol

---

*Alfred Tennyson's marriage to Emily in 1850 had been a stroke of luck for Woolner. Emily greatly warmed to him and was protective towards him – maybe she saw in this brilliant, rough-mannered figure a younger version of her husband. Indeed it is striking, during the 1850s, to see how many of the most lasting friendships in Tennyson's life were actually cemented into place by Emily, rather than Tennyson himself. There is a sense in which Tennyson allowed Emily to be his personal ambassador to the human race.

itself but as a consequence of Britain's bombardment of the Russian naval dockyard near what is now Helsinki.[23]

The campaign was led by Lord Raglan, a veteran who had lost his right arm standing beside Wellington at Waterloo (and who was heard to refer to the Crimean enemy forces as 'the French' despite the fact that he was now fighting the Russians). Raglan's incompetence and neglect underlie the legendary bad management of the army in the Crimea. As news leaked of the British troops suffering from disease (many more men died of cholera than they did in battle), the popular mood soured. Tennyson wrote what is probably still his most famous poem as a result of reading a report in *The Times* on 14 November 1854, of the bungled charge of the Light Brigade at Balaclava. Over 600 men died as a result of inadequate leadership. The tendency to see *Maud* as militarist can only be reinforced by a consideration of 'The Charge of the Light Brigade', which had appeared in *The Examiner*, on 9 December 1854.

The poem is about a disastrous tactical error. Like the retreat from Dunkirk nearly a century later, though, it was one of those defeats that has gone down in legend as an instance of the quintessential spirit of the British. 'Honour the charge they made!' the poem declaims. 'Honour the Light Brigade, Noble six hundred!'[24] Because he had published an enormously popular poem that appeared to support the British army, it was inevitable that the jingoism of the speaker of *Maud* at the end of the monodrama was identified in the popular imagination with Tennyson's own views.

It helped Tennyson to recover from his wounded feelings over the reviews of *Maud* when he learnt that the poem was admired by Robert Browning. Tennyson recognised the technical virtuosity of Browning's dramatic monologues, and if Browning could admire the poem then he could feel that it was held in proper esteem by a man who was an intellectual equal. The friendly correspondence between the poets over *Maud* led to an invitation from Emily Tennyson for the Brownings to visit Farringford. They were unable to do so, but they in turn invited Tennyson and Emily to visit them in London.

Tennyson went on his own. This was increasingly the pattern as he became more famous in the 1850s. Emily loved Farringford, she was happy there, and she had accepted the fact that Tennyson needed company and stimulation in ways that she did not. The marriage remained contented. Ann Thwaite points out that Emily had her own clearly defined role within it: 'She paid the bills and subscriptions, kept the accounts, and dealt with the entire money side of the marriage most of the time'; this included dealing with builders when the house was extended, with the letting of Farringford for their summers away, and with the management of the farm at Farringford (which they took over later, in 1861).[25]

There was an agreement that the Tennysons would often lead their social lives separately from each other. The Brownings entertained Tennyson twice at their rented house. Emily wrote to him from Farringford on 25 September:

> Hallam expressed great sorrow at thy departure and poor little baby sighed over it. Thy wifie, thou knowest, wishes thee back with all her heart but then with half of it she would have thee stay [in London] if there be good or pleasure in staying. 13 Dorset Sq., Baker St. is the Brownings' address. I would not willingly have thee miss seeing such good and great people.[26]

One of the Brownings' parties, on 27 September 1855, was a comfortable and intimate affair for Tennyson, Robert and Elizabeth and Thomas Woolner. Tennyson wrote to Emily the following day: 'I dined yesterday with the Brownings and had a very pleasant evening – both of them are great admirers of poor little *Maud* – made very kind enquiries after thee.' It is striking that Tennyson makes no mention of a fellow poet, Dante Gabriel Rossetti, who arrived (with his brother William Michael Rossetti, chronicler of the Pre-Raphaelite Brotherhood) after dinner. 'Poor little' *Maud* was the centrepiece of the evening. Tennyson was smarting over its reception, and to reassure him, Elizabeth Browning asked him to read it to her guests. D. G. Rossetti covertly made two sketches of him, one of which he afterwards gave to Browning.*

Tennyson was immersed in his own reading and did not notice that he was being sketched. Rossetti's brother William Michael recorded the scene: 'His deep grand voice, with slightly chanting intonation, was a noble vehicle for perusal of mighty verse.' Dante Gabriel's recollection was less reverent: 'I was never more amused in my life than by Tennyson's groanings and horrors over the review of *Maud*.' The story about the anonymous letter signed 'yours in aversion' was repeated 'at least six or eight times', and 'he repeated them to me again, walking

---

*Browning wrote in 1883: 'I remember Tennyson reading the poem one evening while Rossetti made a pen-and-ink sketch of him, very good, which I still possess, and duly value.' (Hood, p. 220.)

home together'.[27] Rossetti noted Tennyson's total absorption in his own words, and his extraordinary comments on the poem as the reading proceeded: 'There's a wonderful touch!' and 'That's very tender', for example. Tennyson had not brought his spectacles, so he had to read the poem holding the book very close to his face. One of Rossetti's two sketches shows him hunched awkwardly to catch the light, his beard and moustache looking improvised (his decision to grow them, following the fitting of the false teeth, was still recent). Rossetti and Tennyson had comparable interests – they were both absorbed in Arthurian romance, they both sought to recreate the medieval world in the modern world – but following this dinner in 1855, they walked through the London night together and found disappointingly little to say to each other.*[28]

One of the most surprising consequences of Tennyson's hurt over *Maud* was his decision to collaborate (in effect) with a medical man living on the Isle of Wight who was also an amateur critic and part-time astronomer. Dr Robert James Mann (1817–86) attracted Tennyson because he could converse easily on a whole range of scientific subjects.[29] He and Tennyson had first met when Tennyson was house-hunting on the island in 1853, and they enjoyed immediate rapport. In 1856 Mann published *Maud Vindicated*, a defence of the poem which greatly pleased Tennyson. Tennyson wrote to Mann in April 1856, 'No one with this essay before him can in future pretend to misunderstand my dramatic poem, "Maud": your commentary is as true as it is full, and I am really obliged to you for defending me.'[30] Tennyson and Mann had spent a good deal of time together while Mann wrote the book, and his account contains passages which are certainly quotations from Tennyson himself. The peculiarity of the poem, Dr Mann wrote, was that its one character revealed to the reader 'his own sad and momentous history, by fits and starts, which are themselves but so many impulsive utterances naturally called forth from a mind strung to the pitch of keen poetic sensibility'. This was wholly naturalistic: 'Nothing can be more exquisitely consonant to the proceedings of nature than that such utterances should be made in fitful and broken strains, rather than that they should march steadily on to the measure of equal lines, and regularly recurring rhymes.'[31]

*   *   *

---

*Although he was inclined to mock Tennyson, Rossetti agreed to contribute to the illustrated volume of Tennyson's poetry published by Moxon in 1857. He delayed over committing himself and found that other artists had been engaged to illustrate the poems that most attracted him.

It is obvious, with the benefit of a long retrospective view, that *Maud* is indeed personal. The story is of a profoundly unhappy man, engaging with a present reality which is wholly disordered, and looking for an external, rather than an internal, object for his aggressions. He finds the external object, but at the cost of losing his humanity and becoming a machine, a doomed soldier (he will certainly be killed in the final battle at the close of the poem: the whole tonality of the piece points to that conclusion, especially in the first – 1855 – ending). The poem is about Tennyson's state of mind for much of his earlier life – a man with a violent sense of entitlement, excluded, angry, ambitious, convinced of the disorder of a world which opposes his will – and brings the marginalised younger self into conjunction with the newly wealthy, established, confident, effective self who was actively supporting British militarism in the 1850s. The Crimean War could give a man like Tennyson a sense of purpose, and of engaging in significant action. Britain in the 1850s was the most powerful civilisation in the world, and yet it was not a happy place. Tennyson himself was becoming one of the most successful figures in a striving and ambitious society, yet he was not a happy man – not yet, perhaps not ever. British society measured its citizens ruthlessly in terms of success or failure, and Tennyson was participating in this, relishing his own authority as he endorsed violence as a way of vindicating manhood.

Although the reviewers of *Maud* were in many cases puzzled and repelled, the public bought the poem so enthusiastically that Tennyson's income became more conspicuously healthy with each passing year. With increasing knowledge of him came increasing demand for personal contact. The great and the cultivated, especially those who attended the emerging salons in London centred on Lady Ashburton at Bath House and on the Prinseps at Little Holland House, all wanted to claim Tennyson as an acquaintance.

At Christmas 1855 Benjamin Jowett, arriving to join the Tennyson household for the holiday, brought with him a pressing invitation from Harriet Ashburton for Tennyson to join her party for the New Year celebrations at the Grange. Immersion in such a world suited Tennyson, despite his protestations of shyness. His way of dealing with the shyness was to read *Maud* to the assembled guests, somewhat to Jane Carlyle's irritation.[32]

He was still smarting over the reception of *Maud* at the time of this house party at the Grange, to which he had been persuaded to go partly because Jowett, at the same time as he delivered the invitation from Lady Ashburton, had written with great tact about *Maud*:

> No poem since Shakespear seems to me to show equal power of the same kind or knowledge of human nature. No modern poem contains more lines which ring in the ears of men. I do not know of any verse out of Shakespear in which the ecstasy of love soars to such a height. The vulgar don't see this psychological truth & they have not imagination enough to fill up the interstices of the tale. They are incapable of feeling the continuous effect of the whole. Also they confound the hero with the poet & yet are disappointed that they cannot absolutely identify them.[. . .] I am truly sorry that in reward for this great effort you should be tormented by those mosquitos the critics.

Jowett was shrewd about Tennyson's sensitivity to his critics: 'If I could hope you would listen to me I would beg of you to make a vow never to read a line of them. They can do you no harm except through yourself.' These men were 'the small fry of minor poets', 'the most unsafe style of people to have to do with: mortified vanity is like a jealous woman'. This was excellent advice, which Tennyson would always find it peculiarly difficult to take, as Jowett knew: 'You cannot avoid being sensitive: all poets are so but you can take away the occasions of sensitiveness.'[33]

Fame had become a problem. The point of Farringford, when he and Emily had first moved there, was that it was relatively inaccessible to the eyes of the curious and of 'lion-hunters'. At the same time Emily made sure that there was a steady stream of congenial guests, old friends such as Jowett, Edward Lear and James Spedding, and agreeable residents of the island such as Sir John Simeon. Part of *Maud* was written in Sir John's garden at Swainston (a cedar of Lebanon, which still stands at Swainston, appears in the poem – Tennyson wrote some of it in the open air in fine summer weather lying beneath this magnificent tree).

Thomas Woolner was a regular and welcome visitor. Emily greatly liked him, and so did the boys – his high spirits and rough charm were infectious, and he was a voluble and communicative correspondent. His visit to the newly married Tennysons at Coniston in 1850 was a golden memory. Late in 1856 he wrote to Emily: 'I always look back upon Coniston with a satisfied poetic love, for the happy week I spent there, now more than 6 years ago. I think it the happiest week I ever spent, it gladdens me even at this time and will I think so long as I live.' His medallion of Tennyson dating from that visit was a precursor of the well-known medallion of 1856. Emily Tennyson replied on 11 November assuring him that she found this medallion a work of 'delicate yet lofty beauty';[34] it would be used as the frontispiece to Moxon's Illustrated Tennyson of 1857.[35]

Of all the Pre-Raphaelites who were to feature in the illustrated edition of 1857, Woolner was the most energetic in his communication with the Tennysons. Late in 1854 he was planning to visit Farringford for sittings to create the new medallion. His admiration for Tennyson was genuine, but so was his business sense, and he knew that he was doing himself no harm with the Tennysons by offering lavish flattery to the Laureate:

> Tell Mr Tennyson it will not require a great deal of time as I am so well acquainted with his features now, and he need not anticipate it as an extraordinarily formidable task: Millais told me he read him some new poems of such marvellous beauty, that they surpassed anything he had ever done before, which of course I find too hard to believe true, as I do not believe perfection can be more than perfect. I am delighted to hear that Rossetti and Millais are going to illustrate the poems, with Hunt, they are the only men who ought to presume to tread upon that enchanted ground.[36]

Emily was eager to promote Woolner's career and his well-being, and she also asked him to help with acquiring some paintings for Farringford. With the earnings from *Maud* they had now been able to buy the house, and she and Tennyson had commissioned a representative to bid for furniture being sold by its previous owners, the Seymours, in a separate sale. As Tennyson himself liked to do, she dwelt on their supposed poverty. She wrote that 'one might soon make the house comfortable again were it not for the ghastly appearance of the drawing room and dining room walls so woefully stained by pictures. Can you recommend him to any pawn brokers for we must not look to finding our oil pictures in a more reputable quarter.' She asked him to look out for her 'Oldest copies of oldest pictures to be sold for one farthing each barring the discount on ready money'.[37]

Tennyson liked him (but would never give enough time to the sittings for the images that Woolner made of him) and Woolner continued to be a vigorous channel of communication, as in this letter of May 1856. He sent a report of some of the images that Millais was making for the Moxon illustrated edition of Tennyson's poems, and followed this with an account of the Royal Academy exhibition of 1856:

It is a pity you have not seen the Exhibition of R.A. this year, Hunt's 'Scapegoat' is wonderful, some of Millais are exceedingly good in colour, one of them, the 'Blind Girl,' is good in expression likewise. Hunt has not sold his picture and is not likely to now for a long time [. . .] Ruskin has been cutting it up and praised some of the worst pictures in the place; he has made such an obvious mess of it this year that his enemies are dancing for delight.

Unlike Woolner, Tennyson and Emily were on good terms with Ruskin (who had admired *Maud*). Woolner plunged ahead recklessly with his disparagement of Ruskin: 'I should like Ruskin to know what he never knew – the want of money for a year or two; then he might come to doubt his infallibility.' If Ruskin were not a rich man, perhaps he would 'give an artist working on the right road the benefit of any little doubt that might arise. The little despot imagines himself the Pope of Art and would wear 3 crowns as a right, only they would make him look funny in London!'[38]

Emily made no comment on this. It is possible that she privately agreed that Ruskin could be a tyrant, but it is more likely that she kept her opinions to herself because she felt that Woolner's energy was good for Tennyson. Woolner was always an enthusiastic and welcome visitor to the house. Emily was able to write to him triumphantly in June 1856 to say that she and Tennyson now owned Farringford. She added that little Hallam had been so struck by Woolner that 'he persists in calling a stranger kind to him, Mr Woolner'. She congratulated Woolner on the steady growth of his reputation: 'The night behind and only the day before you', though Woolner wrote back later in the summer to correct her impression that his fortunes might be improving.*

Woolner's heroic and beardless bust of Tennyson now stands outside the entrance of the Wren Library at Trinity College, Cambridge. Woolner had great hopes of this commission. It was part of the breakthrough of his career (and it also marked a slight moderation of his hostility to Ruskin). He was able to write to Emily in March 1857:

---

*He had been commissioned for a statue of Bacon for the new museum in Oxford (the museum of science and medicine, brainchild of Ruskin and of his friend Henry Acland, soon to be the Regius Professor of Medicine at the university). This important Victorian Gothic building, by the Dublin architects Dean and Woodward, is the best finished example of 'Ruskinian Gothic' that still stands (some of its decorative detail was designed personally by Ruskin). It did not make Woolner's fortune, though: 'the statue of Bacon is for the New Museum Oxford; but it is not a thing I can well be congratulated upon, for 2 or 3 more such commissions would lodge me in prison for debt.' (Woolner, p. 115.)

I have only a few minutes just to tell you that my bust is finished, and send you a card or two, thinking you might know some who would like to see it [. . .] I expect a good many next week, or this week perhaps I should call it; Ruskin came yesterday and was more pleased than anyone, since Millais saw it, has been: he said that he was 'very glad to know that such a thing could be done' and he shook my hand violently several times congratulating me on my 'great success' as he called it, and when he was going away said, 'I consider that bust to be a triumph of Art.' Now if he would say this in print it would make my fortune, but unhappily it quite hurts his feelings to have to praise anything without colour.[39]

Emily loved the bust partly because it was beardless and recalled her husband as he had looked when they married. She pointed up the contrast between the smooth marble and the shaggy reality in her letter of March 1857 to Woolner: 'I wish the public could compel A. by Act of Parliament to cut off his beard!'[40] The question of whether the bust would in any sense make Woolner's fortune was a troubling one. It was displayed at the Manchester Art Treasures exhibition in the summer of 1857, but no buyer came forward for it. Either the National Portrait Gallery or Trinity College were regarded by Tennyson's friends as appropriate destinations for it, and at Trinity in 1858 some younger members of the college, led by one of the Fellows, Montagu Butler (a future master of Trinity), who had been encouraged by his friend Vernon Lushington, combined to raise the purchase price of the bust in order to acquire it. Vernon Lushington was a member of Trinity and a successful London barrister, a brother of Edmund Lushington and thus part of Tennyson's ever-loyal Park House circle. He was the fund-raiser for the purchase of the Tennyson bust, as he explained in a breezy and jovial letter to Woolner early in 1858:

Montagu Butler a friend of mine (and Fellow of Trinity) has written to me proposing that some of us Trinity men should join together, buy your Tennyson and present it to the College Library at Cambridge. What do *you* say to this? Would you be satisfied with your master-piece resting *there* to the end of time? I think you must have seen our Library when you went to Cambridge searching for Bacons [as models for the Oxford Museum sculpture]; and know otherwise what rank our Trinity College as a place of education has and has long had in the sight of all the land. Your Tennyson if it got there would find itself in company of many distinguished heads by undistinguished sculptors; also in the presence of Thorwaldsen's Byron [which is indeed, as Lushington implies, a fine portrait of the poet].

Lushington added as a warning that 'no one cares for Art in Cambridge and your handiwork would seldom be beheld by any seeing eye'.[41] Woolner needed no persuasion; the proposal was a grand and generous one. In practice, though, the raising of the money was frustratingly slow. In August of 1858 he complained to his generous client Pauline, Lady Trevelyan, that the subscription for the bust had been open for five months and that Lushington 'knows how seriously I am in want of the money' but was impeding progress with his (unexplained) 'crotchets'.* Woolner felt that Lushington was being needlessly cautious over the terms of the fund-raising, and in the process was both damaging Woolner's own reputation and preventing other buyers from offering for the Tennyson bust. In addition Lushington's behaviour was 'making Tennyson himself anything but pleased, for he says that it is "disgracing" him, that a subscription should be so long on hand for placing a bust of him in his own College'.[42] All of this was unjust to Lushington. By May 1859 £200 had been raised to buy the bust and the sculpture was at the college. But the Master, Whewell, resisted placing it in the library. The Bursar's minutes of a meeting on 27 May show that the Master and the senior fellows considered the 'Offer of Bust of Tennyson (Poet-Laureate) to be placed in Library. Declined chiefly because he is *Living* Poet'.[43] It was not until 1 November that Vernon Lushington was able to write to Woolner with the final decision:

The mighty Master & his men have at last graciously condescended to accept your *Masterpiece* & even with thanks. Into the College Library itself they won't allow it to go, that being devoted to dead men, but they offer to place it in the *Vestibule* of the Library, to be promoted we hope, in due time, when old Tennyson himself is promoted [i.e. dead; though this 'promotion' of the masterpiece never took place]. To this we offer no objections, seeing no probability of

---

*Woolner had a commission from Lady Trevelyan for a sculpture to be placed in the central hall of Wallington in Northumberland. The piece is called *Civilisation* (also sometimes called *The Lord's Prayer*). It is a substantial work of art: on a plinth a mother teaches her child to recite the Lord's Prayer while below the plinth are scenes of pre-Christian savagery: druids, human sacrifice and the like. Woolner had been engaged on this commission since 1856 but had difficulty finding suitable models for it; it was not finished until 1867, by which time Lady Trevelyan had died.

obtaining better terms, & wishing to have the business settled; so into the Vestibule your Bust goes.[44]

There had been some potentially annoying discussion in the press about the business of the bust, including a comic poem in *Punch*, but the Tennysons were content with the decision.

Woolner was a helpful social lubricant, cheerfully passing on to Emily praise of Tennyson heard in London. J. A. Froude said that 'Carlyle and Tennyson are the only men of the present time whose heads [as busts or medallions] will be cared for 200 years hence'; Francis Palgrave was impressively learned and 'his high regard for the Lord Farringford [Tennyson] is pleasant common ground for us both'. Woolner could be tactless, however, and it is not surprising that in October 1858 we have a sudden reference to a misunderstanding. 'You made a serious mistake,' he told Emily, 'in supposing that you saw my lip curl with contempt when you were criticising my work.'[45] Curled or not, Woolner's lips were seldom sealed, and his generous nature and exuberant volubility clearly overcame whatever this difficulty with Emily had been. They remained very good friends.

As Leonée Ormond has pointed out, Woolner and Tennyson were similar men. Woolner was born in Suffolk, and was the son of a minor post office official:

> Both came from eastern rural counties and had made their way to success from an impecunious start. Neither ever quite regarded himself as belonging to the moneyed public-school world to which both committed their sons. It is significant perhaps that Woolner's two most important contributions to Tennyson's poetry ['Enoch Arden' and 'Aylmer's Field'] were subjects for narrative poems with a rustic setting, not unlike that in which both men had passed their childhood.[46]

The many visitors whom Emily encouraged to visit Farringford, the boisterous Woolner among them, were therapy for Tennyson's loneliness. So was the gardening: Emily's diary shows Tennyson engaging in a surprising amount of work, digging, laying new beds, planting out potatoes, building a shed and so forth – hard physical labour which helped to lift the spirits of the man who had written 'The Two Voices' and other such depressed poems in his youth.

Routine, physical labour, friends, reading steadily to Emily from a very wide range of his favourite texts in the evenings filled his day and helped to keep his depressions at bay. Yet *Maud* is a record of depression – the drama is one of inner anger which at last is turned, violently, outwards. Emily recorded the completion of the revised state of the poem in 1856. In April Tennyson showed 'the new poem' (i.e. new sections of it) to Drummond Rawnsley, from whose house he and Emily had been married six years earlier. On 24 April 'Drummond walks on Afton down with A. & hears a few lines of King Arthur & is shown the new poem in "Maud."'[47]

After the publication of the second and enlarged edition of *Maud* in 1856, Tennyson busied himself with the preparation of his Arthurian poems. He and Emily learnt Welsh together in order to be able to read the source poems. The Arthurian project drew an interesting comment about Tennyson from Arthur Hugh Clough, who had stayed at Freshwater in the late summer of 1856 and had become friendly with the Tennysons. On 13 November 1856, Clough wrote to F. J. Child to say that 'Tennyson is going on with fragments, or idylls as I believe he calls them, on the Morte d'Arthur subjects. Two considerable ones are complete and he seems to be working steadily – studying Welsh moreover – I like him personally better than I do his manner in his verses; personally he is the most unmannerly simple big child of a man that you can find.'[48]

Tennyson was ten years older than Clough, and the unmannerly big child was the object of the younger man's hero-worship. Arthur Hugh Clough (1819–61) was a distinguished poet and a troubled, complex, shy and to some extent self-defeating personality, though he had a great gift for friendship. He knew and corresponded with many of Tennyson's circle of friends, especially Arthur Stanley (later Dean Stanley of Westminster), William Allingham, Thomas Carlyle, Benjamin Jowett, Francis Palgrave and William G. Ward; others of his acquaintance connected with Tennyson included the Cracrofts (the family who had let Harrington Hall to Rosa Baring's family) and Sir John and Lady Franklin, relations of Emily.

As early as 1838, well before Tennyson became famous, the nineteen-year-old Clough wrote of him as the major poet of the day and the standard by which to judge other poets.[49] If Clough had lived longer, this friendship with Tennyson could have come to resemble the earlier friendship between Tennyson and Arthur Hallam. Clough had something of Hallam's style and assumptions; like Hallam before him, he had his finger on the cultural pulse of his time. It was important for Clough to be able to feel that he was liked. There had always been something about him of the earnest schoolboy. In 1835, aged sixteen, he had written to his brother George: 'remember always, that to be liked is not the thing we should wish for on its own account, but only because it will make [it] easier for us to do good, namely to those who like us'.[50] This remained a strong impulse in Clough's adult life, and as he got to know Tennyson better, he would feel a powerful urge to do good to him.

Tennyson was taking his Arthurian research seriously. With Emily he travelled in Wales in the summer of 1857, staying in particular at Caerleon and then following the Wye from Builth to Brecon. In her journal Emily wrote, 'Neither he nor I admired this part of the Wye [toward Brecon] as much as that at Builth.'[51] Travelling, either for profit in this way or simply for pleasure, became increasingly a feature of his life after the publication of *Maud*, together with a London-based sociability which could to some degree compensate him for the isolation of Farringford. In April and May 1857 he stayed with the Prinseps at Little Holland House, leaving Emily on her own at Farringford. This visit to the Prinseps was longer than he had intended (and probably longer than was welcome to his hosts) because he developed a nasty ingrown toenail. As he told Henry Hallam, on 1 May, 'I am laid up with a bad foot and cannot stir out. The nail of the great toe having shot out a spur low down into the flesh causing an inflammation, I have twice had to undergo a rather cruel surgical operation owing to this abnormal fancy of the nail.' But whether he could move much or not at the Prinseps', he continued to have an amusing time there and clearly enjoyed being cosseted as an invalid. The loyal London friends trooped out to see him: 'Hunt and Woolner and Palgrave here,' he wrote. 'Spedding dines here today. I have little or no news except that all people are exceedingly kind.'[52]

The toe cannot have caused much suffering, since distinguished guests were invited by the Prinseps to dine on successive evenings in the following week: John Everett Millais, Richard Doyle and one Burnet Morier (a diplomat, a man of great charm and powerful physical presence, and Benjamin Jowett's closest friend).[53] And when Tennyson was back in Farringford later that May, the house was again 'full of visitors and will be so for some time', which did not prevent him from going to London again on his own to see the Duke and Duchess of Argyll; he gave them a private reading of some new poems including 'Merlin and Nimuë' (the original title of 'Merlin and Vivien'). A bit later he complained to the Duchess that he was anxious about premature exposure for this poem, because a nameless acquaintance to whom he had shown it previously had 'gone brawling about town' expressing hostile views. 'Why should I expose myself to the folly of fools?' the poet wanted to know.[54]

In July 1857, Tennyson and Emily were travelling together once more, this time to Manchester to visit the Art Treasures exhibition (for which a huge structure, rivalling in magnificence London's Crystal Palace, had been built at Old Trafford). This was a massive event, and Tennyson and Emily stayed in Manchester for a week and made five visits to it. Tennyson was something of an exhibit himself, of course, and was treated as such by a brilliant literary American visitor, Nathaniel Hawthorne, who observed him, in company with Thomas Woolner, looking at the paintings. Tennyson was 'the most picturesque figure' that Hawthorne had ever seen, 'dressed entirely in black, and with nothing white about him except the collar of his shirt, which methought might have been clean the day before.'

> He had on a black wide-awake hat, with round crown and wide-irregular brim, beneath which came down his long black hair, looking terribly tangled; he had a long pointed beard, too, a little browner than his hair, and not so abundant as to encumber any of the expression of his face.

Hawthorne did not dare to introduce himself to Tennyson, partly because of the press of acquaintances who were already claiming the poet's attention, and partly because of Tennyson's body language, which was shy and retiring. Woolner had a loud voice and a rough manner; Hawthorne felt that he was somewhat coarse company for the poet:

> Mr Woolner was as unlike Tennyson as could be imagined; a small smug man, in a blue frock and brown pantaloons. They talked about the pictures, and passed pretty rapidly from one to another. Tennyson looking at them through a pair of spectacles which he held in his hand, and then standing a minute before those that interested him, with his hands folded behind his back.[55]

Hawthorne also overheard Tennyson talking in his deep voice ('a bass voice, but not of resounding depth; a voice rather broken as it were, and ragged about the edges') with William Fairbairn, a wealthy Manchester industrialist who had the misfortune to have two deaf and dumb children.[56] Fairbairn was another client of Thomas Woolner, who made a strikingly effective double sculpture of these children (a boy and a girl), bringing out both their physical beauty and the pathos of their situation.

Woolner wrote to William Michael Rossetti on 2 August, describing Manchester itself as fearfully busy and indeed a kind of industrial hell, 'no rest for mind or body, din, clatter, thunder, dust, smoke, showers of black smuts'. All was redeemed however by the magnificence of the exhibition: 'the Art Treasures are worth any amount of inconvenience – wonderful – only too rich – you are bewildered with the amount'. He was immensely pleased that the Manchester visit had been a success for Tennyson: 'Tennyson was delighted with the Art Treasures, liked his reception among the Manchesterians, they have an immense reverence for him'.[57]

In the summer of 1857 the Tennysons spent three months in Scotland and the north of England. They visited the Charles Tennyson Turners at Grasby in Lincolnshire, and attempted a rapprochement with the Tennyson d'Eyncourt family. Tennyson's uncle Charles was away from the house, but his wife Fanny was friendly and showed Alfred and Emily round Bayons Manor, which had now been in development for nearly twenty years and was nearly completed. The expense of Bayons and the pretensions that it represented were still laughed at by Lincolnshire society, and Charles had become a lonely and disappointed man.

Charles Tennyson d'Eyncourt's career in politics had been that of an active and intelligent reformer. He supported the redistribution of parliamentary constituencies, and when the Whig government was elected in 1830 he was appointed Clerk of the Ordnance. In May 1831 he was elected as the radical MP for Stamford, in Lincolnshire. At this point his political career went off track: following his win at Stamford, he fought a duel with Lord Thomas Cecil, the rival candidate (who had been enraged by his electioneering methods). Neither man was hurt, but his reputation was fatally damaged by this. In 1832 he resigned his office of Clerk of the Ordnance, ostensibly because of ill health but in reality because he was effectively in disgrace.

By way of consolation for his loss of office he was made a member of the Privy Council; and as MP for Lambeth he continued to speak on the radical side in debates supporting municipal reform, the repeal of the Corn Laws and some of the demands made by the Chartists. As a Privy Councillor he could reasonably hope to be raised to the peerage, and he wanted the barony of d'Eyncourt (from which the Tennysons were distantly related) to be revived. Lord Melbourne, then prime minister, refused. Despite this, and immediately after his father's death in 1835, Charles Tennyson changed his name to Tennyson d'Eyncourt in accordance, as he always maintained, with his father's wish. In the story of Alfred Tennyson he looks an increasingly failed figure, angered by his nephew's fame and unwisely seeking to emulate his success as a poet.

He wrote a long elegy, in eighteenth-century rhyming couplets, for his dead son Eustace, who had succumbed to yellow fever in Gibraltar in 1842. This was published at his own expense (lavishly got up) in 1851 (the year after *In Memoriam*), as *Eustace: An Elegy*. His need to trump Alfred's elegy for Hallam was obvious. Some of his friends tried to persuade him not to publish; they should have tried harder. By parading his love of his dead son in this way, the poor father invited derision rather than sympathy:

> Lamented EUSTACE! I invoke thy Shade
> These moral Truths – this warning Voice to aid.
> With genius, energy, and Power of Mind,
> Beyond the usual fortune of Mankind:
> Exempt from Passions which the heart deprave:
> Forbearing, constant, generous and brave;
> Gentle, but firm, benevolent and true, –
> Would that my Summons could thy Life renew![58]

Comparison with his nephew's masterpiece was both inevitable and painful. Charles's poem for his son was a genuine expression of love and grief, and it would have invited no mockery if it had been circulated privately among his family and friends.

In 1852, Charles Tennyson d'Eyncourt's public career came to a quiet close; he was defeated at Lambeth in the parliamentary election, and he never stood for Parliament again. Instead he diverted his energy with a kind of manic intensity to the completion of Bayons Manor, which was by this time a remarkable testimony to his understanding of medieval architecture. It divided the family; his children disliked the place and he found his life there increasingly lonely. By the mid 1850s, then, the reverse in contrast of fortunes between Alfred Tennyson's family and that of his uncle had become very clear (and makes Alfred's continuing bitterness in *Maud* over the disinheritance of his father the more remarkable). The rapprochement in 1857 was overdue.

Tennyson and Emily travelled north to Tent Lodge on Coniston Water (the house they had borrowed for their honeymoon in 1850). Here Charles Dodgson ('Lewis Carroll') hunted them down. Dodgson was a mathematician, a 'Student' (equivalent of a Fellow) of Christ Church at Oxford, and an enthusiastic amateur photographer. He visited Tent Lodge with the express purpose of securing some photographs of the poet and his family. Dodgson visited regularly over a period of a week or ten days, took walks with Tennyson and made photographs both of Tennyson and of the boys. He wrote to his sister to say that his subject was 'a strange, shaggy-looking man', whose 'hair, moustache and beard looked wild and neglected', but who was 'kind and friendly from the first'.[59] Clearly Tennyson at this time took to Dodgson, perhaps flattered by attention from this young, intelligent and culti- vated Oxford don, and Dodgson was encouraged by a general invita- tion to visit Farringford at a later date.[60]

After this point the Tennysons' itinerary miscarried in various ways: they were due to visit Alfred's Cambridge contemporary Robert Monteith and his wife in Lanarkshire, but had not given enough notice of their approach. They then travelled through Glasgow towards Inverary Castle, but that also miscarried: the Argylls were away from home, but the Duchess came hastily to find them, having hired a special steamer in order to do so. The processional dignity of their late summer continued, with a successful October visit to the Argylls followed by a delayed visit to the Monteiths at Carstairs, and then a staged return, partly by train. They stopped in Headingley in Yorkshire with the ever-hospitable Marshalls, and were back at Farringford, in the rain, on 4 November.

One wants to ask: why? Why did a man as shy, as intensely literary and devoted to his inner life as Tennyson need to devote so much time and energy to travelling among these grand friends and acquaintances with whom, however well they got on at the personal level, he had very little in common? Perhaps the answer is that none of this mattered. It was all surface; the real activity taking place in him was at a depth that remained undisturbed. Possibly another answer is that the deep social unease of his young manhood was still lingering, and he needed constantly the reassurance of being fêted by the rich and the great.

The hectic travelling of 1857 was too much for Emily. When they returned home, her health, never strong, collapsed and thereafter for several years she did not travel with Tennyson. An unwritten agreement was established whereby he would visit London or the country houses of the grand friends on his own, and Emily would stay in her beloved Farringford and share his life vicariously through his letters. He was good about writing her what were, in effect, letter-journals of his travels and visits.

Emily continued to correspond with Thomas Woolner, who was a favourite with the boys and a reliable source of refreshment to Tennyson; she was very pleased that Woolner had looked after Tennyson so well in Manchester. Woolner's letters to Emily were positively garrulous, with a wealth of detail about his personal affairs and his quest for further commissions – he trusted her completely – while Emily's letters to him were increasingly warm and personal in tone. She wrote to him in December 1857 that she had to go to London with Alfred to stay with the Prinseps at Little Holland House, a prospect over which she had mixed feelings. 'I do badly to stay in a house, and should always like my private house like a snail to moor alongside that of a friend.'⁶¹

Emily's nervous collapse was the subject of a letter from little Hallam Tennyson to Thomas Woolner in April 1858:

> Love and kisses. I used to love you and you used to love me and you played with me. I love you and you love me. What games did you play with me when you were here? Have you forgotten them? Mamma has not been well but now she is better and papa is making a beautiful summer-house, and would you like to come and see it? Mamma has been wheeled in the little carriage and papa draws it, and papa says mamma must come to the summer-house and papa painted the summer-house all by himself.⁶²

The decoration to the summer house that Tennyson built for Emily was skilled, Pre-Raphaelite in inspiration, and lasted well, but as a result of later rough use of the structure for agricultural purposes it has disappeared. It was a tender and probably a guilty gesture from Tennyson, a way of showing Emily how much he cared for her in the illness which had been brought on by his own taste for harvesting the rewards of fame. Emily continued to function as an unpaid secretary, scrupulously answering all the letters that came in to Tennyson from aspiring writers – and there were hundreds of them. Other writers would visit; one such was Algernon Charles Swinburne, who came with a friend to call at Farringford from his home at Bonchurch, also on the Isle of Wight, early in 1858. Swinburne behaved perfectly, as became a member of an ancient Northumberland family (and an undergraduate of Jowett's). 'I thought him a very modest and intelligent young fellow,' wrote Tennyson. 'What I particularly admired in him was that he did not press upon me any verses of his own.'⁶³

Jowett, who understood Tennyson as well as anyone did, spoke of him as 'the shyest person I ever knew, feeling sympathy and needing it to a degree quite painful'.[64] One person who could meet this need was the ever-attentive Francis Turner Palgrave. Palgrave knew enough about the topics that interested Tennyson to be able to hold a conversation with him, and the two men took a holiday in Portugal together in the summer of 1859. At first Tennyson was delighted by this new experience. At this point he was getting on well with Palgrave and with another younger man, Palgrave's friend F. C. Grove, who was accompanying them.*[65]

The holiday began well: on the journey to Southampton they were joined in the carriage by W. H. Brookfield, who got on at Andover 'with great joy on both sides', as Palgrave reported. 'Thus the talk of the two after dinner at Radley's Hotel [. . .] was one continuous stream of lively anecdote and happy remembrance: each speaker seeming to vie with the other in a contest which was really only the result of the pleasure of the moment.'[66] Tennyson and Palgrave were both immune from seasickness and enjoyed the voyage – dolphins accompanied them, and the experience was spacious and peaceful. Tennyson felt like one of his own Lotos-Eaters, 'free from the troublesome exertion of the will; saved thus far from ourselves; carried along without the power of choice, and as it were under "direction"'.[67]

Lisbon was hot, but Cintra was even hotter:

> Cintra disappointed me at first sight, and perhaps will continue to disappoint though to Southern eyes from its evergreen groves in contrast with the parched barren look of the landscape it must look very lovely: but as yet I have not seen much of it. I climbed with Grove to the Pena, a Moorish looking castle on the top of the hill, which is being repaired and which has gateways fronted with tiles in patterns, these gates look very much like those in the illustrated Arabian nights of Lane.†[68]

They found a spectacular convent city with wonderful views: 'This [wrote Palgrave] undoubtedly is one of the great panoramic landscapes of Europe, and I suppose the least visited.' But the heat and above all

---

*Palgrave kept a journal of the holiday; it was subsequently published in 1868, and extracts from it appear in the 'Materials for a Life of A.T.', in Hallam Tennyson's *Memoir* and in the memoir of Palgrave edited by his daughter. (Palgrave, pp. 58–62.)
†Edward William Lane's translation of *One Thousand and One Nights*, first published in monthly parts 1838–40 and in three volumes in 1840, became the version in which these exotic tales were best known to the mid-Victorian reading public. The illustrations to Lane's translation were by the Newcastle-born designer and engraver William Harvey, who had been trained by Thomas Bewick. *One Thousand and One Nights* was Harvey's most successful commission.

the mosquitoes were becoming too much for Tennyson. Palgrave helped him to rig up a mosquito net for himself wherever they stayed. Once twisted into this funnel-like contraption enclosing his bed, Tennyson found that he was unable to smoke unless he summoned a servant. He wanted to light a match but feared that he would set the muslin on fire: 'Hence one night Tennyson, able to command the bell, summoned the waiter. I brought him in through my (contiguous) room with a light; and the man's terror at the spectacle of the great ghost, looking spectral within its white canopy, was delightful.' After this Tennyson gave up the mosquito net but said that he wished he 'had a little baby in bed with him' so that the mosquitoes would attack the baby and not himself.[69]

On 2 September Tennyson decided to cut short the holiday because of 'the heat and the flies and the fleas and one thing and another'[70] and so they sailed home from Lisbon to Southampton on the 7th. Thomas Woolner wrote about the aborted trip to his Northumberland friend and patron Lady Trevelyan:

> He enjoyed tolerably the trip to Lisbon, but was exceedingly ill for some days, brought on by the wine and vile food of the country: Palgrave, who was with him, was in a fright about him for some while: his and Tennyson's fear was lest the fact should get into the papers and frighten Mrs Tennyson at home: she was staying at Maidstone with the Lushingtons while he was away. A few days after their arrival at Lisbon, all the grandees, who had discovered Tennyson's identity, came flocking to pay their compliments and offer him their services. The same thing occurred at Copenhagen last year – the result, you see of becoming famous.[71]

Palgrave was disappointed, and to compensate him Tennyson took him to Cambridge, a city that Palgrave hardly knew. Two Fellows of Trinity entertained them, and Tennyson visited the rooms where Arthur Hallam had lived as an undergraduate, 'with the pathos in his voice of memories distant and dear', as Palgrave put it.[72] Did Tennyson place any value on Palgrave as a friend? His journal-letter to Emily indicates a chilling willingness to use him as a servant. He wrote to her from the Crown Hotel in Lyndhurst in September 1859: 'Palgrave has been as kind to me as a brother, and far more useful than a valet or courier, doing everything.'[73]

Palgrave was certainly pertinacious in seeking out Tennyson's company. In 1856, in the hope that Tennyson might be on holiday at Cauteretz in the Pyrenees (the place sacred to the memory of Arthur

Hallam), Palgrave, who with his father was travelling through the region on his way to Spain, 'hunted through registers and local arrivals' but found no trace of him. As Palgrave put it in his literary way, he had comforted himself 'for finding no notice of you by deciding that whilst I am in the land of Charlemagne and Roland, you are in British or Armorican Arthuria'.[74] But he was regularly a guest at Farringford at Christmas, and he was a welcome travelling companion. Like William Allingham (and, later, James Knowles), Palgrave was serviceable: a loyal lieutenant.

Edward Moxon was loyal to Tennyson, and decidedly long-suffering – but then he had effectively struck oil by becoming Tennyson's publisher, and he was fully aware of that. Between 1832 and 1855, Moxon had published seven volumes of Tennyson's poems. All except the first had made substantial profits. *In Memoriam* had of course met with runaway fame and fortune. The surprise, perhaps, was *Maud*, which in spite of – or perhaps because of – its mixed reviews and consequent notoriety showed such strong sales that Tennyson had the confidence to make an offer for Farringford. It was this commercial success that encouraged Moxon to embark on the de luxe edition, with fifty illustrations from plates by favoured artists of the day, including three founding members of the Pre-Raphaelite Brotherhood: Millais had seventeen plates (competent rather than exciting) in the volume, Holman Hunt six, while Rossetti, who had been dilatory and exacting about his contributions, had five (of which his illustrations to the conclusion to 'The Lady of Shalott' and to 'Mariana in the South' are the most interesting). The full list of artists comprised T. Creswick, Millais, Holman Hunt, Mulready, J. C. Horsley, D. G. Rossetti, Clarkson Stanfield and Maclise.

Moxon had discussed the project with Tennyson as early as 1854, and poet and publisher together had called on Creswick, Mulready, Horsley and Millais, in order to engage them for the project.[75] Landseer, Stanfield, Maclise and Frost were also recruited. Tennyson's recent and warm acquaintance with Ruskin (following the latter's enthusiasm for *Maud*) led to the addition of Rossetti and Holman Hunt in 1855. Ultimately, though, Tennyson was disappointed by Rossetti's illustrations. The contributor he liked best was Millais. His lines were clean, his images clear, picturesque, and on the whole faithful to Tennyson's text. Rossetti, by contrast, created images which are strong in themselves (his 'St Cecilia' from 'The Palace of Art' is particularly striking), but for

Tennyson they bore an oblique and puzzling relationship to the text. Moreover, Rossetti demanded more money than the other artists did.

In February 1857, Moxon wrote a defensive letter to Emily:

I am sorry to hear that with few exceptions you would not care to have the illustrations at [*sic*] a gift. All I can say is that neither labour nor expense has been spared in the getting up of the book – the best artists have been employed, and for the designs and engraving alone I have paid upwards of £1500. The price of the book will be either 30/- or 31/6. Mr Routledge it is true makes the price of his annual volumes a guinea, but your friends should bear in mind that he pays *nothing* for the copyright.[76]

Moxon was absolutely right to draw attention to the lavishness of the volume. It is richly and prolifically illustrated, and the artists were all well-known names of the day. Moxon had indeed worked hard to create something magnificent, and Tennyson's reaction was little short of curmudgeonly. Millais' illustrations to 'The Dream of Fair Women' are somewhat dark, perhaps, but he did make a large number of images which do faithfully represent the incidents from the poems for which they were designed, especially those for 'Locksley Hall' and 'St Agnes' Eve'. Mulready's illustration to the rollicking London ballad written in 1837, 'Will Waterproof's Lyrical Monologue', is lively and full of faithful incident. ('Waterproof' is writing his poem, and in a thought bubble above his head appears the Cock flying with the 'some-thing-pottle-bodied' boy.[77] This is a reference to the inn sign for the Cock Tavern in Fleet Street, a favourite place for literary men, much frequented in the 1830s by Tennyson and some of his Cambridge friends such as James Spedding.) The poem was essentially a piece of fun acknowledging Tennyson's own liking for drink. It had been sent to Fitzgerald to read in 1837 and was first published in 1842. 'Will Waterproof' is a more drunken version of Tennyson himself:

> Head-waiter, honoured by the guest
>   Half-mused, or reeling ripe,
> The pint, you brought me, was the best
>   That ever came from pipe.
> But though the port surpasses praise,
>   My nerves have dealt with stiffer.
> Is there some magic in the place?
>   Or do my peptics differ?

For since I came to live and learn,
　　No pint of white or red
Had ever half the power to turn
　　This wheel within my head,
Which bears a seasoned brain about,
　　Unsubject to confusion,
Though soaked and saturate, out and out,
　　Through every convolution.

And through the haze of drink and fantasy the ballad makes a friendly nod to the actual head waiter at the Cock:

Head-waiter of the chop-house here,
　　To which I most resort,
I too must part: I hold thee dear
　　For this good pint of port.[78]

One of the best images in the volume is Holman Hunt's memorable plate illustrating 'Out flew the web and floated wide; / The mirror cracked from side to side; / "The curse is come upon me," cried / The Lady of Shalott'.[79] It beautifully captures the wilful destruction that the Lady has brought upon her world. The web that she has been weaving and her own hair are in wild disorder: they dominate the image and frame the ecstatic and suicidal central figure. Hunt has certainly caught the spirit of the poem's crisis, but Tennyson disliked it ('I didn't say her hair was blown about like that').[80]

Rossetti's plate of the Lady lying dead (while Lancelot looks down on her in resignation) is overcrowded, but so are the final stanzas of the poem in its 1842 state (and in the 1832 state they had been even more so: 'Out upon the wharfs they came, / Knight and burgher, lord and dame [. . .] They crossed themselves, their stars they blest, / Knight, minstrel, abbot, squire and guest.')[81] Rossetti's images for the volume are more interesting and more distinguished than Tennyson was prepared to recognise.

The hope was that the book would cover additional expenses for the newly purchased property, Farringford, but difficulties with some of the illustrators meant that it missed the Christmas market in 1856, and came out at the less propitious date of May 1857.[82] Despite the love and labour that had gone into it, the cherished illustrated edition, for which Moxon had secured the best engravers and the most noted and fashionable artists, was a commercial failure. Initial sales were promising, and Moxon was able to write to Emily

Tennyson early in July 1857 saying, 'we have sold 1300 of the illustrated edition, which is I think a fair number to begin with'. But sales fell off sharply, and by 22 July Moxon had written to Tennyson offering for his 'interest in the edition' a lump sum of £2,000. He, Moxon, would bear the remaining loss.[83] Moxon died the following year, and Holman Hunt reported that 'it was said when, soon after, Moxon quitted this world of worry and vexation, *the book* had been the death of him!'[84]

After Moxon's death, his business was run by Bradbury & Evans, Printers (who were also the trustees of his will). In 1858, Bradbury & Evans claimed over £8,000 from Tennyson following the failure of the illustrated edition. By this time Tennyson had recruited a family member – Emily's brother-in-law Charles Weld – to deal with the publisher, and Weld vigorously resisted this claim on his behalf. Bradbury & Evans climbed down (after a long correspondence and consultation of legal opinion), but there was further dispute over the illustrated edition of *The Princess*, with plates by Maclise. Tennyson said that he had never agreed to the illustrated *Princess*, but when he saw how deeply the firm had already invested in the project, he reluctantly agreed that it should go ahead, much though he disliked Maclise's illustrations.[85] The illustrated *Princess* was in fact a very handsome, expensively produced volume. The embossed blue and gold cover proclaimed that this was a prestigious object to own. As always, Tennyson's Oxford DCL and his appointment as Laureate were prominent. The solemnity of the title page was part of the joke, given that what followed was a 'medley', a fantasy, a comedy and a love story: THE PRINCESS: / A MEDLEY / BY / ALFRED TENNYSON D.C.L. / POET LAUREATE / WITH TWENTY-SIX ILLUSTRATIONS ENGRAVED ON WOOD BY DALZIEL, GREEN, THOMAS, AND E. WILLIAMS, FROM DRAWINGS BY DANIEL MACLISE, R.A. / LONDON: EDWARD MOXON AND CO. DOVER STREET. / 1860.

By 1857, Tennyson had become grand. Edward Fitzgerald, who had been born into social grandeur and on the whole disliked it, was dismayed by this development in his friend. In May 1857 he was in the London Library when Tennyson suddenly arrived, 'bearded, and seeming very well but staying at a great House in Kensington with which I won't meddle'; this was actually Little Holland House, home of the Prinseps, which was scarcely a 'great House', more an overgrown country cottage. Fitzgerald added a wistful hope that he and Tennyson would meet soon in Spedding's rooms, where he would have felt again on equal terms, but that meeting did not materialise.[86]

Fitzgerald himself was going through a particularly bad patch. On 4 November 1856, he had made the disastrous mistake of marrying Lucy Barton, the daughter of an old friend, William Barton, the Woodbridge poet and bank clerk. His motives for marrying seem to have been helplessly altruistic and high-minded, but the reality of the situation was that soon after securing this ungainly and unpresentable wife, who was forty-eight years old at the time of the marriage, he began to hate her. Fitzgerald was homosexual if he was anything, and he had no sexual experience at all. Nor did Lucy. This marriage was even more doomed than the tragic match between John Ruskin and Effie Gray (with which it has often been compared). By May 1857 Fitzgerald knew that he had to extricate himself; the final separation from Lucy took place in August of that year. The couple did not divorce, but Fitzgerald stipulated that in return for a regular income, Lucy should have no further contact with him.[87] Tennyson, by sharp contrast, was happily married, and Fitzgerald's distaste for the influence that Emily had over him was by this time quite marked. He was not alone in this: some of Tennyson's siblings and old friends experienced Emily as an unwelcome rival presence. But there can be no doubt that since his marriage Tennyson had become healthier, far more prosperous and far less prone to periods of depression and despair than before, and it seems certain that without Emily's care he would not have lived as long as he did.

With the fame and security that he now enjoyed went a heightened level of responsibility for his extended family. His indulgent and adoring mother, Elizabeth, liked nothing so much as to be surrounded by her striking sons and handsome daughters (a Mrs Gould, who knew the whole family, said that the youngest of the family, Horatio, was 'the most beautiful man I had ever seen'). Three of the daughters had married and were thus provided for (while poor disabled Matilda lived with her mother and later with Alfred and Emily). But too many of the sons showed neither interest in leaving home nor a desire to earn their own livings.

Arthur, who wrote sensitive poetry, seems to have trained for a while as an artist but did not persist at it, and lived with his mother, first at Somersby and then at High Beech. He became an alcoholic and spent the year 1842–3 in an institution for the treatment of alcoholism (and insanity). Thereafter he lived for a while in Italy with his oldest brother, Frederick, who was now married to an Italian and was able to live comfortably on the capital that he, exceptionally (as the oldest son), had inherited from Old George. In the 1850s, Arthur returned from Italy and lived for a while with his gentle and indulgent brother Charles Tennyson Turner in his parish of Grasby, and in 1860 he settled down into marriage (with Harriet West, sister of the vicar of a neighbouring Lincolnshire parish). Although he never took orders, Arthur worked as a kind of unpaid priest, devoting himself to good works in the parish. He looked like an artist 'floating down the garden path, his picturesque figure clothed in an ample cloak with a large collar open at the neck and a wide artistic hat over his somewhat unkempt locks'.[88]

Septimus had been a promising youngster, with sharp wits and more readiness and capacity than was displayed by any of his brothers. He was apprenticed to a land agent (land agency had been one of the planks of Old George's prosperity), but this did not last, and in 1834 he was instead apprenticed to an apothecary (as great-grandfather Michael Tennyson had been). After receiving his modest inheritance following Old George's death in 1835, Septimus gave up work altogether. With Arthur he went to Florence to live with Frederick, but this did not last. Like the others, Septimus was a poet, and some able sonnets of his have survived; but he sank into what must have been deep and incurable depression, and died in 1866, aged fifty-one, having achieved nothing.[89] Rossetti said that once:

> When calling at the Henry Hallams' house in Wimpole Street, he was ushered into the drawing room which he thought was empty, until a huge, untidy, shaggy figure rose from the hearth rug on which it had been lying at full length, and advanced towards him with outstretched hand, saying 'I am Septimus, the most morbid of the Tennysons.'[90]

The story of the youngest brother, Horatio, is not as sad. He took his small capital out to Tasmania in order to make his fortune farming. Before long the hard reality of farming in a raw colonial outpost defeated him; Horatio came back to England and for some years lived either with Alfred and Emily or with Charles Tennyson Turner. Subsequently he would marry and have four children; his first wife died young, which devastated him for a while, but he would in due course make a second happy marriage.

By writing the *Idylls of the King*, Tennyson was throwing down a gauntlet. Despite the furore over *Maud*, he retained a commanding position among poets of the 1860s, but with his Arthurian projects he was aware that he would be negotiating his way among a shoal of long poems: Bulwer Lytton's *King Arthur* of 1849; Martin Tupper's *Proverbial Philosophy*, which sold particularly well in 1855; William Morris's distinguished and major contribution to Arthurian poetry, *The Defence of Guinevere*, 1858; Elizabeth Barrett Browning's celebrated verse novel *Aurora Leigh*, 1860; and in due course Robert Browning's masterpiece *The Ring and the Book*, which would establish Browning's reputation on its publication in 1869. Tennyson's *Idylls*, then, had not only to refuse to be an 'epic', but also to compete for attention with verse novels, homiletics, and stifling (but popular) works of domesticity such as Coventry Patmore's relentlessly complacent celebration of married love, *The Angel in the House*, published in four volumes 1854 63. Each volume of this poem by Patmore comprises twelve 'Cantos', so the epic ambition of the whole is self-evident.

Martin Tupper enjoyed success and reputation on a bewildering scale. His career demonstrates how violently many early Victorians could welcome simple confidence, piety, assurance and egotism. 'I am rejoiced to tell you,' Tupper wrote to W. E. Gladstone (who was a personal friend) in 1842, 'that literature thrives with me, and threatens to make me rich, as well as – pardon my folly – famous.'[91] The first and second editions of *Proverbial Philosophy*, 1838 and 1842, had been sensational best-sellers. Although the tide turned against him in 1859, the work would eventually sell one and a half million copies, at the rate of at least 5,000 copies a year, until the outbreak of the First World War.[92]

In 1860, a visit to Devon and Cornwall was planned with the serviceable Palgrave, who was good at smoothing out travel arrangements and making sure that everything would be comfortable and fitting. On this occasion, however, the arrangements went wrong because Palgrave decided to linger in Oxford for a week with his brother – then due to travel to Syria – and Tennyson was put out. Woolner was in Oxford as well, and so, of course, was Jowett, who by this time was Master of Balliol. Tennyson was invited to lunch with Jowett in the Master's lodgings and read a new work to the distinguished classical scholar. Jowett was becoming somewhat formidable in these years: he listened gravely to the poem and then said, 'I think I wouldn't publish that, if I were you, Tennyson.' After a moment of frigid silence Tennyson answered: 'If it comes to that, Master, the sherry you gave us at luncheon was beastly.'[93]

Thomas Woolner had said that he was too busy for this holiday, but now he kindly agreed to change his plans and travel with Tennyson to the West Country, where they would wait for Palgrave. Emily wrote to him on 18 August to praise him for his goodness in giving up his work to accompany Tennyson on the holiday. Tennyson and Woolner were good companions for each other; Palgrave by contrast was something of an irritant. Once Palgrave had arrived to join the party at Tintagel, Woolner had intended to get back to work, but Tennyson begged him to stay with them. Woolner wrote to Emily on 25 August, about this change of plan:

> prudence, desire to get to work, hatred of continuous wet, and everything gave way and I consented to stay a short time longer. I hope that now I am so near I shall be gratified by a sight of the Land's End; for that I have the greater part of my life longed to see, although I know perfectly well it will be much like many rocky scenes of my experiences; but I am rather like a baby and want to do something that sounds grand.[94]

They walked steadily at least ten miles a day despite the continuous rain, visiting Bideford, Clovelly, Bude and Tintagel, and swimming wherever they could. But Palgrave developed an irritating habit of following Tennyson too closely and 'protecting' him at every turn, because Emily had particularly asked him to take care of her husband. Tennyson's poor eyesight was a legitimate reason for her to worry about him having a fall. At Helston they were joined by Holman Hunt and Val Prinsep, who were painting, and had some reasonably sociable evenings together. But Tennyson became impatient with what he felt was Palgrave's excessive fussiness and decided to go home.

The holiday yielded visual memories of Arthurian sites for the *Idylls of the King*; it also, importantly, yielded a major monument to Victorian literary taste and judgement in Palgrave's *The Golden Treasury of Songs and Lyrics*. This volume was conceived in Cornwall, and Palgrave started work as soon as the holiday was over. By October 1860 he was able to write to Tennyson: 'since I returned I have worked steadily for two or three hours a day at making the collection of English Lyrical Poems which we discussed in Cornwall; and I have spoken about it to Macmillan, who gives a conditional assent to act as publisher'.[95] Palgrave had worked remarkably quickly. Thomas Woolner wrote to Emily on 9 December:

Palgrave has nearly finished making his selections from the Poets, and has throughout shown the most extraordinary interest in his work; in fact he scarcely seems to think of anything else than the work he is engaged upon. He certainly has an astonishingly acute and quick mind in reading an enormous amount and extracting the best things.[96]

The Golden Treasury guided Victorian taste. The idea was developed by Palgrave, but in consultation with Tennyson, and indeed Tennyson made the selections, at the same time stipulating that none of his work should appear in it. His unerring instinct for his own market told him that it was better to be known as an artist still in full creative flood than as one whose *oeuvre* was in some sense fixed. But his preferences for the collection are informative. In the course of his career he wrote very little in the way of critical commentary on the work of other poets, and therefore this book, with its clear indications of which poetry, including that of his own period, should be noticed and which should not, is as close as we come in Tennyson's life to an extended account of what he himself thought of the work of his contemporaries.

The need to depict humanity in a state of ideal moral perfection brought into focus the difficulties of being both a spiritual and a physical being. Earlier, in *In Memoriam* lyric XXVII, Tennyson had written: 'I envy not the beast that takes / His licence in the field of time.' Lyric XXXVI had taken this further. Tennyson would later tell James Knowles that he was thinking of 'the vastness of the future – the enormity of the ages to come after your little life would act against that love'. The point here is that the consolations of love are disabled by our foreknowledge of death, so that without some consoling illusion of our own permanence we cannot experience love at all:

> If Death were seen
> At first as Death, Love had not been,
> Or been in narrowest working shut,
>
> Mere fellowship of sluggish moods,
> Or in his coarsest Satyr-shape
> Had bruised the herb and crushed the grape,
> And basked and battened in the woods.

'Locksley Hall' had similarly stressed the animal in the average sensual man. Amy's brutish husband was presented by Tennyson in uncompromising terms; the 'grossness of his nature' would force her into a subhuman role. The war between the spiritual and the animal in man remained a constant anxiety in *Maud*, where the speaker was deranged in part by the fact that he was a sexual being:

> Most of all would I flee from the cruel madness of love,
> The honey of poison-flowers and all the measureless ill.[97]

The fact that men can be destroyed by the cruel madness of love is a theme of two of the four *Idylls of the King* published in 1859.

Tennyson would advance on the Arthurian materials and then retreat from them, pause, write something completely different, come back to them, pick them up, put them down, meditate on their difficulties; he seemed to perform a kind of dance with himself. The four woman-centred poems which comprised the first set of *Idylls* made a reasonably elegant quartet: 'Enid', 'Guinevere', 'Vivien' and 'Elaine'.* They had found a warm and responsive readership on publication. Gladstone gave the 1859 *Idylls* heartfelt praise which more than compensated for his reservations about *Maud* (in the same essay in the *Quarterly Review*):

> It has every recommendation that should win its way to the homage of a great poet. It is national: it is Christian. It is also human in the largest and deepest sense; and, therefore, though highly national, it is universal; for it rests upon those depths and breadths of our nature to which all its truly great developments in all nations are alike essentially and closely related.[98]

In due course Tennyson would come to say that Gladstone's reading of the *Idylls* was the ablest account published.

A great mind destroyed by lust is the story of 'Merlin and Vivien' (printed for friends in its trial edition as 'Nimuë' in 1857 and published as 'Vivien' in 1859). The poem was composed in 1856, and is of a piece with the disturbed and enraged response to female sexuality which animated *Maud*, published the previous year. 'Vivien' shows the magician surrendering to lust in the full knowledge that such surrender will destroy him ('he let his wisdom go for ease of heart').

---

*These subtitles, four women's names, could be seen as challenges to those readers who had dared to dislike *Maud*.

The luxury and peace the surrender afford to the old man feel more like death than sexual fulfilment (the poem is deliberately blurring the distinction between the two), and the crisis in the action is given so quickly, just two lines, that the impatient reader could miss them completely:

> For Merlin, overtalked and overworn,
> Had yielded, told her all the charm, and slept.[99]

Women in the four *Idylls* were seen entirely in terms of their relationships with men – two of them do damage to men (Vivien and Guinevere), two of them are supportive (Enid and Elaine). Vivien was explicitly contrasted with Enid. Under the earlier version of her name, 'Nimuë', she was balanced against Enid in the trial edition of 1857, called 'Enid and Nimuë: The True and the False'.

Once his four Arthurian women were assembled and published in 1859, Tennyson circled round the problem of how next to proceed, and then found his solution in other projects. The Arthurian story never left him, however, and just as he had written *In Memoriam* over seventeen years, so the *Idylls* fermented away in his mind. The full time span for completion of the *Idylls* from inception in about 1830 to publication of the last book ('Balin and Balan', 1885) was therefore approximately fifty-five years. He was acutely sensitive to his audience and to the nature of the period in which he was living. He was neither lazy nor procrastinating, but the project was felt by him as solemn, daunting, and in places one which it was sacrilegious to handle – he felt that about writing 'The Holy Grail', in particular. And his work on the subject when it was complete filled twelve books, conforming to the traditional proportions of the great classical epics.

A sympathetic study of the Arthurian poems by a medievalist, David Staines, has given a good account of their composition. The indirections and hesitations of the composition are particularly well addressed. Early in his life Tennyson was writing about King Arthur's court. 'The Lady of Shalott', 'Morte d'Arthur', 'Sir Launcelot and Queen Guinevere' and 'Sir Galahad' date from the 1830s. He had written a treatment of the Arthurian story for adaptation for the stage, but in the 1840s he turned to other kinds of narrative. As his grandson Sir Charles wrote, two things spurred him to take up the Arthurian material again: the success of *The Princess* and the news that 'his old enemy, Bulwer Lytton, was bringing out an epic poem [about King Arthur] on the subject which he intended to be his masterpiece'.[100]

In 1861 Tennyson visited once more the valley of Cauteretz, scene of his treasured expedition with Arthur Hallam in 1830. His sons' tutor, Henry Graham Dakyns, had become a valued addition to the family by the time they took their summer tour to France. Dakyns was an excellent classicist who could engage with Tennyson as an equal in his discussions of classical metre; he was fond of Emily and was a success with the boys. Although a small man, he was very physical and athletic, and could divert and engage them in ways that no longer suited Tennyson himself as he grew older.

The holiday in France included Emily, despite the fact that she was weak and ill and found it painful to move about. The holiday lasted ten weeks, from the end of June to mid September. They travelled slowly and in considerable style to the Auvergne and the Dordogne. At Mont-Dore they encountered Arthur Hugh Clough, who was very frail; he was suffering from tuberculosis, and in fact had only three months to live. He was delighted to see them, as he reported to his wife in a letter of 21 July:

> This morning about 8½ going across the *place* to the café, whom should I see but Tennyson? – he and she and Dakins [Dakyns] and the 2 boys and a maid are all here – he and Dakins had been here two days. They go to the Pyrenees and I am to follow them. [. . .] Today I rode with him and Dakins walking and put 'em into the road up to Pic de Sancy which I hope they reached.

The Tennysons had been somewhat disappointed in their trip so far ('inns have been inconvenient etc, etc') and Clough had taken care to set Tennyson and Dakyns on a walk that they would enjoy and remember. Progress was slower than anticipated, and Clough spent a fruitless period of his summer looking for them; he was reunited with them towards the end of August. The boys were unwell, but Tennyson himself lingered in Cauteretz because of the memory of Hallam. Clough wrote to his wife on 2 September: 'Tennyson was here with Arthur Hallam 31 years ago and really finds great pleasure in the place. They staid here and at Cauterets – Oenone, he said, was written on the inspiration of the Pyrenees – which stood for Ida.'[101]

Clough noted that Tennyson became quiet and self-absorbed as they approached the valley. He wrote to his wife on 7 September to say that he had been with Tennyson 'to a sort of island between two waterfalls with pines on it, of which he retained a recollection from his visit of 31 years ago'. In the same letter he showed how protective he felt towards Tennyson: he told his wife that he would like to stay on longer than planned in the Pyrenees, 'for various reasons': 'It would be among other things a charity to these Tennysons; for Dakyns is to go away for a month most likely, perhaps this next week, and A.T. is but helpless by himself and thinks himself even more so than he is.'[102] Tennyson was in reality much tougher than Clough took him for. Like many metropolitan literary men of the time, Clough was misled by Tennyson's appearance and manner to see him as a kind of wild, unsophisticated genius who could barely function in the real world.

Because of his frailty under the burden of tuberculosis, Clough was riding a mule, while Dakyns and Tennyson walked. As they approached Cauteretz itself, the composition of the party changed: Clough in a carriage with Emily, the two boys and a maid, while Tennyson and Dakyns approached the sacred place on foot, Dakyns serving as Tennyson's 'walking stick'. As they entered the valley itself, Dakyns dropped behind, allowing Tennyson to stride on alone with his own thoughts and memories. 'Dakyns isn't a fool,' Tennyson said in the evening to Emily, in his appreciation of this tactful gesture.[103]

Sadly, Tennyson's friendship with Clough was transitory; it seems certain that it would have deepened and become mutually rewarding had Clough lived longer. The two men had already become decidedly comfortable with each other; it is possible that Matthew Arnold, Clough's lifelong friend, disliked this somewhat. Arnold was inclined to be disparaging about Tennyson, regarding him as a man who lacked the intellectual power of Goethe or Wordsworth.* When Clough was firmly established as a friend of Tennyson, early in 1861, Arnold wrote to him that although he promised to send Tennyson his own poems, 'you need not add that I care for his productions less and less'.[104]

A brilliant, troubled and rather lonely young man, Clough, whose parents lived in America, had, in effect, found a foster family in the Arnolds. He was sent back to England for his education at the age of nine, and found security as a boarder at Rugby, the famous public school, which was then in its prime under the legendary Dr Arnold.

---

*Dislike of Tennyson's *Idylls* was a fixed position in Arnold's mind. In December 1860 he had written: 'I have a strong sense of the irrationality of that period and of the utter folly of those who take it seriously and play at restoring it.' Tennyson's *Idylls* could not capture 'the peculiar charm and aroma of the Middle Ages', and Tennyson himself was 'deficient in intellectual power'. (Lang, *Letters of Matthew Arnold*, II, p. 42.)

Dr Arnold became a kind of adopted father to Clough, and his son was Clough's closest companion at the school. The pairing of these two poets, Clough and Arnold, was intimate, intellectual, literary and mutually stimulating and creative, not unlike the pairing of Arthur Hallam and Alfred Tennyson. When Clough resigned his fellowship at Oriel College, Oxford, in 1848, because he was unable to subscribe to the Thirty-Nine Articles of the Anglican Church, he became a living embodiment of the 'honest doubt' which Tennyson had enshrined in lyric XCVI of *In Memoriam*. Matthew Arnold's *Thyrsis*, his moving elegy for Clough, immortalised their friendship in the same way that *In Memoriam* had immortalised that earlier friendship.

This visit to the Pyrenees prompted Tennyson's 'In the Valley of Cauteretz', which gives full and simple expression to his feeling for Arthur Hallam:

> All along the valley, stream that flashest white,
> Deepening thy voice with the deepening of the night,
> All along the valley, where thy waters flow,
> I walked with one I loved two and thirty years ago.
> All along the valley, while I walked today,
> The two and thirty years were a mist that rolls away;
> For all along the valley, down thy rocky bed,
> Thy living voice to me was as the voice of the dead,
> And all along the valley, by rock and cave and tree,
> The voice of the dead was a living voice to me.[105]

Tennyson was disappointed, which was perhaps inevitable, by the changes that had overtaken this valley made sacred in memory. The little village had swollen to become a popular centre for holidaymakers and visitors.

The strange food, the illness before they arrived in Cauteretz, and then a chill contracted while he was there resulted in a stomach upset which meant that Tennyson now had to cut short the tour and get back as quickly as he could. In the railway station at Amiens on the way home, the party saw Browning and his son. Browning was shattered by the recent death of his wife, and pretended not to recognise Tennyson and his family: the contrast between their group and his own state was too much to bear.[106]

As well as Elizabeth Barrett's death, the end of 1861 was marked by the death in November of Clough, who had been their holiday companion so recently. And there was a family death, that of Tennyson's uncle, Charles Tennyson d'Eyncourt. By this time Tennyson was able to feel that the balance of their fortunes had been redressed in his favour. But this did not cancel out the old bitterness over his grandfather's disinheritance of the Somersby Tennysons. In the narrative poem 'Aylmer's Field' (1864), Tennyson would write with undiminished anger about the damage done to the lives of young people by a wealthy and powerful father.

The death of Prince Albert, at the end of 1861, was the immediate cause of Tennyson's closer relationship with Queen Victoria. It was at this point that he wrote his new dedication to *Idylls of the King*. Tennyson knew full well that the great honour of the Laureateship was thanks to the Prince's admiration for his work, and he genuinely regretted that the opportunity had now been missed for becoming a personal friend of a man as intelligent and cultivated as Albert. In *Idylls of the King*, Tennyson was struggling with the difficult problem of how to create a persuasive ideal of conduct, in a literary form, for a secular and materialist society. He saw Albert himself as a modern embodiment of that ideal: 'These to His Memory – Since he held them dear, / Perchance as finding there unconsciously / Some image of himself.'

If we find these lines sonorous and empty, that is a mark of the historical gulf between our respective times. Tennyson meant what he wrote here. Emily persuaded him to send the dedication to Princess Alice, who wrote back on 15 January to say, 'Princess Alice has transmitted the lines to the Queen, who desired her to tell Mr Tennyson, with her warmest thanks, how much moved she was in reading them, and that they had soothed her aching, bleeding heart. She knows also how *He* would have admired them.' (Bursting with pride over this response – perhaps understandably – Emily wrote in her diary for the 16th that this was 'a day to be remembered by us – a letter of thanks to A from Princess Alice telling us that his lines have soothed our Queen, thank God!' It certainly marked a personal success for her.)[107] In February Argyll made his well-known report to Tennyson of the way the Queen had annotated *In Memoriam* so that it referred to her own bereavement,[108] and this chain of events led directly to Tennyson's highly successful audience in April 1862, and the second audience, for Tennyson, Emily and their two sons, in May 1863.

*   *   *

In 1849, Julia Margaret Cameron (1815–79), one of the delightful and eccentric Pattle sisters, became a friend of Henry Taylor, the poet who was best known as the author of a tragic drama set in the Renaissance era called *Philip Van Artevelde*. Tennyson first met Julia Margaret in 1850, shortly after his marriage. Emily Tennyson wrote in her diary that Julia Margaret 'was a delightful picture in her dark green silk with wide open sleeves, the dress fastened by a silk cord round the waist and having the courtly charm of manner [. . .] which became her well'.[109] At this date Tennyson was living in London, and Julia Margaret and Henry Taylor and his wife were close neighbours in Richmond Park. It was through these comfortable and almost casual meetings that Julia became a close friend, especially of Emily. She knew that Emily had lost her first child, and when Emily suddenly went into labour with Hallam, in August 1852, Julia went personally into the city to fetch the doctor for her. Later she was at Hallam's christening.

Julia Margaret and her husband Charles Hay Cameron were part of a decidedly wealthy, striking and successful literary and artistic set based on the Prinsep family at Little Holland House. But from 1859 onwards they were short of money because of the failure of Charles Cameron's coffee plantations in Ceylon. Julia was on a steady descent, socially and economically, during the 1860s, while Tennyson was in an astronomic ascent, yet she showed no sign at any time of resenting this – on the contrary, she remained resolutely loyal, generous and loving. Financial difficulties meant that she made her home on the Isle of Wight rather than continuing in London. She bought two small adjacent houses, built an idiosyncratic tower between to link them to each other, and called the whole 'Dimbola' (which was the name of one of her husband's properties in Ceylon).

The anecdotes about her are many, all of them entertaining. She showered the Tennysons with gifts, most of them useless, inappropriate, unattractive and unwanted, and bullied Tennyson into receiving visitors he did not want to see (especially Americans). She also embarked on her own personal venture to repair the Cameron fortunes, in middle age becoming a professional photographer. This was partly a passionately adopted hobby and partly a money-making venture, and it worked; she made a considerable reputation, and a reasonable income, from her photography. It is an extraordinary feature of this odd but likeable woman that she could cope, in the most improbable ways, with anything that life threw at her. The Camerons rapidly became part of an inner circle which by 1862 had become a kind of court, assembled in deference to Tennyson. The regular visitors to the Isle of Wight who comprised the court included writers such as Edward Lear, Aubrey de Vere and William Allingham; old friends of Tennyson who were also scholars, such as Benjamin Jowett and James Spedding; and the Pre-Raphaelites such as Holman Hunt and Woolner who had also been habitual visitors at Little Holland House.[110]

For much of 1863 Tennyson suffered a mysterious illness. This may have been Julia Margaret Cameron's fault — she persuaded him, much against his instincts, to have himself vaccinated. At the same time he was suffering from gout, and advised to reduce his alcohol intake. The poetry dried up in these adverse conditions, and it was partly for this reason that he was willing to try his hand at versifying two prose narratives given him by Thomas Woolner.

Later in the year his health improved and he felt happy and confident enough to support Julia Margaret in one of her quixotic projects. The novelist William Makepeace Thackeray and Tennyson had known each other since they were young men at Cambridge. The young Thackeray was not among Tennyson's closest circle of friends, but they had considerable regard for each other. Thackeray's life was dogged by a personal disaster, his wife's insanity, which meant that care of his daughters and the struggle for literary success all devolved upon him without another supporting adult. He must have felt keenly the difference between his situation and Tennyson's.

When Thackeray died suddenly at Christmas 1863, the Thackeray girls effectively became orphans, their mother being hopelessly insane. Julia Margaret Cameron, with her characteristic generosity, made a cottage in Freshwater available to them, and Tennyson stirred himself to look after them. It was against his instincts to fill his retreat with people, but for the sake of these Thackeray girls, whose plight touched him, he encouraged the painter George Frederick Watts,* with his wife Ellen Terry, and the Prinseps to visit Freshwater 'until Freshwater seemed an outpost of Little Holland House'.[111]

Thackeray's daughter Annie (later Anne Thackeray Ritchie) gave her own record of Tennyson. In London her father's friends from his student days, now 'grown to be middle-aged', used to come 'from time to time to her father's house, and smoke with him, and talk and laugh

---

*George Frederick Watts (1817–1904) was a successful portraitist, and an artist whose work steadily developed throughout his life. Major recognition came late, but the visionary and symbolic paintings of the 1870s onwards assured him fame and security in his own lifetime. When he married Ellen Terry in 1864 she had not yet reached her seventeenth birthday, and he was thirty years older; the marriage was doomed from the start and lasted little more than a year.

quietly'. She was nine years old, living with her father and sister in Young Street, Kensington, where they had moved in 1846, and Tennyson, still a bachelor and still short of money, was a regular visitor:

> I can remember on one occasion, through a cloud of smoke, looking across a darkening room at the noble, grave head of the Poet-Laureate [though Tennyson was not yet Laureate at this date]. He was sitting with my father in the twilight, after some family meal, in the old house in Kensington. It is [. . .] Tennyson himself who has reminded me how upon this occasion, while my father was speaking to me, my little sister [Minny Thackeray] looked up suddenly from the book in which she had been absorbed, saying, in her soft childish voice, 'Papa, why do you not write books like *Nicholas Nickleby?*'

She then moves on to later memories, from the early 1850s:

> Then again I seem to hear, across that same familiar table, voices without shape or name, talking and telling each other that [. . .] Tennyson was married – that he and his wife had been met walking on the terrace at Clevedon Court [home of Arthur Hallam's relations]; and then the clouds descend again, except, indeed, that I can see my father riding off on his brown cob to the Tennysons' house at Twickenham (Chapel House, with its oak staircase, when the carved figure of a bishop used to bless the passers-by) to attend the christening of Hallam, their eldest son.[112]

At the time of Thackeray's death, Anne was in her twenties. She never forgot Tennyson's kindness to her and her sister Minny when they arrived on the Isle of Wight to stay in one of Julia Margaret Cameron's cottages: 'As we rested aimlessly in the twilight, we seemed aware of a tall figure standing at the window, wrapped in a heavy cloak, with a broad-brimmed hat. This was Tennyson, who had walked down to see us in silent sympathy.'[113] Annie was already embarked on a literary career of her own. Tennyson encouraged her, and she was fully aware, as any young writer at that time would be, that his patronage could be useful to her. Tennyson had no daughters of his own and his two sons were not particularly literary. Annie Thackeray was a surrogate in both these roles: she was a writer and she adopted him as a substitute father. She sought advice about her writing from him and all her memories of him were fond and loyal. She recalled how he responded to her work: 'He read, he said flummery flummery, he corrected a word here & there. I was not Dante but he most assuredly was Virgil & it was joy to have such a convincing lesson in style, simply given & indisputably felt by me.'[114]

Another witness of these years was Ellen Terry. Initially she lived with Watts in Little Holland House, the artistic commune – as it was becoming – created by Mrs Prinsep, sister of Julia Cameron.

Ellen Terry was a strongly independent personality who took a triumphalist view of her own career, and in due course she would become so grand and ascendant in the theatre that comment about her private life – and there was plenty on which to comment – was effectively muted. Still, as Watts's child bride she was certainly very unhappy. The Prinseps brought her, with Watts, to the Isle of Wight, where she was somewhat bullied by Mrs Prinsep. The Tennyson children were a welcome relief from her marriage. She wrote in her memoir that she was just too young for the world into which she had been plunged:

> I was meeting distinguished people at every turn, and taking no notice of them. At Freshwater I was still so young that I preferred playing Indians and Knights of the Round Table with Tennyson's sons, Hallam and Lionel, and the young Camerons, to sitting indoors noticing what the poet did and said. I was mighty proud when I learned how to prepare his daily pipe for him. It was a long churchwarden, and he liked the stem to be steeped in a solution of sal volatile, or something of the kind, so that it did not stick to his lips. But he and all the others seemed to me very old. There were my young knights waiting for me; and jumping gates, climbing trees, and running paperchases are pleasanter when one is young.[115]

Although she saw Tennyson as very old, she loved him for his simplicity:

> In the evenings I went walking with Tennyson over the fields, and he would point out to me the differences in the flight of different birds, and tell me to watch their solid phalanxes turning against the sunset, the compact wedge suddenly narrowing sharply into a thin line. He taught me to recognise the barks of trees and to call wild flowers by their names. He picked me the first bit of pimpernel I

ever noticed. Always I was quite at ease with him. He was wonder-
fully simple.[116]

He was quite different from the rest of the circle in this respect.

Farringford remained the real centre of Tennyson's private life. In
the winter, especially, when there were no intrusive tourists, he could
relax with friends, play with his children, and talk engagingly and
melodiously about poetry. William Allingham recalled visiting
Farringford immediately after Christmas 1863; his diary entry gives
a good instance of Tennyson as a happy family man enjoying
Farringford on a winter day. Francis Palgrave was a visitor as well,
and the three men took one of Tennyson's favourite walks up High
Down towards the eastern point of the Isle of Wight. The sea is
often particularly rough there, and the three men would have had
the full dramatic effect of the Needles' startling chalk pillars standing
out against the churning sea under a wind-blown sky full of circling
gulls.

There was the usual surprisingly early dinner, at six p.m. With
Tennyson's typical pleasure in ceremony, they moved into the drawing
room after dinner for wine and dessert (guests regularly remarked that
this was like the rituals of the senior common room at Trinity).
Tennyson turned the discussion to poetic metre, a reminder that he
remained alert all his life to the technical resources and possibilities
of his craft. The following day was a Sunday.* Allingham played
football with the boys (Hallam was eleven and Lionel was nine): 'Lionel
talks to me; he is odd, shy, sweet, and as his mother says, *daimonish*.
Hallam has something of a shrewd satirical turn, but with great good
nature.' Tennyson then joined them and they all made a slightly
dangerous expedition 'to the cliff edge, then returning we creep up
long slopes of down and rest at the Beacon. Thistles and other growths
crouch into the sward from the fierce sea-winds.' The beacon was the
vantage point at the top of High Down, with a wonderful outlook on
the open sea, and to the west the rolling hills, coves and beaches of
the island. 'We talk of "Christabel." Race down, I get first to the stile.
After dinner more talk of "Classic Metres."' Tennyson delivered his
own metrical invention:

---

*There is no mention of church; Tennyson was never a regular churchgoer, while Emily
was faithful in her observance of Sunday – this was sometimes an issue between them.

> Higgledy-piggledy, silver and gold,
> There's – (*it's nothing very dreadful!*)
> There's a louse on my back
> Seven years old.
> He inches, he pinches,
> In every part,
> And if I could catch him
> I'd *tearr* out his *heart!*

The last line he gave with tragic fury.[117]

In the spring of 1864, Garibaldi came to the Isle of Wight. His first visit was to Mottistone, near Brooke, home of the ancient Seely family (the family of Lord Mottistone), where Tennyson and Emily called on him to pay their respects and invite him to Farringford. Their plan was that he should plant a wellingtonia which had been given to them by the Duchess of Sutherland. The great man arrived and he and Tennyson had a long session up in Tennyson's study. The conversation started in English, but they struggled to understand each other; the dialogue became less sticky when they began to quote Italian texts to each other. There was a comic encounter with Julia Margaret Cameron: 'Mrs Cameron wanted to photograph Garibaldi, and dropped down on her knees before him, and held up her black hands, covered with chemicals. He evidently thought that she was a beggar until we had explained who she was.'[118] Garibaldi planted the wellingtonia (with some awkwardness because there was a high wind), shook hands warmly with everyone present and kissed Hallam and Lionel. The meeting ended amicably, but it is unlikely that the great Italian liberator was able to see any point in his encounter with the great English poet.*[119]

Despite his burgeoning fame, Tennyson remained surprisingly susceptible to easy flattery. The Marquess of Dufferin and Ava had sought out his friendship in the 1850s. In 1858 he sent Tennyson his book,

---

*The encounter with Garibaldi was a mark of the fact that by this date Tennyson had become an institution. As Norman Page has put it: 'The legend grew rapidly quite soon after the move to Farringford and became firmly established in the last thirty years of his life. Partly, of course, it flourished because, like Victoria, he lasted so long: while some of his readers grew old along with him, younger and even middle-aged readers of his later volumes would have been unable to remember a time when he had not been the dominant figure in English poetry. If he had died at the same age as, say, Byron, there would have been no *Princess,* no *In Memoriam,* no *Maud,* no *Idylls of the King,* no "Enoch Arden" [. . .] – and the legend itself would have taken a very different, and surely a less potent, form.' (Page, *Illustrated Life,* pp. 123–4.)

Letters from High Latitudes,[120] and invited him for a yachting trip. An only child, Dufferin adored his mother, Helen Sheridan (a descendant of the playwright), and in 1861 the thirty-five-year-old Marquess had persuaded Tennyson to write 'Helen's Tower' for the decorative 'old-world' tower that he had built in his park and named for his mother. Creating this tower was an intensely literary act: in his appeal to Tennyson to write a poem for it, Dufferin called it his 'Palace of Art'.

> You must know that in my park in Ireland there rises a high hill, from the top of which I look down not only on an extensive tract of Irish land, but also on St George's Channel, a long blue line of Scotch coast, the mountains of the Isle of Man. On the summit of this hill I have built an old-world tower, which I have called after my mother 'Helen's Tower'.[121]

Tennyson sent three versions of a possible poem, of which after some further correspondence he and Dufferin agreed a twelve-line version.[122] It is graceful enough, but given how strong, independent and famous a figure Tennyson was by this date, he did not need this kind of patronage:

> Helen's Tower, here I stand,
> Dominant over sea and land.
> Son's love built me, and I hold
> Mother's love in lettered gold.
> Love is in and out of time,
> I am mortal stone and lime.
> Would my granite girth were strong
> As either love, to last as long!
> I should wear my crown entire
> To and through the Doomsday fire,
> And be found of angel eyes
> In earth's recurring Paradise.[123]

In his genial and generous-spirited study of Tennyson, J. H. Buckley wrote about Tennyson's writing in the 1860s: 'The true sanction for his activity lay deeper than any desire for reward or fame. He was driven most of all by the necessities of self-expression, the will to see his talent, the real warrant of his being, always shine in use.'[124] This rings true, and helps to explain the otherwise unaccountable excursions into exercises in which Tennyson turned subjects offered by friends into narrative poems.

*   *   *

The arrival of Julia Cameron in Tennyson's life marks a point of intersection between the Victorians and Bloomsbury. The forthrightness and sense of entitlement displayed by all the Pattle sisters served Cameron well in her dealings with Tennyson. He too had a sense of entitlement and was capable of being grand and difficult, but Julia Margaret easily overrode any resistance he put up because she simply failed to notice it.

It is refreshing to see Tennyson being selfless and kind in relation to Julia Cameron – he went with her to see her husband and her son off on their emergency voyage to Ceylon in 1859, for example, when their fortunes were foundering and Julia Margaret was seriously upset – and he had also been strikingly kind to Thackeray's daughters and to Ellen Terry during her short-lived and wretched marriage to G. F. Watts. By contrast, some of the younger male companions, such as Dakyns, William Allingham and Palgrave, he used rather than befriended. The degree to which he could dominate them varied according to their pliability. Allingham, for example, quotes remarks made by Tennyson to him which would have caused a more independent or robust man to walk away from the friendship, but Allingham clung to it for his own reasons. He constantly kept alive his hope of escaping from his employment as a customs officer and earning his living by writing, as Tennyson did.

Thomas Woolner was a more resilient and altogether coarser figure, and it helped that Emily Tennyson responded warmly to him and promoted that friendship as much as she could. Palgrave was tough and ambitious in his own way, and Emily relied on him to keep an eye on her husband, which Tennyson naturally resented. Palgrave's over-attentiveness could infuriate him, and indeed at times Palgrave's behaviour was strikingly short of dignity in relation to the older man. Sadness enters into the story when one reflects on Tennyson's treatment of long-standing friends like Edward Fitzgerald and Edward Lear, who were increasingly neglected as his fame grew. Julia Margaret Cameron understood Tennyson's need for privacy. She was also the woman above all others whom he would allow to order him around and call him by his first name. On the question of his need for privacy and his hatred of biographers she was revealing. In a letter of 29 November 1862 she quoted Tennyson as follows:

The desiring anecdotes and the acquaintance with the lives of great men was treating them like pigs to be ripped open for the public; that he knew himself should be ripped open like a pig; that he thanked God Almighty with his whole heart and soul that he knew nothing, and that the world knew nothing, of Shakespeare but his writings; and that there were no letters preserved either of Shakespeare's or Jane Austen's, that they had not been ripped open like pigs.[125]

CHAPTER 8

Idylls of the King and the creation
of Aldworth, 1862–1872

Two dead men have I known
In courtesy like to thee:
Two dead men have I loved
With a love that ever will be:
Three dead men have I loved and thou art
last of the three.

In the 1840s Tennyson had been revered by the Pre-Raphaelites, and now in the 1860s he became associated with a second-wave Pre-Raphaelitism which was vigorously exploiting its new-found favour in the marketplace, as was clearly the case with the increasing sales of Millais' and Rossetti's paintings. The PRB passionately embraced the fashionable Victorian enthusiasm for ancient British history and stirring British myths, as exemplified in the writings of Malory. Thus when Rossetti and William Morris and their friends and disciples devised a decorative scheme for the Oxford Union building, it was Arthurian in theme.

Rossetti had effectively initiated the project; he was a personal friend of the architect Benjamin Woodward (who had played the major part in the design of the Oxford Union building). Rossetti and his team chose the Arthurian theme both because of their enthusiasm for Tennyson's 'Morte d'Arthur', and because they were aware of Wagner's work on stories from the same body of romances: *Lohengrin* (1850) and *Tristan und Isolde* (which was completed in 1859). William Morris was at the same time working on his own distinguished Arthurian poem, 'The Defence of Guinevere'.

The Tennyson who had embarked on *Idylls of the King* was therefore pursuing a theme dear to the hearts of the Pre-Raphaelites. His own Arthurian poems published in 1842, especially 'Morte d'Arthur', had stimulated the artists, and their work in turn stimulated the public appetite for Arthurian stories. When Tennyson began publishing the poems of the *Idylls* sequence he was riding a surge in public taste to which his own earlier work had contributed. This remains true despite the fact that he did not respond particularly warmly to painting and sculpture, and disliked the many illustrations of his own work made by artists. There was a further divergence as well: when the younger generation of writers who interested themselves in Arthurian romance came to read Malory for themselves, they were struck by the contrast between Tennyson's Arthurian poems and the great source text from which he was working.

As an undergraduate at Exeter College in 1853, William Morris had become the first and closest friend of Edward Burne-Jones ('Ned Jones'), and with others formed a kind of Oxford-based second-generation PRB, which indeed called itself 'the Brotherhood'. Other members included William Fulford, Charles Faulkner and a promising poet, later a clergyman, Richard Watson Dixon.

To these men Tennyson was a hero. 'The Lady of Shalott', 'Sir Launcelot and Queen Guinevere', 'Morte d'Arthur' and 'Sir Galahad' were favourite poems for William Morris: he would read them aloud to his friends, emphasising the rhythms and the inherent musicality of Tennyson's verses. For Morris and Burne-Jones Arthurianism 'was not merely an intellectual exercise. They fell upon it as an extension of religion, adopting the chivalric as a rule of life. Embedded in their visions of the San Graal were the memories of the high emotions of those early weeks at Oxford, and their mutual recognition.' Burne-Jones wrote that 'nothing was ever like Morte d'Arthur – I don't mean any book or any one poem – something that can never be written, I mean, and can never go out of the heart'. Their engagement with these stories was

> part of a whole Arthurian cult, following the rediscovery of Malory's *Morte d'Arthur* in the late eighteenth century by Sir Walter Scott. By the time Morris and Burne-Jones arrived in Oxford Victorian Arthurianism was approaching its grand climax. William Dyce had already started painting his cycle of Arthurian frescoes in the Queen's Robing Room in the Palace of Westminster.[1]

Tennyson belonged to that cult. Richard Watson Dixon recalled that in 1853–5 'All reading men were Tennysonians; all sets of reading men talked poetry. Poetry was the thing; and it was felt with justice that this was due to Tennyson.'[2]

Morris himself, though, looked for more meat in the Arthurian stories than Tennyson had offered: he complained that 'Tennyson's Sir Galahad is rather a mild youth.'[3] Morris had bought his own copy of Malory (Southey's edition of the *Morte d'Arthur*). He found in it a much more tough and rugged narrative than the smoothed-out lyrical effects given in Tennyson's poetry.⁴ He was struck particularly by the strength of Guinevere and the ambivalence of her story. His own Guinevere poem ('The Defence of Guinevere' of 1858), in which the Queen is about to be burnt at the stake, is a vivid, passionate, defiant and sexually charged poem, one of Morris's most powerful achievements in verse. This Guinevere, unlike Tennyson's, revels in her adulterous liaison:

> In that garden fair
> Came Launcelot walking; this is true, the kiss
> Wherewith we kissed in meeting that spring day,
> I scarce dare talk of the remember'd bliss,
> When both our mouths went wandering in one way,
> And aching sorely, met among the leaves.⁵

Interest in the material was spurred on by popular re-creations of the Arthurian stories such as *The Quest of the Sangraal* (1864) by Robert Stephen Hawker of Morwenstow. Hawker had helped Tennyson with his Arthurian researches in Cornwall, and Tennyson admired his verse account of the story of the Holy Grail when it appeared. It is an exuberantly noisy work, confidently setting the whole story in Hawker's own beloved Cornish landscape:

> Ho! For the Sangraal! vanished vase of heaven!
> That held, like Christ's own heart, an hin* of blood!
> Ho ! for the Sangraal! . . .
> [. . .]
> Uprose they for the quest! the bounding men,
> Of the siege perilous, and the granite ring!
> They gathered at the rock: yon ruddy tor, –
> The stony depth where lurked the demon-god,
> Till Christ, the mighty Master, drave him forth.
>
> There stood the knights! stately, and stern, and tall;
> Tristan; and Percevale; Sir Galahad:

---

*The antiquarian in Hawker revelled in footnotes, of which he would provide, typically, two or three for every printed page of his poem. A 'hin' was a Hebrew measure for the wine of the sacrifice; the 'ruddy tor' was 'Routor', a red hill thus named for the heath which blossomed near it; the 'logan' was a 'shudding stone': 'A child or an innocent person could move it, as Pliny records, with a stalk of asphodel, but a strong man, if guilty, could not shake it with all his force.' (Hawker, pp. 180–1.)

And he, the sad Sir Lancelot of the Lay:
Ah me! that logan of the rocky hills,
    Pillared in storm, calm in the rush of war,
    Shook, at the light touch of his lady's hand!

There was a scholarly Arthurian revival in the 1860s, particularly in F. J. Furnivall's editions of *The History of the Holy Graal* (1861) and *Le Morte d'Arthur* (1864). Furnivall gracefully acknowledged the stimulus given by Tennyson's work (the Corpus Christi manuscript of *The Holy Graal* had come to light while 'all our English world [. . .] was delighting in "The Idylls of the King"'). At the same time, though, his editions offered corrections to Tennyson. Tennyson was wrong about Merlin and Nimuë, for instance: 'There are several versions of this story; but in none is the lady represented as actuated by such abominable motives as Tennyson has ascribed to her.' Tennyson had also ignored 'the dark background of Arthur's incest', the story of 'the seduction by Arthur, in ignorance, of his own sister Margause, the wife of King Lot [. . .] From this adulterous, not to say incestuous, amour was Modred born.'[6] He had written clearly about Arthur's incest in his early prose treatments of the material, when he was an undergraduate, but when he came to writing the great work out in full, he had taken a conscious decision to present a decorous and morally uncompromised version of the stories of King Arthur.

Tennyson turned aside from King Arthur, though, to write *Enoch Arden* (1864). Emily was worried when he had periods of creative dryness or aimlessness, and she encouraged Thomas Woolner to come up with ideas for him; in December 1860 she wrote to Woolner: 'Beyond all price to me would be a worthy subject for Alfred, one which would fix him whether he would or no.'[7] *Enoch Arden* was based on the narrative that Woolner had written on his way home from Australia, and which he had subsequently worked up into 'The Fisherman's Story'.[8] It was 'a beautiful tale of a poor sailor', of which Woolner gives his synopsis – a sailor leaves his young wife and children behind in his home village to make his fortune, and is wrecked on a desert island. Believing him dead, his wife marries a former sweetheart, but after many years the sailor returns. He sees the domestic happiness his wife has now found and selflessly conceals the fact of his homecoming. Many years later his wife and her supposed husband are both in their graves, and the true husband is found dead on their tomb holding a lock of his wife's hair.

There is a strong coincidental resemblance to Elizabeth Gaskell's

Sylvia's Lovers, which is set in a lightly fictionalised Whitby and was published in 1863. It tells effectively the same story but the similarity with Woolner's narrative is an accident – Woolner had written his story in 1854 and had sent the developed version of it to Tennyson by 1862 (it is discussed in correspondence between Emily and Woolner in February 1862 while Tennyson was writing the poem). It is possible though that the name of the ship on which Enoch sailed, *The Good Fortune*, was suggested by Mrs Gaskell's tale and added at a late stage.[9]

Tennyson's sense of his market had remained sound with this poem. The four women-based *Idylls* published in 1859 had sold well, but *Enoch Arden and Other Poems* sold astonishingly well. It was published in August 1864, sold 17,000 copies on the day of publication and the whole impression of 60,000 copies by the end of the year. Tennyson's payments from Moxon for the volume were £6,664 4s. 2d in January of 1865 and a further £1,400 17s. 8d in June 1865. These were huge sales, especially for a volume of narrative poetry.[10] The simple title contributed to its success. This was nearly not the published title: Tennyson was drawn by the example of *Idylls of the King* to use *Idylls of the Hearth* instead. He was in London working closely with Moxon when Emily wrote twice expressing her surprise and disappointment over this: 'Ally [as she often called him] dearest I see in the Reader the title is to be Idylls of the Hearth. Surely not. Will not "Enoch Arden & Other Poems" be more in thy usual simple style? I dont like this Idylls of the Hearth. Wilt thou not change it?' She pointed out that she was a good judge of titles: '*In Memoriam* has proved a good title so perhaps I may be right in this too.'[11] Emily won this battle, and did Tennyson no harm thereby.

The appeal of the story was in its simplicity: the fisherman at its centre is a figure of pathos and natural nobility. But to reflect on the possible meanings of 'nobility' is to encounter the heart of the problem of this poem. This was well expressed by Walter Bagehot in his unsigned essay in the *National Review* (November 1864) called 'Wordsworth, Tennyson, and Browning; or, Pure, Ornate, and Grotesque Art in English Poetry'. Here the point was that Tennyson did not content himself with displaying the moral nobility of a simple character (as Wordsworth had aimed to do in *Lyrical Ballads*), but wanted to give him social grace as well. His central character was 'a dirty sailor who did *not* go home to his wife', and was forced to look, sound, smell and behave like a member of the English middle class. Tennyson had used 'ornate' art to create something that does not exist in the real world 'but which would seem pretty if it did exist'. In reality 'people who sell fish about the country [. . .] never are beautiful'. But Tennyson 'has given us a sailor crowded all over with ornament and illustration, because he then wanted to describe an unreal type of fancied men – not sailors as they are, but sailors as they might be wished'. As Bagehot's essay proceeded, so its argument became more damagingly accurate. Tennyson's fisherman poem, he concluded, was the work of a poet using the ornate style to cover the imperfection of his material just as the upwardly mobile middle class, 'the sudden *millionaires*' of the day, surrounded themselves with 'aristocratic furniture'.[12] In a private letter to a friend of 10 September 1864, the undergraduate Gerard Manley Hopkins found an even better phrase for the problem with *Enoch Arden*: Tennyson had developed his own 'Parnassian', which Hopkins identified as a stylistic habit. It was the language 'which genius speaks as fitted to its exaltation', but which 'does not sing'.[13] In plain English, the story tells us that Enoch the fisherman goes out visiting houses in his district with a basket of fish to sell. Tennyson's verse expresses this as follows:

> Enoch's white horse, and Enoch's ocean-spoil
> In ocean-smelling osier, and his face,
> Rough-reddened with a thousand winter gales,
> Not only to the market-cross were known,
> But in the leafy lanes behind the down,
> Far as the portal-warding lion-whelp*
> And peacock-yewtree of the lonely Hall,
> Whose Friday fare was Enoch's ministering.[14]

This is skilful, but did the story of Enoch really need it?

This 'Parnassian' and elevated treatment of the story of the fisherman in *Enoch Arden* was part of Tennyson's increasingly idealising habit of mind. He displayed a drive to find something or somebody, preferably somewhat remote and out of focus, that would become the object of veneration in his art. *In Memoriam* had shown signs of this, and in this respect that poem and *Idylls of the King* were continuous with each other. The dead Arthur Hallam, the dead Enoch Arden and the dead King Arthur were all models of manhood and virtuous behaviour. Tennyson believed from deep within himself that perfect human beings could exist, and that one of the functions of

---

*A recall of an impressive gateway at Gunby Hall, in Lincolnshire, which is topped by a lion in profile.

art was to display them as role models in a world that was too often materialist and flawed. The selflessness of Enoch in *Enoch Arden* and the moral intensity of the sermon in 'Aylmer's Field' are both consistent with this seriousness which was by this time part of Tennyson's nature.

'Aylmer's Field' was again a narrative poem based on a prose treatment provided by Thomas Woolner. It was a Suffolk story; Woolner wrote it out, recorded the work in his diary (5 July 1862), and sent it to Emily. Woolner's narrative was entitled 'The Sermon', and according to him the story was a true one, which he had heard talked of by his Suffolk grandfather. It concerned a wealthy baronet whose only child was a beautiful daughter. This young woman fell in love with a man held by her family to be unsuitable, the brother of the rector of the parish. The young woman died as a result of her parents' harshness towards her over the love affair. In the meantime the young man had worked ferociously hard to make a success of himself; and when he heard of her death he killed himself in despair. The clergyman, the young man's brother, was moved by these tragic deaths to preach a sermon of such passion that the baronet and his wife met due punishment as a consequence. As Woolner put it:

His [the Rector's] mind borne on a storm of passion, denounced pride and avarice and hardheartedness and all those dreadful worldly vices that had brought about this dreadful calamity, till there were sobbings and moanings and deep groans through the congregation and great agitation. The mother uttered a sharp cry and fell into a fit, causing a wild commotion throughout the church, while the Baronet sat in a paralysis of stupor seemingly unmindful of everything, and they had to be taken home in their coach.

The mother subsequently died and the baronet over a period of two years became 'almost an imbecile' and also died.[15]

Emily received this narrative with great enthusiasm. She wrote to Woolner on 10 July: 'The story is very grand and very finely told we think. The arrangement and form are so good.'[16] It had promising resonances for Tennyson; several of its details could be directly linked to his own early manhood. The notion of a clergyman's family being regarded as socially inferior by a rich man brought back the wretchedness of Dr Tennyson's disinheritance by Old George and the subsequent triumph of the Tennyson d'Eyncourts. Further, the memory of being seen as an unsuitable suitor for wealthy Rosa

Baring was stirred by Woolner's narrative. The reality, though, was that Tennyson struggled with it. Woolner's prose treatment did not engage him. He took long breaks from it. In December Emily wrote to Woolner that Tennyson was again working on the poem. It helped that he could 'take walks often now that the tourists are gone' (the summer visitors to the Isle of Wight were already a serious nuisance). She herself had doubts about some aspects of the poem: 'my chief objection to it is that it must necessarily be so indignant in its tone'.[17] Tennyson was quoted at the time by a friend as saying 'how incalculably difficult the story was to tell, the dry facts of it so prosaic in themselves'.[18]

Tennyson named the lovers Edith Aylmer and Leolin Averill and gave the story the dramatic date of 1793. (Edith's rich father, Sir Aylmer Aylmer, refers to 'That cursèd France with her egalities!'[19]) The young Tennyson's despair over Rosa Baring, reflected in *Maud*, surfaces again here when Leolin is turned out of the Aylmers' house by Edith's enraged father:

> Insolent, brainless, heartless! [. . .] wealth enough was theirs
> For twenty matches. [. . .] He believed
> This filthy marriage-hindering Mammon made
> The harlot of the cities: nature crost
> Was mother of the foul adulteries
> That saturate soul with body.[20]

Leolin's subsequent attempt to make a success of himself as a lawyer echoes another pair of cruelly separated lovers from Tennyson's youth, his friend Arthur Hallam and his sister Emily Tennyson. Hallam, forbidden to have any contact with Emily, struggled in London with the uncongenial profession for which his father had destined him, that of lawyer. Leolin Averill's labour as a law student could be directly drawn from Tennyson's memory of Arthur Hallam's suffering in London. Young Leolin

> [. . .] toiled
> Mastering the lawless science of our law,
> That codeless myriad of precedent,
> That wilderness of single instances,
> Through which a few, by wit or fortune led,
> May beat a pathway out to wealth and fame.[21]

'Aylmer's Field' was published in the *Enoch Arden* volume of 1864. Tennyson could see that his struggle in the writing had left it dramatically stilted. Certainly poor Edith's death, following 'twenty months of silence', is from an unspecified fever which is a plot necessity, and Leolin's subsequent suicide makes little sense in dramatic terms. Leolin knows of her death from a supernatural message: 'Star to star vibrates light: may soul to soul / Strike through a finer element of her own?' Presumably Tennyson wanted to heighten the tragedy by showing that the intensity of the lovers' feeling for each other overcame all physical barriers, but in sober reality Leolin would in any case have learnt of Edith's death on the following day.[22]

The title of Woolner's prose narrative, 'The Sermon', was also Tennyson's working title for the poem. Leolin's brother, the rector, preaches on the theme of 'My house is left unto me desolate':

> He, when it seemed he saw
> No pale sheet-lightnings from afar, but forked
> Of the near storm, and aiming at his head,
> Sat anger-charmed from sorrow, soldierlike,
> Erect: but when the preacher's cadence flowed
> Softening through all the gentle attributes
> Of his lost child, the wife, who watched his face
> Paled at a sudden twitch of his iron mouth;
> And 'O pray God that he hold up' she thought
> 'Or surely I shall shame myself and him.'[23]

At the climax of the sermon the couple are brought together by their mutual anguish. She reaches out to him and takes his hand, is overcome by her grief and has to be carried out of the church, while he:

> the Lord of all the landscape round
> Even to its last horizon, and of all
> Who peered at him so keenly, followed out
> Tall and erect, but in the middle aisle
> Reeled, as a footsore ox in crowded ways
> Stumbling across the market to his death,
> Unpitied.[24]

Tennyson himself felt that *Enoch Arden* was the more accomplished of the two works; 'Aylmer's Field' 'had given him more trouble than anything he ever did' and he was never fully satisfied with it.[25] Still, the poem had notably successful passages, particularly at the close where the story is all done, the baronet is dead and his great estates have been broken up:

Then the great Hall was wholly broken down,
And the broad woodland parcelled into farms;
And where the two contrived their daughter's good,
Lies the hawk's cast, the mole has made his run,
The rabbit fondles his own harmless face,
The slow-worm creeps, and the thin weasel there
Follows the mouse, and all is open field.[26]

When the volume was published, Woolner was pleased to see the narrative poems based on his stories, naturally enough, but he had reservations about 'Aylmer's Field'. He told Emily that the writing, though often 'exquisite', was at the same time 'too beautiful', and that he would have preferred 'something more stern and craggy'.[27] Tennyson had been less stirred by the subject matter than he had hoped.

The Tennysons were so prosperous and so successful that their way of life had become sedate and complacent; unimaginably different from the life that Alfred had led before his marriage. Emily controlled the finances, found topics for his work, pressed her recommendations for the titles of his volumes, and devoted her own life to his well-being and his writing. Her circle of acquaintance included clergy, particularly senior clergy who might be willing to pay rent for Farringford during the summer months when the Tennysons themselves were in London or abroad. And she was a woman whose confidence in her own opinions grew with each year of marriage. She herself was conventionally and rather narrowly pious, comfortable with the clergy and their wives, and resolutely distancing with people whose opinions were at variance with her own.

An enthusiastic acquaintance of the Tennysons, Mrs Margaret Gatty, sent as a gift an advance copy of her book about a holiday in Ireland;* she must have been taken aback by Emily's reaction: 'Do you know I love not the Irish [.] I think them a nest of traitors with some honourable exceptions [.] . . . patriotism I love [,] nationality I love not. I wish conquered nations could take gracefully the married state upon them.'[28] Mrs Gatty protested and Emily backed down slightly in her next letter: 'I was only speaking in the Irish fashion'; she then

---

*The Old Folks from Home, a Holiday in Ireland (published the following year, 1862). Margaret Gatty was a successful writer of children's books, well known in her day; and she and her husband had established cordial contact with the Tennysons on a visit to the Isle of Wight in the 1850s; the very large number of surviving letters to her from Emily Tennyson indicates that Emily valued this relationship. (Thwaite, Emily Tennyson, p. 337.)

talked about her anger with something said recently by Aubrey de Vere (that remarkably gentle and peaceful soul): 'It is so wicked in those who call themselves Christian gentlemen to keep up old grudges when they know very well that for years England has done all she can for those who are too little inclined to do anything for themselves.'[29]

Mrs Gatty must have regretted embarking on the Irish as a topic when she received this. Tennyson himself had taken gracefully to the married state. Had he been conquered? Did Emily's conventional middle-class piety, social ambition for her children and interest in accumulating wealth represent the transformation of Tennyson into something of a 'lost leader'?

There was a reaction against Tennyson as a public figure after 1860; an inevitable turning of the tide against an artist who had become a monument. A shift was taking place in the habits of the reading public. The great éclat enjoyed by *In Memoriam* in 1850 was a late flowering of the dominance that lyric poetry had enjoyed since the romantic movement. The novel in the hands of Dickens, Thackeray, the Brontës and Elizabeth Gaskell had become the dominant form in the following decade and in the 1860s George Eliot's work intensified its claim to the moral and intellectual – and political – high ground. The novel had become prestigious. Tennyson did not articulate it this way, nor was it anything other than his magnificent instinct for his audience that drove the shift in his own work, but at the same time it is true to say, in simple terms, that his poetry was claiming its own place among these big narrative works. *Idylls of the King* was clearly a huge project which was likely in the long term to keep him active for many years, but he needed smaller projects and different themes in order to keep fluent, to keep his hand in, and importantly to keep the money coming in. Narrative poems based on English stories of the present or recent past, 'English Idylls' as he thought of them, provided an outlet which was an alternative to his Arthurian Idylls. In due course Emily and Woolner between them would help him to write these, but in the meantime he eased the frustration with travelling, some of it seemingly random, restless and contingent.

Tennyson was uneasily aware that literary fashion was now moving away from him. Browning was at last recognised as a major poet, and as having a distinctive and original voice and an artistic daring and energy which compared favourably with the measured decorativeness of Tennyson's work. At the same time Dante Gabriel Rossetti and Algernon Swinburne had found a new, young audience which was impatient of the stateliness, propriety and endorsement of Queen, Country and Empire with which Tennyson's name was by this date irretrievably linked. The new generation was becoming tired of Tennyson; this included some young men who were ostensibly part of his milieu.

John Addington Symonds went as an undergraduate to Balliol College, Oxford, in 1859, 'and was taken under Jowett's wing' – Jowett of course was a close family friend of the Tennysons. Symonds' respect for Tennyson had until he left Oxford been learned chiefly from members of an older generation. In 1862, there was established near the Symonds family home at Clifton a new proprietary school on the model of Arnold's Rugby or Cotton's Marlborough, under its founding headmaster Dr Perceval. One of the first teaching appointments that Perceval made in 1862 was Henry Graham Dakyns, who had earlier been tutor to Tennyson's two sons, and had accompanied Tennyson on his visit to Cauteretz in 1861. Symonds soon got to know Dakyns well, and Dakyns provided a link with Tennyson. Symonds married young, and took his wife on honeymoon, in November 1864, to the Isle of Wight. He had obtained letters of introduction to Tennyson from his old tutor Jowett, and from his new friend Dakyns. Tennyson himself was away from Farringford, but Emily was kind to the young man and he wrote to thank her 'from my wife and myself for your great kindness to us. You have truly given what Mr Jowett wished for us – a happy recollection, to be connected with a great event in our lives.'[30]

A dinner party at Thomas Woolner's house in London in December 1865 gives a telling vignette of Tennyson as a great Victorian locked in gladiatorial combat with another great Victorian – Gladstone. The other guests included John Addington Symonds' father, Dr Symonds of Bristol, who was on a visit to London, and the artist William Holman Hunt. A further group of guests, including the young Symonds and Francis Turner Palgrave, arrived later in the evening. Symonds wrote an account of the evening for his sister Charlotte: 'I was like a man hearing a concerto, Gladstone first violin, Tennyson violoncello, Woolner Bass viol, Palgrave viola, & perhaps Hunt a second but very subordinate viola'.[31] Gladstone quarrelled with Tennyson over the October rebellion in Jamaica, which had been put down with extreme brutality. The governor of Jamaica, Edward John Eyre (1815–1901) was originally a Lincolnshire man; by coincidence he had been a pupil at Louth Grammar School shortly after Tennyson had left it. This Lincolnshire connection may have contributed to Tennyson's surprising support for Eyre.

Tennyson declared that in controlling a violent mob, any degree of cruelty was justified. He repeated himself and delivered his prejudices with increasing emphasis instead of engaging with Gladstone's arguments in favour of dispassionate proportion. 'We are too tender to savages; we are more tender to a black man than to ourselves,' Tennyson declared, and continued: ' "Niggers are tigers, niggers are tigers", in *obbligato, sotto voce* to Gladstone's declamation. "But the Englishman is a cruel man – he is a strong man," put in Gladstone.'[32]

Symonds recognised Tennyson and Gladstone as equally forceful:

both with their strong provincial accent, Gladstone with his rich flexible voice, Tennyson with his deep drawl rising into an impatient falsetto when put out, Tennyson denying with a bald negative, Gladstone full of facts, Tennyson relying on impression, both of them humorous, but the one polished and delicate in repartee, the other broad & coarse & grotesque. Gladstone's hands are white & not remarkable. Tennyson's are huge, unwieldy, fit for moulding clay or dough. Gladstone is in some sort a man of the world, Tennyson a child & treated by him like a child.[33]

In the drawing room later in the evening, Tennyson delivered a long monologue on such matters as the size of the universe, the nature of the soul, prayer, creation, the eternity of punishment, morality, and the existence of evil. He was startlingly naïve for such an intelligent man: 'In all this metaphysical vagueness about matter, morals, the existence of evil, and evidences of God there was something almost childish.' Giving Tennyson the benefit of the doubt, Symonds interpreted his behaviour as 'perfect simplicity' which 'recognises the real greatness of such questions'.[34] Nor was the awkwardness of the evening yet over. Tennyson was persuaded to read part of his blank verse translation of the *Iliad*, and this produced a further contest with Gladstone, who continually interrupted with corrections of Tennyson's understanding of the Greek.

The long evening, hosted by Woolner as a convivial event, had effectively been sabotaged by a collision of mighty egos, though interestingly Tennyson's report of it to Emily the following day ignored the quarrelsomeness: of Gladstone he wrote: 'The great man was infinitely agreeable and delivered himself very eloquently.'[35]

In private, with trusted friends, young Symonds could afford to be critical of Tennyson. Dakyns owed Tennyson a good deal; nevertheless Symonds could confidently write to him (in August 1868): 'The time is come for a return to Byronism in literature [. . .]. I hope we shall free ourselves from the nightmare of Tennyson – not, I mean, of Tennyson himself, but of the evil influence which he has of late exerted by educating finical and fastidious tastes.'[36] By 1868 Symonds could assume that this was now the acceptable view of his generation. Tennyson was past his prime, and had become an obstruction to development in poetry.

Tennyson's success and fame in the mid 1860s created a little episode which was a recall of his earliest years. The bookseller Thomas Jackson of Louth, who when Alfred was an adolescent had published the little volume *Poems by Two Brothers*, now proposed to reissue the volume. Jackson probably felt, not unreasonably, that he was owed something for being the famous poet's very first publisher. In 1864 Moxon's widow took on Bertrand Payne as manager of the firm; from that date onwards Payne was in charge of Tennyson's dealings with Moxon. Payne kept a copy of a letter from a firm of London solicitors giving their view of Thomas Jackson's intentions. Jackson, they pointed out, 'evidently intends, if he can, to make a purse out of the matter'. Jackson believed that on the back of Tennyson's fame he could sell 10,000 copies and clear a profit for himself of £1,000. 'However he is anxious not to do anything contrary to Mr Tennyson's wishes and is open to an offer based on such terms.' Tennyson paid Jackson £1,000 in order to avoid the embarrassment of this early volume reappearing under his name.[37]

Another potential source of embarrassment to the family, if not to Tennyson himself, involved Charles Weld (1813–69), married to Emily's sister Anne Sellwood. Weld was a scientist who became secretary and librarian to the Royal Society in 1843. In 1861 he was forced to resign this post in disgrace. The details were hushed up but the matter is referred to obliquely and regretfully in letters from Emily and other family members. It seems that Weld had 'introduced a lady to his rooms at Burlington House'.

Much of the decade from 1860 to 1870 was spent on the Isle of Wight. Tennyson and Emily had chosen the place for its seclusion, but like most people who love solitude and time to write, Tennyson also loved company, and there was a steady stream of admiring visitors who would keep him up to date with the life of London and of the old Cambridge circle. What Tennyson needed were strong, opinionated men like Gladstone, who would stand up to him and argue with him. What he got, increasingly, were worshippers at the shrine.

Some of Tennyson's friends were becoming disillusioned. Emily remained fond of Edward Lear, who continued to visit Farringford, but Lear was intensely sensitive and easily upset. By the 1860s his relaxed intimacy with the Tennysons had become a thing of the past, and as they became more frequented by the great world so he felt more out of place there. On one of his visits in the early 1860s, Julia Margaret Cameron decided that Emily Tennyson's little upright piano was not good enough for him to play. Lear wrote to Thomas Woolner: 'Mrs Cameron absolutely sent up a grand piano by 8 men from her house [Dimbola, in Freshwater village] for me to sing at !!!!' Extravagant gestures of this kind were all very well, but Edward Lear was shy and quiet, and he wanted a chance to talk intimately with Tennyson about the old days without interruption. Mrs Cameron's busy intrusiveness disturbed this intimacy with an 'odious incense palaver & fuss.'[38]

The incense was driving a wedge between the two friends. At Farringford in 1864 (after the successful publication of the *Enoch Arden* volume), Lear found Tennyson mopping up the flattery and devotion offered to him and reluctant to engage in ordinary conversations; also Mrs Cameron and her friends continued to invade the place. 'One always seems to live in public here,' Lear complained. He managed to secure a walk by the sea in Tennyson's company, but it was no comfort to him. Tennyson embarked on an obsessional monologue about the invasions of his privacy on the Isle of Wight until Lear was provoked into giving him an 'outspoken opinion about his morbid absurdity & unphilosophical botherings'. He left after this visit thinking that in spite of his love of Emily he was unlikely to want to visit the place again. He could no longer put up with the changes that fame and adulation had wrought in Tennyson, 'the anomaly of high souled & philosophic writings combined with slovenliness, selfishness, & morbid folly'.[39]

In 1865, there was speculation in the press about the offer of a title to Tennyson. The *Spectator* carried an article on the subject, and Tennyson and Emily were embarrassed by this. They did not want the Queen to think that they had been talking about it.[40]

Marks of public recognition continued to flow in the 1860s; all of them were welcome, but they were accompanied by a kind of slackening of Tennyson's inner life. He would say of Farringford that its endless peace deadened him, as though he was enjoying an eternal weekend ('Sunday touches Sunday'), and he increasingly needed the buzz and stir of London and its grand institutions (of which he was in some cases becoming a member). His use of geology in both *In

Memoriam and *Maud* (his account in the latter poem of a dinosaur, or 'monstrous eft') had attracted a lot of attention in discussion of those poems, and indeed from his very earliest writing he had shown signs of reading deeply and seriously in biological and geological works. His 'The Kraken', created when he was very young, is a mark of that. His fame, and his friendship with several members of the Royal Society, caused him to be invited to become a Fellow of the Society in 1864. He was clearly surprised, though intrigued and flattered, and he thought it right to decline the invitation. The Fellows were undeterred: the following year they invited him again. This time he accepted, and became thus a member of a community which included Sir John Herschel, Charles Pritchard, Norman Lockyer, John Tyndall, James Paget and T. H. Huxley.

A valiant attempt to see Tennyson's poetry as displaying an understanding of biology and geology would be published years later, in 1910, by Sir Norman Lockyer, *Tennyson as a Student and Poet of Nature*. Adam Sedgwick was among the distinguished list of scientists who contributed to this book.[41] It was a friendly and systematic listing of quotations from Tennyson's poetry which could be taken to indicate accurate scientific observation. If nothing else, it was a remarkably loyal gesture from a friend who was also a Fellow of the Society. Lockyer's objective 'was to collect together the passages in Tennyson's Works which deal with the scientific aspects of nature', and the book does exactly that. Lockyer had been introduced to Tennyson by Thomas Woolner in 1864. Lockyer was an astronomer, and Tennyson loved to explore the heavens through a telescope and have them explained to him by a man of science. Lockyer in turn was pleased and surprised by Tennyson's enthusiasm. 'I was then living in Fairfax Road, West Hampstead,' he explained, 'and I had erected my 6-inch Cooke Equatorial [telescope] in the garden.' (At night Hampstead was still like a country village.) Tennyson was a regular visitor to his observatory. The vastness of the heavens – 'vastness' was itself a favourite word of Tennyson's – reduced humanity to a humble scale. Of a particular configuration of the moon and the stars beyond it Tennyson said: 'What a splendid Hell that would make.' Again after seeing clusters in Hercules and Perseus he remarked musingly, 'I cannot think much of the country families after that.'[42]

Tennyson's knowledge of Lyell's *Principles of Geology* and Chambers' *Vestiges of Creation* was supplemented by his friendships with men such as Lockyer and Sedgwick. His election to the Royal Society was not preposterous, but as with the other clubs to which he was elected in the 1860s, he was not a steady attender. He enjoyed the excitement of his initial introduction to the Society, but he seldom went to its meetings.[43] In March 1865 he was invited to join a celebrated and long-established literary society, 'The Club'. Given that his sponsors in this case were the Duke of Argyll and Monckton Milnes (Lord Houghton), he could scarcely refuse. He was worried though that membership and dining with such grandees would commit him to more expense than he wanted, and, again, once elected, he did not often attend.[44]

There were losses and interruptions from 1865 onwards. The most serious of these was the death of his mother in February. This was a major milestone in Tennyson's life: Elizabeth had been a sweet, saintly and suffering presence throughout his turbulent childhood at Somersby. After his father's death Alfred had effectively become head of the Somersby family, and care of his mother and his younger siblings at home had fallen to him. Between 1837 and 1850 her several homes, in Epping, Tunbridge Wells and Cheltenham, had been his only permanent addresses. Now, with her death, the care of his siblings again fell to him. His sister Matilda, the oddest and, ironically, the longest-lived of the Tennysons, came to live with Alfred and Emily at Farringford, and remained part of their household thereafter.[45] In August 1866 his brother Septimus died, followed a year later by Emily's father. Tennyson seemed remarkably little concerned about the death of Septimus, and it received the sparest of references in Emily's journal: 'A. tells me that Septimus is gone.'[46] The death of Emily's father, Henry Sellwood, received a great deal more commentary. Emily had a telegram summoning her to his bedside, where she sat for much of the day, and she was able to say goodbye to him.[47]

Tennyson was hit hard by his mother's death. 'Ally has not been writing', Emily told Edward Lear in late April 1865. 'He is not yet as he has been.'[48] Other distractions and interruptions flooded in: there was the well-documented and utterly pointless visit of Queen Emma of the Sandwich Islands in the autumn of 1865,[49] and an invitation to stand for election as Professor of Poetry at Oxford in 1866 (wisely Tennyson decided immediately to have nothing to do with that). When his brother Septimus died in Cheltenham, Tennyson did not go to the funeral. Although he said so little about the death of Septimus, it is possible that it reminded him of Arthur Hallam's. He had cared deeply about Arthur but could not face his funeral. With this younger brother whom he had loved as a child, the same feelings may have resurfaced.

His own sons, who now filled the emotional space that had once been occupied by his younger brothers, were growing up, needed attention, and were often causes of anxiety. Emily was desperately reluctant to send the boys to school, and she hung on to them as long as she could. As an older mother whose first baby had died, she invested a great deal of her emotional life in her children, and early photographs show that she kept them with long hair and wearing long clothes (so that they looked like large girls) later than was normal in the period for male children. Farringford would be lonely without them. Benjamin Jowett in particular was tactfully insistent that Tennyson should think about a school for them, and in due course they were sent to a preparatory school kept by a friend, Kegan Paul (who later became a publisher). This was not a success: Lionel was bullied at the school, and developed a speech impediment. In the meantime Hallam, the elder brother, had gone on to Marlborough.

Tennyson chose Marlborough because the headmaster, Dr Bradley, was a friend of his, and also because the Dean of Westminster, Arthur Stanley, had told him that it was 'the best school in England'. Tennyson was feted by the Bradleys, who gave a dinner party for him – a rather grand event for an institution full of adolescent boys. It cannot have displeased him that after dinner 'The Upper Sixth came in, and at their petition he read "Guinevere", refusing however enthronement in a large arm-chair, and asserting it was "too conspicuous".'[50] Because *In Memoriam* and *Maud* had both displayed such a developed interest in the sciences, especially geology, Tennyson was introduced to all the science teachers. But the tension between religion and science present in those poems was not felt on this particular evening. On the contrary, Tennyson insisted on the immortality of the soul.

Hallam suffered from pneumonia while he was at Marlborough, and at one point Emily believed he would die. In 1868, Lionel, always regarded as the more fragile of the brothers (and still stammering), was sent to Eton. It was felt that he was not robust enough for the regime at Marlborough. He was a gifted and creative young man, and his stream of lively and funny letters should have convinced his parents that he was actually the more interesting of their two sons. Given the tragic history of his own father, one might have expected Tennyson, of all people, to guard against the tensions created in a family by preferring one sibling above another. But Lionel could be wayward and undisciplined, and Hallam would always remain Tennyson and Emily's favourite. Tennyson's way of dealing with problems was to withdraw into himself and leave them to Emily, and he could be over-bearing with both his children. Edward Lear found his treatment of them 'brutal and snubbing'.[51]

Tennyson's fame was such that visitors came on pilgrimages to the Isle of Wight simply to see the poet in person. The erosion of privacy was relentless. Hallam Tennyson remembered being with his father and a stranger tapping him on the arm and asking: 'Do you know who it is with whom you are walking?' Hallam replied, 'Yes, my father.' 'Nonsense, man,' said the intruder, 'you are walking with the poet Tennyson.'[52] Tennyson himself brusquely rebuffed strangers, sometimes making errors of judgement in so doing. A party of cultivated Americans, with an introduction from Julia Margaret Cameron, arrived at Farringford to call on the Poet Laureate. They were quiet and courteous, and very conscious that they had been afforded a rare honour. Tennyson refused to have them admitted to the house and they returned to Dimbola forlornly, still holding the letter of introduction that Mrs Cameron had provided. She immediately went to Farringford herself with the group, demanded admission, and said: 'Alfred, these good people have come 3000 miles to see a lion and they have found a bear.' Tennyson then let them in and was introduced to them with good grace.

Osborne House, designed by Prince Albert as a seaside summer retreat for the Queen, and completed by 1851, was also an attraction: the Isle of Wight developed rapidly as a fashionable resort during the 1850s, and by the end of the decade Tennyson and Emily were looking for a house to which they could escape during the summers, when the press of visitors had become so great as to be a serious nuisance. They settled on a region on the Surrey and Sussex border to the south-east of Haslemere and close to Blackdown. The idea of moving there was already developed by 1860, though it took time to acquire the land and the rights of access to it, and to find an appropriate architect.

They habitually took houses in London in the summer; for the summer of 1867, for example, they rented Gore Lodge, Kensington, home of Emily's relation Lady Franklin. A great deal of entertaining took place at Gore Lodge. Robert Browning, Lord Houghton, Carlyle, James Spedding, Venables, the Lushingtons and Gladstone were among the older friends. Those who had joined Tennyson's circle more recently, and were marks of his increasingly elevated social status, were people such as Dean Stanley and Lady Augusta Stanley, Lord Boyd and the Duke and Duchess of Argyll. Lady Stanley of Alderley gave a reception at which Tennyson, Robert Browning, Carlyle and Lord Houghton all stood for a long time in deep conversation with each other. A need in Tennyson for acceptance by a group of which he would be the focus was being met here.[53]

To protect Farringford from prying eyes, and from the unwelcome rash of little houses that had been built near it, the Tennysons had an embankment made between the house and the lane into the village, and surrounded the garden with a screen of trees. The original appeal of the house had been the uninterrupted view from the big window of the drawing room, but with their own attempts to separate themselves from the unwelcome new building around them, that view no longer existed. As a winter refuge Farringford continued to do well enough. William Allingham was by this time a regular and very welcome guest – Tennyson always loved to talk poetry with him, and Allingham was fond of the older man despite his frequent contrariness. Tennyson was increasingly unaware of his impact on other people, and was capable of crass selfishness. In February 1867, Allingham accompanied him on one of his favourite walks down to Brook Bay, where a ship had grounded in a storm. Allingham suffered from vertigo, and he warned Tennyson that he had begun to feel unsteady on the cliff path. They reached the point and saw the steamer which had come ashore, then, in Allingham's words:

> turned up to the downs and came back by a path slanting along the cliff side, like a frightful dream rather, my head being lightish. T. tells of people who have fallen over, and at one place is a monumental stone to commemorate such an accident. I said (walking close behind him) 'suppose I were to slip and catch hold of you, and we both rolled down together,' on which T. stopped and said, 'You'd better go on first.'

On this same walk Tennyson talked about the slow growth of his *Idylls of the King*. He blamed John Sterling's review of the 1842 volumes which had found fault with his 'Morte d'Arthur'.

> T. told me he was prevented from doing his Arthur Epic, in twelve books, by John Sterling's review of 'Morte d'Arthur' in the *Quarterly*. 'I had it all in my mind, could have done it without any trouble. The king is complete man, the knights are the passions.'[54]

After Edward Moxon's death, Tennyson's relationship with his publisher had settled back into relatively harmonious prosperity once the problems of the illustrated edition had been overcome. However, after 1864 the situation deteriorated; Bertrand Payne, the new manager, became high-handed and tactless in his dealings with Tennyson. Payne published a *Selections* from Tennyson's work which annoyed him (it was ornamented in a way that made it look like the fashionable and lightweight annuals). Tennyson's letters to Payne during 1867 are mainly to do with vexations: a lack of courtesy to his American publishers, or Payne's confusing and inaccurate accounts, or disagreement over money actually due. At the same time, and because he was irritated by Payne, Tennyson took to publishing individual poems in periodicals again (much against Emily's advice). Late in 1867, he became worried by rumours of Moxon's financial insecurity and wrote to Payne: 'when it came to a rumour that your house had actually failed I considered that my best and handsomest course was to apply directly to yourself, to ascertain the real state of things'. He added a postscript which was indignant, heartfelt and accurate: 'Seeing that I have stuck to the house of Moxon from the beginning through evil report and good report, and really have been and am the main pillar of it, it seems to me (and I say it with all kindliness) that you cannot but feel that it is not only due to me but also your duty to yourself that I should be fully informed of the state of affairs.'[55] Tennyson was not mollified by the sumptuous 1867–8 edition of *Idylls of the King*, with illustrations commissioned by Payne from Gustave Doré, an artist then very much in vogue. He remained lukewarm towards all attempts to make visual images of his work. Matters were made worse still when Payne decided that Moxon's problems were being exacerbated by the fact that Tennyson had sold copyright for publication in Europe to Tauchnitz. Payne discovered that the Tauchnitz editions of Tennyson were being imported into England by post at a price much cheaper than Moxon's own prices (the example he gave was '10/- *for the whole of Mr Tennyson's works!*'),[56] Tennyson wrote to Disraeli, then prime minister, and to the Privy Council seeking tighter copyright regulations, although the reality – as he recognised – was that he had in part created the problem for himself by selling the rights to Tauchnitz in the first instance.[57]

For Tennyson and Emily the final vexation with the firm of Moxon came in the form of Moxon's advertisement, in 1868, for a new 'Standard Edition' of Tennyson's works in four volumes. The advertisement promised that the volumes would include substantial new work. Both Emily and Tennyson – especially Emily, perhaps – thought that this was dishonest, since there was very little in the proposed volumes that had not already appeared. Emily wrote in her journal:

> What I do really care for is that my Ally should stand before the world in his own child-like simplicity & by this he would be made to appear a mere cunning tradesman. He hates it all as much as I do – only he does not see the consequences as clearly perhaps not having turned his mind to the subject.

Tennyson had not signed an agreement for this 'Standard Edition', and early in the following year, 1869, he withdrew from Moxon. On 15 January 1869, Emily recorded the change of publisher:

> [Strahan] offered £5,000 a year for five years. New works he offered to publish for nothing, but Alfred would not agree to this, and a commission of ten per cent was fixed. Alfred was rather staggered by the £5,000 offer, and told Strahan that he could not possibly make a profit on it. However, the publisher stuck to his point, and the bargain was struck to the satisfaction of both parties.[58]

In 1871 Moxon failed and was sold. By his mishandling of Tennyson, Payne had lost the company its central support. Tennyson got on well with Alexander Strahan, and the firm continued to flourish until 1873, when it, too, failed: fundamentally the problem was Strahan's ineptitude as a businessman, but he and Tennyson remained on good personal terms.[59] Strahan would continue as owner and publisher of the *Contemporary Review*, edited by James Knowles. Even when Knowles and Strahan parted company acrimoniously in 1877, Tennyson managed to retain reasonably cordial relations with both of them.[60]

Tennyson's dealings with publishers were increasingly canny, and he would remain a master of hard negotiations for money. From 1873 he would be published by Henry S. King (on very favourable terms), and when that contract came up for renewal in 1884 and King tried to modify the agreement somewhat, Tennyson signed a ten-year contract with Macmillan. This relationship lasted for the rest of his life.

The young architect and writer James Knowles (1831–1908), ambitious, intelligent, and set on making his way in the fashionable world, had written to Tennyson in 1861 for permission to dedicate to him his own retelling of the Arthurian legend, *The Story of King Arthur and his Knights*. The two men had never met, but Tennyson was willing enough to have the book dedicated to him. He was pleased with it when he saw it, and he recognised Knowles's energy and professionalism. He wrote to Knowles: 'I was from home and ill when your double gift arrived. [Knowles had sent two copies of the book, one specially bound for Tennyson.] Accept my thanks now. Your task seems to me admirably done. My boys of 9 and 7 could think of nothing else but King Arthur and his Knights while reading your book.'[61]

In the early stages of their contact, Tennyson tried to discourage Knowles in case he was just another celebrity-hunter, but Knowles was persistent. He called at Farringford in October 1866 and was lucky to find Tennyson and Emily in a receptive mood. He was invited up to Tennyson's little study to hear some of the poems read, and he and Tennyson took to each other. Knowles's veneration for Tennyson was absolute: 'I was shown upstairs to the top of the house and into an attic which was the Poet's own study, and presently, with my heart in my mouth, I heard his great steps as he climbed up the little wooden stairs. His bodily presence seemed as kingly as I felt it ought to be, though a little grim and awful at first.'[62]

Knowles was busy establishing himself in London in the mid-1860s: he had been elected to the Reform Club in 1865 and his name was becoming known. It is likely that Tennyson heard him well spoken of by mutual acquaintances in London and that this helped the relationship to prosper. In June 1867 Tennyson and Emily visited Surrey in order to make an offer for a plot of land. The plot was the property of a very substantial local landowner, Lord Egmont, and occupied a natural terrace on the southern side of Blackdown Hill, which was otherwise all sloping and wooded. This little clearing where Tennyson was thinking of building a house was currently used to grow potatoes. The hill behind it gave it ideal privacy and a good deal of shelter from bad weather, and heather surrounded it, with foxglove in bloom. It had a wonderful view, which stretched seemingly for hundreds of miles to the sea in the distance. 'It wants nothing,' said Tennyson, 'but a great river looping along through the midst of it.'[63]

The site was perfectly secluded, so it exactly met the Tennysons' requirements. When Tennyson visited again, hoping to gather information from Lord Egmont's agent about his offer to buy, Knowles saw him at Haslemere station. When they had met the previous October Tennyson had said to him, 'I am so short sighted that I shall not know you if I meet you unless you speak to me.' Knowles took him at his word. Emily summarised what happened next: Knowles 'having been told A's errand said I am an architect. A. replied, you had better build me a house & Mr Knowles said on one condition that you take my services freely only paying the journeys. Afterwards this was agreed upon.'[64] (Knowles said simply that Tennyson had 'accepted my terms'.) Knowles had created a magnificent opportunity for himself through this chance meeting. By the end of June the Tennysons had concluded the transaction with Lord Egmont's agent: they paid £1,400 and were now the owners of the site. On 23 April 1868 (Shakespeare's birthday) friends came to witness the laying of the corner stone. Sir John Simeon made a speech and the new owners celebrated with a picnic on the property.[65]

The house was originally to have been a four-roomed cottage, but the ideas of both architect and clients became increasingly ambitious. Indeed, the site was so magnificent that it seemed natural to take advantage of its possibilities as the setting for a grander house. Knowles wrote that Emily had ideas 'which she could not quite express by drawing but which I understood well enough to put into shape'. Tennyson made some drawings as well – these have survived, and although very rough and approximate sketches they are clearly visualisations of part of a two-storey house with a third-floor garret and steep handsome gables. Tennyson liked to joke with visitors that Knowles had imposed his own will, but the truth was that the two men had a number of friendly meetings at the potato patch, and the designs developed gradually.

Aldworth, as it evolved from the creative energies of client and architect, was an Arthurian romance in stone seen through the powerfully transforming medium of a Victorian lens. It was a 'fantasy on the idea of an Anglo-French manor-house', as Knowles's authoritative biographer Priscilla Metcalf has called it:

> The informing idea seems to have been fixed in the period of Caxton's publication, in the precincts of Westminster Abbey on the first English printing-press, of Malory's *Morte d'Arthur*: that is, 1485, liberally construed – the year, too, of that English landmark, Bosworth field. (And Tennyson must have liked the thought that the house was finished precisely four hundred years after Malory finished writing in 1469.) Its Englishness was to include a French strain, as the Arthurian tales did.[66]

The original plan for a four-roomed cottage had long since given way to a house which was very substantial: two main storeys and above a garret with decorative dormers, with an eighty-foot facade (and a depth of about fifty feet). It was disproportionately large for the natural terrace on which it stood, and a number of unwelcome practical problems (malfunctioning drains, insecure parapets and the like) would emerge in the course of the building work. The house followed the centemporary fashion for carved external decorative detail on neo-Gothic buildings.

The site is just over the county border from Surrey into Sussex, and the house was built at a height of about 720 feet with Blackdown rising behind it. There was a large bay window on the first floor facing south, which was covered by a sturdy flat leaded roof that could be accessed from a window in the second-floor garret. This space gave full advantage to the wonderful views that the house was designed to enjoy. Tennyson loved to step out immediately into the sky, as it felt, and stand on this roof. A great many of his guests, including very grand ladies with billowing skirts which had to be squeezed through the window, were brought up there to be impressed.

Tennyson and Knowles kept in close contact with each other over the coming months and Tennyson made regular visits to Knowles's house, the Hollies, Clapham, both to discuss the house and to talk about Tennyson's writing. The writing of a book for the *Idylls* on the legend of the Holy Grail had been bothering Tennyson for a while; he lingered and hesitated over it partly because he felt that such an intensely mystical subject was for a poet who was less questioning in his Christian devotion than he himself had ever managed to be. Emily wanted him to get on with this poem, and Knowles, from her perspective, was a good influence: he was intelligent enough to be a stimulating literary conversationalist and he encouraged the flow of the poet's central activity. By September 1868 Tennyson was writing 'The Holy Grail' after a gap of nearly ten years in the slow cumulative composition of *Idylls of the King*.

Knowles was now in demand as an architect,[67] and in his eagerness to capitalise on his friendship with Tennyson, he now devised another club, or association, specifically for Tennyson to join: this was 'The Metaphysical Society'. Tennyson's brother-in-law, Edmund Lushington of Park House, was interested in metaphysical matters. On 7 August 1866 Emily recorded a day which for her was particularly sad, because the boys went back to their respective schools, Hallam to Marlborough and Lionel, who still had his worrying stammer, to his speech therapist, a Dr Hunt, at Hastings. Edmund and Cecilia Lushington were in residence at Park House, where Tennyson and Edmund talked about metaphysics. 'They have engrossed A. much of late. The materialism of the day has revived his interest in them.'[68] Knowles's proposal for a club fell, then, on fertile soil. In November 1868, while Tennyson was staying at the Hollies, Charles Pritchard, an astronomer, was a fellow guest. Pritchard was distinguished in his field, and was soon to be the Savilian Professor of Astronomy at Oxford. He strongly believed that it was possible to reconcile scientific discovery with the teachings of the Bible. Tennyson himself, as he grew older, increasingly wanted to be able to share this belief.

The idea of the Metaphysical Society arose during a kind of 'triangular duel' between Knowles, Pritchard and Tennyson on religious and philosophical questions. Tennyson said of James Knowles that he did not know a concept from a hippopotamus, but despite this Knowles took it upon himself to set up a society if both Tennyson and Pritchard were willing to join it. The list of members assembled by Knowles was long and impressive. It comprised two of the country's most distinguished Roman Catholics (Archbishop Manning and W. G. Ward, the latter a close friend of Tennyson), two Broad Churchmen (Tennyson's friends Dean Stanley and F. D. Maurice), a well-known Unitarian (James Martineau), several rationalists (W. R. Greg, W. K. Clifford and Fitzjames Stephen), scientists (Huxley and Tyndall, and also in this category the ever-loyal Duke of Argyll), the agnostics John Morley and Sir Leslie Stephen (editor of the *Dictionary of National Biography*), and other major figures of the day, including Gladstone, Froude, Ruskin, Henry Sidgwick, Walter Bagehot and R. H. Hutton.[69]

It was typical of Tennyson that he refused to go to the first meeting of a society which had been created entirely round and for him. Knowles wrote a few days before the inaugural date (in May 1869):

(The Hollies, Clapham Common May 19th 1869) I do trust that you may feel moved to be there and thereby ensure the genial tone of the first meeting. [R. H.] Hutton is to read a paper about Herbert Spencer and we have written to ask Herbert Spencer to be present accordingly. Yesterday I read to Hutton as you gave me leave to do 'the higher Pantheism' which gave him wonderful delight. He begged me to ask you whether he might have a copy of it for his & wife's own sole perusal – and he also begged me to beg of you most earnestly to let it be read – if you will not come and read it yourself – at our next Wednesday meeting. It would make it historical he said – to open with such a piece as that – which he declared was as grand as anything you have written – He said 'It would do more to convert the atheists than all our arguments.' Do pray kindly give me your authority just to read it to our members – if you should not be there yourself to do so. It would be so immensely graceful and generous of you to allow it [. . .] in Hutton's words 'it would go straight to the hearts of the men.'[70]

Tennyson replied, 'I am not coming up for your meeting.' He reluctantly agreed that the poem should be read, provided it was 'stated surely that I have but ceded to your strongly expressed desire'. He was not sure that the poem was yet finished, and he was anxious about Knowles's delivery: 'It wants to be read in a big voice. Can you make yours big enough?'[71] 'The Higher Pantheism', written in 1867 (and not yet published), was duly read by Knowles at the first formal meeting of the Metaphysical Society, 2 June 1869. It is a somewhat half-hearted rehearsal of the argument from design with which Tennyson had been familiar since he had studied Paley's work as an undergraduate. Compared with his speculation about such questions in *In Memoriam*, it is a low-key and unmemorable piece of work.

The Metaphysical Society would meet, dine and discuss sporadically over a period of ten years; Tennyson himself attended eleven of its meetings. It ceased to meet partly because Tennyson lost interest in it. The conversations that he had enjoyed as an active member had done him good, contributing to his increasing breadth of understanding and tolerance in religious matters. However, when the club ceased to meet, he complained that in 'ten years of strenuous effort no one had succeeded in even defining the term "Metaphysics"'.[72]

There were features of his life at Farringford, where he was surrounded by working farms and the rhythms of country life, that Tennyson would miss at Aldworth. A friend and neighbour in the new setting, James Mangles, later quoted Tennyson as saying: 'The view [from Aldworth] was magnificent; but he missed, he said, the country sounds, whetting of scythes, reapers' songs, & sheep & cattle – and the birds, he said, don't seem to care to come so high. "This fellow," pointing to the architect [James Knowles], "makes me have all this. I should be contented with something much simpler".'[73] James Mangles was trained as a lawyer but by this date had become a celebrated horticulturalist who specialised in the cultivation of rhododendrons. His small private estate, Valewood, was within a short walk of Aldworth. Tennyson was willing to talk to him with a freedom and lack of constraint which he would probably not have shown if Mangles had been a literary man (Mangles knew very little about literature). Tennyson was happy to be rude about distinguished men of letters who were among his acquaintance, since Mangles was unlikely to meet them:

> He described how he had been once introduced to Macaulay. Two other men (Hallam [the historian, father of Arthur Hallam] and Guizot [also an historian]) were present to whom he spoke (or rather preached) for two hours. When they left, he turned to me & said he was glad to see me. I thought he had been a deuced time finding that out & skedaddled as quickly as I could.[74]

(In Hallam Tennyson's *Memoir* there is a slightly different version of this: Tennyson had quoted Macaulay as turning to him and saying,

'Good morning, I am happy to have had the pleasure of making your acquaintance,' before he strode briskly away.)[75]

When Mangles first met him in 1870, Tennyson was still suffering from eczema which he believed had been caused by the inoculation forced on him by Julia Margaret Cameron. He was required to stick to a sugar-free diet in the hope of curing it. On a visit to Mangles' house (without Emily) he talked about the eczema and pulled down his stocking to show that the offending leg had improved somewhat. He had scratched it: 'No luxury like scratching – beats fornication all to pieces.'[76] In July he was suffering from gout as well as eczema, and his son quoted him, more decorously, as saying: 'The doctor says that I mustn't scratch my leg, but I can't help it, and last night I scratched it till I could have shrieked with glory.'[77] He talked with Mangles about the preposterous Martin Tupper, and recalled that his and Thackeray's nickname for him was 'farting Tupper'. He also talked to Mangles about his frustrations with Freshwater and his hatred of new building near his house there. Outside his gate at Aldworth he pointed to the beautiful view of the brow of the hill:

'There, they might build a whole crescent of houses on that brow, and spoil all that.' I remarked that that was not likely. Oh yes, he said, not less unlikely than they should build at Freshwater when first I went there. What would that waste land sell for, do you think? I said that I feared that its price might have been raised by his living so near.[78]

On 20 September 1870, Mangles noted – without comment – a particularly sad aspect of the Tennyson regime. 'I walked across the common about 11 o'clock & found Mrs T writing letters. She writes, she says, for nearly 7 hours a day – answers all her husband's letters for him.'[79] (Four years later she was to suffer a complete breakdown in health from the pressure of her work for Tennyson.) Tennyson's ruthlessness in his treatment of other people is felt in this entry. Given what would happen later, the reference to his sons has a muffled ruthlessness about it as well. Tennyson was talking to Mangles about the public schools to which he had sent the boys – Marlborough for Hallam and Eton for Lionel. A public school, he said, 'teaches to govern as well as to obey. His eldest "Hallam" was the most useful at Marlboro' in keeping order in his house. Spoke of Lionel, as his handsome son.'[80] Hallam was polite and pliable, and on the whole his parents seemed to favour him in preference to the lively but more troublesome Lionel. Here, though, one can experience a momentary pang of pity for Hallam, being contrasted with the handsome son while he remained the stolid, dull, 'useful' son, like Ulysses' boring ('blameless' and 'decent') son, Telemachus, as he appeared in the poem that Tennyson had written nearly forty years earlier. Lionel was indeed a magnificent-looking boy. The young John Addington Symonds had called him 'a splendid creature, tall and lithe, with long curls & a pear shaped face extremely beautiful'.[81]

In March 1871 Tennyson was on his own at Aldworth, Emily staying behind at Farringford so that Lionel could visit her there. For this short period Tennyson was – unusually – far less comfortable than his wife was. He had left the Isle of Wight earlier than usual because there were a number of issues involving unsatisfactory building work at Aldworth: the drains had been laid badly and did not function properly, a section of stone balustrade fell away when gently pushed, and there were other problems. Knowles, the architect, was not to blame for these; the man directly responsible was a builder from Farnham called Duke (the subject of imprecations and dark threats from Tennyson). Tennyson was obviously a bit lonely, and he welcomed Mangles' company. Mangles and his wife invited him to dine and to sleep at their house. He gratefully accepted, and came with a copy of *Idylls of the King* which he inscribed for them, telling Mangles that King Arthur represented the conscience. (Emily later wrote to Mangles and his wife to thank them: 'I hope he is the better for his little visit to Aldworth tho' but for yourselves it would have been for the most part wretched enough.')[82] At the same time he praised Darwin's recent book *The Descent of Man*, published in February. Darwin had visited Tennyson and Emily at Farringford in 1868 and they both found him reassuring. Tennyson said to him: 'Your theory of Evolution does not make against Christianity.' Darwin replied: 'No, certainly not.'[83] Rather surprisingly, Tennyson found it easy to accept the central thesis of *The Descent of Man* and was untroubled by it, and he told Mangles that he had found Darwin 'a thoroughly good honest & sterling man.'[84]

In 1870 there was a sudden little spat with Charles Dodgson, with whom Tennyson had hitherto had a relationship that was cordial though never close. Tennyson had liked Dodgson's photographs of himself and his family, taken at Tent Lodge in 1857; Dodgson had had some successful visits to Farringford and had been a hit with the boys. Things began to go wrong when he wrote, punctiliously, to Tennyson about a manuscript copy of 'The Lover's Tale' which a cousin had shown him. Tennyson's reaction was to say that he did not want the poem circulated, and he therefore asked Dodgson to destroy the manuscript. Tennyson was easily roused to fury over what he saw as abuse of his unpublished or privately printed works, and matters came to a head when Dodgson wrote again asking for permission to keep and show to friends a privately printed copy of 'The Window' (a song cycle that Tennyson had written for Arthur Sullivan to set to music).[85] Tennyson had come to regret keeping his promise allowing the young Sullivan to set his verses, and as a consequence of his vexation and tangled feelings over this song cycle he prompted Emily to write a sharp letter to Dodgson: 'No doubt "The Window" is circulated by means of the same unscrupulous person whose breach of confidence placed "The Lover's Tale" in your hands.' The letter ends with a deliberate insult: 'A gentleman should understand that when an author does not give his works to the public he has his own reasons for it.'[86]

Tennyson was being grandiose and unreasonable. Dodgson kept his temper and replied: 'you first do a man an injury, and then forgive him'; he followed this with a poised and witty mock-dialogue illustrating the point:

'Sir, you are no gentleman.'

'Sir, you do me grievous wrong by such words. Prove them, or retract them!'

'I reiterate them. Your conduct has been dishonourable.'

'It is not so. I offer a full history of my conduct. I charge you with groundless libel: what say you to the charge?'

'I once believed even worse of you, but begin to think you may be a gentleman after all.'

'These new imputations are as unfounded as the former. Once more, what say you to the charge of groundless libel?'

'*I absolve you.* Say no more.'

Dodgson concluded with angry dignity:

I accept what you say, as being in substance, what it certainly is not in form, a retractation (though without a shadow of apology or expression of regret) of all dishonourable charges against me, and an admission that you had made them on unsufficient grounds.[87]

Because their house in London was being refurbished, the novelist George Eliot (Mary Ann Evans) and George Henry Lewes, her partner, stayed at Shottermill, near Haslemere, from 2 May to 1 September 1871, and were therefore now neighbours of the Tennysons. She was 'very gentle, tho' masculine looking, with a big nose'. Lewes was separated from his wife, but was unable to divorce her; consequently his relationship with George Eliot was a marriage in all but name. This cast a shadow over the couple, and Tennyson was generously impatient with the social ostracism that they suffered. On 25 August he told Mangles that the problem was that 'ladies would not allow her to come to his house. Very hard! She had been the making of Lewis [*sic*].'[88] 'Ladies' here did not include Emily; she and Alfred called on George Eliot the following day. On 3 September Tennyson pointed out to Mangles that George Eliot 'had done nothing morally wrong – Lewis [*sic*] could not get a divorce tho' his wife had eloped'. She had 'been received by Lady Houghton & others'. She and George Lewes had asked Tennyson to read 'Guinevere' to them, which (given that it was about an adulterous woman) he had thought an odd choice 'under the circumstances'. George Lewes 'shed tears copiously' during the reading, and Tennyson wondered whether the separation of Arthur and Guinevere might have stirred up feelings about his own failed marriage.[89]

The Mangles friendship came at a time when Tennyson felt threatened by the advance of the younger writers. Swinburne and Rossetti were 'all in a clique' with William Morris: 'they praise one another in the most fulsome ways'. This was a nagging vexation: he was complaining in these terms in September 1870 and he returned to the theme in late March 1871, noting that the admirers of Swinburne had all turned against him, and that press notices of him now teemed with insults and abuse. He thought Swinburne's recently published *Songs before Sunrise* were blasphemous, while his 'Hymn to Proserpine' was no more than 'sing song'.[90] There were indeed pungently hostile accounts of Tennyson's work now in print, notably those by Alfred Austin in *The Poetry of the Period* (1870) and a bilious essay by J. H. Friswell, later collected into his book *Modern Men of Letters Honestly Criticised* (1879). Friswell started with Tennyson's physical appearance:

> Look at his photograph. Deep-browed, but now deep-lined; bald, but not grey; with a dark disappointment and little hopeful feeling on his face; with hair unkempt, heaped up in the carriage of his shoulders, and with his figure covered with a tragic cloak, the Laureate is pourtrayed, gloomily peering from two ineffectual and not very lustrous eyes.

He then noted how unfairly fortune had favoured Tennyson. 'Poetry pays,' he sneered. 'The Queen salutes the Laureate with respect; it has been said, and has been denied, that he has been offered and refused a baronetcy [. . .] He is sugar sweet, pretty-pretty, full of womanly talk and feminine stuff. Lilian, Dora, Clara, Emmeline – you count up thirty such pretty names, but you cannot count any great poem of the Laureate's.'[91]

Alfred Austin's* attack on Tennyson was a patently shabby affair. The terms on which Tennyson had parted company with Moxon in 1867 had been acrimonious, and Payne, the manager of the firm, had persuaded Austin to write an attack on Tennyson's poetry for *Temple Bar*. Austin's judgements were snarling and venomous:

> Even now, whilst he is still alive, and his adulators are naturally averse from stultifying themselves by recanting the more fulsome praises they have so often and so confidently lavished on him, our Poet Laureate is beginning to totter on his throne. The signs of mutiny against his long unchallenged supremacy are unmistakable.[92]

Tennyson's work, in this view, was 'feminine', while Browning's was so desk-bound and scholarly that he could not be seen as a poet at all.[93] The field was therefore clear for Swinburne, who was himself second-rate: 'Had a really great, adequate poet been alive, Mr Swinburne would have failed to attract much attention.'[94] Swinburne at least avoided Tennyson's boring topics, the farm, the mill, the dining room and the deanery (Austin was taking a shot at Tennyson's 'English Idylls' here), and his deep knowledge of the classics could have yielded the kind of poetry that Austin sought. But Swinburne's poetry fatally eliminated from the ancient world all that was masculine ('and what a masculine epoch it was!').[95]

Tennyson reacted with a couple of effective squibs, the second of which he included in a letter to Frederick Locker-Lampson, saying that Payne 'has lately bribed his bully to write me down'.[96] Payne became Pistol, companion of the ruffian Poins (in *Henry IV Part II*):

> Ancient Pistol, peacock Payne,
> Brute in manner, rogue in grain,
> How you squeezed me, peacock Payne![97]

---

*After Tennyson's death in 1892, Lord Salisbury, a man notoriously indifferent to the arts, would appoint this same Austin to succeed as Poet Laureate.

Frederick Locker, later known as Frederick Locker-Lampson,* was part of the small interlocking upper echelon of London society to which Tennyson and Emily now belonged. Locker's wife, Lady Charlotte, was the sister of Lady Augusta Stanley, close friend of the Queen and wife of the Dean of Westminster.

Friswell behaved like Uriah Heep, obsequious and violently resentful simultaneously. He had dedicated a volume of his own poems, published in 1865, to Tennyson. And in 1870 he reissued his essays called *The Gentle Life* and published *Modern Men of Letters Honestly Criticised*. Tennyson took the 'gentle life' title as the starting point for a brief, private attack on Friswell (it survived in Harvard Notebook 45).

> *Gentle Life* – what a title! here's a subject
> Calls aloud for a gentleman to handle!
> Who has handled it? he, the would-be poet,
> Friswell, Pisswell – a liar and a twaddler –
> Pisswell, Friswell – a clown beyond redemption,
> Brutal, personal, infinitely blackguard.[98]

The piece was in hendecasyllabics, the metre of the little poem published in the *Cornhill* in December 1863, which had taken on reviewers as a species:

> O you chorus of indolent reviewers,
> Irresponsible, indolent reviewers,
> Look, I come to the test, a tiny poem,
> All composed in a metre of Catullus,
> All in quantity, careful of my motion,
> Like the skater on ice that hardly bears him,
> Lest I fall unawares before the people,
> Waking laughter in indolent reviewers.[99]

This is a brilliant, witty, sharply engaged formal exercise in a difficult classical metre – a tiny display of virtuosity tossed off, almost casually, by a master. It is good to be reminded of Tennyson's formidable technical skills.

*   *   *

---

*Lady Charlotte Locker died in 1872, and in 1874 Locker took his second wife's name, Lampson, in order to succeed to her family estate. Locker-Lampson became a family member of the Tennysons by virtue of the marriage, in 1878, of his daughter to Lionel Tennyson.

Tennyson and Emily had now been married twenty years. They had been on the threshold of middle age at the time of their marriage, and by 1870 – in which year Tennyson was sixty-one and Emily fifty-eight – they had established a pattern that would change little in the future. It had never been a particularly passionate marriage. By the time they took possession of Aldworth and spent their first autumn there, in 1869, the relationship had become one of deep mutual understanding, and also a highly successful business partnership. With her intelligence, dedication, strict moral principles and strong will, Emily was the perfect foil for Tennyson. Her management of him was excellent, in the sense that he was productive, prosperous, usually in good health, and full, much of the time, of confidence and self-esteem. The toll on Emily herself was very great. Her objective was to ensure that he was free to write. To that end she took on most of the burden of his literary and business correspondence, and of their very extensive (and expensive) social life. To achieve all this she made very considerable personal sacrifices. Edward Lear loved her, and for her part she understood his deep personal insecurity and emotional unhappiness. She became fond of him, and often confided in him, as in this letter from Blackdown of 1 September 1869 (by which date Aldworth had been fully adopted as their second home):

> Thou ask me how I like Blackdown. For my own private opinion I much prefer Farringford as to its beauty. The absolute solitude of this place at present is not displeasing to me or would not be if there were not so many workmen about [. . .] and if the terrace were green instead of a waste of sand and if there were flowers growing instead of lime and trees [. . .] boards and shrubs instead of stones. But all these things will be in time, let us hope.

When a wealthy man decides to build a country house in a remote place, he is well advised to seek the cooperation of the local landowner in advance. This Tennyson had failed to do. There were not only difficulties with the drains in the new house but also, very late in the day, a serious problem with Lord Egmont, who refused permission to build a road up to Aldworth. Emily was defiant about this ('I don't care so much for want of the road which Lord Egmont denies as most people would, I suppose')[100] and negotiation between the two parties continued until June of the following year, when she was able to write to Tennyson (who was in London having treatment for the persistent eczema on his leg): 'The agreement for the road is signed by Lord Egmont's agent and by ours and our bit of road may be begun any day.' Emily was conducting tough negotiations – via the Tennysons' solicitor, a Mr Simmons – with Lord Egmont's agent. 'I told him I had no idea of yielding to a crotchety old man and my parting advice was please hold your head a little high and Mr Simmons has acted on it and has been "very stiff" as he expresses it [. . .] Lord Egmont's agent seemed rather astonished at the ground taken but I have no doubt this is the way to deal with my Lord and his agent.'[101]

In 1868, Tennyson took a holiday in Europe with Frederick Locker-Lampson. The friendship blossomed and in due course Tennyson took rooms in Albert Mansions (the building in London recently completed by James Knowles), partly in order to be close to the Locker-Lampsons, who lived at 91 Victoria Street. They took two European holidays together, in December 1868 and again in June and July 1869. Locker-Lampson indulged Tennyson's unpredictability and wilfulness. Of the December 1868 trip to Paris he wrote:

He should pick me up at 91 Victoria Street, that we should catch the 4.30 p.m. train at Victoria Station (you see we were precise), and that we should sleep at Dover. At four o'clock on the day appointed, when I was sitting ready packed and expectant, a message arrived that Tennyson's cold was so severe he could not possibly start, and further that he was to be heard of at Mr Knowles'. I swallowed my disappointment, went to church next day, forgave Tennyson his cold, and on the Monday drove down to Clapham [Knowles's house]. It was then and there that we solemnly agreed to set off on Wednesday, the 2nd December, which we actually did.

On the second trip, Tennyson behaved better. They travelled in France and Switzerland, admiring the mountains and waterfalls, and Tennyson talked speculatively about the nature of the universe. Although he was an irregular attender of its meetings, it was clear that the concerns of the Metaphysical Society were preoccupying him:

Mürren 19 June We were looking toward the higher Alps, and Tennyson said that perhaps this earth and all that is on it – storms mountains, cataracts, the sun and the skies – are the Almighty: in fact, that such is our petty nature, we cannot see Him, but we see His shadow, as it were a distorted shadow.

As always when travelling, Tennyson was capable of being childishly peevish over any slight disappointment. The falls of Schaffhausen 'were very impressive' but it was a hot day.

> They took refuge in a hut, which stank ('of cheese'). 'This is my usual luck,' says Tennyson, 'I never go to see anything which is very impressive, without encountering something mean or repulsive. Now, this sublime cataract, and this disgusting stench, will for ever dwell together in my memory.'

They discussed posterity, and this stirred up another of Tennyson's pet hates, the activity of biographers. He wrote in Locker-Lampson's commonplace book:

> While I live, the owls!
> When I die, the GHOULS!!![102]

Among Locker-Lampson's notes is a brief but striking reflection on Arthur Hallam, the perfect man, the poet, courtier and prince of his friend's memories. If he had lived, Tennyson said, he would have been 'one of the foremost men of his time, *but not as a poet*'.[103]

As the autumn of 1869 drew in, Emily longed for the mildness of the Isle of Wight. She confided a good deal in her older son. In August she wrote to Hallam that Tennyson disliked his workroom in the new house, and in September she complained to him about the press of visitors (although they were people she had herself invited): 'It is astonishing how little time we have alone here on what seems our lonely hill. This evening and tomorrow I hope we may calculate on, for Mr Lear has gone this morning and Mr Knowles does not come before Thursday or Friday.'[104]

Alfred's sister Matilda had lived with the Tennysons since the death of Elizabeth Tennyson. Emily often complained about 'Aunt Tilly' to her sons. On 19 October she wrote to Hallam: 'Thou wilt be glad to hear that Aunt Tilly leaves me much more to myself than she used to do. She fortunately greatly prefers the dining room to *our* room, as I call the library.'[105] In November Matilda seemed to be planning to go to Edinburgh (instead of travelling with the Tennysons to Farringford for Christmas) and Emily's spirits rose, as she told Hallam: 'Certainly a little time alone with Papa and our boys would be very precious but no doubt that which is kindest to other people is in fact best for ourselves though it may not seem so.'[106]

While Aldworth was being built, the Tennysons also added to Farringford a substantial extension comprising a large new 'ballroom' for parties (and indeed for dancing) and above it a handsome well-lit study for Tennyson with plenty of space for his steadily growing collection of books. The ballroom has been absorbed into the dining room of the hotel that now occupies Farringford, but Tennyson's study has been carefully maintained and still looks much as it did when he worked in it. The surroundings have changed a great deal since the Tennysons first saw the house in 1853, but many of those changes took place in Tennyson's lifetime.

Tennyson was increasingly disturbed in these years by the way in which the sexual drive could derail human designs. This is the central narrative theme of the completed twelve books of *Idylls of the King*: the brilliant, courageous and noble court of King Arthur, devoted to a Christian ideal of male chastity and martial valour, was to be slowly destroyed by the corrosive effects of Guinevere's adultery with Lancelot. The whole huge work turns on this, with elaborate and on the whole restrained deliberation. There is no such restraint in Tennyson's 'Lucretius' (1868), one of the most startling of his poems of the 1860s. Here Lucretius's wife, Lucilia, has sought to restore some passion to her marriage by feeding her husband a potion. The effect of this is described with striking precision:

> the wicked broth
> Confused the chemic labour of the blood,
> And tickling the brute brain within the man's
> Made havoc among those tender cells, and checked
> His power to shape: he loathed himself.

The violence and lack of control that had characterised the Somersby household of Tennyson's adolescence and young manhood were now well in his past, but he had never forgotten the damage they could do. Tennyson could not share Wordsworth's confidence in the nurturing and healing force of the natural world. Nature, red in tooth and claw in the elegy for Hallam, reappeared in 'Lucretius' as 'Great Nature' to which the vanquished Lucretius feels he must now surrender himself, because he has lost human control of his own mind. ('Nature' – that is, the laws governing the known physical universe – is the subject of Lucretius's only surviving work, the *De Rerum Natura, c.*50 BC.)

An uncomfortable truth about the human condition was increasingly hateful to Tennyson as he grew older: the noble mind of man shared its physical base with the 'brute brain' of the animal from which he was descended. Tennyson liked Darwin personally, and had managed to persuade himself that his work was not a threat: the fact that Darwin was so obviously a 'gentleman' helped. Nevertheless the impact on High Victorian culture of Darwin's bombshell, *On the Origin of Species by Means of Natural Selection*, published in 1859, would reverberate for the rest of the century. The shock was not in the theory itself, but in the irrefutable demonstration that it was true. It confirmed what geologists and biologists had been considering since the late eighteenth century: man could not be a unique creation, and a central teaching of Christianity was simply wrong. Darwin's second bombshell, *The Descent of Man, and Selection in Relation to Sex* (1871), would make explicit as its central finding the fact that man was an animal. Tennyson had feared this for many years: the possibility of it had haunted some of the most troubled lyrics of *In Memoriam*.

The title and subtitle of Darwin's *Descent of Man* could have served as headings for the nightmare that Tennyson explored in 'Lucretius': that man's 'descent' was a matter of steep moral decline in which his brute nature would reassert itself and he would be helplessly in thrall to his sexuality. 'Lucretius' dramatised the horror felt by a civilised man acknowledging his loss of control. The lustful images have usurped his mind:

> These prodigies of myriad nakednesses,
> And twisted shapes of lust, unspeakable,
> Abominable, strangers at my hearth.

The process by which they have arrived there is physical assault by a grotesque being:

> But now it seems some unseen monster lays
> His vast and filthy hands upon my will,
> Wrenching it backward into his.[107]

Lucretius's radical solution to this dreadful loss of control is to kill himself. Tennyson's solution was to write poetry that addressed it directly. His own 'will', the ability to control his creative processes and to *keep writing*, regularly and constantly, had come under strain earlier in the 1860s (hence the somewhat mechanical metrical treatment of stories provided for him by friends like Woolner). In other words, Lucretius's central problem – not sexual frenzy, but lack of command of his own faculties – is one that Tennyson was experiencing personally during this decade. The writing of the poem probably exorcised some of that creative dryness and dependency on others. It is a distinguished and powerful poem in itself, and a forceful reminder that in this decade we are still reading the work of a major poet.

In 1870 came a bereavement that in Tennyson's mind became linked with the loss of Arthur Hallam all those years earlier. This was the death of Sir John Simeon, landowner and Roman Catholic convert, a man with no great interest in the arts and at first sight a surprising person to become one of Tennyson's most important and intimate friends; but there is no doubt that that was what the relationship was. Emily wrote to Hallam from Aldworth on 24 May 1870. 'A very sad parting from Farringford for but an hour before we left we heard the news of our dear friend Sir John which the papers have probably told you before this. [. . .] We have lost one of our dearest friends. Papa's dearest I think and most trusted.'[108] She was not exaggerating. The two men had seen each other regularly and with increasing affection during Tennyson's Farringford years. At Tennyson's pace, and given his love of walking, Swainston, Simeon's country seat in the Isle of Wight, was within easy reach of Farringford. The walk would have taken well over an hour, but for Tennyson that was a moderate stretch for the daily walks in which he composed his poetry.

On 31 May, Tennyson made the journey back from Aldworth to the Isle of Wight in order to be at the funeral at Swainston. Emily reported him as saying that it seemed all the more sad for the fact that it was a beautiful day: 'the sun shone & the roses bloomed profusely. A great many people there. A [Alfred] went as a mourner. The poor heart-broken widow & Louy see him for a minute.'[109] Roses were climbing the walls of Swainston's medieval chapel,* lilacs were blooming and nightingales were singing; the natural world was gently celebrating the beautiful weather, and in the midst of this were the black-suited rituals of the occasion.[110] (Tennyson always hated the deep mourning typical of Victorian funerals.) On this day or shortly afterwards he wrote 'In the Garden at Swainston', in which his love

---

*Swainston's chapel still stands; it survived the Second World War incendiary bombs that damaged much of the main house as Tennyson would have known it.

and veneration for Simeon are clearly felt. Simeon was 'the very Prince of Courtesy',* as Tennyson called him in a letter to Lady Simeon, 'the only man on earth, I verily believe, to whom I could, and have more than once opened my heart and he also has given me, in many a conversation at Farringford in my little attic, his utter confidence. I knew none like him for tenderness and generosity.'[111]

The poignancy and hard-won emotional restraint of the poem speak for themselves:

> Nightingales warbled without,
>   Within was weeping for thee:
> Shadows of three dead men
>   Walked in the walks with me,
>   Shadows of three dead men and thou wast one of the three.

> Nightingales sang in his woods:
>   The Master was far away:
> Nightingales warbled and sang
>   Of a passion that lasts but a day;
>   Still in the house in his coffin the Prince of courtesy lay.

> Two dead men have I known
>   In courtesy like to thee:
> Two dead men have I loved
>   With a love that ever will be:
>   Three dead men have I loved and thou art last of the three.[112]

Soon after this there was another, very different funeral: that of the most famous novelist of the day, Charles Dickens, who had died prematurely, aged fifty-eight, with *The Mystery of Edwin Drood* left unfinished. This was a national event which took place in Westminster Abbey. Tennyson could reasonably have felt a chill at the thought of the similar funeral that might well be held in the same place following his own death. Tennyson was himself a principal feature of Dickens's funeral, somewhat to his dismay: children were held aloft so that they could see him over the heads of the congregation. When the service was over, the congregation ought to have left in sober silence, instead of which Tennyson found himself effectively mobbed by the throngs

---

*Robert Bernard Martin (*Tennyson*, p. 495n) suggested that this carefully retained Arthur Hallam as higher in Tennyson's affections: in *Balin and Balan* his mythical Arthur was the 'king of courtesy'.

in the Abbey, who pushed towards the west of the building where he was sitting in order to have a glimpse of him. Given that he hated funerals and had a horror of becoming a spectacle, this was a depressing experience for him.[113]

There was always Knowles; he could invariably lift Tennyson's spirits. And in the early days of their life at Aldworth, Tennyson and Emily increasingly made friends with George Eliot. After Dickens's death, Alfred found pleasure in the company of this brilliant novelist who was rapidly becoming as famous as Dickens had been. His Farringford life was also enlivened by a new friend. If George Eliot had in a sense replaced Dickens (who had never been more than a cordial acquaintance), then William Ward could be said to fill the space left by Sir John Simeon. Ward owned a large house called Weston Hall near Freshwater and was thus now a close neighbour. Like Simeon he was a devout Roman Catholic, and Tennyson liked the simplicity and directness of his faith. Ward was a modern embodiment of the male virtues that Tennyson wanted to display in his *Idylls*: honour, generosity of spirit and unwavering moral courage. He had been in Anglican orders and had held a fellowship at Balliol College, Oxford (where he was Arthur Hugh Clough's friend and tutor). As a devoted follower of John Henry Newman, he was at the heart of the convulsions of the Oxford Movement which came to a head in the 1840s; hence his resignation from his Fellowship in 1845.

There was comfort for Tennyson in the friendships among his Isle of Wight circle as other men's reputations grew in London. Fitzgerald wrote to him on 12 October 1870 asking: 'Is Mr Rossetti a Great Poet, like Browning & Morris? So the Athenaeum tells me. Dear me, how thick Great Poets do grow nowadays.' Tennyson would have welcomed neither this nor the many similar reminders from his old friend that his own poetry was facing challenges from younger men. Another letter from Fitzgerald of 7 April harps on the same theme: 'I have been again reading Lord Houghton's Life of Keats – whose hastiest doggerel should show Browning, Morris and Co. that they are not what the newspapers tell them they are.' (Houghton – Richard Monckton Milnes – had of course been an Apostle and was a friend of both Tennyson and Fitzgerald.) Fitzgerald was an addicted and incontinent letter-writer, and on the following day quoted his own letter to Tennyson in a letter directed to Houghton himself:

I wonder Messrs. Browning, Morris, Rossetti, etc., can read Keats's hastiest Doggerel and not be ashamed at being trumpeted as 'Great Poets' in the Athenaeum and elsewhere. Only to mention Tennyson alone, to compare themselves with: who used not to think himself equal to Keats at all. I don't know what he thinks now after so much Worship has been offered him.

The aside about 'Worship' demonstrates the sad gulf that was opening up between the friends, although Tennyson did in fact write to Fitzgerald on 11 April, asking for a copy of his *Omar Khayyám* to replace one that Tennyson had lost.[114]

CHAPTER 9

The completion of the *Idylls* and the aspiring playwright, 1872–1886

Arthur, my lord, Arthur, the faultless king,
That passionate perfection, my good lord –
But who can gaze upon the Sun in heaven?
He never spake word of reproach to me,
He never had a glimpse of mine untruth.

If the Arthurian poems were a huge self-imposed task which started at the time of Arthur Hallam's death, then the long works for which Tennyson is now most famous (*In Memoriam* and *Maud*) were digressions from this task. His obsession with Arthurian material began as early as 1833. Notes on the characters* in the story of King Arthur are on fols 20v and 21r of Notebook 16 (the Trinity College notebook which contains the earliest drafts of *In Memoriam*). Despite his Arthurian poems of the 1830s, the final shape of the big work to be based on the Arthurian stories would take a long time to become clear to him.[1] The friend of Arthur Hallam who was twenty-four when he began writing about King Arthur was a very different man, now in his fifties, by the time he was working on his twelve-part Arthurian poem.

'Morte d'Arthur', completed in 1834, was part of Tennyson's shocked grieving for Hallam. 'The Epic' was written later, possibly in 1835, and is boisterously comical in tone. The writing of 'The Epic' was imagined as a learned game played by Cambridge undergraduates staying in a handsome country house during the Christmas vacation. It frames 'Morte d'Arthur' and belongs to a young masculine culture.

---

*The Arthurian figures named in these notes include 'son by Arthur. Mordred'; in Malory Mordred was the product of Arthur's incest with his sister. In Tennyson's finished *Idylls* he was Arthur's 'nephew', and the fact that he was also his son was suppressed. Other figures in the notes were Guinevere and 'Nineve', who was reworked as 'Nimuë' and finally as 'Vivien' in the *Idylls*. The young Tennyson also planned a five-act drama based on the story of King Arthur. This projected work for the stage got no further than a substantial synopsis, which was reproduced in Hallam Tennyson's *Memoir* (II, pp. 124–5).

The frame invites us to think that the young Tennyson was hesitant about adopting so mighty a story as that of King Arthur. And indeed any young poet would hesitate. To recreate Malory's world was to compete with a central medieval figure who was the basis of a founding national myth, and to write a large-scale work with such an ambition was to match oneself against Homer and Virgil. One of the drafts for the first lines of this frame plunges directly into the central challenge that the young poet confronted:

> Why, what you ask – if any writer now
> May take the style of some heroic age
> Gone like the mastodon – nay, why should he
> Remodel models rather than the life?
> Yet this belief was lately half-unhinged
> At Edward Allen's – on the Christmas Eve[2]

The final state of 'The Epic' somewhat weakens the immediacy and impact of this challenge by embedding it in a dramatic narrative: we are at Sir Francis (not Edward) Allen's. The girls are 'all kissed' and have (presumably) gone to bed. Four men sit late round the fire: Francis or Frank, the host; a poet, Everard Hall; Holmes, a parson ('Now harping on the church-commissioners, / Now hawking at Geology and schism'); and the unnamed narrator. The narrator teases Everard with his reputation for being a heavy drinker at college, but at the same time reminds him of his literary ambition from those days and asks what became of it. The answer is melancholy: '"You know," said Frank, "he burnt / His epic, his King Arthur, some twelve books" – / And then to me demanding why? "Oh, sir, / He thought that nothing new was said, or else / Something so said 'twas nothing – that a truth / Looks freshest in the fashion of the day."' The poet Everard Hall agreed that it was a mistake to adopt the fashions of the past. He himself would steer clear of archaisms.

> 'Why take the style of those heroic times?
> For nature brings not back the Mastodon,
> Nor we those times; and why should any man
> Remodel models? these twelve books of mine
> Were faint Homeric echoes, nothing-worth,
> Mere chaff and draff, much better burnt.'

Given that Tennyson would later embark on a huge archaism, Homeric echoes and all, in the style of heroic times, this is permissibly artful, not to say disingenuous. And in any case one book of Everard's epic has been rescued by a friend (just as Tennyson's own manuscripts were frequently rescued by friends).

> 'But I,'
> Said Francis, 'picked the eleventh from this hearth
> And have it: keep a thing, its use will come.
> I hoard it as a sugar-plum for Holmes.'

It is not clear why the tiresome parson needs a sugar-plum (nor indeed why he is in the scene at all). But that is beside the point. What matters here is the engaging self-portrait of Tennyson, as Everard, reading his own work to his eager and ever hungry and appreciative friends:

> He laughed, and I, though sleepy, like a horse
> That hears the corn-bin open, pricked my ears;
> For I remembered Everard's college fame
> When we were Freshmen: then at my request
> He brought it; and the poet little urged,
> But with some prelude of disparagement,
> Read, mouthing out his hollow oes and aes,
> Deep-chested music, and to this result.[3]

Another self-portrait exists among the cancelled drafts of *The Princess*, written a bit later, in one of the early Harvard notebooks (number 23). This is again full of the feeling of a group of young men at Cambridge sitting round to idolise their Alfred:

> The next that spoke was Arthur Arundel
> The Poet: rough his hair but fine to feel,
> And dark his skin but softer than a babe's,
> And large his hand as of the plastic kind,
> And early furrows in his face he had:
> Small were his themes – low builds the nightingale –
> But promised more: and mellow was his voice,
> He pitched it like a pipe to all he would
> And thus he brought our story back to life.[4]

'Morte d'Arthur' of 1842, the 'eleventh' book of the lost 'epic', will turn out in due course – many years later – to be the major part of the twelfth and final book of the *Idylls*. And its central figure is, of course, Arthur Hallam, disastrously dead yet immortalised as this mythic Christian king.

Thomas Carlyle and Alfred Tennyson had been friends since their first meeting (when Carlyle had responded memorably to the 'bronze-coloured', 'shaggy-headed' vagabond in Tennyson).[5] Carlyle was an excellent reader of poetry. In a personal letter to Tennyson he wrote one of the most tender and appropriate responses to 'Ulysses'. He quoted:

> It may be that the gulfs will wash us down;
> It may be we shall touch the Happy Isles,
> And see the great Achilles, whom we knew.

'These lines do not make me weep,' Carlyle said, 'but there is in me what would fill whole Lachrymatories as I read.'[6]

The word 'epic' had stirred Carlyle to one of his characteristic overstatements. He was dazzled by the raw power of the 'industrial aristocracy': 'What an Aristocracy; on what new, far more complex and cunningly devised conditions than that old Feudal fighting one!'* This was written the year after Tennyson had published his 'Morte d'Arthur'. Carlyle liked to pretend that he had a low opinion of poetry as a vocation, but this was manifestly untrue: an important lecture in his sequence of lectures published as *Heroes and Hero-Worship* is devoted to 'The Poet as Hero'. His ideal poet displayed a capacity for virile action in all spheres: 'I have no notion of a truly great man that could not be *all* sorts of men. The Poet who could merely sit on a chair, and compose stanzas, would never make a stanza worth much. He could not sing the Heroic warrior, unless he himself were at least a Heroic warrior too.'[7] Carlyle's canvas here was huge and he painted with a broad brush; his heroic poets were 'World-Poets', Homer, Dante and Shakespeare, but he was also thinking of Goethe: 'the Poet has an *infinitude* in him; communicates an *Unendlichkeit,* a certain character of "infinitude", to whatsoever he delineates'.[8]

Despite Carlyle's paradoxical claim that the English are a 'dumb people', *Idylls of the King* is, by his definition, heroic poetry. Tennyson's great poem was composed in the firm belief that it was possible to

---

*He added, 'The English are a dumb people [. . .] *their* Epic Poem is written on the Earth's surface.' (Carlyle, *Sartor Resartus,* pp. 266, 195.)

write a big national work which reflected, or expressed metaphorically, the aspirations of the age and the forces driving it. By taking a medieval story and reworking it, he shared Carlyle's conviction that the great men of the nineteenth century needed to understand the remote past if they were to engage successfully with the present.*

The image of the arch in 'Ulysses', admired by both Carlyle and Matthew Arnold ('all experience is an arch wherethrough / Gleams that untravelled world, whose margin fades / for ever and for ever when I move'),† contained a metaphor which expressed the way in which the long Arthurian poem worked. *Idylls of the King* opened up archways of memory and legend. Tennyson's audience could look back at a world whose story underpinned their own sense of themselves: Christian, responsible, troubled, belonging to an older culture that had itself been both noble and fragile.

As a free-standing early poem, the 'Morte d'Arthur' of 1842 displayed simple male virtues: warrior loyalty, noble aspiration and grand sombre death. Bedivere's anguish as his king died was a painful mix of love and duty. He was losing Arthur, but if he disobeyed and kept possession of Excalibur, then at least he could have a tangible memory of the dead man. He risked Arthur's anger by hiding the sword twice. When the order to throw it in the lake was repeated again, he obeyed, finally, with a headlong, unthinking desperation which was admirably caught in the verse:

> Then quickly rose Sir Bedivere, and ran,
> And, leaping down the ridges lightly, plunged
> Among the bulrush-beds, and clutched the sword,
> And strongly wheeled and threw it.

The sword was caught by an arm 'Clothed in white samite, mystic, wonderful', and withdrawn into the water. From this point the poem became the story of Bedivere's emotional growth, from angry adolescent to grieving adult. He carried Arthur to his funeral barge, where 'all the decks were dense, with stately forms / Black-stoled, black-hooded, like a dream', and there took leave of him.

Bedivere's final desolated speech and Arthur's historic response to it are among the more successful parts of the poem:

---

*In the story of Abbot Sampson from Carlyle's *Past and Present*, the institution controlled by the medieval Abbot of Bury St Edmunds is a model to the modern world of how organisations should be run by a hard-working manager.

†Arnold wrote: 'These three lines by themselves take up nearly as much time as a whole book of the *Iliad*.' (Quoted by Ricks, *Tennyson*, p. 116.)

'[. . .] now the whole ROUND TABLE is dissolved
Which was an image of the mighty world;
And I, the last, go forth companionless,
And the days darken round me, and the years,
Among new men, strange faces, other minds.'

King Arthur speaks as though already beyond the grave, ushering in an inscrutable future; a future which is the present in which his Victorian audience now lives.

'The old order changeth, yielding place to new,
And God fulfils himself in many ways,
Lest one good custom should corrupt the world.'[9]

Sir Bedivere is the wrong knight to be Arthur's last companion. The true friend and the closest comrade was Lancelot, the same man who fatally betrayed Arthur and destroyed his kingdom by falling in love with his wife. It remained Lancelot for whom Arthur's feeling, as presented in the *Idylls*, was strongest. It has been said that 'the great absence' among the paired episodes of the *Idylls* ('Gareth and Lynette', 'Geraint and Enid', 'Merlin and Vivien', 'Lancelot and Elaine') is an episode called 'Lancelot and Arthur'.[10] Early in 'The Coming of Arthur', these two men declare their love for each other. Arthur has secured his first victory:

So like a painted battle the war stood
Silenced, the living quiet as the dead,
And in the heart of Arthur joy was lord.
He laughed upon the warrior whom he loved
And honoured most. 'Thou dost not doubt me King,
So well thine arm hath wrought for me today.'
'Sir and my liege,' he cried, 'the fire of God
Descends upon thee in the battle-field:
I know thee for my King!' Whereat the two,
For each had warded either in the fight,
Sware on the field of death a deathless love.[11]

Tennyson is on record as saying that the figure in the poem that he really loved was not the King but the man who cuckolded him. 'My father loved his own great imaginative knight, the Lancelot of the *Idylls*,' wrote Hallam Tennyson,[12] and indeed this figure's emotional torment is brought out movingly in the most successful of the woman-centred Idylls of 1859, 'Elaine' (the poem's title became 'Lancelot and Elaine' for the 1870 edition). His face is marked by his conflicted passions, and it is this troubled, lived-in as well as battle-scarred look which attracts Elaine.

> The great and guilty love he bare the Queen,
> In battle with the love he bare his lord,
> Had marred his face, and marked it ere his time.

The conflict is at times physical torture:

> His mood was often like a fiend, and rose
> And drove him into wastes and solitudes
> For agony, who was yet a living soul.[13]

The dramatic date of the Elaine poem is fairly far on in the internal chronology of the *Idylls*: Lancelot and Guinevere are mature lovers, and their love is well known to the whole court – though not to the saintly King. It is this saintliness which prompts in Guinevere an account of her sexual feelings that sounds strikingly authentic. Speaking to Lancelot – weary as they both are of the constraints of an adulterous relationship – she echoes the impatience that some readers are bound to feel with Arthur's perfections:

> 'Arthur, my lord, Arthur, the faultless king,
> That passionate perfection, my good lord –
> But who can gaze upon the Sun in heaven?
> He never spake word of reproach to me,
> He never had a glimpse of mine untruth.'

Arthur belongs to the world of male nobility. He is:

> 'Rapt in this fancy of his Table Round,
> And swearing men to vows impossible,
> To make them like himself: but, friend, to me
> He is all fault who hath no fault at all:
> For who loves me must have a touch of earth;
> The low sun makes the colour.'[14]

'All fault who hath no fault at all' – the poem is in part a revisiting of 'The Lady of Shalott', a young man's poem written at a time when Tennyson lived a life far less ordered than his life as a married man in the 1850s. Lancelot rides anonymously in the joust and wears Elaine's favour – believing that no one will recognise him. The Queen, though, learns what he has done, and her sexual anguish is powerfully dramatised:

> [She] sharply turned about to hide her face,
> Past to her chamber, and there flung herself
> Down on the great King's couch, and writhed upon it,
> And clenched her fingers till they bit the palm,
> And shrieked out 'Traitor' to the unhearing wall.[15]

No good comes to people who disguise themselves. Lancelot is horribly injured by his own kinsmen (who see him as an unknown rival to their lord). In this scene Tennyson was working within what had been since Sir Walter Scott's day a stock romantic topos – the appeal of a strong warrior in pain – and Elaine's passion for the sick man need not surprise us. She tends Lancelot 'in the cell wherein he slept' and is stirred by

> His battle-writhen arms and mighty hands
> [which] Lay naked on the wolfskin, and a dream
> Of dragging down his enemy made them move.
> Then she that saw him lying unsleek, unshorn,
> Gaunt as it were the skeleton of himself,
> Uttered a little tender dolorous cry.[16]

When Tennyson says that he loved the knight, we may draw the implication that he admired rather than loved his King. And indeed the poet's study of Arthur becomes ever more resolutely unlovable as it progresses. He seems fastidiously self-regarding as he punishes his adulterous Queen:

> I cannot take thy hand; that too is flesh,
> And in the flesh thou hast sinned; and mine own flesh,
> Here looking down on thine polluted, cries
> 'I loathe thee:' yet not less, O Guinevere,
> For I was ever virgin save for thee,
> My love through flesh hath wrought into my life
> So far, that my doom is, I love thee still.
> [. . .]
> But hither shall I never come again,
> Never lie by thy side; see thee no more –
> Farewell![17]

Few readers would continue to be engaged by this figure. Yet the logic of the drama here requires us to believe that his curse is a disaster for Guinevere, just as the adultery itself has been a disaster for his fabled kingdom.

For his contemporary audience Tennyson was helped by the fact that Malory's great text was seen as coarse, barbaric and severely in need of tidying up by a modern hand. Fitzgerald quoted Tennyson as saying: 'There are very fine things in it, but all strung together without art.'[18] Among the many copies of Malory in Tennyson's own collection now held in the Tennyson Research Centre in Lincoln is one volume (of two) of a modernised version of Malory, with Caxton's preface, inscribed 'Alfred Tennyson from Leigh Hunt'. Tennyson marked a number of passages, drawing attention in particular to the visionary parts of the narrative and, oddly, the place names (some of the cities referred to in the then Roman Empire, for example, are given their modern Italian names).

Much of this is done to indicate passages for future reference: notably magical episodes – enchantments, dream, faerie in general; which on the whole did not get into the *Idylls* – and topographical details (Winchester as the setting for the Round Table, for example, and Glastonbury as the site of Arthur's grave, both from Caxton's preface). The volume has been dropped into water at some stage in its life – at Cambridge, while walking by the Cam with Arthur Hallam? Tennyson was already thinking of a five-act drama of King Arthur, and it may be that he marked these passages for possible use there: for example the exotic scene in which Arthur is enchanted, deluded into thinking that he is in a sumptuous chamber but wakes up in a prison, and the whole episode of the pulling of the sword from the stone. Neither of these was used in the final *Idylls*. All the wickedness of Morgan le Fay is carefully marked, and some of that reappears in the enchantment of Merlin by Vivien.[19]

John Sterling wrote in his review of the 'Morte d'Arthur' in 1842 that 'the miraculous legend of "Excalibur" does not come very near to us, and as reproduced by any modern writer must be a mere ingenious exercise of fancy'.[20] Tennyson always said that he was discouraged by this, and it put him off writing his long poem. He did not go back to his Arthurian narrative poems until 1857. The *Idylls* grew slowly over two decades, with 'The Coming of Arthur', 'The Holy Grail', 'Pelleas and Ettarre' and 'The Passing of Arthur' in 1869, 'The Last Tournament' and 'Gareth and Lynette' in 1873, and 'Balin and Balan' written in 1874 but not published until ten years later.

Many literary men were disappointed by Tennyson's Arthurian narratives; Browning for example said of them: 'Here is an Idyll about a knight being untrue to his friend and yielding to the temptation of that friend's mistress after having engaged to assist him in his suit. I should judge the conflict within the knight's soul the proper subject to describe: Tennyson thinks he should describe the castle, and effect of the moon on its towers, and anything *but* the soul.'[21] Sterling, whose review still itched like a wasp sting in Tennyson's recollection, had actually written moderately about the 'Morte d'Arthur'; he felt that the poem was less rich and colourful than Tennyson's other work and that it missed the central significance of the death of Arthur, 'the departure from earth of the whole old Gothic world'.[22] Tennyson ought to have taken comfort, though, from the fact that the whole review put him in the company of Coleridge and Wordsworth.

'Gareth and Lynette' displays the court of King Arthur when it was unsullied, valiant and full of hope, while 'The Last Tournament' charts 'the progress of disintegration preceding the final calamity'.[23] *Idylls of the King*, comprising eleven narrative poems, was published as 'complete' in the *Library Edition* of Tennyson's works in 1873, with a new Epilogue addressed to the Queen spelling out the comparison that Tennyson wanted to make between his idealised version of King Arthur and the Queen's equally idealised recollections of her husband.

Tennyson found it convenient – against Emily's advice – to publish in periodicals, but the only section of *Idylls* to appear in a periodical was 'The Last Tournament', in the *Contemporary Review*.[24] Knowles had taken over as editor of the *Contemporary Review* in 1870, securing the first publication of 'The Last Tournament' for the Christmas edition in December 1871, which considerably enhanced the periodical. It also spurred Tennyson on. Knowles later angled for other parts of the *Idylls*, including, in 1873, the Epilogue addressed to the Queen, but Tennyson drew back from that suggestion because the Queen herself had not yet seen the poem. On the other hand, Tennyson would later give considerable support to Knowles's new venture of 1877, the successful periodical known as *The Nineteenth Century*.[25] Emily remarked to her son Hallam in May 1869: 'Papa has been very cheerful' as a result of a visit from the Knowleses: 'He has a great fancy for them. I am thankful to say that Mr Knowles has the power to encourage him in his work.' But she could also find them intrusive. In October 1871, she was enjoying a Farringford completely free from visitors, but this peaceful interlude did not last. Two days free from guests 'lifts me above the petty cares of life. Infinite refreshment. 21ˢᵗ [October] Mr & Mrs Knowles come.'[26]

At what point had it become clear to Tennyson that he was not writing an 'epic' and that he needed to spell this out for his public? He wrote to his American publisher in 1858: 'I wish that you would disabuse your own minds and those of others, as far as you can, of the fancy that I am about an Epic of King Arthur. I should be crazed to attempt such a thing in the heart of the 19ᵗʰ century.'[27] In his early notes on the Arthurian stories in the 1830s, an epic had certainly been one of his projected ways of treating the stories (a stage tragedy was another). And the century proceeded to see his *Idylls* as filling an epic-shaped space within the national literary landscape. Tennyson was still complaining about this in the 1870s, in a letter to George Grove, the celebrated musician, about an essay on his work by R. H. Hutton. Hutton had referred to the Arthurian poems as 'epic': 'I am not going to criticise the criticism, though I may say that his calling the Idylls an Epic which they are not, is to me a misnomer and may set my foes blaming.'[28] Hutton had understandably found the word 'idyll' altogether perplexing in relation to the Arthurian poems. He saw it as 'applied', but 'misleadingly', to Tennyson's 'greatest work'. (He was writing before the creation of the final three books of the poem.) He complained that the word had been wrenched out of context, and that the idyll proper was 'a *picture* coloured by a single emotion, and intended to give a perfect illustration of that emotion. The power which makes Tennyson's idylls so unique in their beauty is, I think, his wonderful skill in creating a perfectly real and living scene.'[29] This is a polite way of saying that the Arthurian poems are disappointingly static and short of action. Tennyson responded to this and other readings of his work with some richly suggestive phrases, quoted by his son in the *Memoir*:

> They [the reviewers and essayists] have taken my hobby, and ridden it too hard, and have explained some things too allegorically, although there is an allegorical or perhaps rather a parabolic drift in the poem. [. . .] Poetry is like shot-silk with many glancing colours. Every reader must find his own interpretation according to his ability, and according to his sympathy with the poet.

Tennyson liked to say that the central meaning of the Arthurian poems was straightforward: 'The whole is the dream of man coming into practical life and ruined by one sin. Birth is a mystery and death is a mystery, and in the midst lies the tableland of life, and its struggles and performances. It is not the history of one man or of one generation but of a whole cycle of generations.'[30]

No other work of Tennyson's has divided critical opinion so violently as has *Idylls of the King*. Those who see the later Tennyson as a romantic who has betrayed his identity are still inclined to agree with Harold Nicolson, who saw the poem as a sad abuse of Tennyson's talent. Christopher Ricks disliked most of it, isolating just three of the Idylls which he regarded as successful both in style and as wholes: 'Merlin and Vivien', 'The Holy Grail' and 'The Passing of Arthur'.[31] Others have praised it, seeing it not as a literary equivalent of one of Gilbert Scott's neo-Gothic public buildings but as a new creation making appropriate use of its medieval sources, a poem of 'consummate art' to rank with *The Faerie Queene*, *Paradise Lost* and *The Prelude*,[32] or as a 'doom-laden prophecy of the fall of the West'.[33] An influential essay by Kathleen Tillotson, 'Tennyson's Serial Poem', made a considered case for the work as one which grew over a long period, and which as it grew created the audience that was then able to read it:

A man of fifty reading the accumulated series of ten in 1873 would recall reading the *Morte d'Arthur* as an undergraduate; but he would be over sixty before he saw the last instalment and nearly seventy before he read the last additional line. [. . .] In 1842, Arthurian story was still strange to the ordinary reader, and even felt to be unacceptable as a subject for poetry; and this was undoubtedly one reason for the first long-interval of seventeen years between the serial appearances. Here the spread of time and the slow deepening of the impression are particularly important. For by 1873 the Arthurian story had become a household word; and part of the responsibility was Tennyson's, from the delayed effects of his own earlier work. There is no clearer instance of a poet creating the taste by which he was enjoyed; that taste also eventually recoiled upon him, through his imitators, his rivals, and his sources themselves.[34]

In his attack on Tennyson written in 1870, the ham-fisted Alfred Austin protested that Tennyson's poetry was like a tame and safe garden. He invoked Nature (thus capitalised) as the measure of truly great poetry (Shakespeare, Keats, Byron, Shelley, Wordsworth): 'Their concern is with the permanent aspects of Nature – human nature included; with the sea, the sky, the mountains, the far-stretching landscape, stormy winds that fulfil His Word, the planets, the intolerable thunder, grim murder, vaulting ambition, mad revenge, the intolerable and Promethean discontent. These are enduring.' Tennyson's poetry, by contrast, 'is exceedingly pretty, soothing, elegant; but is not grand'.[35] Austin's remarks were little more than envious sneering, but he made one palpable hit in this comment on the inertia of taste: 'It is natural enough that the age, having got in Mr Tennyson a poet that it vastly likes, should want to persuade itself that he is a great poet. Self-love impels it to nourish the delusion [. . .] Our attempts to glorify ourselves by over-exalting him can do no possible good to anybody.'[36]

In the 1880s some rapprochement would be achieved between Alfred Tennyson and Alfred Austin. By this time Tennyson's position was unassailable and he could afford to be gracious. He generously sent a message to his former adversary inviting him to Aldworth. Austin's first impressions were sympathetic: 'He was no longer young, save in mind, and I noticed, when I entered at tea-time – I found him seated at the tea table, and Lady Tennyson lying on the sofa, not far from him – that his hands were crippled with gout.' Austin was understandably nervous about this meeting, and Tennyson put him at his ease, though he acknowledged the past by saying: 'you once did abuse me, and said I had taken one of my lines from Keats.' (This was the least aggressive of the things Austin had written.) Austin made a cumbersome attempt to retrieve the situation: 'I observed that every great Poet is the child and descendant of preceding great Poets, at least for a time, and until he gets his own voice completely, and that Keats seemed to me, as to many others, his more immediate ancestor. This seemed to satisfy him.'[37]

Gerard Manley Hopkins' complaint that Tennyson's *Idylls* should have been called *Charades from the Middle Ages*[38] was a great deal more apt and witty than anything that Alfred Austin could come up with, but Hopkins was wrong to treat the whole project dismissively. He was reacting against the work's topicality and timeliness; however, those are among the qualities that make it a major poem. Malory's King Arthur had been embraced by the Tudors as endorsing and legitimising their claims to the crown. Tennyson's stories of King Arthur endorsed the Empire, the Queen and the sacred memory of Prince Albert. It is a work of its time and as a whole it moves with the rhythm and the triumphalism – and the unease – of the 1880s, the decade in which the whole text was presented in its final form. No responsible account of late-Victorian culture can fail to take it seriously. As a large, sombre and finally pessimistic musical structure it gathered up, reflected and helped to define the way in which the period saw itself.

In 1870 Tennyson was increasingly out of fashion but at the same time increasingly commercially successful. He was also consolidating himself in personal terms: creating a kind of fortress comprising his family, his most trusted friends and his two grand country houses. By 1871 the gap created by Sir John Simeon's death helped him to welcome the arrival near Farringford of other members of his inner circle. The Prinseps' lease of Little Holland House had expired. With warm encouragement from Tennyson, they moved to a house called The Briary, very close to Farringford (the money was provided by their constant companion G. F. Watts, who had for many years been effectively a family member in the Prinsep household):

> Alfred became an almost daily visitor at the Briary whenever he was at Farringford, for he dearly loved old Thoby [Prinsep], who never allowed the blindness which overtook him in his old age to diminish his interest in men and things. Hour after the hour the two would sit together discussing politics and literature; or Alfred would read aloud and Thoby, in return, would spout Persian translations of Alfred's poems.[39]

The Queen's pleasure in the poem restored personal contact with the poet: she invited Tennyson to Frogmore to visit the new mausoleum that she had built for Prince Albert. It was highly inconvenient for Tennyson and he did not want to go, but he could scarcely disobey.[40] He was staying in London with Frederick Locker-Lampson (Locker-Lampson's wife had died recently and the visit was a matter of support and condolence). A letter to Emily of 28 February 1873 showed some welcome spirit over the invitation to visit the mausoleum: 'sore I wanted to shirk it – so I said "Deuce take all Kings and Empresses and Deuce take the Prince"! – but I suppose I shall have to go'.[41]

Social aspiration and the desire to consolidate his wealth were clearly part of the drive to complete *Idylls of the King*. Another part was Tennyson's ingrained appetite for work. Although he suffered long periods of inspirational 'dryness', he hated to find that he was not writing poetry at all, and he kept going despite the constant demands on his time from visitors and responsibilities. Emily's determination to fill their two country houses with guests is surprising. She herself was always in very poor health. Tennyson was perfectly willing to be admired, but he made a point of keeping to his own hours and sticking to his own timetable, and the guests were forced to fit in. At Farringford he would breakfast alone, work on the poetry, and then there would be a walk of at least two hours (usually from eleven until one) accompanied by dogs and whichever guests were currently regarded as in favour. In the evening he would work again, dinner was early, and then he would receive guests in his study (and read them his poetry; a convenient way of milking them for applause while at the same time not having to make conversation with them). The Aldworth timetable was similar, but because London was accessible by train, there was an even greater flow of visitors. It often seemed to the guests that the houses, the lavish hospitality and the loyal court assembled around him were arranged by Emily with regard to his needs and comfort to the exclusion of the needs of anyone else.

Throughout the 1870s Tennyson was restless. He was now wealthy as well as famous, and could keep up his two country houses and the various addresses that he rented for stays in London, but the restlessness meant that invitations to visit other parts of the country were always acceptable. Thus in 1871 he travelled north to Naworth Castle, Cumberland, to visit Mr and Mrs Howard (later Lord and Lady Carlisle). On the train up from London a fellow guest (Mary Jeune, Lady St Helier) noted that the poet 'was in a state of great irritation and discomfort from some cause or other'. The problem was that he had severely burnt his mouth on hot bread and milk because he had been in a hurry to catch the train. 'Like many great men, he bore small misfortunes with less heroism than more serious ones.' But he also gave a memorable reading of *Maud* to the Howards' assembled guests 'in his wonderful sonorous voice, with its deep vibration and all its endless shades of expression'.

Tennyson went on to visit Hadrian's Wall and Brancepeth Castle, on which he had inadvisedly drawn for his 'gew gaw' castle in *Maud* (now the property of his aunt Russell's son-in-law, Lord Boyne), which he found 'rather triste after Naworth';[42] and then back to London, where he found a welcome letter from Walt Whitman, containing a photograph. Whitman was admired by Swinburne and the Rossettis, so Tennyson might well have been wary of him, but the American had initiated contact the previous year by sending him some books as a gift. Tennyson recognised the strength of his work, and Whitman was to be one of the few Americans for whom he had lasting respect. He was enthusiastic about the photograph: 'I was well pleased with the rough outward Man of W.W. not altogether unlike what I had pictured him in my fancy.' He reciprocated with a photograph of himself, which

Whitman liked, and teased Whitman a bit about the possibility that America, that pure young country, 'may turn out the most immoral the world had ever seen'.[43]

There was a good deal of rough outward man about Tennyson himself, of course, and these two strong poets were clearly intent on showing good will to each other. The friendship blossomed over the years and yielded mutual strong support (by letter), and the pair died within a few months of each other in 1892. Tennyson responded with great warmth to an essay about him published by Whitman in January 1887, in which Whitman claimed him as an indelible force in American culture: 'he has entered into the formative influence of character here, not only in the Atlantic cities but inland and far West, out in Missouri, in Kansas, and away in Oregon, in farmer's house and miner's cabin'. The following year Whitman remarked in private to a friend that while his contact with Tennyson was always cordial, 'I don't think he ever quite makes me out: but he thinks I belong: perhaps that is enough – all I ought to expect.'[44]

One odd feature of Tennyson's surviving letters to Whitman is the sense that Tennyson tended to write as though he was constantly on the move and in a hurry. In later letters he is always immediately off on a European tour, or a visit to London, or the like. Perhaps he liked to adopt a breezy, active manner in response to Whitman's robust man-of-action masculinity. In a letter tentatively dated September 1872, he wrote from Aldworth explaining that a letter from Whitman had not yet had a reply because 'I have been on the Continent for several weeks.'[45] If the date is right, this cannot be true. On the other hand, if the letter was actually written in September 1873 – when he had indeed been away for a long Swiss and Italian tour – then his reply to Whitman was over a year late.

By 1874 Emily was suffering from exhaustion – her work as Tennyson's secretary and general factotum had overwhelmed her. In the summer of that year he took her away for a holiday to France in the hope that she would make a recovery. Lionel, the younger son, was left in Tours to be a companion to Emily, and Tennyson and Hallam together visited Cauteretz once more. On 4 September Tennyson was admired for his energy by a chamois hunter: 'You are climbing a diable of a mountain and the old gentleman at 65 (meaning A.T.) has diablement legers pieds.' On 6 September they reached Cauteretz itself, 'thirteen years to the day since he had walked into it with Dakyns and just over forty-four years since he had left it on his first visit' (with Arthur Hallam).[46] Hallam Tennyson remembered that his father said: 'in 1830 I remember the exquisite shadows on the mountains, cast by the morning light, in this valley, some of "Oenone" was composed here'.[47]

The holiday did not refresh Emily as Tennyson had hoped. On 16 October he wrote from Farringford to Palgrave:

> My wife I am sorry to say from overwork and over-letterwriting is still obliged to lie flat and must not exert herself in any one thing (the Doctor says) if she be to recover: and so a good deal of the work falls on me, who, you know, abhor letterwriting. We had not much of a tour.[48]

By 1875 Emily was unable to continue as amanuensis and Hallam had to leave Cambridge and take over.

The adolescent Tennyson had been a budding actor-playwright. His unfinished piece *The Devil and the Lady* was a brilliantly precocious burlesque; he created dramas for the family to perform at home in Somersby and he enjoyed undergraduate theatricals at Cambridge. His friends loved him to perform, on stage and off: with his beautiful deep voice and his striking good looks he was their bard and orator.

Tennyson's decision to turn playwright at the age of sixty-five was not, then, a fresh departure. It was compatible with his ambition and his sense of his own national role. By writing *Idylls of the King* he was keeping company with Malory's *Morte d'Arthur* and Spenser's *The Faerie Queene*. By turning to the theatre and writing big historical verse dramas, as well as pastoral comedies which made use of English legends, he was keeping company with Shakespeare.

Tennyson saw his big historical plays as a trilogy portraying the making of England. *Queen Mary* (1875) dealt with the downfall of Catholicism and the birth of Protestant England; *Harold* (1876) depicted the conflict of Saxons, Danes and Normans for supremacy and forecast 'the greatness of our composite race'; and *Becket* (1879) covered the struggle between Crown and Church. Tennyson had explored a number of other possibilities before settling on these topics. He had thought of writing on the Armada, on Lady Jane Grey and on William the Silent, and had wondered also about his ancient ambition to write a play about King Arthur, but decided rightly that there was no need to work further on the materials of *Idylls of the King*.[49] Michael Slater considers that:

Tennyson's chief motivation for turning playwright seems to have been patriotic, appropriately enough for a much-looked-up-to Poet Laureate. He sought, in his three major dramas, to portray 'the making of England', and to fill in some major gaps in the chronological line of his revered Shakespeare's English History Plays.[50]

Queen Mary, the first of these historical verse dramas, was initially written for publication rather than performance. Jeffrey Richards summarises the plot of the play in its full published state:

The play opposes the idea of revolt against legitimate authority. Elizabeth refuses to participate in plots against Mary. Wyatt raises his revolt not against the Queen but against the Spanish marriage. It is strongly patriotic. When Gardiner suggests saving money by reducing the Calais garrison, Mary exclaims: 'I am Queen of England; take mine eyes, mine heart, but do not lose me Calais.'[51]

Tennyson read deeply in the period as he researched the reign of the Catholic Queen, her recruitment of Cardinal Pole to lead an English Counter-Reformation and her tragically childless marriage to King Philip of Spain. His major source was chapter 6 of J. A. Froude's monumental *History of England*, and he followed carefully both Froude's sensitive and sympathetic portrayal of the Queen herself and his broad panorama of the men who jostled for position during her reign. He also incorporated the story of the Wyatt rebellion and of Cranmer's struggles to maintain his integrity and his final martyrdom at the stake. The result is a very long text divided into five acts with forty-five speaking parts and a crowd of extras. The whole work smells all too thoroughly of the lamp.

Froude himself was delighted by the way the play assaulted papal aggression against the Anglican Church. He wrote to Tennyson with his congratulations:

Beyond the immediate effect, you will have hit Manning and Co. a more fatal blow than a thousand pamphleteers and controversialists – besides this you have reclaimed one more section of English history from the wilderness and given it a form in which it will be fixed for ever. No one since Shakespeare has done that.[52]

Tennyson was also attracted by the personal tragedy of the Queen's circumstances:

He pitied the poor girl, who was not only cast down by her father from her high estate, but treated with shameless contumely by the familiar friends of her childhood. What wonder that a nature originally bright should thus have been clouded![53]

There are striking dramatic moments. In Act 1, the Queen, at this point still moderate in her aspiration to convert England back to Rome, refuses to have Jane Grey executed, saying, 'I am English Queen, not Roman Emperor.' This line, which survived into the final staged version of the play, drew spontaneous applause from the audience at the first night. The *Illustrated London News* speculated that this had to do with current debate about Disraeli's wish to confer on the Queen the title of 'Empress of India'; the Lyceum audience's applause could lead to a 'final settlement of this vexed question'.

By the end of Act II, though, in a shocking reversal which must have worked well on stage, Mary has sentenced Jane Grey and her husband, and her own sister – the future Queen Elizabeth – to death. So relentless is her iteration of the death sentence that she begins to sound a bit like Lewis Carroll's Queen of Hearts. This particular scene (Act II, scene iv) does not end a moment too soon. There are though some beautiful isolated lyric passages in *Queen Mary*, some of which remind us of the poet who wrote 'Mariana'.*

Although it was written and published as a reading text, it was natural that Tennyson should want to see his play performed. Negotiations opened with Henry Irving and with a Mrs Bateman, the American manager of the Lyceum. There would be difficulties, and at times open war, between the playwright and the company over the production. Initially Tennyson refused to take responsibility for creating an acting version of the play. The fact that it was forthcoming had been announced prematurely by Irving (from the stage of the Lyceum Theatre, where he was playing Hamlet), before agreement between Tennyson and the company had been reached. He was also asked to reduce the length drastically, and complied by resorting to a cut-and-paste operation, the results of which can be seen in the Tennyson Research Centre. Both the story of Wyatt and the whole of the Cranmer plot had to go. A friend wrote to Tennyson's brother Frederick to say that the next stage was that the 'Yankee Manageress Mrs Bateman [. . .] slashed at it with her bowie knife – & has reduced it to 2 scenes

---

*Especially the soliloquy from Wyatt the younger, reflecting on the life of his father, Wyatt the poet. (Alfred Tennyson, *Queen Mary*, I, v, pp. 54–5; II, i, p. 63.)

an act, & all the dramatis personae to 7 or 8!'[54] As well as Cranmer and Wyatt, Cardinal Pole and twenty other characters were removed. The work was now a domestic drama focused on Mary – she became 'a sentimental heroine who would appeal to Victorian audiences'.[55]

Tennyson added some text to heighten the theatrical impact of some of the scenes. 'Papa has written a splendid finale for Miss Crowe,' Hallam wrote to James Knowles (in January 1876), 'in order that she may die on the stage.' Miss Crowe was Kate Bateman, one of the manageress's daughters, who was cast as Mary. But Tennyson clearly had little control at this stage: he had also added a scene which Hallam called 'the centre-piece of the play' (Philip and Mary newly married) but Mrs Bateman cut it out.[56]

Tennyson gave Charles Villiers Stanford* sole rights to write settings for two songs in *Queen Mary*. Stanford also wrote a score for the play. This became a source of friction with Mrs Bateman, who had promised the commission to the conductor of the Lyceum orchestra. She told Tennyson that Stanford's score required more performers than the orchestra pit would hold, and refused Tennyson's proposal that she should remove the first two rows of the stalls and that he would pay for the lost income from the ticket sales for those seats. Stanford's music was not performed.[57]

On the first night of *Queen Mary*, 18 April 1876, the playbill announced that it had been 'arranged for Dramatic Representation expressly for the Lyceum Theatre'. Friends of Tennyson who loyally came to this first night included Robert Browning and a recent acquaintance, the ardently admiring Mrs Sabine Greville. Tennyson himself refused to go to the first night, and he had not witnessed any of the rehearsals either. The 'Dramatic Representation' could thrive or otherwise without him. Browning wrote to him to say that it had been really well received: 'abundant "encores" of half the speeches'.[58]

The play as performed was obviously a heavily compromised text, and it had mixed notices. *The Times* reviewer thought it unwise of Irving to address the audience directly at the end of the performance to say that he had telegraphed Tennyson to report its great success. The reviewer in *The World* was bitterly disappointed by the changes:

> Much of the stir and action distinguishing the original has been elim-
> inated from the stage edition of the work. *Queen Mary* has been
> wrecked indeed, and its least dramatic constituents are among the

---

*The young Irishman had been organist at Trinity College, Cambridge, and became known to Hallam and Lionel through this connection.

salvage [. . .] Almost the entire weight of the drama [. . .] devolves upon a heroine who cannot command the sympathies of a theatrical audience, or move them to interest in her proceedings.

This reviewer also felt that the actress did nothing with the part: 'The art of Miss Bateman has strict limitations. Her voice is hollow, her delivery is monotonous, her manner is conventional; her histrionic method is wanting in variety and in light and shade.'[59]

In dramatic terms, however, the coldness of Philip towards his Queen worked effectively. In her memoir Ellen Terry singled out this aspect of the text – and Henry Irving's performance in the role of the Spanish King – as the strongest features of the play on stage. A crucial scene, in which the Queen presses and presses for a declaration of love from her husband, ends with him callously turning away from her and addressing a servant. Ellen Terry in her memoir recalled: 'The horrid, dead look, the cruel unresponsiveness, the indifference of the creature! While the poor woman protested and wept, he went on polishing up his ring!' and then he closed the scene with the single line: "Is supper ready?"' [60]

James Knowles was not at the first night, but he wrote to Tennyson in April to congratulate him on the play's opening and assured him that he had heard that it was '*most* successful and *sure of a long run*'. Tennyson replied distancing himself from the production.[61] When Knowles actually saw the Lyceum adaptation, he was horrified. On 7 May 1876 he wrote to Tennyson referring to *Queen Mary* as Mrs Bateman's 'Mary and Philip', 'adapted by her from Tennyson's "Queen Mary"', and promised to give a personal debriefing on the production: 'have much to say about it when I do next see you'.[62]

Tennyson's conviction that he could still be a successful national playwright led him to a long treatment of the Norman Conquest – *Harold* – which was not performed in his lifetime; and then to an extremely cumbersome attempt to dramatise the story of Robin Hood in *The Foresters*. This includes a good deal of laboured comic effect, with a lot of Shakespearean cross-dressing and gendered disguise, though devoid of Shakespearean magic or suggestiveness, and some truly horrible writing.

Tennyson liked small-scale dramas, and two of his plays were effectively curtain-raisers. *The Falcon*, which had just four characters, the two major ones played by Fanny Kemble and her husband at the St James's Theatre, was based on a story in Boccaccio; the plot turned on the noble altruism of a poverty-stricken nobleman who cooks his last remaining possession, his falcon, to feed the son of a woman who calls on his charity. 'Two people reconciled to Love over a roasted

Hawk', as Fitzgerald called it. The falcon used in the first few performances strangled itself on its chain and had to be replaced by a stuffed bird.[63]

A second short drama, much more commercially successful, was *The Cup*, a spectacular two-act vehicle for Henry Irving and Ellen Terry, performed at the Lyceum Theatre in 1881. The source of *The Cup* was a story (by Plutarch) from the time of the Roman Empire; Tennyson had come across it in W. E. H. Lecky's *History of European Morals*. Camma (Ellen Terry), the wife of Sinnatus, the Tetrarch of Galatea, is pursued by a former Tetrarch, Synorix (Henry Irving), who seeks to destroy her husband by disclosing his supposed disloyalty to Rome. In the ensuing struggle Sinnatus dies and Camma becomes a priestess of Artemis; she then agrees to marry Synorix, her husband's killer, but at their wedding invites him to drink from the cup that he has given her. They both drink; she has poisoned the wine, and as they die, Camma predicts a better future for the province of Galatea.[64]

Tennyson's text was cumbersome and melodramatic, but the production was an elaborate affair. The designs were largely by Ellen Terry's former lover (and father of her children), E. W. Godwin, with some specialist support on the architectural effects from James Knowles, who in turn sought help for the Greek details from an expert at the British Museum. The commercial success of the piece onstage owed everything to the lavish spectacle it offered. A reviewer in *The Weekly Dispatch* praised it as:

> The greatest triumph of scenic art within our remembrance. When the doors are thrown open, and the bright crimson rays of the morning sun stream on the solid columns and throw into deeper shade the mysterious recesses of the building where the colossal figure of Artemis looms darkly on us all, as the procession of torch-bearing men and flower-laden maidens and children assumes every instant some new groupings of beauty and picturesqueness, we surrender ourselves delightedly to the spell, and feel that the eye and the intellect are receiving equal gratification.[65]

Gladstone, a loyal admirer of Henry Irving (and of Tennyson, though with reservations), attended the first night of *The Cup*; his reaction to it is not known, but he probably appreciated the care that had been devoted to the scenery.

* * *

Mrs Bernard Beere, 'the one tragic actress of the moment',[66] had taken a lease of the Globe Theatre, and had been persuaded by the financial success of *The Cup* to take on Tennyson's play *The Promise of May*. This was a play of ideas, set in a village, and written in prose (much of it laboured Lincolnshire dialect, phonetically rendered). The first night was, famously, a horrible disaster. Loyal friends came, as usual. Gladstone, one of the busiest men in England, went with his wife and his daughter Mary, and Hallam Tennyson and Lionel were both there. Tennyson himself did not go, which was probably just as well. There was a rowdy audience and the performance started very late.

> Care and thought had been bestowed upon every detail of the production. But before the end of the first act the fate of the play was decided. The first murmurs of disapproval grew into loud and continued derision, and the principal actor [Hermann Vezin, playing Philip Edgar the agnostic] could with difficulty carry his part to an end. When the curtain fell, *The Promise of May* was irretrievably ruined.[67]

Mary Gladstone recorded in her diary that they 'jeered and hissed and greeted with peals of laughter the special points of pathos, morality or tragedy.'[68] The fourth performance, 14 November, was interrupted by Lord Alfred Douglas's preposterous father, Lord Queensberry.

> An eye-witness of the scene which astonished the audience at the Globe Theatre, on November 14th, 1882, has given the present writer a description of the circumstance. Early in the first act, while Mr Hermann Vezin was speaking, a gentleman leapt excitedly to his feet from one of the stalls, and cried, 'I beg to protest: I beg –' A murmur for silence interrupted him, and he sat down, saying, 'I beg your pardon: I will wait till the end of the act.' As soon as the curtain had fallen, he again sprang up, exclaiming, 'I am an agnostic, and I protest against Mr Tennyson's gross caricature of our creed.'*[69]

Queensberry had misunderstood the play – Philip Edgar is an amoral young sensualist, not a principled agnostic – but it is not surprising that he was misled given that the play itself was a depressing muddle.

* * *

---

*Arthur Waugh (the father of Evelyn Waugh), writing a biography of Tennyson immediately following the poet's death in 1892, quoted a first-hand account here.

Queen Mary was the only play from the historical trilogy to be performed in Tennyson's lifetime. Becket was not at first intended for performance. Tennyson included a disclaimer of any hope that it would 'in its present form, meet the exigencies of our modern theatre'. Yet in 1892 Tennyson was discussing the possibility of a staged version of Becket with Irving and Bram Stoker (who would become known in 1897 as the author of Dracula). At this time Stoker was working as Irving's theatrical manager. Tennyson was too frail to go into details and he died at an early stage of the discussion. It was not until 1893 that Irving published an acting edition of the play and then gave it what turned out to be a triumphant staging, with himself in the leading role. The somewhat wooden Harold had to wait until the 1920s before it found a company to perform it.

Both the romance of English history and the force and conflicts of the nineteenth-century Evangelical movement helped to mould Tennyson's work for the theatre. Carlyle wrote in Heroes and Hero-Worship:

> The whole Past [. . .] is the possession of the Present; the Past had always something *true*, and is a precious possession. In a different time, in a different place, it is always some other *side* of our common Human Nature that has been developing itself. The actual True is the *sum* of all these; not any one of them by itself constitutes what of Human Nature is hitherto developed.[70]

Tennyson enlisted the legend of King Arthur, together with the key events at the centre of his three ambitious history plays, to establish a notion of England that has the dignity of underpinning by big ancient narratives. Together with this he believed in an England which was morally upright, and in this he reflects the strength of the Evangelical movement, which established the cult of respectability and what has been called 'the call to seriousness': 'Between 1780 and 1850 the English ceased to be one of the most aggressive, brutal, rowdy, outspoken, riotous, cruel and bloodthirsty nations in the world and became one of the most inhibited, polite, orderly, tenderminded, prudish and hypocritical'.[71]

Tennyson certainly heard and believed the call to seriousness. His Arthur is a Christian hero, Queen Mary is a Protestant text, and Becket reminded his audience of the foundations of the Christian society in which they lived. By extension, therefore, these can all be seen as works which underpinned the idea of the British Empire, itself in part a reflection of the Evangelical movement. The work of the Empire was *moral*. The Queen was Empress of India by divine right, rescuing the subject races from their tendency to confusion and doctrinal darkness. From this perspective Tennyson's plays can be seen as the culmination of a process in British society that had been in place since the 1780s or thereabouts.

In September 1876 Tennyson and Hallam were touring in Norfolk and Suffolk. On Thursday the 14th, without giving him any notice, they called in on Edward Fitzgerald at Woodbridge, leaving him a note – the first personal communication that his steadfast friend had had from Tennyson for many years – which read in its entirety: 'Dear old Fitz, I am passing through and will call again.'[72] Fitzgerald was astonished and delighted to see them, but also flustered by the fact that he had had little time to make any preparations to entertain them. He took them to the Bull Inn in Woodbridge rather than trying to accommodate them in his house; they stayed until Sunday and had a warm and festive time together. Fitzgerald wrote on the 19th that 'immediately it was as if we had parted only twenty days instead of twenty years: with our old Jokes, Banter, Comparisons of Taste, etc.' It was poignant for him: 'He looked as well as I had ever seen him, and was in all other ways unaltered. What astonished me was, our feeling not the slightest hesitation in taking up our intercourse just as easily as we had it twenty years ago: and I still rather wonder at this.' On the 21st, though, he wrote to Fanny Kemble in a more sombre tone: 'I suppose I may never see him again: and so I suppose we both thought as the Rail carried him off: and each returned to his ways as if scarcely diverted from them.'[73]

In this decade Alfred and Emily Tennyson regularly rented houses in London for the winter so that they could go to dinner parties and catch up with all their acquaintance. Number 7 Upper Wimpole Street, small, comfortable and convenient, was rented for the winter of 1876–7. The poet was so famous now that his every move was news, and friends and acquaintances faithfully recorded their sightings of him. In February 1877 Robert Browning recalled that he and Tennyson were walking from Wimpole Street together in order to have their photographs taken (for a new periodical, *The Portrait*) when they were accosted by a 'dissipated-looking' stranger:

'Now *you* are Mr Tennyson; I know you from the photos.' 'Well, if I am' said T., 'that is no reason why I should be stopped in the street in this way.' 'Mr Tennyson' said the other 'I've been dead drunk half a dozen times this week; if you'll only shake hands with me I'll never get drunk again.' So conjured Tennyson had nothing for it but to comply, though of course without any faith in the efficacy of his touch as a cure for this kind of King's evil.[74]

In October 1878 Henry James, to whom all doors of any distinction would open, was staying near Aldworth with Mrs Sabine Greville ('a well-connected and wealthy follower of the arts with an undiscriminating passion for literature, celebrities, and the theatre').[75] James liked to mock Mrs Greville ('amiable and clever, but fantastic and ridiculous') and at the same time was genuinely fond of her. 'She is not young, and she is ugly; but she has a touch of genius.'[76] He and Mrs Greville were invited to lunch at Aldworth, and Tennyson saw the young James as an appropriate audience for his poetry. He took him up into his study and read aloud ('not very well') 'Locksley Hall' from beginning to end. One wonders whether Tennyson singled out for this gruelling privilege guests whom he had decided he did not wish to see again. James's steely self-possession was more than a match for Tennyson's egotism, but he did not enjoy the experience of the reading, and on this occasion he found Tennyson was personally 'less agreeable than his works – having a manner that is rather bad than good'. The lunch party afforded an incident of a peculiarly Jamesian kind. Innocently boastful, Mrs Greville referred to a grand French relation of hers, 'Mademoiselle Laure de Sade'. To Tennyson the name of the marquis was a red rag to a bull, and he proceeded to list the 'most notorious' of the Marquis de Sade's 'titles to infamy'. Mrs Greville listened to this in bewilderment ('with the blankest grace'), and as the Tennysonian thunder continued, it became clear to Henry James that with the exception of himself none of Tennyson's party had any idea what he was talking about.[77]

Concurrently with Tennyson's adventures in the theatre, the indefatigable Knowles had founded another periodical, and saw the involvement of Tennyson as a key to its prospects. Alexander Strahan, Tennyson's publisher until 1873, had been the owner of Knowles's previous periodical, the *Contemporary Review*, which had flourished under Knowles's editorship. Strahan's mismanagement of the *Contemporary* provoked an angry breach with Knowles late in 1876. Early the following year the two men had parted company and Knowles had set up his own new periodical.[78] He wrote Tennyson several very long and excited letters about *The Nineteenth Century*. This one is typical in its urgency (and in its glaring self-interest and opportunism):

Everybody tells me one and the same thing about 'the XIX Century'
– Get Mr Tennyson to give you something – however small – &
whatever It may be for your first number & your success is certain.
It will make it known everywhere in a way which nothing else
whatever can do – & give it a stamp which will *make it*. I feel that
this is so true and that you have been and are so really my friend
– and I feel besides so nervous at embarking on this big venture all
by myself & with my own capital – that I overcome my repugnance
to seeming like a beggar.[79]

Tennyson agreed, and wrote a prefatory sonnet for the new periodical. With its image of old seagoing companions setting out on a new
voyage, it partly recalls the subject of 'Ulysses', and is a workmanlike
piece:

> Those that of late had fleeted far and fast
> To touch all shores, now leaving to the skill
> Of others their old craft seaworthy still,
> Have chartered this; where, mindful of the past,
> Our true co-mates regather round the mast.[80]

This sonnet gives a welcome indication of Tennyson's ability to keep
his distance from Knowles. The first five lines would cause trouble. In
February Knowles wrote in a 'cold perspiration of dismay' to Tennyson
asking him to change line three, where he referred to Strahan's periodical, the *Contemporary Review*, as the 'old craft seaworthy still', but
Tennyson ignored the request.[81] He did not wish to be seen to be
taking sides in Knowles's quarrel with Strahan.

Gladstone had several times proposed Tennyson for a title, and had
considered the House of Lords for him but was misled into thinking
that Tennyson would not be able to afford the personal expenses that
such an honour would entail. On 23 March 1873 Gladstone wrote
(at considerable length, and in his own hand) offering a baronetcy:

> It is the highest honour we have, unclogged with legislation & other
> public functions such as would probably be uncongenial to you; and
> it would survive in the person of your descendants as a note of
> Royal & national acknowledgement for the great services which by
> your works you have conferred upon your country.[82]

Emily was much disappointed: 'I had quite hoped he would be offered a Peerage. When the Dean [Stanley] spoke of it to G[ladstone] there was something in G's manner which made the Dean think that G. personally would wish to offer something more than the baronetcy, so much so that I primed the Dean with all the history, as far as I knew it, of the D'Eyncourt title [. . .] I think he had better take the B[aronetcy] for our friend Hallam's sake'. [83] Indeed Tennyson did write on 28 March 1873 accepting the baronetcy, but then wrote again on 30 March declining it.

Personal relationships meant less to Tennyson as he grew older. Increasingly he venerated his own mind and his own methods. Mary Gladstone noted that he talked about religion a lot, but in an heretical and egocentric way. 'T. does not appear to be much of a Christian, and I suspect is no theologian, but really very religious' (by which she clearly meant 'mystical', as indeed he was). Much of her record of her first meeting with him (at the Gladstone family home, Hawarden, in 1876) has to do with amused recognition of his self-centredness. 'At six came Tennyson and his son Hallam, tired and cold. Sat between the two at dinner. He snubbed me once or twice, but was afterwards very amiable. He is exactly like Shakespeare to look at.' She added later that he was 'not altogether good-tempered' during this visit.

Late the following morning Tennyson read the whole of his play *Harold* to the assembled company. Mary thought that her father fell asleep during the reading; his son Willy had a fit of the giggles; his daughter Helen disciplined herself by focusing intensely. Eleanor Locker, Lionel Tennyson's fiancée and a fellow guest, was politely 'rapt'. Mary herself was hungry: 'We were forced to take no need of such earthly things as luncheon.'[84] Gladstone's own account of the visit in his diary noted politely that 'Tennyson read to us his Harold: it took near 2½ hours.' On the day after the reading, Gladstone engaged Tennyson in a conversation about hell. (If this was a hint about having being forced to sit through the whole of *Harold*, Tennyson missed it.) Later he wrote in his diary: 'Conversation with Tennyson on future Retribution, and other matters of theology: he has not thought, I conceive, systematically or thoroughly upon them, but is much alarmed at the prospect of the loss of belief.'[85]

Mary also recorded a party that the Tennysons gave at a house they had rented in Wimpole Street in March 1877. The company, which included Robert Browning and the famous violinist, Joachim, was 'very higher ground', despite which Tennyson failed to recognise some of his guests: 'Tennyson forgets everybody and growls out "Haven't an idea who you are," very embarrassing for a shy individual.'[86] Henry

James found himself dining at the Athenaeum on 28 March in the company of Tennyson, Gladstone and Lord Houghton. Tennyson was 'very swarthy and craggy, and strikes one at first as much less handsome than his photos: but gradually you see that it's a face of genius. He had I know not what simplicity, speaks with a strange rustic accent and seemed altogether like a creature of some primordial English stock, a thousand miles away from American manufacture.'[87]

By 1878, only the grandest of British institutions could do justice to major Tennyson family occasions. The marriage of his younger son, Lionel, to Eleanor Locker, in February 1878, was one such occasion, and took place in Westminster Abbey. The couple were very young but they had already been pledged to each other for three years, since the summer holiday of 1875. The Tennysons had coincided with the Lockers at Pau, and romance had blossomed. It was the kind of connection about which the Tennysons could feel comfortable, indeed complacent. Hallam Tennyson said of the engagement that it 'had not been in any way foreseen; but it was as welcome as so anxious an event can be to those whose life has been with and for their children'.[88]

Early in 1876 Tennyson wrote to the Duke of Argyll with the news: 'Tell the Duchess if she do not know it that Lionel, my youngest son, is engaged to Miss Eleanor Locker.' He referred to Eleanor as descended from a Bruce and a London Lyric, by which he meant that her mother was Lady Charlotte Locker (née Bruce) while her father was a writer (among other things). 'The Queen has been very kind about it,' he was able to say with satisfaction.[89] Naturally Dean Stanley (as Dean of Westminster and a relation by marriage of the bride) had been invited to conduct the wedding, but he was taken ill so that it was celebrated instead by Frederick William Farrar. Farrar recorded in his diary that Tennyson and Emily were late because the door through which they were to have entered was locked. 'I did not see the father, mother, and brother of the bridegroom; but they might be easily overlooked in such a multitude, and I naturally assumed that they were present. The service began, and it was only when I came to the sentence, "I pronounce that they be man and wife together" that I noticed the Tennysons entering.'[90] In addition to the parents of the young people, the signatories to the register were Robert Browning, Lord Argyll and Gladstone. Alfred Domett (1811–87), former Prime Minister of New Zealand and a prominent champion of Browning, wrote of the occasion:

> Tennyson had chosen them, I suppose (though Browning did not of course say so) as it was pleasant to leave on the register on such an

occasion, the names of the most famous poet, next himself, the most literary and perhaps most talented member of the House of Lords, and the celebrated Prime Minister.[91]

That winter Tennyson and Emily took a house in Eaton Square, where they held a very considerable soirée on 30 March. Robert Browning was one of the guests, and he and Tennyson were on excellent form; as Mary Gladstone recalled, they 'hurled ridiculous epitaphs at each other'. The dinner party itself was small (it was completed by the Duke of Argyll and Frederick Locker), but afterwards other guests arrived ('all sorts of Big Wigs', in Mary Gladstone's phrase), including Joachim, Matthew Arnold, William Allingham and his wife, and Burne-Jones.[92] To permit audience to as many as possible, the sequence of a small dinner party followed by a larger reception was by now the established pattern. Mary Gladstone was there again some two weeks later: 'off to Tennyson's *great* fun'. The 'fun'(to the sharp eyes of a young satirist) was afforded by Lord Acton, George Eliot and Thackeray's elder daughter ('oh how affected she was'). Tennyson agreed to read – he never took much persuasion – and gave them 'Boadicea', much of *Maud*, and 'The Revenge'. On this occasion Mary Gladstone was not bored: indeed 'The Revenge' was 'perfectly splendid. He reads it in an ever increasing rush, and shouting out the climax.'[93]

An inevitable feature of the ageing process is that one's friends and contemporaries fall away. George Eliot's beloved partner G. H. Lewes died on 30 November 1878 (Tennyson and Emily had become close to George Eliot and were genuinely sorry for her). A much more grievous loss was that of Alfred's brother Charles Tennyson Turner, the other serious poet in the family and the brother to whom he had always been closest. Charles had lived a quiet, diligent life as a clergyman, humbly caring for the flock in Grasby, Lincolnshire, and slowly writing the carefully crafted sonnets that are still a lasting reminder of his very real talent. His opium addiction had dogged him throughout his life. His wife Louisa Sellwood, Emily's sister, had separated from him for a while, but was reconciled to him in later years and joined him in his good works. An obvious sadness for them both was that they had no children. Charles had been unwell throughout the winter of 1878–9 and died, to no one's surprise, on 25 April 1879.

The following year Tennyson's son Hallam and his and Charles's old friend James Spedding published a beautifully presented volume of Charles Tennyson Turner's collected *Sonnets*. James Spedding's introductory essay is one of the most discerning pieces on the work of a minor writer. Many of Charles's sonnets had been devoted to religious and ecclesiastical matters. As a religious sceptic James Spedding naturally preferred the sonnets that showed direct continuity from the early romantic poets. Still, his summing-up of Charles's achievement was scrupulously balanced, giving equal weight to both sides of his talent:

> Whatever we take to be the distinguishing mark of the true poet – whether imaginative sympathy with nature, as Wordsworth used to maintain, or application of moral ideas to questions concerning man and nature and human life, as Mr Matthew Arnold rules it, or the power of casting beautiful thoughts into forms which are accepted at once and remembered for ever, which I take to be the common opinion – we have a true poet here.[94]

To balance such losses Tennyson increasingly encouraged young favourites, especially Gladstone's talented and vivacious daughter Mary. She did not feel threatened by his obvious partiality, but it was clearly very marked. Tennyson and Emily had again taken a London house (in Eaton Place, a house rented from the widow of Tennyson's friend Sir John Simeon), and Mary Gladstone recorded visiting them there in the early spring of that year, March and April 1879. Tennyson gave a reading of *Maud* on 22 March, and this time Mary was no longer inclined to laugh at him: 'It was wondrous the fire and fervour and despair he alternately put into it. More like a passionate youth than a worn-out old man.' Tennyson was sixty-nine and was certainly not 'worn-out', but he liked to play the old man when it suited him. On 5 April he took leave of Mary Gladstone: 'The old fellow came to the door and was very affte. "Goodbye, dear, be happy – till I die, and afterwards."'[95]

In June of the same year, Mary stayed with the Tennysons at Farringford. It was her first visit there, and she felt appallingly shy. The routine at Farringford was dauntingly elaborate, though lightened by moments of frivolity: 'Dinner was at 6.30 and went off pretty well, the evening was like 6 rolled into one; as it is the fashion here continually to move into a fresh room and begin again – altogether 4 different moves – the last sit employed in backgammon [*sic*].' Tennyson 'was such a funny wayward child over the game, and when we got up for bed suddenly startled me by asking earnestly, "What colour *are* yr. eyes, I cannot make out."' The flirtatiousness made her uncomfortable. 'He suddenly began to stroke my nose, having discovered it was a "petit nez retroussé," and declared it meant all sorts of naughty things.' Two days later he took Mary to his study and kissed her. Her 'alarm' at this was understandable. The flirtatious teasing was still going on as she left: Tennyson 'called me a "hard little thing" for not crying'.*[96]

The teasing and playfulness masked grief for his brother Charles. This death had left Tennyson quite shaky, and looking noticeably older. James Russell Lowell, who was invited by the Tennysons to lunch at Eaton Square in March 1880, remarked that he was 'getting old and looks seedy',[97] and the ever-mischievous Henry James, who was at the same party, made Tennyson's absent-mindedness on this occasion the basis of another of his feline anecdotes. Lowell and Tennyson both sat at table in complete silence, neither addressing the other. At last Tennyson leant across and asked, 'Do you know anything about *Lowell*?' which was 'crowned at once by Mrs Tennyson's anxious quaver: "Why, my dear, this *is* Mr Lowell!"'[98] (Despite this gaffe, Tennyson and Lowell were thereafter in warm and friendly correspondence with each other.)

Tennyson became increasingly frail following Charles's death. During the early summer of 1880 he suffered from a liver complaint and, more seriously, heard ghostly voices talking to him. Froude wrote of him (in a letter to Hallam Tennyson):

> Spiritually he lives in all our minds (in mine he has lived for nearly forty years) in forms imperishable as diamonds which time and change have no power over. The mortal case of him is of frailer material, and, as I believe he takes extremely little care of it himself, the charge falls on you.[99]

The liver complaint was a result of Tennyson's drinking. Port, which he loved, was particularly bad for him. Since Emily's collapse in the early 1870s, the burden of being his father's secretary had fallen on Hallam, and as his parents grew older Hallam also had to become in effect their carer. It was he who liaised with doctors, took advice, and made appropriate arrangements. In the summer of 1880, Sir Andrew Clark, the physician treating Tennyson, advised cutting out the port and recommended another European tour to divert him from his grief over Charles's death. Hallam organised a visit to Venice. The journey took the two men to Munich, then to the Tegernsee, where they visited Lord Acton; thence to Innsbruck, the Dolomites and Cortina. They

---

*Other young girls were the objects of his clumsy and teasing affection as he grew older: Margot Asquith, who was a friend of Lionel Tennyson, was made to sit on his knee while he read *Maud* to her, and another girl was almost pushed off his knee when she said that the bird in 'the high Hall-garden' was a nightingale ('No, fool! . . . rook!'). Margot Asquith, *Autobiography*, 2 vols (London: Penguin, 1936), I, pp. 167-8.

arrived at Venice in a storm accompanied by a torrential downpour. 'Having dreamt all his life of this city on the sea', Tennyson found the reality of Venice disappointing. The Grand Canal lived up to expectations, but the side canals were narrow, crowded and disorderly, and the paintings in the many churches that they visited were in such dim light he could barely see them. They returned home via Verona, which Tennyson found more rewarding: 'my father was enchanted by the romance of its situation, nestled among vine-clad hills, with the Adige rushing round the walls, and by the beautiful Giusti garden'. The tour was leisurely, and brought them back via Lake Garda and Milan. The most fruitful stopping place was Sirmio, where Tennyson began the elegy modelled on Catullus for his brother Charles, 'Frater Ave atque Vale'.[100] He allowed James Knowles to publish this most beautiful and personal poem in *The Nineteenth Century* in March 1883.[101]

Row us out from Desenzano, to your Sirmione row!
So they rowed, and there we landed – 'O venusta Sirmio!'
There to me through all the groves of olive in the summer glow,
There beneath the Roman ruin where the purple flowers grow,
Came that 'Ave atque Vale' of the Poet's hopeless woe,
Tenderest of Roman poets nineteen-hundred years ago,
'Frater Ave atque Vale' – as we wandered to and fro
Gazing at the Lydian laughter of the Garda Lake below
Sweet Catullus's all-but-island, olive-silvery Sirmio![102]

In 1880 Tennyson appeared to have turned away from playwriting and back to his first art, and he pleased his audience with *Ballads and other poems*. One of the most successful pieces was 'Rizpah, or the Bones', a testament to the violence of a mother's love. It is a dramatic monologue spoken by an old woman on her deathbed. Tennyson based the ballad on a true story about a young Sussex man executed for theft in 1793. His body was hanged on a gibbet above the cliffs ('so high / That all the ships of the world could stare at him, passing by') and attacked by crows and ravens ('God 'ill pardon the hell-black raven and horrible fowls of the air, / But not the black heart of the lawyer who killed him and hanged him there').[103] As the flesh rotted and the bones fell to the ground, the young man's mother gathered them up and secretly laid them to rest in consecrated ground. The grotesque handling of the theme recalled 'St Simeon Stylites', with the difference that in this poem the macabre was being mined for pathos rather than satire.

In March 1881 Tennyson lost James Spedding, who died some days after being run over by a cab. At Trinity he had been second only to

Arthur Hallam in Tennyson's eyes, and when Hallam died Spedding effectively took his place as literary facilitator and unofficial agent, the man who showed the best judgement and understanding of where Tennyson's work was going. Spedding was in St George's Hospital, near the house that the Tennysons had taken in Belgravia. Tennyson visited the hospital once but was not allowed to see the injured man. After this one attempt he did not bother to visit again (in his final days Spedding asked several times if Tennyson would visit – Hallam went to his bedside but his father stayed away). Tennyson did not go to Spedding's funeral, either, and the letters and journals find him at a number of dinner parties and other occasions in March, always the centre of attention, and making, it seems, no reference to his old friend.[104]

It is astonishing that Tennyson was so unmoved by Spedding's horrible death. As a young man Spedding had been a constant, loyal and discriminating presence, a man whose suggestions for Tennyson's poetry were never wrong, and who knew the young poet so well that his mind moved to the rhythms of Tennyson's creative processes. Yet since Tennyson's marriage and fame, Spedding had been increasingly left out. Tennyson joked that the problem was that Spedding had moved out of London to a suburb where he lived forlornly among his nieces, a clean family man instead of the comrade of old. But beyond the nieces Spedding had no attachments, he had never married and he lived a single and intellectual life as though he was still an exceptionally solemn undergraduate. He had always been available if Tennyson had chosen to seek him out.

Other friends died in the same year: Drummond Rawnsley, the Lincolnshire friend from whose house at Shiplake the Tennysons had married in 1850, and who had visited them annually in Farringford; and Dean Stanley, a friend who belonged more to the London and Laureate aspects of Tennyson's life, but who for all that had been a valued intimate. In 1882 his close friend on the Isle of Wight, W. G. Ward, the convivial and rumbustious Roman Catholic convert, also died, leaving Tennyson feeling that old comrades were deserting him one by one.

In June 1883 Edward Fitzgerald died. Sir Charles Tennyson wrote that Fitzgerald was 'perhaps the dearest of his old friends', and loyally claimed long after the event that there had been no estrangement, despite the fact that Tennyson and Fitzgerald had seen so little of each other in recent years.[105] But the evidence seems to show that Tennyson had neglected this friendship, treated Fitzgerald hurtfully and allowed the old affection to die. His grandeur and the huge social demands on him at all times were of course not compatible with the retired single life in East Anglia that Fitzgerald had created for himself, but Fitzgerald wrote to him regularly, at least twice a year, asking for news. Tennyson would never answer his old friend himself; the task was delegated to Emily or to Hallam. And this was to a man who had helped him financially – liberally – when he was at a low ebb in the 1830s. Perhaps the hard fact is that very successful men find it convenient simply to erase from the record early friendships and obligations.

Yet Tennyson had thought of his old friend, and was in the process of writing a carefully considered poem for him when the news of Fitzgerald's death reached him. Fitzgerald died on 14 June, on a visit to his executor, the Rev. George Crabbe (grandson of the poet), who lived at Merton in Norfolk. On the 17th, Tennyson wrote from Farringford: 'Dear old Fitz – I had no truer friend – he was one of the kindliest of men and I have never known one of so fine and delicate a wit.' He then revealed the painful irony of the timing of Fitzgerald's death: 'I had written a poem to him within the last week – a dedication – which he will never see. There are now left to me only two or three of my old college companions, and who goes next?'[106]

The friendship could become warm and real again to Tennyson once he had internalised it and was working it into art in the safety of his study; but actual contact with the living man who had been thus internalised had become too awkward and uncomfortable for him to confront. This birthday greeting, addressed 'To E. FitzGerald', was published in 1885 as a dedication to 'Tiresias'. Here he praised Fitzgerald's '*Omar Khayyám* and hailed him as from one old poet to another:

> But we old friends are still alive,
> And I am nearing seventy-four,
> While you have touched at seventy-five,*
> And so I send a birthday line
> Of greeting; and my son [Hallam], who dipt
> In some forgotten book of mine
> With sallow scraps of manuscript,
> And dating many a year ago,
> Has hit on this, which you will take
> My Fitz, and welcome, as I know
> Less for its own than for the sake
> Of one recalling gracious times,
> When, in our younger London days,
> You found some merit in my rhymes,
> And I more pleasure in your praise.[107]

---

*Not quite accurate: Fitzgerald was seventy-four when he died.

Even here an old grievance was allowed to surface: Fitzgerald had been unable to admire Tennyson's poetry written since the 1830s, and had been tactless enough to persist in making that clear. This had undoubtedly contributed to the sad cooling of the friendship.

The Queen's view of her own position meant that relations with her subjects, even one as distinguished as Tennyson, were unlikely to be other than formal. In the summer of 1883 she indicated that Tennyson would be welcome to a personal audience at Osborne. This was a matter of obedience: if Her Majesty indicated that she wished to see him, he had no choice, nervous although he always was about such things. He visited on 7 August, and was received in what had been Prince Albert's room. The Queen was warm and friendly in manner. Protocol required that the honoured visitor should stand throughout a private audience, but on this occasion the Queen wrote that she had waived that convention, saying, 'You and I, Mr Tennyson, are old People, and like to sit down.'[108] She wrote in her journal that Tennyson had 'grown very old – his eyesight much impaired – and he is very shaky on his legs. But he was very kind.' The Queen liked to dwell on bereavement and immortality, and Tennyson could relate to both of these themes. 'He talked of the many friends he had lost and what it would be if he did not feel and know that there was another World, where there would be no partings; and then he spoke with horror of the unbelievers and philosophers who would make you believe there was *no* other world, no Immortality.'[109] Tennyson was not just telling the Queen what she wanted to hear; as he grew older, he had become increasingly interested in the supernatural.

In 1883 Tennyson's claim to a peerage was reinforced by a two-week sea excursion – almost a royal progress – that he and Hallam took together with Gladstone and his wife and a whole host of other guests. The owner of the yacht, a magnificent new ship called the *Pembroke Castle*, was a wealthy shipping magnate (and MP for Perthshire) called Sir Donald Currie. He had invited the party for a trial cruise which took in the west coast of Scotland and then Norway. Tennyson himself suggested that the journey should be extended to Denmark; he had never seen Elsinore.[110]

In Copenhagen there was a lavish entertainment on the yacht. As Mary Gladstone put it in her diary: 'All the crowned heads accompanied by their children came to luncheon, 48 strong, rather bewildering, but a real success.' The crowned heads included the Tsar of Russia and his wife and eldest son, the kings of Denmark and Greece and their families, and a number of the British royal family including the Princess of Wales, for whom Tennyson had written 'A Welcome to Alexandra' in 1863. Tennyson was persuaded by the Princess to read to some members of this galaxy of guests ('senior Imperial and Royal Personages crowded together into a small cabin on the Deck to hear Mr Tennyson read two of his poems', as Gladstone put it in a letter to the Queen). Tennyson's reputation for being socially inept was endearingly enhanced by a small faux pas. He was sitting next to the Princess of Wales, and on the other side of him sat a lady whom he could not identify. She complimented him on his reading. 'I patted her on the shoulder very affectionately, and said, "My dear girl, that's very kind of you, very kind." I heard the czar chuckling mightily to himself, so I looked more nearly at her, and, God bless me! 'twas the czarina herself.'*[111]

Sir Edward Hamilton, one of Gladstone's private secretaries, was also a guest on the *Pembroke Castle*. Tennyson talked to him over breakfast one morning, and mentioned the offers of a baronetcy that had been made to him in the past. 'He concluded by saying that were the offer again made, and made by Mr Gladstone, he should return a different answer.' Hamilton acted immediately on this heavy hint: 'I thought it right to let Mr Gladstone know this. He at once said that he would willingly offer a Baronetcy to Mr Tennyson if he knew the offer would not be rejected as it had been on previous occasions. I then asked him whether he did not think he might go a step further and offer Mr Tennyson a peerage. His first answer was characteristic: "Ah! Could I be accessory to introducing *that hat* into the House of Lords?"'[112]

The hat, and the general sense of Tennyson as a man whose manner could be rough and unpredictable, were not the real impediments. There was the question of Tennyson's willingness to be an active member of the Lords: would he vote 'if an urgent question of state-policy required it'? Would he be able to afford the expenses associated with a peerage? Gladstone made discreet enquiries, and may well have been surprised to discover how secure Tennyson was financially. Nevertheless, having looked carefully into relevant precedent, Gladstone decided that the patent fee of £500 normally required of new peers would be waived in the case of Tennyson. Macaulay had paid the fee 'but he was a confirmed bachelor & there was no succession'.[113]

*   *   *

---

*The Princess of Wales – Alexandra – and the Tsarina – Dagmar, known as Minnie – were sisters, daughters of the King of Denmark.

Tennyson was moving towards 'Baron of Aldworth and Farringford' as his preferred title.* The correspondence shows that he had explored vigorously the possibility of reviving the name and title of 'd'Eyncourt' for himself. This is a painful demonstration of the degree to which the old bitterness over his father's disinheritance had corroded Tennyson's judgement. There was a generous letter from the senior d'Eyncourt cousin (Rear Admiral Edwin Clayton Tennyson d'Eyncourt) raising no objection to the title 'Tennyson d'Eyncourt', but adding, reasonably enough: 'Personally I should have preferred his title of Baron Tennyson thereby continuing and handing down to posterity his renowned and familiar name.'[114] In the event a long and detailed letter arrived in December 1883 from Sir Albert William Woods, Garter King of Arms, which firmly ruled out any claims Tennyson might have thought he had to the d'Eyncourt title. After a bit more tinkering with possible styles, he settled on 'Baron Tennyson, of Aldworth, in the county of Sussex, and of Freshwater, in the Isle of Wight', and this was confirmed by the Queen on 15 January.[115]

There was widespread hostile comment. Sir Edward Hamilton recorded that 'the announcement has been received coldly and with scant favour', and he quoted James Knowles as saying that the literary world 'pitied the Poet Laureate for having fallen a victim to the ambition of his wife and eldest son'. This was reflected in the family. Tennyson's brother Frederick wrote to his own son:

> Mrs – now Baroness T. of Aldworth and Freshwater – has not been laid upon her back most of her life without nursing ambitious dreams, now realised. She, of course, will plead the advantages accruing to her children, and theirs. Many years ago the Queen – whose heart he had gained by poetical incense offered to the late Prince Consort – would have done the same – but he did not seem to regard it in any other light than an empty adjunct to an already honoured and illustrious name. But doubtless he has been drawn into his wife's worldliness.[116]

Frederick's jealous dislike of Emily looks sad and badly timed when put side by side with two letters to him from Emily and Tennyson later in this same month. Frederick's wife had died, and Emily wrote

---

*He was not an active peer, as Arthur Waugh (pp. 264–5) observed: 'Lord Tennyson's attendances in the House were very few; his vote was only registered on two occasions. He voted in support of the bill for extending the County Franchise, and paired in favour of the bill which advocated the legalization of marriage with a deceased wife's sister.'

a personal and warmly expressed letter of condolence on 25 January. Tennyson's letter to his brother, whom he certainly loved, was shorter, but heartfelt: 'Neither you nor I can have long to wait before we join those whom we have lost. I myself feel every day as though I stood at the gates of Death and the light of morning is not always upon them.'[117]

Hallam, the older of the two Tennyson sons, married considerably later than did his younger brother Lionel. By June 1884, the time of Hallam's marriage to Audrey Boyle, Tennyson had been raised to the House of Lords and Hallam was therefore 'the Honourable' and the heir to a peerage. The marriage took place in Henry VII's chapel at Westminster and was, like Lionel's, appropriately grand, and unlike Lionel's, free of mishap. Emily travelled to the ceremony but was so unwell that she could not attend the signing of the register, and had to be carried in a chair from place to place. Still, the event was clearly one that filled her with appropriate pride: she and Tennyson had come a very long way. The Allinghams, delighted to be invited to the wedding (and taking notes as usual), recorded the occasion, and noted the figures who made up the congregation: Matthew Arnold, Robert Browning, Lord Houghton, the historian Lecky, and to their pleasant surprise Matilda and Cecilia Tennyson, the latter with her husband Edmund Lushington. 'Mr Lushington, after all these years, recollected me well and some talk we had together (which I have forgotten) – he looks little older, and bears his age like a cheerful wise man.'[118]

These family events gave Tennyson a sense of dynasty as well as much more innocent and obvious forms of satisfaction. Lionel's sons, Alfred, born in 1878, and Charles, born in 1879, were important in the lives of Tennyson and Emily.[119] From a visit to Aldworth in September 1884, William Allingham recalled the pleasure that Lord Tennyson took in playing with the children, now aged six and five:

H. [Helen Allingham] and I to Aldworth. In the drawing-room we find Lady Tennyson – then T comes in. His two little grandsons run in. Tennyson went to his bedroom and returned with a soap-dish and piece of soap, which he rubbed into a lather, and proceeded to blow bubbles, himself much delighted with the little crystal worlds and their prismatic tints – 'Never was anything seen so beautiful! You artists (to H) can't get such colours as these.'

The children jumped and laughed, and we fanned the bubbles to the ceiling and watched them burst in various parts of the room.

Then T., inverting his pipe, blew up a magic cluster of diamond domes on the saucer, which rolled over and wet his knees, till we put a newspaper to save him. Next he took his trusty tobacco pipe, lighted it and blew opaque bubbles which burst with a tiny puff of smoke, like shells over a besieged fortress.[120]

Tennyson was now in his seventies, rich, famous and recently ennobled. Both his sons were settled in their marriages, and he could play with these little children with every prospect of his family steadily prospering and expanding. The boy who had lived with so much disorder in the troubled family at Somersby had become a serenely confident patriarch. It is good to be able to stabilise this sweet domestic scene and hold it in the mind for a while, in view of what was to come.

CHAPTER 10

Tragedy and resolution, 1886–1892

Peace, let it be! for I loved him, and love him for ever:
the dead are not dead but alive.

Tennyson had at one time been a friend of Coventry Patmore. The fragile egos of both men meant that the friendship had never been close, but after a very long silence Patmore attempted in June 1881 to put things right with a careful and detailed letter to Tennyson explaining the reason for the initial breach between them some twenty years earlier.[1] Tennyson was unlikely to respond to a reminder of a long-forgotten grievance, and Patmore's letter was clumsy and ill-judged, but he was undoubtedly in the right. He explained that he had been prompted to get in touch by Woolner, who had told him 'that you were never aware of the last steps I took in order to maintain a position among your friends'. He referred back to 1862, when he had been offended by an application for money made on his behalf by the Tennysons to the Royal Literary Fund. Patmore was distraught because his wife had just died, and his pride was hurt: he was vexed by the offer of 'an assistance which, as it happened, I did not need, and which, had I needed it ever so much, I should not have sought'. He had written to Emily explaining that he did not need help, and separately to Tennyson with an invitation to his house in Hampstead, 'But I never heard again from you.' He now wanted to say that he believed that his second letter was never delivered.[2] Tennyson's reply could scarcely have been more chilling: 'As I am perfectly certain that I never received any such letter as you allude to, I can only regret that this long estrangement has taken place.'[3] Patmore tried once more to break the ice by sending Tennyson his latest publication. He received an aloof and impersonal acknowledgement, and thereafter did not contact Tennyson again.

Tennyson's poems about friendship were more lasting than the friendships themselves. The publication of *Tiresias and Other Poems* in 1885 marked in an ironic and indirect way another friendship that had been allowed to cool. Tennyson had begun the title poem in 1832, extended it considerably after Arthur Hallam's death in 1833 and made further additions to it shortly before its publication in 1885.* One is reminded of his habit of looping back to his much younger self, in creative terms.

The source narrative for 'Tiresias' was brutal in its simplicity. Tiresias, who as a young man was blinded by Athene for witnessing her bathing, was granted at the same time the gift of accurate prophecy, but was doomed not to be believed. As an old man he has to advise on the saving of Thebes from destruction, and he knows that the only way this can be achieved is by human sacrifice. It was Cadmus who first offended the god Ares, and Tiresias has the terrible duty of telling a descendant of Cadmus that he must sacrifice his own life. In the sources this descendant, the young Menoeceus, is the son of King Priam of Thebes. In Tennyson's treatment of the story Priam is not mentioned, and Menoeceus is addressed as though (spiritually or figuratively) he were Tiresias's own son. The story as given by Tennyson here then became a prefiguring of Christianity; God the Father required the sacrifice of his own son to save the world. The barbaric story became in Tennyson's hands a stately and decorous narrative. The most striking – and painful – moment in the poem is the evocation of the last scene that the young Tiresias is permitted to see:

> There in a secret olive-glade I saw
> Pallas Athene climbing from the bath
> In anger; yet one glittering foot disturbed
> The lucid well; one snowy knee was prest
> Against the margin flowers; a dreadful light
> Came from her golden hair, her golden helm
> And all her golden armour on the grass,
> And from her virgin breast, and virgin eyes
> Remaining fixt on mine, till mine grew dark
> For ever.[4]

A detached and intelligent visitor, Lord Carnarvon, visited the Tennysons at Aldworth in July 1888. He brought out well the narrowing of Tennyson's horizons. Tennyson now lived in books, he said, or in a

---

*'Tithonus' and the *Idylls* had displayed the same husbanding of material which he knew would be used at some later date. In the same way 'Oh that 'twere possible' existed in the 1830s and was knitted up into *Maud* in 1855, and the first arresting line of 'The Revenge' rested on its own in a notebook – occupying the centre of an otherwise blank page – for several years before Tennyson saw his way to writing the whole poem for publication in *The Nineteenth Century* in 1878.

very small world of his own, and had become exclusively self-revolving: 'he brings everything back to himself. His own writings are the central point of all his thoughts.' After dinner Tennyson had read the 'Ode on the Death of the Duke of Wellington' and the new Locksley Hall poem, 'Locksley Hall Sixty Years After'. With the latter work 'he was very anxious to make me understand that there was no inconsistency between the early poem and the later one; but that this second was "dramatic" – that it was the soliloquy of an old man who has passed through a succession of changing moods'. To Carnarvon this claim was unfounded. Although Tennyson was 'desirous of avoiding the charge of inconsistency', he had in fact become a fixed conservative. 'He hates the modern Radicals, he has lost any admiration he may have had for Gladstone, and if he expresses an occasional belief in human or social progress it is a very frigid and doubtful profession of faith.' Carnarvon greatly regretted the loss of Tennyson's youthful self: 'In him one sees the two natures in conflict – the impulsive, hopeful, sanguine believer in progress of former days, and the timid Conservative of the present who fears the tendency of modern times.'[5]

Friends meanwhile were developing a resistance to Emily. In the early 1870s, for example, Anne Gilchrist, the widow of Blake's biographer, told William Michael Rossetti that Emily 'attaches to position and appearances a certain value beyond what you do: and I can most cordially say that in this matter I agree with you, and not with her'. Anne Gilchrist wrote to Rossetti in May 1871 to say that 'my conscience smote me for having spoken depreciatingly' (of Emily Tennyson). She added:

> Underneath that soft, languid manner there lurks a clear-headed, acute, energetic, strong-willed character. She devotes herself with the most unwearied zeal (spite of fragile health) to realizing in her husband's home her ideal of what a [Poet Laureate's] home should be.

'What a mistake it all is,' was Mrs Gilchrist's judgement of Emily's care of Tennyson. The consequence, in the poet himself, was his 'profoundly *ennuyé* air and utter lack of the power of enjoyment'. The problem lay in Emily 'watching him with anxious, affectionate solicitude'; she 'surrounds him ever closer and closer with the sultry, perfumed atmosphere of luxury and homage in which his great soul – and indeed any soul would – droops and sickens'.[6]

Lionel Tennyson was working at the India Office in London, somewhat unhappily; he found the work tedious and the prospects unattractive.

Tennyson and Emily used their contacts to find him a more interesting posting. When the Marquess of Dufferin and Ava was appointed Viceroy and Governor-General of India in 1884, Tennyson wrote to him exploring the possibility that Lionel might be appointed his private secretary. That post had already been filled, but further letters resulted in the London India Office itself transferring Lionel to India, where, as Dufferin wrote, 'his abilities would have a wider field than at home, and which would give me an opportunity of pushing him on in his career'.⁷ The future now looked very bright indeed for Lionel and Eleanor, and they left Aldworth on 6 October 1885 in order to sail to India.

In February 1886 Dufferin wrote to Tennyson to report that Lionel was suffering from some kind of fever: 'we regard attacks of this kind pretty much in the same light as we do colds in England, so you need not be uneasy'. But the illness progressed: Lionel underwent surgery, which left abscesses. They became infected and made his situation worse. At the beginning of April, he and Eleanor were put on a ship to return to England under the care of an English doctor who was also coming home. Lionel had grown a beard, and although he was still a young man he had come to look very like his father as he lay on his sickbed on deck; the hope was that he would benefit from cool sea breezes calming his fever.

The Queen wrote to Tennyson about Lionel's illness: 'I am indeed grieved beyond measure for you and your dear wife.' She also remarked that she 'cannot in this letter allude to politics, but I know what your feelings must be'. Here she was referring to Gladstone's attempt to secure Home Rule for the Irish, a measure to which she was bitterly opposed. Tennyson too was opposed to it. In his reply, written 'in this pause, as it were, between life and death', he found space to agree with Her Majesty about Ireland. He was writing on 18 April, by which date he knew that Lionel would probably die, but he still needed to play the courtier.⁸ Lionel was delirious on board much of the time, and unaware that he was seriously ill. Eleanor sent a series of telegrams to Tennyson and Emily, culminating in her telegram of 20 April in which she reported Lionel's death. He was buried at sea the same evening.

Tennyson's distress was uncontrollable, and took the form of involuntary weeping and desperate self-blame. He felt that he had always been guilty of showing preference for Hallam, and had allowed Lionel to grow away from him. It is more accurate to say that Lionel had been a somewhat rebellious teenager and was now an independent adult who preferred not to be as absorbed by his parents as Hallam had been. Both his early marriage and his choice of a career which was unconnected with anything literary had shown his need to break away.

Lord Dufferin, who served as Viceroy of India 1884–8, was a long-standing friend of Tennyson. It had been Lionel's own adventurous spirit that had taken the young man out to India, but none the less Dufferin felt that he had some responsibility for his death. In 1888 Tennyson wrote 'To the Marquess of Dufferin and Ava', a memorial poem for Lionel, in the stanza form of *In Memoriam*; obviously this brings together the deaths of these two young men, Arthur Hallam and Lionel Tennyson. With remarkable courtesy and restraint it aims to console Dufferin by reminding him that the decision to go to India was Lionel's own. And it also serves, as *In Memoriam* had done, to make grief manageable by organising it into a work of art. As in the earlier poem, mythologising and patterning the experience of loss created a defence from the intensity of its pain. Lionel went out to India because he was adventurous and courageous. Like Arthur Hallam, he showed magnificent promise:

> vii
> A soul that, watched from earliest youth,
> > And on through many a brightening year,
> > Had never swerved for craft or fear,
> By one side-path, from simple truth;

> viii
> Who might have chased and claspt Renown
> > And caught her chaplet here – and there
> > In haunts of jungle-poisoned air
> The flame of life went wavering down.

At the personal level, the poem's deepest regret is that Tennyson was not there to witness his son's burial at sea. But this also reminds us of the odd fact that Tennyson chose, all those years ago, not to go to Arthur Hallam's funeral, nor indeed to the funerals of many friends. Imagination is powerful enough to provide a controlled alternative to the unbearable reality. It successfully makes present to the bereaved father that moment:

> xi
> [. . .]When That within the coffin fell,
> Fell – and flashed into the Red Sea.[9]

Memories of that earlier death were fresh in Tennyson's mind because of a recent long letter he had had from his sister Emily, who had been engaged to Arthur Hallam. She wrote to him in March asking him to remind her of the name of the 'fair ship' which had brought Hallam's body home from Trieste. 'I have been asked more than once lately,' he replied, 'I cannot remember having heard the name.'[10]

Lionel's death intensified Tennyson's interest in spiritualism and the afterlife. He went to a seance, and asked the spirit, 'Are you my boy Lionel?'[11] These interests brought him closer in sympathy than he had been recently with his brother Frederick, whose belief in the world of the spirits was always intense. Browning recalled visiting Frederick when he lived in Jersey to find him 'wholly addicted to spirit-rapping and [spirit-]writing'.[12] Because Frederick lived abroad, first in Italy and then in the Channel Islands, the brothers seldom met, but in the summer of 1887 Tennyson chartered a yacht, belonging to Sir Allen Young, taking Hallam and his wife Audrey with him as companions. The cruise took them first to Wales, then to Jersey, where they stopped at St Helier to visit Frederick. 'The two brothers gossiped lovingly a whole day, finding when Frederick was free of Emily's presence that their concord was as complete as it had been in Somersby. The older he got, the more convinced Frederick became of the spirit world and of the ghosts in whom he believed with the credulous innocence of the great boy that he had always remained.'[13]

In 1886 Tennyson published 'The Promise of May' and 'Locksley Hall Sixty Years After' (in the same volume). Friends worked loyally to admire the play, which was, obviously, a disaster, and the poem, which was not. The poem, however, because it explicitly invites comparison with 'Locksley Hall', shows Tennyson hardening and stiffening into a series of fixed attitudes. He was now nearly eighty, and there is no doubt that he was turning in on himself and increasingly oblivious to other people or indeed other topics. The volume also included his jingoistic poem – much derided by his enemies – called 'The Fleet'. The volume was dedicated to Emily, almost as though she was the one person left in the world whom he could trust not to disagree with him politically.

'Locksley Hall Sixty Years After' is full of rage and despair over the condition of the contemporary world. Tennyson became indignant when it was suggested that it reflected his own views, but it is hard to see how it can be said not to. The old man who speaks the poem has had a son, 'Leonard', who died young as Lionel did, and he reverts to his frustrations as a young man over his relationship with 'Amy', whose role in the original 'Locksley Hall' had closely resembled the role of Rosa Baring in Tennyson's own life.

In April 1888 he wrote angrily to the translator of the German-language edition of the poem ('Locksley Hall sechzig Jahre später'):

> I object strongly to the statement in your preface that *I* am the hero in either poem. I never had a cousin Amy. Locksley Hall is an entirely imaginative edifice. My grandsons are little boys. I am not even white-haired. I never had a gray hair in my head. The whole thing is a dramatic impersonation, but I find in almost all modern criticism this absurd tendency to personalities. Some of my thought *may* come out in the poem but am I therefore the hero? *There is not one* touch of *autobiography in it from end to end.*[14]

The curmudgeonly and ranting figure who speaks the poem is easily identified with many of Tennyson's attitudes at this date. His touchiness over his poetry was compounded by his vexations with any critic who dared to suggest that some of his work was derivative. The scholarly John Churton Collins – Professor of English Literature at Mason College, Birmingham, and a tragic figure who would later commit suicide when he was not appointed to a chair at Oxford – found many references to the classical poets in Tennyson's work, and published his findings in an influential article. Edmund Gosse, who had some slight acquaintance with Tennyson and was greatly in awe of him, had been savaged in print by Churton Collins in the *Quarterly Review* in 1886. There are two versions of what Tennyson said to Gosse about Churton Collins. In one version (transmitted by Osbert Sitwell) Gosse recalled that 'happy, never-to-be-forgotten afternoon, when, still smarting from the murderous attack made upon him in the *Quarterly* a day or two earlier by Churton Collins – one whom he had considered a friend – he had arrived, in fulfilment of a promise made long before, to stay with Lord Tennyson'. Tennyson said that Churton Collins was 'a Louse upon the Locks of Literature'. In fact Gosse had invented this, as Ann Thwaite has shown. In reality Tennyson's remark was made two years later than Collins's attack on Gosse, when Gosse visited Aldworth in August 1888. 'Tennyson said: "How's Churton Collins?" and then "Would you like to know what I think of him?" Of course Gosse said he would. "Well he's a jackass. That's what he is. But don't say I said so."'[15] Churton Collins would inflame Tennyson even further by collecting his findings about the poet's allusions and quotations into his book *Illustrations of Tennyson* (1891).

Tennyson's old rival Gladstone was particularly annoyed by 'Locksley Hall Sixty Years After'; he was vexed both by its content and by its timing. His essay, '"Locksley Hall" and the Jubilee' is a magisterial rebuke to Tennyson in the course of which Gladstone set the seal on his own 'Whig' view of the progress of Britain. He believed that Britain in the 1880s was a well-managed society and a good place in which to live, and that Tennyson's bilious view of it was simply wrong; Britain had improved as a civilisation in the sixty years since the first 'Locksley Hall'. Education had spread, the condition of the poor had improved, 'fallen' women were cared for better than they had been (Gladstone himself had been particularly active in this field, and had attracted much adverse publicity for it). Social reformers such as Ruskin's friend Octavia Hill had transformed British society, and at the same time the 'imposing magnitude' of the Empire enabled that society to be a force for good throughout the world.[16] 'Will it be too audacious to submit to the prophet of the new "Locksley Hall" that the laws and works of the half-century that he reviews are not bad but good?' asked Gladstone (who then listed representative reforms in the fields of slavery, the Poor Law, combination laws, and a criminal code 'which disgraced the statute book'). 'Science and legislation have been partners in a great work' of addressing what Carlyle had earlier called 'the Condition of England question'. Tennyson had obstinately ignored the progress that had been made:

> I observe that, in the sphere of the State, the business of the last half century has been in the main a process of setting free the individual man, that he may work out his vocation without want or hindrance, as his Maker will have him do. If, instead of this, Government is to work out his vocation for him, I for one am not sanguine as to the result.

Identifying Tennyson as a 'Prophet', Gladstone wrote that:

> The multiplication and better formations of the institutions of benevolence among us are but symptomatic indications of a wider and deeper change: a silent but more extensive and practical acknowledgement of the great second commandment, of the duties of wealth to poverty, of strength to weakness, of knowledge to ignorance, in a word of man to man. And the sum of the matter seems to be that upon the whole, and in a degree, we who lived fifty, sixty, seventy years back, and are living now, have lived into a gentler time; that the public conscience has grown more tender, as indeed was very

needful; and that, in matters of practice, at sight of evils formerly regarded with indifference or even connivance, it now not only winces but rebels: that upon the whole the race has been reaping, and not scattering; earning, and not wasting, and that, without it being said the old Prophet is wrong, it may be said that the young Prophet was unquestionably right.

The Queen had now reigned for sixty years, and as his parting shot, Gladstone observed that 'Justice does not require, nay rather she forbids, that the Jubilee of the Queen be marred by tragic tones.'[17]

After Lionel's death, the number of people whom Tennyson was able to trust, or willing to tolerate, steadily dwindled. His daughter-in-law Eleanor had not been particularly happy in her marriage to Lionel (there had been infidelity on his part, possibly also on hers). When she became engaged to Augustine Birrell, there was much the same hostility as there had been many years earlier when Emily Tennyson, after Arthur Hallam's death, chose to marry her courageous but unexciting husband Captain Jesse. In his boorish way Tennyson accosted Augustine Birrell, asking, 'Why do you want to force an entrance into my family?' It was apparently a relief to Eleanor when she was finally free of her connection with the Tennysons. There is no indication of a break or quarrel, but her letters to them dropped any pretence of intimacy and became chiefly communications about her sons by Lionel. Emily was particularly resentful about Eleanor's second marriage. She told the obedient Hallam that 'Poor Eleanor has deeply wronged us & it is, no doubt, difficult to be just to her.'[18]

In September 1888, Tennyson had a setback brought on chiefly by exposure to damp and miserable weather at Aldworth. He had always had gout; this now became arthritic gout, which in turn gave way to two months of serious illness. His established routine now was that he would spend the summer at Aldworth but the winter back at his beloved Farringford, and this year the return to Farringford was later than usual – he could finally travel (by special train) in November. But his residual strength was remarkable. After a difficult winter in Farringford, where he lost a great deal of weight and became very weak, he was strong enough in the spring of 1889 to borrow a yacht from another of his wealthy friends – Lord Brassey – and explore again his favourite Arthurian country, the coast and rivers of Devon and Cornwall. For his eightieth birthday, celebrated at Aldworth in August of that year, he made a special effort, as old men like to do, to appear youthful and energetic, and he was as excited as a child by the hundreds of letters and telegrams of congratulation that came in from his public. 'I don't know what I have done to make people feel like that towards me,' he is quoted as saying.[19]

In July of 1889 there was a distressing episode involving two of Tennyson's friends, one living and the other now dead. Aldis Wright brought out a *Literary Remains of Edward Fitzgerald*, which included a private letter written by Fitzgerald in 1861 about the death of Elizabeth Barrett Browning:

> Mrs Browning's Death is rather a relief to me, I must say: no more Aurora Leighs, thank God! A Woman of real Genius, I know: but what is the upshot of it all? And her Sex had better mind the Kitchen and their Children; and perhaps the Poor: except in such things as little Novels, they only devote themselves to what men do much better, leaving that which Men do worse or not at all.[20]

Browning was bitterly, savagely hurt* by this and immediately published a short, pithy verse attack on Fitzgerald's memory in *The Athenaeum*: 'You, FitzGerald, whom by ear and eye / she never knew, "thanked God my wife was dead".' His pain toppled his judgement: 'How to return your thanks would task my wits: / Kicking you seems the common lot of curs.'[21] Browning immediately regretted publishing this ('I believe I might preferably have left the thing to its proper contempt'), but it was too late. Tennyson was distressed by the living friend's fury with the dead and wanted to smooth the matter over. Browning was not to be mollified. He wrote to Emily to ask how she would feel if Fitzgerald had written about her husband with 'a thankfulness for the relief felt that an illness of their author guaranteed no more annoyance from "Idylls" and "In Memoriams" (the exact parallel is too abhorrent for me to think out and write out)'.[22] Emily tried to calm him: 'Ally [Tennyson] bids me say with his love that Fitz never meant what you have him to mean.'[23]

Browning glanced obliquely at his own pain when he wrote to Tennyson to congratulate him on his eightieth birthday (6 August 1889): 'your poetry will be a wonder and delight to all those appointed

---

*He had a brief spurt of rage against Tennyson himself, because when he first saw Fitzgerald's offending letter he thought it had been addressed to Tennyson, 'whose adulatory lick-spittle he always was'. (Hood, p. 321.) Fitzgerald was never a lickspittle; some of his reservations about Tennyson's work were printed in the *Remains*, but Tennyson had long been aware of his views and was not bothered.

to come after'.[24] *Your* poetry, unlike poor Elizabeth's; but Tennyson did not pick this up, and replied simply (and truthfully), 'I thank you with my whole heart and being for your noble and affectionate letter, and with my whole heart and being I return your friendship'[25].

In October 1889 Tennyson crossed from Lymington to Yarmouth, on what was now his annual migration from the summer at Aldworth to the winter at Farringford. While the boat was bringing him the short distance across the Solent and over the sandbank, he suddenly composed the single lyrical sentence of 'Crossing the Bar'. This is a poem which has become part of the culture, still often requested to be read at funerals. By this stage of his life Tennyson had moved steadily away from the 'honest doubt' which gives *In Memoriam* welcome tension and energy, and this poem is securely Christian in a robust and direct way.

A nurse was now in full-time employment and she – Nurse Durham – was the first person to see the poem. Hallam Tennyson was the second. Hallam created a consciously historic moment – much quoted subsequently – in which he told his father that the poem was 'the crown of your life's work'. In reality, though, he said, 'That is one of the most beautiful poems ever written', which is less sonorous, but higher praise. Tennyson answered, 'it came in a moment',[26] and instructed Hallam that it was to be placed last in all editions of his poems.[27]

Demeter and Other Poems therefore duly had 'Crossing the Bar' in its position as the last poem. Many of the poems in the volume were elegiac either in subject or in tone. The deaths of contemporaries were increasingly threatening to leave Tennyson the sole survivor of his generation. Browning's *Asolando* was published on the same day as *Demeter*, and with stark and brutal timing that was also the day of Browning's death. Tennyson stirred himself and brought his influence to bear on the decision to bury Browning in Westminster Abbey, and he was invited to be a pall-bearer. His frailty was such that Hallam acted for him. Soon after that came the death of William Allingham, whom Tennyson had befriended, rescued from his intellectual isolation in Ireland and found a reliable and genial companion for many years. Tennyson felt increasingly alone.

Tennyson suffered an illness which he himself referred to as 'rheumatic gout' which weakened him and caused him a great deal of pain: there were exhausting episodes in the winter of 1888 and then again for most of the summer of 1889. He was carefully tended by Hallam and by Emily, and also by the faithful, irreverent Nurse Durham. Nurse Durham teased him and could bully him a bit, and this treatment was probably better for him than the anxious ministrations that Emily and Hallam sought to offer. He often seemed close to death, and all vexations or obligations were taken from him by his ever-attentive son. In August 1889 he was in touch with a correspondent for *The Times*, one Franklin L. Burr, saying, 'I have had nine months of rheumatic gout, which my doctor says at my age would have made an end of nine men out of ten, says too that for the present I had better write no letters.'[28] Writing no letters, of a business kind, had in fact been a luxury that he had afforded himself for many years, his wife and then his son having taken over that responsibility.

By the early spring of 1890 he had recovered. He was now eighty years old, and had reached a stage of his fame and a time of his life when every sighting of him seemed worth recording for posterity. His distinguished Cambridge friend Montagu Butler, whom Tennyson had known since the 1850s (and who was by this date Master of Trinity) called on him on 28 March 1890.

> We went to tea at Farringford, and found him in his little sun-trap of a summer-house, the evening sun playing full upon us, and bringing into perfect beauty the green lawn, the spreading trees, and the clumps of daffodils. He began by speaking of himself as depressed, but soon smiled away all such symptoms, and made us laugh with a story of the Duke of Wellington.[29]

He had recently published 'Crossing the Bar' (in *Demeter and Other Poems*, December 1889), and liked to remind friends that the lyrical impulse had not deserted him with that poem – he had written it in about twenty minutes.

The *Demeter* volume of 1889 contains a remarkable poem in which Tennyson seemed to sum up his writing life, 'Merlin and the Gleam'. He wrote that the Gleam 'signifies in my poem the higher poetic imagination'. 'Elegiac Stanzas suggested by a picture of Peele Castle', a Wordsworth poem that Tennyson loved contained the haunting line:

> add the gleam
> The light that never was, on sea or land,
> The consecration, and the Poet's dream.[30]

The gleam is the vision or promise granted to all great poets, Keats, Wordsworth and Coleridge among them, convincing them of the authentic truthfulness of the imagination. There is no reference to these other poets in the poem's text, though. Its dramatic figures are Merlin the dying magician and the young Mariner, just embarking on adventure, who in his innocence and optimism feels like a youthful Ulysses:

> O Young Mariner,
> Down to the haven,
> Call your companions,
> Launch your vessel,
> And crowd your canvas.[31]

The mature Ulysses of Tennyson's youthful poem had also figured his vision as 'gleam': 'Gleams that untravelled world, whose margin fades.'

The poem does not work as a chronological account of Tennyson's writing career, and indeed all attempts to order Tennyson's writing into a neat chronology are bound to fail. The fact that seventeen years elapsed between the writing of the earliest completed stanzas of *In Memoriam* and the publication of the whole poem demonstrates the problem. (The relationship between the twelve discrete parts of *Idylls of the King* displays the same problem, over an even longer period.) In this late poem Tennyson himself seems to brush the problem aside. Hallam Tennyson printed an inner chronology of this poem based on his father's own authority. In his account section III of the poem refers to the hostile reviews ('the croak of a Raven') of the 1832 volume of *Poems*, while in section VII the death of Arthur Hallam deprived him of all motivation:

> Clouds and darkness
> Closed upon Camelot;
> Arthur had vanished
> I knew not whither,
> The king who loved me,
> And cannot die.[32]

But there is an obvious problem with this: Hallam died in 1833. To resolve it, Sir Charles Tennyson thought that section III, beginning 'once at the Croak of a raven who crossed it', referred to 'the family troubles which followed Dr Tennyson's death in 1831, and the attempts made by the old man of the Wolds to divert Alfred from his determination to devote himself to poetry'. In this reading, much of the poem, sections III to VI, would then have to refer to Tennyson's outpouring of new work during the most fertile period of his friendship with Hallam, and sections VII and VIII would refer to the setback of his bereavement and then his ability to resume work and develop further.[33] While that sequence is possible, it seems more likely that the poem simply displays the asynchronic nature of the poetic imagination. All the events obliquely referred to in the poem had contributed to Tennyson's growth as an artist, and the order in which they happened mattered less than the fact that the memories were still vividly with him.

Arthur Hallam, present in 'Merlin and the Gleam' as 'the king who loved me [me being Tennyson] and cannot die', reappears with remarkable emotional force in 'Vastness', a poem which is another striking instance of the energy that Tennyson could summon at this advanced age. The theme is one he had explored since his young manhood: if death is the end, has human life any meaning at all? It is an uneven poem, but every line of it is sincerely meant, and it closes with a passionate recollection of Arthur Hallam:

> What is it all, if we all of us end but in being our own
>   corpse-coffins at last,
> Swallowed in Vastness, lost in Silence, drowned
>   in the deeps of a meaningless Past?
> What but a murmur of gnats in the gloom,
>   or a moment's anger of bees in their hive? –
>   * * * *
> Peace, let it be! for I loved him, and love him
>   for ever: the dead are not dead but alive.[34]

In early 1890, Tennyson became ill at Farringford, and because he was so famous, each stage of his illness was now a national event to be recorded (and amplified) in the press. As the weather improved he steadily recovered, and by May he was taking exercise and walking up to Beacon Hill above Freshwater with his dogs as he had done for many years. In May he was visited by representatives of Thomas Edison's company, bringing with him their recording device, and Tennyson recorded 'Blow, bugle, blow', 'The Charge of the Light Brigade' and 'Come into the garden, Maud'. Of these, 'The Charge of the Light Brigade' can be heard most clearly by listeners in the twenty-first century. The reading is like the performance of a singer, metrically careful and displaying remarkable breath control. The sense of the poem disappears under the organ-roll of the reading.

Back at Aldworth and visiting London in the summer of 1890, Tennyson formed a kind of rapprochement with Gladstone. The two old men had been distant from each other since Gladstone's review of 'Locksley Hall Sixty Years After', but now they sought reconciliation. At the time of Lionel's death in 1886, Tennyson had been heavily influenced against Gladstone by the Queen's prejudices, but now he even came to acknowledge that Gladstone had been right to pursue Home Rule for Ireland. Gladstone later wrote: 'He and I had both lived with great loneliness after beginning in the midst of large bands of friends.' They both recognised that the similarities between them outweighed the differences.[35]

The old man was increasingly dependent upon his wife, and his love for her was correspondingly deepening. This is marked obliquely in 'Romney's Remorse', based on a story found in one of his late friend Fitzgerald's letters, which had just been published in his *Letters and Literary Remains* (1889). The story set out by Fitzgerald was that the artist George Romney, having married young, then lived most of his life apart from his wife, having been over-persuaded by Sir Joshua Reynolds' remark that 'marriage spoilt an artist'. As an old man Romney goes back to his wife and she nurses him until he dies. Tennyson may have been recognising that he had inflicted pain on Emily. The very long engagement had not been entirely a matter of financial circumstance, and they could have married several years earlier than they did had Tennyson not hesitated to commit himself. The poet had needed solitude, independence and the somewhat vagrant life that he was living in the 1830s and 1840s. Again, after their marriage he sought life away from her in long independent visits to London to immerse himself in its social and literary life or tours and holidays apart from her. This was partly a matter of her physical frailty and partly his choice (which she would never question). He certainly saw something of himself in the artist Romney, who now in old age says to his wife, 'I love you more than when we married.'[36]

In the last of his published volumes, *The Death of Oenone*, he offered Emily a tribute in the form of a dedicatory poem. Farringford, the most loved of his homes, was reasserting its claims, and he wrote 'June Bracken and Heather' for their forty-first wedding anniversary in the setting of the high sunny downs of the Isle of Wight. This poem's lyrical outpouring within a single sentence shows astonishing strength and energy.

There on the top of the down,
The wild heather round me and over me June's high blue,
When I looked at the bracken so bright and the heather so
  brown,
I thought to myself I would offer this book to you,
This, and my love together,
To you that are seventy-seven,
With a faith as clear as the heights of the June-blue heaven,
And a fancy as summer-new
As the green of the bracken amid the gloom of the heather.[37]

Tennyson's good health continued into early 1891, and his spirits rose. His personality was changing – guests at Farringford in the winter of 1891–2 noticed how gentle he had become, how the rages and bursts of prejudice were now abating. In June, he and Hallam borrowed a yacht to visit the Channel Islands, and he visited his brother Frederick again. Once back at Aldworth, however, he found that he had become more frail and could not take his usual walks. In July he had a recurrence of the gout, and this time the illness persisted and he weakened steadily through the late summer. Hallam and Emily were both aware that he would now probably not recover, and as news of his frailty spread, a steady stream of visitors came to Aldworth. Among them was the ever-loyal Henry Graham Dakyns, now an established family man, who had retired from teaching to a handsome house near Haslemere.

Tennyson's eighty-third birthday, in August, prompted a flood of greetings. He was now seen as a national hero, and these valedictory gestures were appropriately triumphal in tone. Proofs of *The Death of Oenone*, to be published by Macmillan, were brought to him from London to check. He had chosen to place the poem for Emily, 'June Bracken and Heather', as the first in the volume, to be followed immediately by a loving tribute to his friend Benjamin Jowett, 'To the Master of Balliol'. Among the poems he had decided to include were several in which he was openly preparing for his own death: 'Doubt and Prayer', 'Faith' and 'God and the Universe', and the volume closed with a last Laureate poem – an elegy for the Duke of Clarence (Queen Victoria's grandson, dead at the age of 28) – in which he urged death as a transition, not an ending:

The face of Death is toward the Sun of Life,
His shadow darkens earth: his truer name
Is 'Onward.'[38]

He was thinking of all those who were no longer there to visit him – Arthur Hallam, his son Lionel, his brother Charles, James Spedding, Sir John Simeon, Henry Lushington and Edward Fitzgerald among them – when he wrote the shortest and most striking of these meditations on death. In this lyric, 'onward' – the thought, if not the word – is again the motif. 'The Silent Voices' addresses the dead:

> When the dumb Hour, clothed in black,
> Brings the Dreams about my bed,
> Call me not so often back,
> Silent Voices of the dead,
> Toward the lowland ways behind me,
> And the sunlight that is gone!
> Call me rather, silent voices,
> Forward to the starry track
> Glimmering up the heights beyond me
> On, and always on!³⁹

He continued to worry about the production of his plays. Bram Stoker had been Henry Irving's secretary and touring manager since 1878 and in that capacity had had regular dealings with Tennyson over his plays. He visited in late September to talk about plans for a possible production of *Becket*: Tennyson was strikingly frail, 'wearing a black skull-cap, from under which his long dark hair fell down thin and straggling'. The visit and the thought that the play would be staged lifted his spirits.⁴⁰ (*Becket* would be produced by Irving in London in February the following year, and thereafter had a successful tour in America.) On Monday 3 October he asked Hallam to give him his Shakespeare. He held the volume, wanting to read a scene from *Cymbeline*, but was distressed to find that he could not see it clearly.

The doctor who treated him at Farringford, Dr Dabbs, was now in attendance at Aldworth. On 3 October Dabbs visited London, and when he returned he told Tennyson that he had seen Irving. Tennyson immediately wanted news about the plans for *Becket*: 'It will be successful on the stage with Irving,' he said, adding 'I suppose I shall never see it.' Some of his old anger about adverse criticisms surfaced. 'They did not do me justice with *The Promise of May*, but,' he said, 'I can trust Irving – Irving will do me justice.'⁴¹

On 5 October he was much weaker, and he asked for his Shakespeare again. He raised the book and opened it at one of his favourite scenes: the moment of reconciliation in *Cymbeline* where Posthumus and Imogen have at last come to a full understanding. The evening of that day found no change in him. Emily, Hallam and Hallam's wife Audrey stayed with him, and he died at two in the morning of Thursday 6 October, Shakespeare still in his lap.

'Crossing the Bar' is much more than a famous anthology piece. Its imagery recalls 'Break, break, break' and 'Ulysses'; indeed, it complements and completes 'Ulysses'. Its relationship with that brief early masterpiece is reminiscent of the oblique connection between the marriage poem which Tennyson placed at the end of *In Memoriam* and the main body of that complex and contradictory set of elegies. 'Crossing the Bar' gently but firmly declares that it is Christian, but permits us to listen to the pagan tonality of all the great poetry that preceded it. As in 'Ulysses' all those years earlier, strength coexists with stoical acceptance of the death that is approaching, and the final journey towards it is still controlled by the heroic voyager's will:

> Sunset and evening star,
>   And one clear call for me!
> And may there be no moaning of the bar,
>   When I put out to sea,
>
> But such a tide as moving seems asleep,
>   Too full for sound and foam,
> When that which drew from out the boundless deep
>   Turns again home.
>
> Twilight and evening bell,
>   And after that the dark!
> And may there be no sadness of farewell,
>   When I embark;
>
> For though from out our bourne of Time and Place
>   The flood may bear me far,
> I hope to see my Pilot face to face
>   When I have crost the bar.

Epilogue: The poet and the pageant, 1892

The bridal garland falls upon the bier,
The shadow of a crown, that o'er him hung,
Has vanish'd in the shadow cast by Death.
  So princely, tender, truthful, reverent, pure –
Mourn! That a world-wide Empire mourns with you,
That all the Thrones are clouded by your loss,
Were slender solace. Yet be comforted;
For if this earth be ruled by Perfect Love,
Then, after his brief range of blameless days,
The toll of funeral in an Angel ear
Sounds happier than the merriest marriage-bell.

This is the first part of the brief elegy, 'The Death of the Duke of Clarence and Avondale', written for Albert Victor, 'Prince Eddy', the oldest son of the Prince of Wales (and thus second in line as heir to the throne), who had died suddenly in an influenza epidemic in January 1892. Tennyson was fragile himself at this date, but this young man's death was poignant for him as all such endings were, following the disaster of Lionel's death, and the poem is appropriately pitched for the emotional needs of the grieving Queen. Prince Eddy had recently become engaged to marry Princess Mary of Teck. The Queen wrote to Tennyson to thank him for the poem, and expressed her anguish over the sheer symmetry of the situation: 'Was there ever a more terrible contrast? A wedding with bright hopes turned into a funeral in the very chapel where the former was to have taken place.'[1]

Tennyson was making this death into part of a pageant. Literature, history, mythology, the particulars of his own life and the large canvas of the monarchy's public life were coinciding in his mind. In this last year of his life the sick old man had constructed the small, opinionated, narrow-minded monarch into a kind of deity, and in the process he was turning himself into a mythological being. The playing of the role of poet, so important to him when he embraced his romantic Spanish self-image in the early 1830s, had adapted itself into the playing of the role of bard, an Olympian chronicler of portentous historical events. Everything in his private experience was now being woven into this process. He was the great lonely survivor of the mid-Victorian giants, he had outlived Carlyle, Dickens, Browning, Thackeray, Trollope and George Eliot, and literary fashion at the time of his death had taken up the wholly alien figure of Oscar Wilde.

After two world wars and the violent diminution of everything that Tennyson meant by the word 'Britain', it is hard to enter into the state of mind that takes his patriotic visions seriously. But in his day his visions were accepted unquestioningly. In 1878, a prosperous and straightforward Newcastle man, David Richardson, wrote to Tennyson, in complete seriousness, urging him to visit the house that he had built for himself. He lived in the (then) fashionable west end of Newcastle, where the mansions of the successful had an agreeable view of the Tyne and their wives were not troubled by the smoke and noise from the shipyards in which the city's wealth was generated. The letter is from The Gables, Elswick Road, Newcastle-on-Tyne, 'within ½ hours walk of the Railway Station'. Richardson urged Tennyson if he ever should visit Newcastle to come to his house:

> To look at the staircase-window of this house, you would be pleased with the Lessons drawn from the 'Idyls of the King' which are here shown. They are in 6 pictures in coloured glass, made some two years ago, by one of the best makers of stained glass in this town [. . .] [he gives the subjects and quotations from the poetry accompanying them:] King Arthur Crowned Merlin persuading him to take the sword, Edyrn overthrown by Geraint, The quest for the Sweet Vision of the Holy Grail – setting out from the gateway, Percival & the Hermit in the Valley of Humiliation – Galahad standing by – the Vision, Dagonet & Sir Tristram – the doorway of the great Hall – the jester point [sic] to the sky, The sword cast away – the king in the barge wounded, discourses with Sir Bedivere, moonlight.[2]

He ends modestly and with dignity, saying that he does not expect a reply but that he would welcome the poet any time that he cared to come. This letter shows how deeply Tennyson's vision of the world coincided with, and was fed by, the expectations of a sturdy middle-class audience which felt enhanced and ennobled by the decorous pageantry of his medievalism. Wagner's historical and mythological music dramas were transforming the German people's vision of themselves in the same way in the same period, and often with overlapping material from Arthurian romance (as in *Parsifal* and *Tristan und Isolde*). The newly wealthy and powerful peoples of Europe needed to feel that their wealth and power were the culmination of a great history, and these artists gave them that history. The destruction of all this was already on its way, and had been coming with the inevitability of a slow avalanche since the Franco-Prussian War of 1870. From that stemmed the growing aggressiveness of Bismarck's newly unified Germany and the threat felt by the rest of Europe. Those flexible enough to read the evidence could see already that Britain was about to lose its pre-eminence as a world power. From that point of view the dates of Tennyson's birth and his death could not have been more propitious and opportune. He was born at the inception of Britain's century of greatness and he was spared the spectacle of its conclusion.

The Queen, who at the time of Tennyson's death was the living figure who had become central to his mythical vision of Britain, said decent things about him immediately after his death. Hallam Tennyson composed a lengthy telegram to the monarch:

> My Father's last conscious effort was to call 'Hallam' and whisper to my Mother, 'God bless you my joy.' As he awaited death the full moon poured through the oriel window on his grand face and on his hand clasping the Shakespeare which he had been reading. Outside the window was the great landscape that he could see from where he lay flooded with glory. It was the noblest imaginable picture of the passing of King Arthur.

One could wish that Hallam had given a more personal and authentic expression of loss. His grief for his father was real, but what he offered the Queen was further pageantry, a theatrical set piece which might have been scripted for one of Henry Irving's lavishly expensive productions. The Queen herself was slightly more down to earth. She wrote in her diary: 'I heard that dear old Ld Tennyson had breathed his last [. . .].' But relishing pageantry as she did, she also chose to quote Hallam's deathbed scene in her diary: 'He died with his hand on his Shakespeare, and the moon shining full into the window, and over him.'³

Tennyson himself hated 'the gloomy pomp of funerals, black plumes, black coaches, etc.' and because of his known feelings there was some hesitation over whether he should be buried in Westminster Abbey or should have a simple funeral at Farringford. Emily and Hallam's preference was clear, though. The funeral in Westminster Abbey, where Tennyson was interred close to Chaucer and Robert Browning, was effectively a state occasion; the dislike of 'black plumes' meant that the coffin travelled from Waterloo station to Westminster Abbey 'on a simple, covered van'.[4]

The occasion was reported in detail to the Queen by Hallam Tennyson (who, having inherited his father's barony was now himself Lord Tennyson) in a letter of 13 October 1892:

> We took him from our home by the light of the sunset and the stars in one of our carriages lined with moss and flowers and covered with a white pall woven by the Workwomen of the North at Keswick and embroidered with a wreath of the ancient poet's bay, wild roses, and the last stanza from his 'Crossing the Bar.' We did not venture to trouble your Majesty, but through Sir Dighton Probyn, the Prince of Wales gave us permission to cover my Father's coffin with the Flag of England. Your Majesty's Guards gave us one of theirs and it was buried with him.
>
> The service today was most beautiful and impressive, simple and heart up lifting. Old Balaclava heroes, Gordon boys from the Gordon home at Woking, and English, Scottish, and Irish Volunteers lined the nave.[5]

It is not clear that the Queen wanted or needed all the detail that Hallam gave here, and 'one of our carriages' (as Hallam gives it) was actually a simple waggonette (in keeping with what Tennyson himself would have preferred). The old man who had died was neither King Arthur nor any other kind of hero; he was a visionary and a supreme craftsman who pursued wealth and fame in ways that his age applauded. The piety and propriety of his relationship with the Queen operated in the same way as did the pious prologue and epilogue to his own masterpiece, *In Memoriam*. They anchored him within his period, but they could not contain or compromise the strangeness, the strength, the individuality and the timelessness of his extraordinary talent.

In this year Emily Tennyson was increasingly alone. She had lost not only her husband but also a number of those closest to her; her beloved cousin Catherine Rawnsley* died shortly before Tennyson, and Edmund Lushington, Benjamin Jowett and Anne Weld, Emily's sister, followed soon after. Emily now preferred to be known as Emily, Lady Tennyson, in order to distinguish herself from her daughter-in-law Audrey, who

---

*Whose husband, Drummond, had married Alfred and Emily in 1850.

as Hallam's wife was now Lady Tennyson. Emily had been delighted when Hallam married Audrey, but their years of living together – the older and the younger Tennysons – had caused tensions between the two women.

Emily invested her energy in her music as well as in her family. She had always had her own creative life in parallel with Alfred's; her musical talent was minor, but it meant a lot to her. She played the piano quite well and wrote a number of compositions, many of them settings of her husband's verses (she wrote settings of songs for *The Foresters*, but in the event new versions by Arthur Sullivan were used in the actual production). However, through the enthusiasm of a young Polish pianist, seven of Emily's settings had a public airing at St James's Hall in 1891, and received a respectful reception.[6] Once Tennyson was dead, though, her remarkable will and energy were devoted to the *Memoir* of Tennyson. This was Hallam's work, but mother and son in fact created it jointly. The *Memoir* suppressed some things, and highlighted others. Ann Thwaite says that Emily was 'quite often less inclined to censorship than Hallam was',[7] and that the pageantry of the *Memoir* arose from his choices and judgements rather than his mother's.[8] Nevertheless, she and Hallam agreed on one thing: the *Memoir* would include nothing personal, nothing that the poet himself would have regarded as private, and nothing at all that glanced at a private life before or outside his marriage. To this end they contacted family and friends from as wide a circle of correspondents as they could, and many of these people agreed, if often reluctantly, to surrender the letters they had received from Tennyson, thousands of which were then destroyed. Emily and Hallam were doing what they thought Tennyson might have wished; at the same time they were creating a version of the poet which suited their own preferences. The Tennysons were now unassailably grand; Somersby was very far in the past. The version of Tennyson that they created was 'Victorian' in both the strong and the limiting senses of that word.

Emily also oversaw in great detail the four printed volumes of 'Materials for a Life of A.T.', set up in print as Tennyson had set up his own 'trial editions' for private reflection and revision before committing a work to the public gaze. A new edition of *The Works of Alfred Lord Tennyson* appeared in 1895, to her satisfaction; by then she had finished checking the proofs of the 'Materials', and the grandchildren could take up more space in her life. There were five boys. Lionel and Eleanor had had three children, Alfred ('Ally') Browning Stanley (b. 1878), Charles Bruce Locker (b. 1879, author of the 1949 biography of Tennyson) and Michael Sellwood (b. 1883). Michael Sellwood was kept out of sight and mind by the family; he was disabled, he could not develop normally and he spent his life being cared for in institutions. Because Hallam had married much later than Lionel, his two sons had been born towards the end of Tennyson's life: Lionel Hallam (b. 1889) and Alfred Aubrey (b. 1891). In 1896 Hallam fathered a third baby, the sixth grandson, Harold Courtney Tennyson; this was a source of great pleasure to Emily, now frail and visibly sinking.

Alfred and Charlie, the two teenage grandsons, had been brought up by Emily and Alfred after Lionel's early death, and they were close to their grandmother; in August 1896 they were at Aldworth for their school holidays. Hallam's little boys, Lionel and Alfred Aubrey, had always made their home with their grandparents. Audrey, their mother, knew that Hallam had much more consideration for his parents than he did for her and his children, and she quietly suffered as long as she had to stay in this situation.

Emily Tennyson was a stoic; she became ill with influenza in August 1896 but concealed her state of health from her family as long as she could. Her lungs became congested, and the family doctor, still the faithful Dr Dabbs, told Hallam on 9 August that she could not recover. She died the following day. Hallam recorded that:

> Emily [. . .] asked to see her grandsons, Lionel and [Alfred] Aubrey. A few moments before the end she spoke again: 'I tried to be a good wife', she said, and when Hallam assured her that none could have been a better wife to his father, she answered, 'I might have done more.'9

Emily was buried at Freshwater; her body travelled from Aldworth by train and then boat. The church at Freshwater is a small, beautiful parish church, and the tomb for Lady Tennyson out in the churchyard is a very handsome one; she lies by the memorial for her son Lionel, who had been buried at sea in 1886.

The intention behind Hallam's work on the *Memoir* and the 'Materials' was to confer immortality on a great man. The effect of it has tended towards the opposite, by binding Tennyson closely into his period and making him look more solidly Victorian, in the pejorative sense, than he actually was. The *Memoir* is a compromised text. Still, Hallam as the only surviving son had memories that no one else could provide. Some of his monument to his father is well written, and much of the information in it is available from no other source. In that it is the first biography of Tennyson, it is unquestionably a major book. One can only imagine the wealth of papers that Hallam and his mother had in front of them as they prepared this work.

To give so much labour to the posthumous public image of Tennyson, though, was to obscure what he actually was. This poet, the heir of Keats and Shelley, the lyricist of unsurpassed emotional force and metrical versatility, needs to be released from the massive carapace of his Victorian reputation. It is this poet who claimed, when he was probably about eighteen years old, that poetry has its own absolute authority and that the poet's vision is given to him as though by nature's amoral and imperative forces:

> Vex not thou the poet's mind
>   With thy shallow wit:
> Vex not thou the poet's mind;
>   For thou canst not fathom it.
> Clear and bright it should be ever,
> Flowing like a crystal river;
> Bright as light, and clear as wind.*[10]

Tennyson was far more than a Victorian. His early work arose directly out of the romantic movement, and after the accession of Victoria herself in 1837 he existed on the fringes of the society of which she was head; a romantic in an anti-romantic age. At the same time, the historical context is absolutely necessary for the understanding of his life as a whole. Everything that makes Tennyson 'Victorian' – the hunger for money and status, together with the pageantry of the Arthurian poems and the well-upholstered ponderousness of the historical plays – is essential to the story. To keep both versions of Tennyson firmly in mind enables us to see the personal, social and economic forces that made him what he was.

---

*This echoes Keats's *Lamia*: 'Do not all charms fly / At the mere touch of cold philosophy?'; 'Philosophy will clip an Angel's wings.'

Bibliography

UNPUBLISHED MATERIAL

Collections of Tennyson manuscripts at Trinity College, Cambridge; Cambridge University Library; the Fitzwilliam Museum, Cambridge; the Houghton Library, Harvard; Boston Public Library; the Beinecke Rare Book and Manuscript Library, Yale; the Tennyson Research Centre, Lincoln.

Documents deposited at the Lincolnshire Archives Office by Sir Charles Tennyson on behalf of the Lord Tennyson (relating to the Turner and Tennyson families).

Dr Tennyson's Commonplace Book, Tennyson Research Centre, Lincoln.

J. M. Heath, A Pocket Commonplace Book, Fitzwilliam Museum, Cambridge.

John Kemble, 'The Kemble Letters' (letters among Cambridge friends, June 1827–October 1831), Dunedin, New Zealand; photocopies in the Tennyson Research Centre, Lincoln.

John Rashdall, Journal, 1833–1835. Bodleian Library, Oxford.

'Materials for a Life of A.T.', n.d. 4 vols [1895], eds. Hallam and Emily Tennyson.

PUBLISHED SOURCES

Allen, M. D. *Essay on the Classification of the Insane*. London: John Taylor, 1838.

Allen, Peter. *The Cambridge Apostles: The Early Years*. Cambridge: Cambridge University Press, 1978.

Allingham, Helen, and Paterson, Arthur. *The Homes of Tennyson* (with 24 plates by Helen Allingham). London: A. & C. Black, 1905.

Allingham, William. *A Diary 1824–1889*. Harmondsworth: Penguin, 1985 (ed. John Julius Norwich).

Aplin, John. *'A True Affection': Anne Thackeray Ritchie and the Tennysons*. Lincoln: The Tennyson Society, 2006.

Argyll, George John Douglas Campbell, Eighth Duke. *Geology: Its Past and Present. A lecture delivered to the members of the Glasgow Athenaeum, January 13, 1859*.

Argyll, Ina (Dowager Duchess of Argyll) (ed.). *Autobiography and Memoirs of George Douglas, Eighth Duke of Argyll, K.G., K.T.*

(1823–1900), 2 vols. London: John Murray, 1906.

Asquith, Margot. *The Autobiography of Margot Asquith* (first published 1920), 2 vols. London: Penguin, 1936

Austin, Alfred. *The Autobiography of Alfred Austin, Poet Laureate.* London: Macmillan, 1911.

Austin, Alfred. *The Poetry of the Period.* London: Richard Bentley, 1870.

Batchelor, John. *Lady Trevelyan and the Pre-Raphaelite Brotherhood.* London: Chatto & Windus, 2006.

Beer, John (ed.). *Coleridge's Poems.* London: Dent, 1963.

Blocksidge, Martin. *A Life Lived Quickly: Tennyson's Friend Arthur Hallam and His Legend.* Brighton: Sussex Academic Press, 2011.

Bradley, A. C. *A Commentary on Tennyson's 'In Memoriam'.* London: Macmillan, 1901.

Brendon, Piers. *Hawker of Morwenstow.* London: Jonathan Cape, 1983.

Brookfield, Frances. *The Cambridge Apostles.* London: Isaac Pitman, 1906.

Browning, Robert. *Men and Women.* (eds. Ian Jack and Robert Inglesfield). Oxford: Clarendon Press, 1995.

Buckley, J. H. *Tennyson: The Growth of a Poet.* Cambridge, Mass.: Harvard University Press, 1960.

Campbell, Nancie. *Tennyson in Lincoln: A Catalogue of the Collections in the Research Centre*, 2 vols. Lincoln: Tennyson Society, 1971, 1973.

Cannon, John (ed.). *The Oxford Companion to British History.* Oxford: Oxford University Press, 1997.

Carlyle, Thomas. *The Life of John Sterling.* London: Chapman and Hall, 1897.

Carlyle, Thomas. *Sartor Resartus, Lectures on Heroes, Chartism, Past and Present.* London: Chapman and Hall, 1888.

Carroll, Lewis. *Alice's Adventures in Wonderland* [1865] and *Through the Looking-Glass* [1871]. Oxford: Oxford World's Classics, 2009.

Chambers, Robert. *Vestiges of the Natural History of Creation* [1844]. Edinburgh: W. and R. Chambers, 1880.

Champneys, Basil. *Memoirs and Correspondence of Coventry Patmore.* London: Bell, 1900.

Cheshire, Jim (ed.). *Tennyson Transformed: Alfred Lord Tennyson and Visual Culture.* Farnham: Lund Humphries, 2009.

Cohen, Morton N. (ed.). *The Letters of Lewis Carroll*, 2 vols. London: Macmillan, 1879.

Collins, John Churton. *Illustrations of Tennyson.* London: Chatto & Windus, 1891.

Cronin, Richard. 'The Palace of Art and Tennyson's Cambridge', Essays in Criticism, 43 (1993).

Daniell, Christopher. 'Edward Tennyson in York, 1832–33', Notes and Queries, NS 34 (1988) 1, and 'Edward Tennyson in York, 1833–1890', Notes and Queries, NS 35 (1989) 3.

Desmond, Adrian, and Moore, James. Darwin. London: Penguin, 1992.

Douglas-Fairhurst, Robert, and Perry, Seamus (eds). Tennyson Among the Poets. Oxford: Oxford University Press, 2009.

Dyson, Hope, and Tennyson, Charles (eds). Dear and Honoured Lady: The Correspondence between Queen Victoria and Alfred Tennyson. London: Macmillan, 1969.

Faber, Geoffrey. Jowett: A Portrait with Background. London: Faber, 1957.

Fitzgerald, Edward. Euphranor: A Dialogue on Youth. London: William Pickering, 1851.

Fitzgerald, Edward. Rubáiyát of Omar Khayyám: the Astronomer-Poet of Persia, translated into English Verse. London: Bernard Quaritch, 1859.

Ford, Colin. Julia Margaret Cameron: 19th Century Photographer of Genius. London: National Portrait Gallery, 2003.

Friswell, J. H. Modern Men of Letters Honestly Criticised. London: General Books (electronic reprint), 2009).

Fuller, Hester Thackeray. Three Freshwater Friends: Tennyson, Watts & Mrs Cameron. Brighstone: Hunnyhill Publications, 2003.

Furnivall, F. J. (ed.). The History of the Holy Graal. London: J. B. Nichols, 1861.

Furnivall, F. J. (ed.). Le Morte d'Arthur. London: Macmillan, 1864.

Gladstone, W. E. '"Locksley Hall" and the Jubilee', The Nineteenth Century, 21 (1887).

Gray, J. M. Thro' the Vision of the Night. Edinburgh: Edinburgh University Press, 1980.

Hagen, June Steffensen. Tennyson and his Publishers. University Park: Pennsylvania State University Press, 1979.

Hallam, A. H. Unsigned review of 'Poems: Chiefly Lyrical', Gentleman's Magazine (August 1831), 616–28.

Hallam, Henry (ed.). Remains in Verse and Prose of Arthur Henry Hallam (2nd edn). London: Murray, 1863.

Hawker, Robert Stephen. The Cornish Ballads: and other Poems. London: Parker, 1869.

Hayter, Alethea. A Sultry Month: Scenes of London Literary Life in 1846. London: Faber, 1955.

Heffer, Simon. Moral Desperado: A Life of Thomas Carlyle. Oxford: Clarendon Press, 1980.

Hibbert, Christopher (ed.). *Queen Victoria in her Letters and Journals.* Harmondsworth: Penguin, 1985.

History of King Arthur, The. London: Walker and Edwards, 1816. [Anon.]

Hoge, James O. (ed.). *Lady Tennyson's Journal.* Charlottesville: University Press of Virginia, 1981.

Hoge, James O. (ed.). *The Letters of Emily Lady Tennyson.* University Park: Pennsylvania State University Press, 1974.

Hood, Thurman L. (ed.). *Letters of Robert Browning Collected by Thomas J. Wise.* London: John Murray, 1933.

Hudson, Derek. *An Unrepentant Victorian: the Rise and Fall of Martin Tupper.* London: Constable, 1949.

Hutchings, Richard J. *Idylls of Farringford.* Brighstone: Hunnyhill Publications, 2002.

Jenkins, Elizabeth. *Dr Gully.* London: Michael Joseph, 1972.

Jenkins, Elizabeth. *Tennyson and Dr Gully.* Lincoln: The Tennyson Society, 1974.

Johnson, E. D. H. *The Alien Vision of Victorian Poetry.* Princeton: Princeton University Press, 1964.

Jordan, Elaine. *Alfred Tennyson.* Cambridge: Cambridge University Press, 1988.

Jowett, Benjamin. *The Interpretation of Scripture: and Other Essays.* London: Routledge, 1906.

Jump, John D. (ed.). *Tennyson: The Critical Heritage.* London: Routledge, 1967.

Kennedy, Ian. 'Alfred Tennyson's *Bildungsgang:* Notes on his Early Reading', *Philological Quarterly,* 57 (Winter 1978).

Killham, John. *Tennyson and 'The Princess': Reflections of an Age.* London: Athlone, 1958.

Kincaid, J. R. *Tennyson's Major Poems: The Comic and Ironic Patterns.* New Haven: Yale University Press, 1975.

Knies, Earl A. (ed.). *Tennyson at Aldworth: The Diary of James Henry Mangles.* Athens, Ohio: Ohio University Press, 1984.

Kolb, Jack (ed.). *The Letters of Arthur Henry Hallam.* Columbus: Ohio State University Press, 1981.

Lang, Cecil. *Tennyson's Arthurian Psychodrama.* Lincoln: The Tennyson Society, 1983.

Lang, Cecil Y. (ed.). *The Letters of Matthew Arnold* (6 vols). Charlottesville: University of Virginia Press, 1996–2001.

Lang, Cecil Y., and Shannon, Edgar F. (eds). *The Letters of Alfred Lord Tennyson* (3 vols). Oxford: Clarendon Press, 1982, 1987, 1990.

Lockyer, Sir Norman and Winifred L. *Tennyson as a Student and Poet of Nature*. London: Macmillan, 1910.

Lowry, H. F. *The Letters of Matthew Arnold to Arthur Hugh Clough*. London: Oxford University Press, 1932.

Lyell, Charles. *Principles of Geology* (4th edn, 4 vols). London: John Murray, 1835.

MacCarthy, Fiona. *William Morris: A Life for Our Time*. London: Faber, 1994.

Martin, Robert Bernard. *Tennyson: The Unquiet Heart*. Oxford: The Clarendon Press, 1980.

Martin, Robert Bernard. *With Friends Possessed: A Life of Edward Fitzgerald*. London: Faber, 1985.

Massey, Gerald. 'The Poetry of Alfred Tennyson', *Hogg's Instructor*, 5 (July 1855).

Matthew, H. G. C. *Gladstone* (2 vols). Oxford: Clarendon Press, 1986, 1995.

Merriam, Harold G. *Edward Moxon: Publisher of Poets*. New York: AMS Press, 1966.

Metcalf, Priscilla. *James Knowles: Victorian Editor and Architect*. Oxford: Clarendon Press, 1980.

Milnes, R. Monckton. *Life, Letters and Literary Remains of John Keats*. London: Moxon, 1848.

Morris, May (ed.). *The Collected Works of William Morris* (24 vols). London: Longmans, Green, 1910–15.

Motter, T. H. Vail (ed.). *The Writings of Arthur Hallam*. New York: Modern Language Association of America, 1943.

Mulhauser, F. L. (ed.). *The Correspondence of Arthur Hugh Clough* (2 vols). Oxford: Clarendon Press, 1957.

Mulhauser, F. L. (ed.) *The Poems of Arthur Hugh Clough*. Oxford: Clarendon Press, 1974.

Napier, George. *The Homes and Haunts of Alfred Lord Tennyson*. Glasgow: MacLehose, 1892.

Nicolson, Harold. *Tennyson: Aspects of his Life, Character and Poetry*. London: Constable, 1923.

Noakes, Vivien. *Edward Lear: The Life of a Wanderer*. London: Collins, 1968.

Noakes, Vivien (ed.). *Edward Lear: Selected Letters*. Oxford: Clarendon Press, 1988.

North, Christopher. 'Noctes Ambrosianae', *Blackwood's Edinburgh Magazine*, 30 (February 1832), and 'Tennyson's Poems', *Blackwood's Edinburgh Magazine*, 31 (May 1832).

Northampton, Lord (ed.). *The Tribute: a Collection of Miscellaneous*

Unpublished Poems by Various Authors. London: John Murray, 1839.

O'Gorman, Francis. 'What is Haunting Tennyson's *Maud?*', *Victorian Poetry,* 48 (2010), 3.

Olsen, Victoria. *From Life: Julia Margaret Cameron and Victorian Photography.* London: Aurum Press, 2003.

O'Neill, Michael (ed.). *The Cambridge History of English Poetry.* Cambridge: Cambridge University Press, 2010.

Ormond, Leonée. *Alfred Tennyson: A Literary Life.* Basingstoke: Macmillan, 1993.

Ormond, Leonée. *Tennyson and the Old Masters.* Lincoln: The Tennyson Society, 1989.

Ormond, Leonée. *Tennyson and Thomas Woolner.* Lincoln: The Tennyson Society, 1981.

Paden, W. D. *Tennyson in Egypt: A Study of the Imagery in his Earlier Work.* New York: Octagon Books, 1971.

Page, Norman (ed.). *Tennyson: Interviews and Recollections.* London: Macmillan, 1983.

Page, Norman (ed.). *Tennyson: An Illustrated Life.* London: Allison & Busby, 1992.

Paley, William. *A View of the Evidences of Christianity.* Cambridge: 1795.

Paley, William. *Natural Theology: or Evidence of the Existence and Attributes of the Deity, collected from the appearances of nature.* Oxford: Oxford University Press, 2008.

Palgrave, Gwenllian F. (ed.). *Francis Turner Palgrave: His Journals and Memories of his Life.* London: Longmans, Green, 1899.

Patmore, Coventry. *The Angel in the House* (vols 1 and 2). London: John Parker, 1858.

Pattison, Robert. *Tennyson and Tradition.* Cambridge, Mass.: Harvard University Press, 1979.

Perry, Seamus. *Alfred Tennyson.* Tavistock: Northcote, 2005.

Pettigrew, John (ed.). *Robert Browning: The Poems* (2 vols). Harmondsworth: Penguin, 1981.

Pope-Hennessy, James. *Monckton Milnes* (2 vols). London: Constable, 1949, 1951.

Rader, R. W. *Tennyson's Maud The Biographical Genesis.* Berkeley: University of California Press, 1963.

Rawnsley, H. D. *Memories of the Tennysons.* Glasgow, MacLehose, 1900.

Renton, J. D. *The Oxford Union Murals.* Privately printed, n.d.

Richards, Jeffrey. *Sir Henry Irving: A Victorian Actor in his World.* London: Hambledon and London, 2005.

Ricks, Christopher (ed.). *The Poems of Tennyson* (2nd edn, 3 vols). London: Longman, 1987.

Ricks, Christopher. *Tennyson.* Basingstoke: Macmillan, 1989.

Ritchie, Anne Thackeray. *Records of Tennyson, Ruskin and Browning.* London: Macmillan, 1892.

Rosenberg, John D. *The Fall of Camelot: A Study of Tennyson's 'Idylls of the King'.* Cambridge, Mass.: Harvard University Press, 1973.

Rupke, N. A. *The Great Chain of History: William Buckland and the English School of Geology.* Oxford: Clarendon Press, 1983.

Sacks, Peter M. *The English Elegy: Johns Hopkins University Press,* 1985.

Sait, James E. 'Edward Tennyson: Two Letters and a Poem', *Tennyson Research Bulletin,* 2 (1974) 3, 137–8.

Scott, P. G. 'John Addington Symonds and the Reaction against Tennyson', *Tennyson Research Bulletin,* 2 (November 1974).

Scott, Patrick. 'Tennyson, Lincolnshire and Provinciality: The Topographical Narrative of *In Memoriam*', *Victorian Poetry,* 34 (1996).

Secord, James A. *Victorian Sensation: The Extraordinary Publication, Reception, and Secret Authorship of Vestiges of the Natural History of Creation.* Chicago: University of Chicago Press, 2000.

Shannon, Edgar F. 'The Critical Reception of Tennyson's "Maud"', *PMLA* (1953).

Shannon, Edgar Finley. *Tennyson and the Reviewers.* Cambridge, Mass.: Harvard University Press, 1952.

Shatto, Susan. 'Byron, Dickens, Tennyson and the Monstrous Efts', *The Yearbook of English Studies,* 6 (1976).

Shatto, Susan (ed.). *Tennyson's 'Maud'; A Definitive Edition.* London: Athlone Press, 1986.

Shatto, Susan, and Shaw, Marion (eds). *Tennyson, 'In Memoriam'.* Oxford: Clarendon Press, 1982.

Slater, Michael. *Tennyson in the Theatre.* Lincoln: The Tennyson Society, 2000.

Staines, David. *Tennyson's Camelot.* Waterloo, Ontario: Wilfrid Laurier University Press, 1982.

Sturman, Christopher, and Purton, Valerie (eds). *Poems by Two Brothers: The Lives, Work and Influence of George Clayton Tennyson and Charles Tennyson d'Eyncourt.* Stamford: Paul Watkins, 1993.

Tennyson, Alfred. *Locksley Hall: Sixty Years After.* London: Macmillan, 1886.

Tennyson, Alfred. *Poems by Alfred Tennyson, D.C.L., Poet Laureate (with illustrations by Millais, Stansfield, Creswick, Mulready, Horsley)*. London: Moxon, 1866.

Tennyson, Alfred. *Poems of Tennyson: 1830–1870 (with ninety-one illustrations by Millais, Rossetti, Maclise and others)*. Oxford: Oxford University Press, 1940.

Tennyson, Alfred. *Poetical Works: Including the Plays*. Oxford: Oxford University Press, 1953.

Tennyson, Alfred. *The Princess: A Medley* (with twenty-six illustrations by Daniel Maclise). London: Moxon, 1860.

Tennyson, Alfred. *Queen Mary: A Drama*. London: Henry S. King, 1875.

Tennyson (later Tennyson Turner), Charles. *Sonnets and Fugitive Pieces*. Cambridge: Bridges, 1830.

Tennyson Turner, Charles. *Collected Sonnets: Old and New* (ed. Hallam Tennyson with an introduction by James Spedding). London: Kegan Paul, 1880.

Tennyson Turner, Charles. *A Hundred Sonnets* (selected with an introduction by Sir Charles Tennyson and John Betjeman). London: Rupert Hart-Davis, 1960.

Tennyson, Sir Charles. *Alfred Tennyson*. London: Macmillan, 1949.

Tennyson, Sir Charles. *Farringford*. Lincoln: The Tennyson Society, 1976.

Tennyson, Sir Charles. 'James Spedding and Alfred Tennyson', *Tennyson Research Bulletin*, 2 (1974), 3, 96–105.

Tennyson, Sir Charles (ed.). *Shorter Poems of Frederick Tennyson*. London: Macmillan, 1913.

Tennyson, Sir Charles. 'The Somersby Tennysons', *Victorian Studies* (December 1963), Christmas Supplement.

Tennyson, Sir Charles, and Dyson, Hope. *The Tennysons: Background to Genius*. London: Macmillan, 1974.

Tennyson, Hallam. *Alfred Lord Tennyson: A Memoir* (2 vols). London: Macmillan, 1897.

Tennyson, Hallam (ed.). *Tennyson and his Friends*. London: Macmillan, 1912.

Terhune, Alfred McKinley and Annabelle Burdick (eds). *The Letters of Edward Fitzgerald* (4 vols). Princeton, N.J: Princeton University Press, 1980.

Terry, Ellen. *The Story of my Life*. London: Hutchinson, 1908.

Thompson, Brian. *The Nightmare of a Victorian Bestseller: Martin Tupper's Proverbial Philosophy*. London: Short Books, 2002.

Thwaite, Ann. *Edmund Gosse: A Literary Landscape, 1849–1928*. London: Secker & Warburg, 1986.

Thwaite, Ann. *Emily Tennyson: The Poet's Wife*. London: Faber, 1996.

Tillotson, Geoffrey and Kathleen (eds). *Mid-Victorian Studies*. London: Athlone, 1965.

Tucker, Herbert F. *Epic: Britain's Heroic Muse, 1790–1910*. Oxford: Oxford University Press, 2008.

Tucker, Herbert F. *Tennyson and the Doom of Romanticism*. Cambridge, Mass.: Harvard University Press, 1988.

Turner, Paul. *Tennyson*. London: Routledge, 1976.

Victorian Poetry, 47 (2009), I, *Tennyson at Two Hundred*. West Virginia University Press

Waller, John O. (ed.). *A Circle of Friends: The Tennysons and the Lushingtons of Park House*. Columbus, Ohio: Ohio State University Press, 1986.

Warren, T. Herbert (ed.). *The Centenary of Tennyson: 1809–1909*. Oxford: Clarendon Press, 1909.

Waugh, Arthur. *Alfred Lord Tennyson: A Study of his Life and Work*. London: Heinemann, 1892.

Weld, Agnes. *Glimpses of Tennyson and Some of his Relations and Friends*. London: Williams & Norgate, 1903.

Wilton, Andrew, and Upstone, Robert. *The Age of Rossetti, Burne-Jones & Watts*. London: Tate Gallery, 1997.

Woolner, Amy (ed.). *Thomas Woolner, R.A., Sculptor and Poet*. London: Chapman and Hall, 1917.

Notes

Prologue: The Tennysons and the Queen, 1862–1863

1 Hallam Tennyson, *Memoir*, I, pp. 334–5.
2 Dyson and Tennyson, p. 30.
3 Quoted in ibid., pp. 31–2.
4 Ibid., pp. 28–9.
5 Ibid., pp. 52–7.
6 Lang, *Letters of Matthew Arnold*, II, pp. 122–3.
7 Lang and Shannon, II, p. 301 and n; Dyson and Tennyson, p. 69. See also Ina Argyll.
8 Quoted in Dyson and Tennyson, p. 69.
9 Hallam Tennyson, *Memoir*, I, p. 485.
10 Quoted by Martin, *Tennyson*, p. 444.
11 Dyson and Tennyson, p. 75.
12 Letter to her sister, Anne Weld, in Hoge, *Letters*, p. 172.
13 Dyson and Tennyson, p. 76.
14 Ibid., p. 79.

CHAPTER I

Somersby, 1809–1827

1 Dyson and Tennyson, pp. 20–1.
2 Ibid., p. 27.
3 Hallam Tennyson, *Memoir*, I, p. 15.
4 Quoted in Sturman and Purton, p. 1.
5 Ibid., p. 2.
6 Ibid., p. 7.
7 Hallam Tennyson, *Memoir*, II, pp. 147–8.
8 For examples of Dr Tennyson's poetry in the Commonplace Book, see Sturman and Purton, pp. 63–81.

9 Dr Tennyson's Commonplace Book, TRC N 15. This became the property of Alfred Tennyson, and has the name A. Tennyson inscribed on the inside front cover, following the formal inscription in his father's hand.
10 Sir Charles Tennyson, *Alfred Tennyson*, p. 18.
11 Willingham Rawnsley, 'Tennyson and Lincolnshire', in Hallam Tennyson, *Friends*, pp. 25–6.
12 Lang and Shannon, I, p. xxvii.
13 Hallam Tennyson, *Friends*, p. 28.
14 Martin, *Tennyson*, pp. 29–30.
15 Hallam Tennyson, *Memoir*, I, p. 5.
16 Ibid., I, pp. 14–15.
17 Ibid., I, p. 19.
18 Ricks, *Poems*, I, pp. 13–72.
19 Quoted in ibid., I, p. 14.
20 Harvard notebook 1 MS Eng 952.
21 Ricks, *Poems*, I, p. 20.
22 Hallam Tennyson, *Memoir*, I, p. 15.
23 Dyson and Tennyson, p. 52; this comic poem is quoted in full in Sturman and Purton, pp. 64–9.
24 Sir Charles Tennyson, *Alfred Tennyson*, p. 16.
25 Dyson and Tennyson, p. 33; Sir Charles Tennyson, *Alfred Tennyson*, pp. 5–7, 19–22.
26 Quoted in Sturman and Purton, pp. 8–9.
27 Quoted in ibid., pp. 12–13.
28 Quoted in ibid., p. 16.
29 Quoted in ibid., pp. 20–1.
30 Quoted in ibid., p. 21.
31 Quoted in ibid., p. 24.
32 Dyson and Tennyson, pp. 27–31, quotation p. 31.

33 Quoted in Sturman and Purton, pp. 24, 28.
34 Ibid., p. vii.
35 Ricks, *Poems*, I, p. 181 (but Ricks gives the date of this poem as 1828).
36 Ibid., I, p. 184; Heath MS, Fitzwilliam Museum; Allen notebook, Trinity College, Cambridge. It is dated 1828 in the Heath Commonplace Book.

CHAPTER 2

Cambridge, 1827–1830

1 Quoted in Lang and Shannon, I, p. 14.
2 Sturman and Purton, pp. 28–9, 31.
3 Dyson and Tennyson, p. 70.
4 Sir Charles Tennyson, *Alfred Tennyson*, pp. 59–61.
5 Dyson and Tennyson, p. 72.
6 Quoted in Lang and Shannon, I, pp. 29–30.
7 Ibid., I, p. 42.
8 Letter to John Frere, Sturman and Purton, p. 34.
9 Lang and Shannon, I, pp. 22–3.
10 Hallam Tennyson, *Memoir*, I, p. 35.
11 Lang and Shannon, I, p. 40 and n.
12 Motter, pp. 45–6.
13 Kolb, pp. 368, 369, 371.
14 Ibid., pp. 26–7.
15 Quoted from a letter to Gaskell's mother (1830) in ibid., p. 197n.
16 Ibid., p. 266.
17 Ibid., p. 354.
18 Quoted in ibid., p. 59.
19 See ibid., p. 337n.
20 It contains manuscript copies made by John Heath of poems by Arthur Hallam, Alfred, Edward, Septimus and Frederick Tennyson.
21 Quoted in Lang and Shannon, I, p. 43.
22 Harvard Notebook 7 MS Eng 952.

23 Peter Allen, p. 138.
24 Here I am quoting and paraphrasing the invaluable account of Hallam's thought given in ibid., pp. 154–8.
25 'Essay on the Philosophical writings of Cicero', in Henry Hallam, pp. 146–210 (p. 173).
26 Quoted by Peter Allen, p. 3.
27 Brookfield, pp. 308–9.
28 Ibid., pp. 309–10.
29 Paden, p. 27.
30 Martin, *Tennyson*, p. 45; Ricks, *Poems*, I, pp. 94–160.
31 Lang and Shannon, I, pp. 8–15.
32 Paden, p. 18 n 44.
33 Hallam Tennyson, *Memoir*, I, p. 23.
34 Lang and Shannon, I, pp. 39, 41.
35 Hallam Tennyson, *Memoir*, I, pp. 45–6.
36 Kolb, pp. 318–19.
37 Quoted in Lang and Shannon, I, p. 39.
38 Hallam Tennyson, *Memoir*, I, p. 46.
39 Kolb, p. 334.
40 Hagen, pp. 10–15.
41 Kolb, p. 363.
42 Charles Tennyson, *Sonnets and Fugitive Pieces*.
43 Coleridge's notes were reprinted in Tennyson Turner, *Collected Sonnets*. Some of Coleridge's notes on the volume reappeared in Tennyson Turner, *A Hundred Sonnets*, pp. 127–8.
44 Tennyson Turner, *Collected Sonnets*, p. 40 and n.
45 Kolb, pp. 365–7 and n.
46 Carlyle, *John Sterling*, pp. 64–5.
47 Ricks, *Poems*, I, p. 168.
48 Hallam Tennyson, *Memoir*, I, pp. 51–4.
49 Kolb, p. 375.
50 Photocopies of the Kemble letters are in the Tennyson Research Centre, Lincoln, and several of

them are quoted in Marion Shaw's essay, 'Friendship, Poetry, and Insurrection', in Douglas-Fairhurst and Perry, pp. 214–15. This letter is quoted by Shaw, pp. 222–3, though with a misreading: 'high spirits at the prospect of our speedy hanging' is given in the essay as 'high spirits at the prospect of our speedy departure'.

51 Kolb, p. 382.
52 Hallam Tennyson, *Memoir*, I, p. 54.
53 Kemble letters, number 85, 27 March 1831, to Kemble.
54 Carlyle, *John Sterling*, pp. 69–70.
55 Marion Shaw, in Douglas-Fairhurst and Perry, pp. 223–4.
56 Quoted in Kolb, p. 378n.
57 Lang and Shannon, I, pp. 45–6.
58 Kolb, p. 387.
59 Quoted in ibid., pp. 388–9n.
60 Douglas-Fairhurst and Perry, pp. 214–15.
61 Ricks, *Poems*, I, p. 236.
62 Ibid., I, p. 384.
63 Ibid., I, pp. 571 and 569n (headnote).
64 Peter Allen, p. 168.
65 Ricks, *Poems*, I, p. 216.
66 Ibid., I, p. 638.
67 Ibid., I, pp. 320, 318, 309.
68 Ibid., I, pp. 202–3.
69 Ibid., I, pp. 243–4 and n.
70 Quoted in Paden, n. 176, pp. 149–50.
71 Ricks, *Poems* I, pp. 254–5.
72 Lang and Shannon, I, p. 84.
73 Kolb, p. 688.
74 Ricks, *Poems*, I, pp. 364–5, 368–9.
75 Ibid., I, pp. 380–1.

CHAPTER 3

Somersby and Arthur Hallam, 1831–1833

1 Dyson and Tennyson, pp. 118–20.

2 Daniell (1988), pp. 32–5; (1989), pp. 315–17.
3 Lang and Shannon, I, pp. 48–9.
4 Ibid., I, pp. 51, 53.
5 Ibid., I, pp. 57–8.
6 Kolb, p. 416. In the event, the owner and patron of the livings of Somersby and Bag Enderby, William Burton, allowed the Somersby Tennysons to remain there until 1837 (by which date the living was needed for one of Burton's sons).
7 Lang and Shannon, I, p. 25.
8 Dyson and Tennyson, p. 28; Hallam Tennyson, *Memoir*, I, p. 12.
9 Ibid., I, pp. 59–61.
10 Sir Charles Tennyson, *Alfred Tennyson*, p. 116.
11 Ibid., pp. 109–10.
12 Martin, *Tennyson*, p. 100, discusses the case for this date for the meeting as against a later date, in 1830, proposed by Jack Kolb.
13 Kolb, pp. 421, 423, 431.
14 A. H. Hallam, in Motter, pp. 182–98 and reproduced and discussed in Jump, pp. 34–49 (the five virtues are listed on p. 42).
15 Kolb, p. 508.
16 Ibid., pp. 536–7.
17 Ibid., p. 539.
18 Lang and Shannon, I, p. 71
19 Quoted in Kolb, p. 538.
20 North, 'Noctes Ambrosianae', pp. 190, 255–88; 'Tennyson's Poems', pp. 194, 724–41.
21 Lang and Shannon, I, p. 75.
22 Ibid., I, pp. 76–7.
23 Martin, *Tennyson*, pp. 149–55.
24 Merriam, p. 1.
25 Ibid., pp. 13–21, 27.
26 Ibid., p. 29.
27 Kolb, pp. 459–60.
28 Ibid., p. 646.
29 Quoted in ibid., p. 653n.

30 Ibid., p. 413.
31 Ibid., p. 616.
32 Ricks, *Poems*, I, pp. 500–1.
33 Kolb, p. 618.
34 Ibid., p. 706.
35 Ibid., pp. 622–3 and n.
36 Ibid., pp. 639–40.
37 Ibid., p. 599.
38 Quoted in ibid., pp. 661, 602 and n.
39 Ricks, *Poems*, I, p. 386.
40 Ibid., I, pp. 449–50.
41 Ibid., I, p. 507.
42 Ibid., I, p. 468 and n.
43 Ibid., I, pp. 473, 475.
44 Quoted in Jump, pp. 71, 74, 81.
45 Kolb, p. 775.
46 Ibid., pp. 784–5.
47 Ibid., p. 4.
48 Hoge, *Letters*, p. 249.
49 Hallam Tennyson, *Memoir*, I, pp. 105–6.
50 Ibid., I, p. 106.
51 Quoted in Ricks, *Poems*, II, p. 312, headnote to *In Memoriam*.
52 Ibid., II, p. 24.
53 Ibid., II, pp. 374, 326, 332–3, 331.
54 Waller, pp. 117–18, 124–6.

CHAPTER 4

Wandering, tribulation and lost love, 1833–1845

1 Martin, *Tennyson*, pp. 149–50.
2 Ibid., p. 150.
3 Turner, p. 61.
4 Ricks, *Poems*, III, p. 150.
5 Rawnsley, pp. 62–3.
6 This poem was written out by Francis Palgrave with the title 'Early Verses of Compliment to Miss Rose Baring', and was first printed in full by K. W. Gransden in *The Book Collector* iv (1955), pp. 160–1; see Ricks, *Poems*, II, pp. 60–1. It is quoted in Rader, p. 32.
7 Quoted by Rader, pp. 28–9, and in Ricks, *Poems*, II, pp. 75–6.
8 Quoted by Rader, pp. 36–7.
9 Ibid., p. 29.
10 Ricks, *Poems*, II, pp. 78–9.
11 Ibid., II, p. 62.
12 Ibid., II, p. 77.
13 Rader, pp. 41–2.
14 Ibid.
15 Ricks, *Poems*, II, p. 122; Yale MS.
16 Ricks, *Poems*, II, p. 129.
17 Ibid., p. 122; Yale MS.
18 Quoted by Rader, p. 42.
19 Ricks, *Poems*, II, p. 125.
20 Kirstie Blair has discussed this in an intriguing essay, 'Tennyson and the Victorian Working-Class Poet', in Douglas-Fairhurst and Perry, pp. 276–95.
21 Ricks, *Poems*, II, pp. 125–6.
22 Ibid., II, p. 130 and n.
23 Lang and Shannon, II, p. 155.
24 Ricks, *Poems*, II, pp. 524, 525n, 540.
25 Harvard Notebook 17; see Ricks, *Poems*, II, pp. 320–1n.
26 Harvard Notebook 16; finished state in Ricks, *Poems*, II, pp. 327–8.
27 Ricks, *Poems*, II, p. 392.
28 Lang and Shannon, I, p. 107.
29 Sir Charles Tennyson, *Alfred Tennyson*, p. 157.
30 Ibid., pp. 157–8.
31 Lang and Shannon, I, p. 135.
32 Ibid., I, p. 138.
33 Ibid., I, p. 140.
34 Ibid., I, p. 142.
35 Ibid., I, p. 134.
36 Hallam Tennyson, *Memoir*, I, p. 148.
37 See Thwaite, *Emily Tennyson*, p. 58.
38 Lang and Shannon, III, pp. 290–1 and n.
39 Ricks, *Poems*, II, pp. 421–2, 426–7.
40 Martin, *Tennyson*, p. 232.
41 Hallam Tennyson, *Memoir*, I, p. 157.
42 Lang and Shannon, I, p. 146.

43 Ibid., I, pp. 147–8.
44 Ricks, *Poems*, II, p. 21.
45 Lang and Shannon, I, p. 158.
46 Ibid., I, p. 157.
47 Ibid., I, p. 173.
48 Martin, *Tennyson*, pp. 234–5.
49 M. D. Allen. (Confusingly, '1836' is pencilled on the title page of the *Essay* in Tennyson's library, Tennyson Research Centre, Lincoln, no. 406. The printed publication date of this volume is 1838.)
50 Ibid., p. xi.
51 Ibid., pp. 59–60.
52 Lang and Shannon, I, p. 159.
53 Ibid., I, p. 161.
54 Ibid., I, p. 176.
55 See the reproduction in Cheshire, p. 72.
56 Martin, *Tennyson*, p. 234.
57 Lang and Shannon, I, pp. 168–9. The editors dated this as either 1839 or 1840; Ann Thwaite regarded 1840 as more likely.
58 Thwaite, *Emily Tennyson*, pp. 137–8.
59 Quoted in Rader, p. 70.
60 This is set out in detail in ibid., pp. 71–3.
61 Quoted in Sir Charles Tennyson, *Alfred Tennyson*, as December 1839; but Lang and Shannon suggest that this letter belongs to the summer of 1840: I, pp. 182–3.
62 Thwaite, *Emily Tennyson*, p. 143.
63 Sir Charles Tennyson, *Alfred Tennyson*, pp. 182–3.
64 Ricks, *Poems*, II, p. 170.
65 Hallam Tennyson, *Memoir*, I, pp. 183–4.
66 Quoted in ibid., I, p. 187.
67 Quoted in Martin, *Tennyson*, p. 258.
68 Quoted in Peter Allen, pp. 162–3.
69 Hallam Tennyson, *Memoir*, I, pp. 129–30.
70 Ricks, *Poems*, I, pp. 395–6.

71 Quoted by Hallam Tennyson, *Memoir*, I, p. 193n.
72 Ricks, *Poems*, I, pp. 396–7.
73 Peter Allen, p. 163.
74 Quoted in Ricks, *Poems*, I, p. 387, headnote.
75 Ibid., I, p. 392.
76 Jordan, p. 57.
77 Ricks, *Poems*, I, p. 393.
78 Ibid., I, p. 395 and n.
79 Ibid., I, pp. 269–70.
80 Quoted in Kolb, pp. 392–3.
81 Ricks, *Poems*, pp. 207, 209.
82 Ibid., I, p. 392.
83 Ibid., I, pp. 475–6.
84 Ibid., I, p. 436 (headnote).
85 Cronin, pp. 195, 200.
86 See Ricks, *Poems*, I, pp. 311–12 (headnote and text).
87 Ibid., I, p. 456.
88 Cronin, p. 205.
89 Jump, p. 143.
90 Lang and Shannon, I, p. 177.
91 Terhune, I, p. 246.
92 Lang and Shannon, I, p. 179.
93 Ibid., pp. 181–2.
94 Ibid., I, pp. 171–2.
95 Waller, pp. 93–4.
96 Ibid., p. 108.
97 See Reginald Bligh's letter from London to 'Mr Turner, Queen's [*sic*] College', 7 May 1775, Tennyson family archive, Lincolnshire County Libraries.
98 Waller, p. 109.
99 Ibid., pp. 110, 113.
100 Paraphrase of the account in ibid., pp. 122–3.
101 Dyson and Tennyson, pp. 149–59.
102 Lang and Shannon, I, pp. 183–4.
103 Ibid., I, p. 188.
104 Ibid., I, pp. 190, 199, 200.
105 Tennyson Research Centre 7712, letter of 14 July 1842.
106 Tennyson Research Centre 7714 to Matthew Allen, mid July 1842, and Lang and Shannon, I, pp. 205–6.

107 Lang and Shannon, I, p. 204.
108 Ibid., I, pp. 213–14.
109 Terhune, I, p. 479.
110 Ricks, *Poems*, II, pp. 592–3.

CHAPTER 5

Growing reputation and *The Princess*, 1845–1850

1 Ormond, *Literary Life*, pp. 90–3 and ff.
2 Quoted by Ricks, *Tennyson*, p. 168.
3 Lang and Shannon, I, pp. 242–3.
4 Headnote and text in Ricks, *Poems*, II, pp. 178–9.
5 See Tennyson's letter to his aunt Elizabeth Russell, 18 April 1828, Lang and Shannon, I, p. 23 and n; Kennedy, pp. 82–103.
6 Shannon, *Tennyson and the Reviewers*, p. 17.
7 Hallam Tennyson, *Memoir*, I, pp. 244–5.
8 Ricks, *Poems*, II, p. 183.
9 Dedication to *Harold* quoted here from Alfred Tennyson, *Poetical Works*, p. 607.
10 Lang and Shannon, I, p. 246.
11 Ibid., I, pp. 247–8.
12 Ibid., I, p. 249.
13 Ibid., I, p. 250.
14 Quoted in ibid., I, pp. 250–1.
15 See Mulhauser, *Poems*, pp. 45–93, 592–4.
16 Ibid., p. 93.
17 Waller, pp. 140–2.
18 Ricks, *Poems*, I, pp. 307–8.
19 Ibid., II, p. 188n.
20 Ibid., II, p. 192.
21 Ibid., II, pp. 200–1n; Houghton Library, Harvard.
22 Ricks, *Poems*, II, p. 264.
23 Ibid., II, p. 265.
24 Ibid., II, p. 232 and n.
25 Ibid., II, pp. 219–20 and headnote to *The Princess*, p. 186.
26 Ibid., II, pp. 293–4.
27 Ibid., I, p. 481n.

28 Ibid., II, p. 208.
29 Ibid., II, pp. 290–1.
30 Ibid., II, pp. 12–17.
31 Quoted in Waller, pp. 142–3.
32 Quoted in Lang and Shannon, I, p. 238.
33 Quoted in ibid., I, p. 237.
34 Ibid., I, p. 237 and n.
35 These journal entries, in the Houghton Library at Harvard, are also printed in ibid., I, pp. 258–60.
36 Ibid., I, pp. 260–1.
37 Ibid., I, p. 264.
38 Waller, p. 151.
39 Lang and Shannon, I, pp. 273–4.
40 Quoted by Martin, *Tennyson*, p. 242.
41 Letter from Carlyle to Emerson quoted in Lang and Shannon, I, p. 228.
42 Letter from Jane Carlyle to Helen Welsh, 31 January 1845, quoted in ibid., I, p. 233.
43 Martin, *Tennyson*, p. 242.
44 Jenkins, *Tennyson and Dr Gully*, Jenkins gives a summary of Tennyson's state at this date: 'The annihilating loss of Arthur Hallam in 1833, the – to us – veiled spectre of his rejected love for Rosa Baring, the disposal of his grandfather's property, overwhelmingly in favour of the other branch of the family, the loss of his small patrimony in the failure of Allen's scheme for mechanical wood-carving, the engagement to Emily Sellwood, broken off in 1840 and not completed till ten years later, had brought him, by the age of thirty-eight, to the condition of a nervous invalid. In the spring of 1847, he tried the fashionable water cure at Umberslade Hall outside Birmingham, an establishment which had been set up by Dr

Edward Johnson the previous year; he must have felt some benefit, for later in 1847 he tried the cure again, but this time in its celebrated head quarters in Malvern.' See also Jenkins, *Dr Gully.*

45 Terhune, I, p. 623.
46 Quoted in Sir Charles Tennyson, *Alfred Tennyson*, p. 225.
47 Terhune, I, p. 604.
48 Hallam Tennyson, *Memoir*, I, p. 274 and n.
49 Sir Charles Tennyson, *Alfred Tennyson*, pp. 227–9; Brendon, passim.
50 Sir Edward Bulwer-Lytton, Bt, *King Arthur*, 2 vols (Leipzig: Tauchnitz, 1849), Introduction and pp. 36-7.
51 Lang and Shannon, I, pp. 297–8, where 'rigorous' has been read as the less distinctive 'vigorous'.
52 Allingham, p. 55. See also Lang and Shannon, I, p. 297n.
53 Those are now in Trinity College, Cambridge, and the Tennyson Research Centre at Lincoln.
54 Rawnsley, pp. 121–2.
55 Lang and Shannon, I, p. 311.
56 Ibid., I, p. 312.
57 Waller, pp. 154–5.
58 As is argued in Thwaite, *Emily Tennyson*, pp. 182–5.
59 Quoted in Rawnsley, pp. 123–4.
60 Lang and Shannon, I, pp. 322–4 and n; Jump, pp. 173–85.
61 Lang and Shannon, I, p. 316.
62 Thwaite, *Emily Tennyson*, p. 190.
63 Rawnsley, p. 126.
64 Lang and Shannon, I, p. 235 and n.
65 'Materials for a Life of A.T.', 4, p. 41.
66 Lang and Shannon, I, pp. 236–7 and n.
67 Ricks, *Poems*, II, p. 452.
68 Lang and Shannon, I, p. 331 (Forster), p. 330 (Monteith).

69 Ibid., I, p. 257 and n.
70 Ibid., I, p. 328.
71 Ibid., I, p. 166.
72 Ricks, *Poems*, II, p. 330.
73 Ibid., II, p. 426.
74 Ibid., II, pp. 420–5.

CHAPTER 6

In Memoriam, marriage and the Laureateship, 1850–1854

1 Sir Charles Tennyson, *Alfred Tennyson*, p. 145.
2 Ricks, *Poems*, II, p. 310.
3 Ibid., I, p. 611n.
4 Ibid., III, pp. 595–6.
5 Hallam Tennyson, *Memoir*, I, p. 371.
6 Shatto and Shaw, p. 194.
7 Ormond, *Old Masters*, p. 21.
8 Ricks, *Poems*, II, pp. 349–50.
9 Ibid., II, p. 398, gives this word as 'wall'.
10 Ibid., II, pp. 397–402.
11 James Knowles, 'A Personal Reminiscence', in Page, *Interviews and Recollections*, p. 96.
12 Ricks, *Poems*, II, pp. 408–9 and n.
13 Ibid., II, pp. 427, 428–9.
14 Ibid., II, pp. 436–7.
15 Ibid., II, pp. 453–4.
16 Lyell, vol. 1, p. 3.
17 Quoted in Martin Rudwick, 'Sir Charles Lyell', *DNB*.
18 For a full discussion of the book's impact, see Secord.
19 Quoted in Desmond and Moore, p. 322.
20 See Batchelor, pp. 46–9.
21 Chambers, p. 324.
22 See Hallam Tennyson, *Memoir*, I, p. 223; Ricks, *Poems*, II, pp. 438–9n.
23 Ricks, *Poems*, II, pp. 438–9.
24 Ibid., II, pp. 457–8.
25 Ibid., II, pp. 411–13 and n.
26 See Shatto and Shaw, pp. 242, 255.

27 Ricks, *Poems*, II, pp. 372–3 and n.
28 Ibid., II, p. 340.
29 Ibid., II, pp. 325–6.
30 Ibid., II, p. 24.
31 Ibid., II, pp. 403–4.
32 Shannon, *Tennyson and the Reviewers*, pp. 141–2; Sir Charles Tennyson, *Alfred Tennyson*, pp. 247–8.
33 Shannon, *Tennyson and the Reviewers*, pp. 142, 144, 145.
34 Champneys, I, p. 336.
35 Waller, pp. 168–9.
36 Quoted in Lang and Shannon, I, p. 339.
37 Ibid., I, p. 340.
38 Lang, *Letters of Matthew Arnold*, I, p. 170.
39 Waller, pp. 170–2.
40 Lang and Shannon, II, pp. 3–4 and n.
41 Ibid., II, pp. 13–14.
42 Hallam Tennyson, *Memoir*, I, pp. 340–1.
43 Pettigrew, I, p. 410.
44 Quoted in ibid., I, p. 1091.
45 Martin, *Tennyson*, pp. 359–61.
46 Ricks, *Poems*, II, pp. 494–5.
47 'Materials for a life of A.T.', 4, p. 288.
48 Ibid., 4, p. 291.
49 As described by Martin, *Tennyson*, p. 357.
50 Allingham, pp. 60–3.
51 Martin, *Tennyson*, p. 365.
52 Quoted in Lang and Shannon, II, p. 26.
53 Ibid., II, p. 50; Martin, *Tennyson*, p. 368.
54 Lang, *Psychodrama*, pp. 1, 3.
55 Martin, *Tennyson*, p. 367; Tennyson Research Centre, letter 6001 from James Spedding.
56 Tennyson Research Centre; also quoted in part in Noakes, *Life*, p. 127.
57 Noakes, *Life*, p. 130.
58 Ibid., pp. 132–52.
59 Terhune, II, pp. 82–3.

60 Letter of 15 February 1853: Lang and Shannon, II, p. 60.
61 Ibid., II, p. 64.
62 Allingham, p. 65.
63 Hoge, *Journal*, p. 30.
64 Lang and Shannon, II, p. 67.
65 Ricks, *Poems*, III, p. 402.
66 Lang and Shannon, II, pp. 67–8.
67 Hoge, *Journal*, pp. 31–3.
68 Sir Charles Tennyson, *Alfred Tennyson*, p. 277.
69 Sir Charles Tennyson, *Farringford*, p. 5; Hutchings, p. 19.
70 Sir Charles Tennyson, *Farringford*, p. 6.
71 Hoge, *Journal*, p. 32.
72 Lang and Shannon, II, p. 86.
73 Ibid., II, pp. 75, 83.
74 Quoted from William Michael Rossetti's diary, in Page, *Interviews and Recollections*, p. 20.
75 Lang and Shannon, I, p. 340.
76 Ricks, *Poems*, II, p. 580 and n.
77 Ibid., II, pp. 529–30.
78 Ibid., II, p. 565.
79 Hoge, *Journal*, p. 48.
80 All quotations from Ricks, *Poems*, II, pp. 513–84.

CHAPTER 7

The reception of *Maud* and the problems of fame, 1855–1862

1 Hallam Tennyson, *Memoir*, I, p. 384.
2 Quoted in Knies, p. 48n. The anecdote about 'Did your mother . . .' is reported in Warren, p. 9.
3 Knies, p. 46.
4 See Ina Argyll.
5 See George Argyll.
6 Letter from Carlyle to Fitzgerald, December 1850: Terhune, I, p. 691.
7 Ibid., I, p. 696.
8 Ibid., III, p. 487.
9 Massey, p. 6.
10 Ibid., pp. 7–8.

11 Quoted here from the headnote to *Maud* in Ricks, *Poems*, II, p. 517.
12 All quoted in the invaluable essay by Shannon, 'Critical Reception', p. 398.
13 Lang and Shannon, II, p. 119n.
14 Ibid., II, pp. 137–8.
15 Ibid., II, Appendix B, pp. 560–1.
16 Lang, *Letters of Matthew Arnold*, I, p. 322.
17 Quoted in Martin, *Tennyson*, p. 390.
18 Quoted in Jump, pp. 244, 248.
19 Quoted in Shannon, 'Critical Reception', p. 399.
20 Quoted in Jump, p. 188.
21 Tennyson Research Centre (numbered 6101).
22 Quoted in Hallam Tennyson, *Memoir*, I, p. 411.
23 Adapted from Stephen Badsey, 'Crimean War, 1853–6', in Cannon, p. 260.
24 Ricks, *Poems*, II, p. 513.
25 Thwaite, *Emily Tennyson*, p. 273.
26 Hoge, *Letters*, p. 82.
27 Lang and Shannon, II, p. 128 and n.
28 Martin, *Tennyson*, pp. 392–4, 395.
29 Lang and Shannon's opinion in II, 73n.
30 Ibid. II, p. 147.
31 Quoted in Jump, pp. 198–9.
32 Martin, *Tennyson*, pp. 399–401.
33 Tennyson Research Centre, Letter 5581, Balliol 29 December [1855].
34 Woolner, pp. 122–3.
35 Ibid., pp. 8–10.
36 Ibid., p. 105.
37 Tennyson Research Centre (this appears in part in Hoge, *Letters*, pp. 99–100).
38 Woolner, p. 114.
39 Ibid., pp. 130–1.
40 Ibid., p. 132.
41 Ibid., p. 173.
42 Quoted in Lang and Shannon, II, p. 206.
43 Quoted in Ormond, *Thomas Woolner*, p. 12.
44 Ibid., pp. 11–14; Woolner, p. 177.
45 Woolner, pp. 147, 149, 151.
46 Ormond, *Thomas Woolner*, p. 7.
47 Hoge, *Journal*, p. 67.
48 Mulhauser, *Correspondence* II, pp. 521–2.
49 Ibid., I, p. 73.
50 Ibid., I, p. 21.
51 Quoted in Lang and Shannon, II, p. 160.
52 Ibid., II, p. 174.
53 Ibid., II, p. 175n.
54 Ibid., II, p. 179.
55 Quoted in Ormond, *Thomas Woolner*, p. 19.
56 Quoted in Lang and Shannon, II, p. 184.
57 Woolner, p. 135.
58 Quoted in Sturman and Purton, p. 117.
59 Cohen, I, p. 34.
60 Martin, *Tennyson*, p. 417.
61 Woolner, p. 138.
62 Ibid., p. 148.
63 Quoted in Martin, *Tennyson*, p. 419.
64 Quoted in Lang and Shannon, II, p. 271.
65 See ibid., II, p. 239.
66 'Materials for a life of A.T.', II, p. 224.
67 Ibid., II, pp. 224–6.
68 Lang and Shannon, II, pp. 239–40.
69 Palgrave's journal, quoted in Hallam Tennyson, *Memoir*, I, pp. 441–2.
70 Ibid., I, p. 441.
71 Quoted in Lang and Shannon, II, p. 141n.
72 'Materials for a life of A.T.', II, pp. 234–5.
73 Hallam Tennyson, *Memoir*, I, p. 442.
74 Quoted in Palgrave, p. 55.
75 Merriam, pp. 182–3.
76 Quoted in Hagen, p. 105.

77 Ricks, *Poems*, II, p. 96, headnote.
78 Ibid., II, pp. 99, 103.
79 Ibid., I, pp. 392–3.
80 Quoted in Martin, *Tennyson*, p. 414.
81 Ricks, *Poems*, I, p. 395.
82 Hagen, pp. 104–6.
83 Ibid., p. 106.
84 Merriam, pp. 185–6.
85 Hagen, p. 108.
86 Terhune, II, p. 272.
87 Martin, *Edward Fitzgerald*, pp. 193–200.
88 Mrs Gould is quoted in Dyson and Tennyson, p. 127.
89 Ibid., p. 121.
90 Quoted in ibid., p. 120.
91 Quoted in Thompson, p. 39.
92 Ibid., pp. 48–9.
93 Quoted (from Sir Charles Tennyson) by Martin, *Tennyson*, p. 433.
94 Woolner, p. 198.
95 Quoted in Ricks, *Poems* II, pp. 438–9.
96 Woolner, p. 203.
97 Ricks, *Poems*, II, pp. 345, 352n and 353, 122, 532.
98 Quoted in Jump, p. 250.
99 Ricks, *Poems*, II, pp. 420, 422.
100 Sir Charles Tennyson, *Alfred Tennyson*, pp. 218, 224–5, quoted in Staines, pp. 24–5n. After the publication of *The Princess*, Tennyson had travelled to Cornwall looking for the legendary haunts of King Arthur. He 'began to study the epical King Arthur in earnest': Hallam Tennyson, *Memoir*, II, p. 125.
101 Mulhauser, *Correspondence*, II, pp. 591, 602–3.
102 Ibid., II, p. 603.
103 Sir Charles Tennyson, *Alfred Tennyson*, pp. 331–2; Martin, *Tennyson*, pp. 437–41.
104 Lowry, pp. 46, 154.
105 Ricks, *Poems*, II, p. 618.
106 Martin, *Tennyson*, p. 441.
107 Quoted in Dyson and Tennyson, p. 65.
108 Ibid., p. 67.
109 Quoted in Olsen, p. 91.
110 Ibid., pp. 127–8.
111 Martin, *Tennyson*, p. 447
112 Ritchie, pp. 39–40.
113 Hallam Tennyson, *Friends*, pp. 153–4; Aplin, pp. 1–2.
114 Quoted in Martin, *Tennyson*, p. 448.
115 Terry, pp. 53, 56.
116 Ibid., p. 55.
117 Allingham, pp. 84–5.
118 Hallam Tennyson, *Memoir*, II, p. 2.
119 Martin, *Tennyson*, pp. 449–50.
120 Hallam Tennyson, *Memoir*, I, p. 427.
121 Lang and Shannon, II, pp. 278–9.
122 Ibid., II, Appendices E and F.
123 Ricks, *Poems*, II, p. 622.
124 Buckley, p. 152.
125 She was writing to Sir Henry Taylor: quoted in Lang and Shannon, II, pp 319–20.

CHAPTER 8

Idylls of the King and the creation of Aldworth, 1862–1872

1 MacCarthy, p. 58.
2 Quoted in ibid., p. 61.
3 Quoted in ibid., p. 62.
4 Ibid., p. 92.
5 William Morris, *The Defence of Guinevere*, in Morris, I, p. 5.
6 Quotations from preface to Furnivall, *Holy Graal*, and from Herbert Coleridge's preface to Furnivall, *Morte d'Arthur*.
7 Woolner, p. 202.
8 Ibid., pp. 90–2, 208–12.
9 Ricks, *Poems*, II, p. 626n.
10 Hagen, p. 112.
11 Hoge, *Letters*, pp. 180, 181.
12 Quoted in Jump, pp. 288–92.

13 Quoted in ibid., p. 279.

14 Ricks, *Poems*, II, pp. 628–9.

15 Woolner, pp. 219–25.

16 Ibid., p. 225.

17 Ibid., p. 230.

18 Ricks, *Poems*, II, p. 657n.

19 Ibid., II, p. 666.

20 Ibid., II, p. 669.

21 Ibid., II, pp. 670–1.

22 Ibid., II, pp. 674–5.

23 Ibid., II, p. 678.

24 Ibid., II, p. 681.

25 Hallam Tennyson, *Memoir*, I, p. 495; Frederick Pollock, quoted in Ricks, *Poems*, II, p. 658n.

26 Ricks, *Poems*, II, p. 682.

27 Woolner, p. 252.

28 Gatty Collection, Boston Public Library; also in Hoge, *Letters*, p. 162 (with different punctuation).

29 Gatty Collection, and Hoge, *Letters*, p. 163.

30 Quoted in P. G. Scott, p. 87.

31 Quoted in ibid., pp. 87–8; the *Century Magazine* version of the same phrasing is quoted in Lang and Shannon, II, p. 417.

32 Quoted from the *Century Magazine* in Lang and Shannon, II, p. 415.

33 P. G. Scott, p. 88.

34 Lang and Shannon, II, pp. 418–19.

35 Ibid., II, p. 421.

36 Quoted by P. G. Scott, p. 90.

37 Lang and Shannon, II, p. 391n.

38 Woolner (1917), p. 196, and Martin, *Tennyson*, p. 431.

39 Quoted in ibid., p. 456.

40 Ibid., p. 463.

41 Prof. J. B. Farmer, FRS, Professor of Botany, Royal College of Science, London; Rear Admiral A. Mostyn Field, FRS, late Hydrographer to the Navy; Dr H. O. Forbes, FRGS, Director of Museums to the Corporation of Liverpool;

W. F. Kirby, Esq., FLS, late Assistant in Zoological Dept., British Museum (Nat. History), South Kensington; Dr P. Chalmers Mitchell, FRS, Secretary to Zoological Society of London; Captain H. F. Oliver, RN, MVO; Lt Col. D. Prain, IMS, CIE, FRS, Director of Royal Botanic Gardens, Kew; Prof. Adam Sedgwick, FSS, Professor of Zoology, Imperial College of Science and Technology; Dr W. N. Shaw, FGS, Director of the Meteorological Office.

42 Lockyer.

43 Martin, *Tennyson*, p. 462.

44 Ibid., p. 461.

45 Ibid., p. 464.

46 Hoge, *Journal*, p. 251.

47 Ibid., p. 266.

48 Martin, *Tennyson*, p. 465.

49 Ibid., p. 463.

50 Hallam Tennyson, *Memoir*, II, p. 35.

51 Quoted in Martin, *Tennyson*, p. 466.

52 Quoted in Fuller, p. 15.

53 Martin, *Tennyson*, pp. 466–7.

54 Allingham, pp. 159–60.

55 Lang and Shannon, II, p. 467.

56 Ibid., II, p. 487.

57 Ibid., II, pp. 488–90.

58 Quoted in Hagen, p. 117.

59 Ibid., pp. 119–31.

60 Ibid., p. 121.

61 Lang and Shannon, II, p. 288.

62 Quoted in Metcalf, p. 191.

63 Quoted in ibid., p. 199.

64 Quoted in ibid., p. 200.

65 Martin, *Tennyson*, p. 472.

66 Metcalf, p. 201.

67 Ibid., p. 202.

68 Hoge, *Journal*, p. 251.

69 Sir Charles Tennyson, *Alfred Tennyson*, pp. 380–1; the Minute Book of the Metaphysical Society.

70 Tennyson Research Centre, Lincoln.
71 Lang and Shannon, II, p. 526.
72 Martin, *Tennyson*, pp. 483–4.
73 Knies, p. 29.
74 Ibid., p. 51.
75 Hallam Tennyson, *Memoir*, I, p. 458.
76 Knies, p. 72.
77 Hallam Tennyson, *Memoir*, II, p. 99n.
78 Knies, p. 46.
79 Ibid., p. 58.
80 Ibid., p. 71.
81 Quoted in ibid. from Symonds' *Letters*, I, p. 512.
82 Quoted in ibid., p. 64n.
83 Hallam Tennyson, *Memoir*, I, p. 57.
84 Knies, p. 67.
85 Cohen, I, pp. 150–1.
86 Lang and Shannon, II, pp. 543–4 and n.
87 Cohen, I, pp. 152–3.
88 Knies, pp. 91–2.
89 Ibid., pp. 102–3 and n.
90 Ibid., pp. 49, 62–3.
91 Quoted in Jump, p. 12. Friswell's piece was reprinted in his *Modern Men of Letters Honestly Criticised*, p. 67.
92 Austin, p. 39.
93 Ibid., p. 82.
94 Ibid., p. 81.
95 Ibid., pp. 85, 88.
96 Lang and Shannon, II, pp. 522–3.
97 Ricks, *Poems*, III, pp. 8, 11 and n.
98 Ibid., III, p. 13 and n.
99 Ibid., II, pp. 652–3.
100 Hoge, *Letters*, p. 239.
101 Ibid., pp. 261–2.
102 Hallam Tennyson, *Memoir*, II, pp. 66–8, 75, 74.
103 Ibid., II, p. 70.
104 Hoge, *Letters*, p. 240.
105 Ibid., p. 244.
106 Ibid., p. 248.
107 Ricks, *Poems*, II, pp. 709, 715, 718.
108 Hoge, *Letters*, p. 256.
109 Hoge, *Journal*, p. 306.
110 Martin, *Tennyson*, p. 488.
111 Lang and Shannon, II, p. 551.
112 Ricks, *Poems*, III, p. 1.
113 Sir Charles Tennyson, *Alfred Tennyson*, p. 389.
114 Terhune, III, pp. 243, 342, 344–6.

CHAPTER 9

The completion of the *Idylls* and the aspiring playwright, 1872–1886

1 Staines, pp. 1–9.
2 Ricks, *Poems*, II, p. 2n.
3 Ibid., II, pp. 2–3n.
4 Ibid., III, p. 588.
5 Quoted by Martin, *Tennyson*, pp. 241–2. See also Heffer, p. 203.
6 Quoted by Martin, *Tennyson*, p. 267.
7 Carlyle, *Sartor Resartus*, p. 243.
8 Ibid., p. 246.
9 Ricks, *Poems*, III, pp. 556–9.
10 Jordan, p. 166.
11 Ricks, *Poems*, III, p. 270.
12 Quoted in ibid., III, p. 562n.
13 Ibid., III, p. 429.
14 Ibid., III, p. 426.
15 Ibid., III, p. 440.
16 Ibid., III, p. 445
17 Ibid., III, p. 544.
18 Hallam Tennyson, *Memoir*, I, p. 194.
19 *History of King Arthur*, vol. I; Tennyson Research Centre, Cat. 453, pp. 113, 125–7.
20 Quoted in Jump, p. 120.
21 Hood, p.134.
22 Quoted in Jump, pp. 119–20.
23 Sir Charles Tennyson, *Alfred Tennyson*, p. 399.
24 Lang and Shannon, III, p. 18; Metcalf, pp. 239, 258–9.
25 Metcalf, p. 261.
26 Quoted from Emily's letters and journal in Metcalf, p. 256.
27 Lang and Shannon, II, p. 212.

28 Ibid., III, p. 44.
29 Revised state of the original 1872 essay in Jump, pp. 355, 357.
30 Hallam Tennyson, *Memoir*, II, p. 127.
31 Ricks, *Tennyson*, p. 254.
32 Gray, p. 2.
33 Rosenberg, p.1.
34 Kathleen Tillotson, 'Tennyson's Serial Poem', in Tillotson, pp. 81–2.
35 Austin, *Poetry*, pp. 17, 25.
36 Ibid., pp. 29–30, 35, 37.
37 Austin, *Autobiography*, vol. 2, pp. 220–1.
38 Letter to Richard Watson Dixon, 27 February 1879, quoted in Jump, p. 334.
39 Sir Charles Tennyson, *Alfred Tennyson*, pp. 393–4.
40 In Chapter 15 of his biography of his grandfather Sir Charles Tennyson (ibid., pp. 393–401) brought together two preoccupations of 1871–2 in Tennyson's life: Tennyson's (and Emily's) increasing interest in the question of an appropriate honour to be conferred on him by the Queen, and the provisional completion of *Idylls of the King* in 1872 ('provisional' because the addition of yet another Idyll, later, meant the final state of the poem was not published until 1888).
41 Lang and Shannon, III, p.52. See also Sir Charles Tennyson, *Alfred Tennyson*, p. 400.
42 Lang and Shannon, III, p. 15.
43 Ibid., III, pp. 12–16.
44 Ibid., III, pp. 348–9 and n.
45 Ibid., III, pp. 35–6, but dated in this edition September 1872, which seems unlikely.
46 Martin, *Tennyson*, p. 503.
47 Lang and Shannon, III, pp. 83–5.
48 Ibid., III, p. 87.
49 Richards, pp. 334–40.
50 Slater, p.1. Slater's essay puts Tennyson's playwriting into its practical context: 'In the course of this grand project he wrote some fine poetry, like Queen Mary's poignant "Magnificat" when she believes she is to bear a son (*Queen Mary*, Act 3, sc. 2) but my concern is not with the literary qualities of these works but to offer a survey of their actual production (and the production of his four other plays) seeing them as very much part of the endlessly fascinating story of the Victorian theatre with its mega-star actors and actresses, technological virtuosity, spectacular effects and boundless, lavish energy and inventiveness.'
51 Richards, p. 339.
52 Quoted in ibid., p. 445.
53 Hallam Tennyson, *Memoir*, II, p. 178.
54 Quoted by Martin, *Tennyson*, p. 523.
55 Phyllis Grosskurth, 'Tennyson, Froude and Queen Mary', *Tennyson Research Bulletin*, ii (1972–6), 44–54.
56 Lang and Shannon, III, p. 120.
57 Ibid., III, p. 124n. Sir Charles Tennyson, *Alfred Tennyson*, pp. 429–30 and Martin, *Tennyson*, p.513, both give an opposite view of this episode. Martin's version reads: 'Tennyson had asked that the music for the play be entrusted to the young composer Charles Villiers Stanford, a friend of Hallam's. His first suggestion to Stanford was that he rearrange some of Beethoven's music to accompany the drama, and Stanford tactfully pointed out that it would no more do to excerpt Beethoven than it would for Tennyson to put one of Lady Macbeth's speeches in Queen Mary's mouth. Bateman, who disliked Stanford's music, cut out

most of it and wanted to put Stanford and a tiny band under the stage. When Tennyson heard of this, he immediately offered to pay for the sixty seats in the stall that Bateman claimed would have to be removed to provide a sufficient orchestra pit. Bateman then backed down, the seats remained, and Tennyson did not have to pay.'

58 Hallam Tennyson, *Memoir*, II, p. 185.

59 Quoted in Richards, pp. 340–1.

60 Terry, pp. 122–3; Alfred Tennyson, *Queen Mary*, III, vi, p. 179.

61 Tennyson Research Centre Letter 3849 (Knowles to Tennyson), 20 April 1876; Lang and Shannon, III, p. 128 and n.

62 Tennyson Research Centre Letter 3850 (Knowles to Tennyson), 7 May 1876.

63 Martin, *Tennyson*, p. 524.

64 Richards, pp. 203–4.

65 Quoted by ibid., p. 207.

66 Waugh, p. 256.

67 Ibid., p. 257.

68 Quoted in Lang and Shannon, III, p. 236.

69 Waugh, p. 261.

70 Quoted by Richards, p. 321

71 Harold Perkins, quoted by ibid., p. 392.

72 Lang and Shannon, III, p. 131 and n.

73 Terhune, III, pp. 705, 707.

74 Lang and Shannon, III, pp. 161–3.

75 Martin, *Tennyson*, p. 509.

76 Lang and Shannon, III, p. 164.

77 Ibid., III, pp. 164–5.

78 Metcalf, pp. 228–73.

79 Tennyson Research Centre Letter 3852 (Knowles to Tennyson), 20 January 1877.

80 Ricks, *Poems*, III, p. 23.

81 Metcalf, p. 277.

82 Tennyson Research Centre, Gladstone's letters to Tennyson:

Letter 3711, 11 Carlton House Terrace S.W., 23 March 1873 [in Gladstone's handwriting].

83 Lang and Shannon, III, p. 56n.

84 Quoted in ibid., III, pp. 135–6.

85 Matthew, II, pp. 72–3.

86 Quotations from Alfred Domett and from Mary Gladstone in Lang and Shannon, III, p. 143.

87 Quoted from Henry James in ibid., III, p. 144.

88 Hallam Tennyson, *Memoir*, II, p. 212.

89 Lang and Shannon, III, p. 122.

90 Ibid., III, pp. 152–3.

91 Quoted from Alfred Domett's diary in ibid., III, p. 153n.

92 Ibid., III, pp. 155–6, 157.

93 Ibid., III, p. 158.

94 James Spedding, 'Introductory Essay', in Charles Tennyson Turner, *Collected Sonnets*, pp. 29–30.

95 Lang and Shannon, III, pp. 170–1.

96 Ibid., III, pp. 174–7.

97 Ibid., III, p. 186n.

98 Quoted in ibid., III, p. 187.

99 Quoted in Hallam Tennyson, *Memoir*, II, p. 244.

100 Ibid., II, pp. 244–8; Lang and Shannon, III, pp. 192–3n.

101 Metcalf, p. 368.

102 Ricks, *Poems*, III, p. 71.

103 Ibid., III, p. 32 and headnote p. 30.

104 Martin, *Tennyson*, pp. 535–6.

105 Sir Charles Tennyson, *Alfred Tennyson*, p. 467.

106 Tennyson to Sir William Pollock: Lang and Shannon, III, p. 247.

107 Ricks, *Poems*, III, pp. 107–8.

108 Lang and Shannon, III, p. 250n.

109 Quoted in ibid., III, p. 249.

110 Matthew, II, p. 266.

111 Quotations from Mary Gladstone and other sources in Lang and Shannon, III, p. 259.

112 Quoted in ibid., III, pp. 254–5.

113 Matthew, II, pp. 266–7.

114 Lang and Shannon, III, p. 272n.

115 Ibid., III, pp. 275–8 and n.
116 Ibid., III, p. 273n.
117 Ibid., III, p. 279.
118 Quoted from William
   Allingham's diary in ibid., III,
   pp. 292–3 and n.
119 Alfred Browning Stanley
   Tennyson (1878–1952) and
   Charles Bruce Locker Tennyson
   (1879–1976): ibid., III, p. 298n.
120 Quoted from Allingham's diary
   in ibid., III, p. 298.

CHAPTER 10

Tragedy and resolution,
1886–1892

1 Martin, *Tennyson*, p. 534.
2 Lang and Shannon, III,
   pp. 210–11.
3 Ibid., III, p. 212.
4 Ricks, *Poems*, I, p. 625.
5 Quoted in Lang and Shannon, III,
   pp. 370–1.
6 Ibid., III, p. 5 and n.
7 Hoge, *Letters*, p. 333 and n.
8 Lang and Shannon, III, pp. 335–7.
9 Ricks, *Poems*, III, pp. 200–1.
10 Tennyson Research Centre Letter
   2483, 17 March 1886.
11 Quoted in Martin, *Tennyson*,
   p. 558.
12 Hood, p. 101.
13 Martin, *Tennyson*, p. 563.
14 Lang and Shannon, III, pp. 386–7.
15 Quoted by Thwaite, *Edmund
   Gosse*, pp. 295–7.
16 Gladstone, pp. 7–8.
17 Ibid., pp. 9–10, 17–18.
18 Aplin, p. 4.
19 Martin, *Tennyson*, p. 569.
20 Fitzgerald's letter was to an old
   Trinity friend, W. H. Thompson;
   clearly it was never his intention
   that it should be seen by a third
   party, let alone published to all
   the world as in Aldis Wright's
   edition. Terhune, II, pp. 407–8.
21 Pettigrew, II, p. 972.

22 Sir Charles Tennyson, *Alfred
   Tennyson*, p. 512.
23 Hoge, *Letters*, p. 342.
24 Hood, p. 315.
25 Lang and Shannon, III,
   p. 402.
26 Hallam Tennyson, *Memoir*, II,
   p.367; 'Materials for a life of
   A.T.', 4, p. 233.
27 'Materials for a life of A.T.', 4,
   p. 234.
28 Lang and Shannon, III, p. 403.
29 Ibid., III, pp. 413–14.
30 Headnote to 'Merlin and the
   Gleam', Ricks, *Poems*, III,
   p 205.
31 Ibid., III, p. 216.
32 Ibid., III, p. 209.
33 Sir Charles Tennyson, *Alfred
   Tennyson*, p. 517n.
34 Ricks, *Poems*, III, p. 137.
35 Martin, *Tennyson*, p. 575.
36 Ricks, *Poems*, III, p. 216.
37 Ibid., III, p. 235.
38 Ibid., III, p. 245.
39 Ibid., III, p. 251 and headnote.
40 Sir Charles Tennyson, *Alfred
   Tennyson*, p. 531.
41 Quoted in ibid., p. 535.

Epilogue: The poet and the
pageant, 1892

1 Quoted in Dyson and Tennyson,
   pp. 137–8.
2 Prinsep papers, Beinecke Library,
   Yale, Box 1, folder 52.
3 Dyson and Tennyson, pp.
   139–40.
4 Hallam Tennyson, *Memoir*, II,
   p. 429n.
5 Quoted in Dyson and Tennyson,
   p. 143.
6 Thwaite, *Emily Tennyson*, p. 591.
7 See ibid., p. 599.
8 Philip L. Elliott, *The Making of
   the Memoir* (Lincoln: The
   Tennyson Society, 1993), passim.
9 Hoge, *Letters*, p. 372.
10 Ricks, *Poems*, I, p. 246.

Index